The Great AMEN
of the Great I-AM

Other books by the author:

The Burning Green (Wipf & Stock, 1996)
The Setting in Life of 'The Arbiter' by John Philoponus
(Wipf & Stock, 1997)

The Great AMEN
of the Great I-AM

*God in Covenant with His People
in His Creation*

JOHN EMORY MCKENNA

ARTWORK BY RUSS MILLER

RESOURCE *Publications* · Eugene, Oregon

THE GREAT AMEN OF THE GREAT I-AM
God in Covenant with His People in His Creation

Copyright © 2008 John Emory McKenna. All rights reserved. Except for brief quotations in critical publications or reviews, no part of this book may be reproduced in any manner without prior written permission from the publisher. Write: Permissions, Wipf and Stock Publishers, 199 W. 8th Ave., Suite 3, Eugene, OR 97401.

Wipf & Stock
A Division of Wipf and Stock Publishers
199 W. 8th Ave., Suite 3
Eugene, OR 97401

www.wipfandstock.com

ISBN 13: 978-1-59752-847-4

Manufactured in the U.S.A.

Contents

Artwork by Russ Miller vii

Foreword ix

1 An Explanation 1

2 The Great I-AM 40

3 The 'Little Credo' of the Great I-AM 73

4 The Beginning of the Generations 108

5 These Are the Words—A People for the Land 166

6 The Great I-AM of the Kingdom of God 192

7 The King, His Kingdom, and the Light of the World 248

8 The Church and the World 272

9 The Person of God in the World 320

10 In Our Time 355

Addendum & Suggested Reading 380

Artwork

by Russ Miller

Chapter 1 Rough Beast 39

Chapter 2 Cosmic Pen 72

Chapter 3 Bull in Snow 107

Chapter 4 Cosmos 165

Chapter 5 Heart 191

Chapter 6 Pouring Into Light 247

Chapter 7 Cross 271

Chapter 8 Calvary 319

Chapter 9 Light Bearer 354

Chapter 10 Extended Hand 379

Foreword

I NEED TO THANK more than a few people. None of them are responsible for the argument I have made in this book, yet I could not have made it without them.

I need most of all to thank my wife, Mickey. Her devotion to me for more than thirty-five years of marriage has been boundless. She has weathered with me storm after storm, time and time again. Our meeting in Laguna Beach in 1972, two creatures thrown together from the subcultures of the Sixties in our nation to become a husband and a wife, solid citizens now, has been a steady struggle. Together, we became a part of the Jesus Movement in Southern California. When we moved from Laguna to attend in Los Angeles the Jesus Christ Light and Power House, a Bible School where Hal Lindsey and Bill Counts sought to teach the movement the prophecy and commands of the Bible, Mickey made good on her vow to me to go where I went, through thick and thin. She followed me then to Fuller Theological Seminary, where I spent ten years earning a Master of Divinity and a Doctor of Philosophy in Historical Theology. It was hard work and she never gave up on a man who was 50 years old when he finished his doctorate. She is still with me as I write, still vital in our ministry, and I cherish her life and love more than I am able to say.

Mickey's son, Paul Drew, has also been through it all with us. He knows firsthand our struggles, and he continues to be a great source of comfort to us. Like his mother, he accepted the Lord in the early 70s, a boy very much damaged by the drugs so prevalent in the subcultures of the times. He, too, has had to learn to endure some very great sea changes. He has experienced and endured one storm after another also. Yet, thanks to the great grace and truth of our Lord in his life, he is free from his past today. Although we were all almost utterly destroyed, the great grace and truth of our Lord has been sufficient for us. This grace and truth is thus the subject of my book. We may yet struggle against the deadly habits of our pasts, perhaps still a bit dumb in the dread depths of the darkness we knew so well then, but we have also known the victories of the faithfulness of this grace and truth with us. Exotic phantoms, mystical moments, the deep splits in the pits our lives experienced, do not keep us from the space where as sinners we have learned to cry out to our Lord and our God. This is where the Good Lord saw fit to find us, even in the midst of that subculture where no one would choose to go, and gave us hearts to participate as red-blooded mainstream Americans in the way of our nation in the world.

It is a long way, indeed, and I am afraid we are still seeking to find our paths in it. Sometimes the distances seem very great, but often near enough to keep us hopeful, and to know the comfort and the tender mercies of the Almighty. Through our Lord's compassion and passion, with the great power of the word of his grace and truth, we are made able somehow to walk with Him. I hope my reader will read about us, with some similar forgiveness, and hear in our testimony the Great Amen He has caused us to hear. I thank Mickey and Paul for listening to me these many years, for being the gifts they are to me. I thank Mickey especially for her beauty and intelligence, her outrageous courage, and her grateful witness to our Lord. I thank Paul for the kindness he has for strangers, for his steady concern for the less seemly members of Christ's Body. We know that estranged people, outsiders in our society, along with the rich and the poor are marked for redemption in our time, and we hope the readers of this book will take heart with us in the glad Amen of the Great I-AM the Lord God is with us, so wonderfully patient and merciful and faithful. I hope my reader will become amazed in the face of his grace, in the light of his truth for us. The older we get, the more sufficient His grace appears to us. We have some friends, the Mohorko's of Oxnard, California, whose children once wrote a song that they sing in their churches, entitled, Sin ti, yo soy nada, 'Without you, I am nothing.' Their song has become a vital part of the impetus for my book. I will attempt to say in its chapters that we are not nothing, that we are who we are because He is who He is with us and for us in this world.

Dr. Suk Kim has been my interpreter at Azusa Pacific University and the World Mission University and my many Korean students. He is a veteran of the Korean conflict, when he first learned English, interpreting for the U.S. Army, and I am privileged to have this refugee from North Korea as a friend and the translator of so much of my teaching. We have been together for more than ten years now. After the Korean action, Suk worked some years in Vietnam and then in Saudi Arabia, and finally as a pastor

Foreword

in the Korean Church in the United States. I am grateful that, upon his retirement, he found it in his heart to work to introduce my theology to a new generation of Korean students here. We hope that this new generation of pastors will be able to move this wonderful people in a direction that can lead their movement towards the formation of a church in the world that may truly witness to the grace and truth that is Jesus Christ and his Revelation of the Trinity of God. One of our students, Byung-Ho Jeon, has translated a collection of my published essays into book form, entitled 'An Ear for His Word.' I am told it contributes to their passionate efforts to witness to Christ in the world. Because of it, I understand that my reputation among Korean speaking people is far more than it is among my English speaking friends. Suk and Byung-Ho have held up my arms on behalf of the Gospel in our times together, and I thank them for their efforts. When we are weak, such people indeed strengthen us.

I also need to thank my teachers at Fuller Theological Seminary, William Sanford LaSor, David Allan Hubbard, Frederick W. Bush, and Geoffrey Bromiley. They took me up as a an old and rather raw student and tried to do more for me than any student might expect of a professor. I remember them as much as friends than as teacher. It seemed that God had given them his compassion for a man much wounded in the wilderness, longing to know God in the Jesus Movement and at the Jesus Christ Light and Power House, and they tried as best they could to mend my broken wings and to teach me to fly. Professor Hubbard was also president of the Seminary, and he made me his special assistant during his final years at the seminary, hoping to domesticate me for service in the Church. Professor Bromiley astonished me with the work he did for me when he mentored my dissertation on John Philoponus. Because of them, I gained at Fuller a broad vision of the Body of Christ in the world today, for which I am grateful. Also because of them, I was able to meet in 1982 the Very Reverend Professor Thomas F. Torrance of Edinburgh University. He came from Scotland to Pasadena to deliver the Payton Lectures that year, and thankfully he became for me a mentor as well as a friend. I considered him an angel sent from the Lord to help me understand the vital problems in theology in our time. Without his lead, without the many challenges his wonderful books have been to me, I do not know that the life of my witness would have ever been able to get up off the ground. As I continue to seek to answer the call of God upon my life, Professor Torrance's life and works continue to challenge me in the most satisfying and gratifying of ways, ways I am happy to associate with flying or riding the waves of the waters of the world. As I write, he lives, recovering from a stroke, with all of his more than 90 years in a nursing home in Edinburgh. I have visited twice with him there, surrounded by the love and care of his wife and family, and I continue to be amazed at his love for the Lord, our God. During my last visit, he said that, if he did not return to his home on Braid Farm Road in Edinburgh and to his wife, Margaret and his son Thomas Spear Torrance, he was very much looking forward to going to heaven. He told me then that one of the first things he would do, when he got to heaven, was ask Karl Barth what he thought about the direction in which he had taken his beloved mentor's thought (cf. Church Dogmatics). The second thing he would do was to ask God why he did not give James Clerk Maxwell, the great Scottish physicist and inventor of dynamic field theories in the nature of the universe, more years upon the earth. Professor Torrance has championed in our time the need to grasp afresh the cognitive interface that must exist between Christian Faith and our Scientific Culture, that the Redeemer-Creator of our theology must be understood as the One who is the Lord of space-time and all of created reality. He would challenge us to seek for a new integration of faith and reason in our time, a new reformation in our cultures, a new significance for the contingent orders and freedoms we are to understand as resting upon the divine freedom and the power of love we may find with the Almighty. I hope that I have understood Professor Torrance well enough to name him as my mentor, and to seek to pass on to my readers some of the deep and profound concerns with which this man of God has faced us. I hope my book will reflect what he has sought to champion. I believe the Gospel of Jesus Christ and the Kingdom of God is the only source for the kind of deep healing our wounded generation needs. I believe that, if we are to 'amen' the 'Great Amen of the Great I-AM', Mickey, Paul, and I and all of us come to know the 'YES' He is for us in our time. Together, I believe, we may give thanks to God and thanks for the Torrance Clan in Edinburgh, Scotland!

Also, I need to thank the Worldwide Church of God. The miraculous transformation of her liberated fellowship as God's children in His Kingdom has been the source of surprising support for us. I am not yet sure why God has put us together, a wounded generation from the subculture with a prophetic community of questionable understanding, but I do know that WCG's transformations and my own somehow have been

Foreword

made to resonate with one another. Healing the fantasies of drugs and the aberrations of church dogma for the Glory of His Kingdom in this way makes a supreme sense of making out of the old new things in this world. As WCG has sought to learn to articulate and witness her newly found freedom for the Gospel of Grace, she has provided a freedom for my own healing and growth, and I have come to cherish her for this freedom. The WCG's journey away from the legalism of her past, the metaphysical bondage she has endured, with its many aberrations, through a tremendous wilderness experience towards a new and fresh grasp of God's grace and truth has been a wondrous miracle that even the most evangelical of faith has recognized in our time. Dr. Joseph Tkach's account of her transformations, entitled Transformed by Truth, and Dr. J. Michael Feazell's book entitled The Liberation of the Worldwide Church of God well represent her efforts to communicate her pain and joy in the sea-changes of her journey. To share with these leaders the struggles of this newly forming church in the world is a privilege, as I continue to exhort her not to throw her baby out with her wash. I believe we can, the Worldwide Church of God and a wounded generation, well embrace together the saying of the Apostle, St. Paul, 'I am what I am by the Grace of God.' Most recently, Mr. Terry Akers of the WCG has been a great encouragement to me and with his wife Nancy have helped me to shape the manuscript of this book into a publishable form.

The World Mission University of Los Angeles remains too a steady support for my work. President Dong Sun Lim, with his board and professors, have made me one of their vice presidents and engaged my teaching with grace and faithfulness. I am happy to report at this time that they have achieved accredited status among the theological schools of our nation, and it has been a privilege to serve them and to enjoy their steady effort to proclaim the Gospel with a vision for theological education across the globalization of our world.

There are many others. Mike Montgomery with his 'communion' in Laguna Beach, Ron Whitson with his 'Walk in the Son' at the Laguna Beach Outreach House gave good substance and foundation during our Jesus Movement experience beside the sea where artists claimed its water and light for their own. They helped Mickey and Paul Drew and I find our way to the Jesus Christ Light and Power House in Los Angeles, and our first systematic study of the Scriptures. The Merritt's and the Bussjaeger's from those Laguna days continue to offer us their support. Friends also from our pasts, from Princeton University in New Jersey and from Flintridge Sacred Heart High School in La Canada, have proven more willing than we supposed to help us restore our relations with them. Most recently one of my U.S Army Security Agency buddies, John Paris, with whom I served in Bad Aibling, Germany, has helped me to try to remember. The freelance artists, Russ and Janice Miller, from our student days at Fuller and now from Arizona, have never forgotten to keep in touch with us. We need to thank them for the illustrations they have provided for this book. They deserve a whole page of special thanks. There are also friends from our childhoods in Cleveland, Ohio and South Pasadena, California that pray for us today. If I were to try to express my gratitude to them all, I would never get on with this book. We trust that you know who you are and that you will continue to go on forgiving us. We could have been better friends, we know, as we knows the world could have been a better place, but we thank you all just the same. Thank you for allowing us, for better or for worse, to be the forgiven children we are. Most of my life has happened too late, and these thanks also come too late, but as they say, better late than never.

1

An Explanation

... Apart from me you can do nothing.
John 15:5b

WHY READ A BOOK about an ex-alcohol and drug addict, come out from under the volcanic eruptions of a self-destructive existence for life as a Jesus Freak? Are not the stories of such conversions tired forms of some practical Narcissism rabid as dogs in the wilderness of our society? My critics also tell me that I am as this one too difficult to understand. My thought is too obscure. My writing is too dense. Whatever it is that I am trying to say is not said with the simplicity that is required by ordinary human beings everywhere. I am sure the critics are right. I ought not to write my book. Yet I must speak, however pathetically. There is a call upon my life. I must write it down on paper. Never mind how complex it is. Who can heal his or herself in any case? However poor the words of this book are, they are what they are as witnesses to their Lord and God.

I say that with real human frailties we move towards all that truly matters, like it or not, with the tender mercies of the One who is who He is in all of his simplicity and complexity and mystery. I would say that, though we appear to spend our times upon this earth on a great river of time, like fish in the water, or specks among the stars of the galaxies, known and unknown, with astonishingly perishable and explosive existences, though we move silently in an impressive vastness that dwarfs any meaning we may want to give ourselves, our significance is something that really matters. There is something moving in the world that would take us quite beyond ourselves, something truly resolute, answering what and how and why and where in the questions of our lives. We are "not-nothing" here. But the way to understanding this '*something-ness*' is resolutely unique, a clearly particular reality, one that somehow possesses a patently universal significance. I will write about why we are "not-nothing" in this case.

I mean to speak that which takes us quite beyond ourselves. I want to see us as individuals in community with what and who it is that lives beyond our own existences. I intend to tell of a freedom, which, as both divine and created human freedom, belongs to the Lord of the New Creation. I would proclaim that we belong to all that matters, to the New World of our God. Especially for terribly perishing people in a very perishing universe are the new dimensions of the new nature of this world absolutely valuable. I would take us on a trip that would point us to the time and space where human life is given to bear witness to the One who truly is the One He is, the Lord God among us, under the heavens and upon the earth. I mean to ask my reader to take this journey with me, to go on this ride, on paths or waves where we may hear and see the Eternal Life God Himself is among us. I mean for us to hear and see what we cannot tell ourselves, what we cannot ourselves image. I mean for us to travel along lines that will allow to think what cannot by thinking be thought. I mean for us to discover a freedom that finds the impossible is actual. We need to discover that space and time in which we truly matter, God's own space and time for us. We need to be able to say about ourselves that we are by the grace of God who we are. We need to tell He is His grace for us in our time.

My argument will attempt to frame a witness to the grace and truth that God is as taught us in the Holy Scriptures. I will claim that it is not impossible to know the One who is who He is, the Great I-AM He is in His Revelation, as truly the Lord and God of our world, a world that is created and made and sustained in its existence with his divine freedom, with his holy love, and with the mysterious being of his wisdom and grace and truth. I would argue that our freedom is meaningless unless we are free in his freedom to be who He is with us, that the significance of our freedom is rooted in the ground the freedom of his being, the mysterious and wonderful being whose way of with his very own freedom, love, and wisdom would give us the grace to think openly and freely of his living presence in this world. I will that he is free to make himself present and known within the created structures and creative freedoms we enjoy with our experience under the stars and upon the lands beside the seas. I will seek to persuade my reader that we are under his command here, even when we will not to believe him. I will argue that we need to know him

An Explanation

for who he truly is as his grace for us, and not as another, not as somebody we imagine for our selves in this world. I will seek to understand him in his divine freedom and holy love and mysterious wisdom then as taught in the Bible with us. I would like to speak of the freedom he is as his grace even with the Holy Scriptures. I would like to speak freely as a free man, a man who has been set free by the truth of the grace he is. Even while all things created, great and small, are perishing in our experiences in the world, we need to hear this One in his divine freedom speaking with us and for us in our times. Without this speaking, we may tell only of the dusts of death in this world, the 'nothingness' that seems to surround this world with a silence we may taste in our lives.

We live in God's Creation and not elsewhere. Here is the place where God's Life has been revealed for us. This is the space where God's Light shines in time and times, giving direction to our destinies with him. In precisely this world, we have been made to hear God's Word, to go to the One who calls us, to worship him as the One He is for us. But who in their freedom hear this One, who among us believes His Voice? Who can believe what they have heard about him? I certainly could not. For 37 years, I lived not merely without him but at times consciously against him. I lived a self-destructive existence as if it were a righteous life, a barfly living as a volcano able to spew forth the burning leave of a primordial rage that exist very clearly and plainly in our times. (To all those who knew me, I ask, "Who but God can forgive us?") In those days I carried around with me an image, drawn by a drinking buddy, of a man in a glass bottle. The bottle is sailing on the waves of a sea. The man's head has been severed from his body and serves to cork the bottle upon the waves. His nerves extend down from the cut of his neck, falling like lightening towards his nude body at the bottom of the bottle. In his hands, he holds a wilting lily, as if the artist wished to send a message in this bottle of a man doomed on the waters. I carried the image around with me for years. I hung it in rented rooms from town to city. I thought that it spoke of my existence in the world. I was a homeless mariner on a sea of troubles no matter where I lived. I was never sure what the lily meant. But near dead from alcohol, cigarettes, carousing, and drugs, in this loveless glass upon the waters of a troubled world, more than 35 years ago now, in the Mission District of the City of San Francisco, the Lord delivered me from the bottle, healed me from my tormented life, and freed me to become a man at home in this world. Two things I knew immediately about this Lord and God. He was almighty and he was very tender. As the almighty, he was compassionately forgiving. As his tender mercy, he was passionate about doing the impossible and becoming our Savior. He sent His Word to me in the midst of those days. He sent His Light and healed me. He filled me with the joy of his salvation and a longing to know him as the One he truly is. I was no more a man alone in this world. I was not that creature in the glass bottle drawn by my artist friend. I was a man who needed to learn of him. I have now spent more than 35 years learning of him. As this tender and almighty Lord God, he is more than I ever could imagine.

With the Light of His Word comes the freedom to see and to follow Him. With this freedom, I am not the same man that I once was. I have come to cherish the gift of this freedom, more than I can say, and I have learned to live my life beyond the bitter rage, the hours of tortured emptiness and loneliness, to be free from their torment and pain, to be able to live with a joy that only He can speak into our lives. From elsewhere than the abyss comes this unspeakable condition in which life knows its origin in God. I can speak of it only as the tender mercies of the Almighty, as the truth that belongs only to the Word of His Being for us in this world. With this freedom, the Almighty touches our lives, makes the One He truly is known to us, and in the midst of our rage makes us to know that we belong to Him. We belong to his divine freedom to be with us. In this freedom, he has forgiven me. He fills us with his joy, and for me this meant that I knew that I was not alone in this world with all my aberrations in its nothingness.

I remember the night I came back to my rented room in the Mission District of San Francisco, when I bowed down there for the first time to thank Him for the mighty thing He had done in my life. I actually looked around me in that barren space to make sure that nobody was watching me. It was not thought manly for a man to be seen weeping for joy down on his knees to God, our Father. We are such strange creatures. Even free to be who we are in this world with God, we can fear what others might think of us. In any case, I knew I was no longer alone, and now even as I write this book, I still prefer that people should not see me down on my knees in tears before Him. I would prefer that my reader see me as a heroic witness to His Salvation. But these are but vain wishes. I am learning to stuff them back into the bottle from where they come, out upon the waters of the seas. What I really need to say cannot be said except upon my knees, not without tears of joy. I must seek to say what our Father has given me to say to my reader, as one of those poor creatures He has forgiven.

An Explanation

It is like being carried down the rapids of the waves in the waters of a great river, tossed and turned and thrown about in a whirling turbulence taking one rapidly towards toward the sea. It is like being sucked by riptides by an anomalous energy down to the depths of the dread darkness, being shaped by the pulls and pushes of the unpredictable powers of wind and storm. It's like being drawn beyond the horizon of a black hole, down into the exotic forces that shred with journey what has mattered, lost in wormholes from infinite curves of space and time vanished onto a singularity as yet unimagined by any physical law we know. That is what life in the Life of the Spirit of the Word of the Father seemed at first to be for me. How do you learn to walk upon the waters of a chaos that appears to be homeless? How can you survive the tides and rip tides of the indifferent oceans out of which we must climb? How may we learn to hear what we cannot see? How may we seek to walk the wild side of boundaries whose definitions mostly escape our attention? How may we talk about the One who heals us? How may we understand the grace of His truth and the truth of His grace for us? Perhaps I should entitle this book *The Great Peace of the Great River*, where running though His creation is a singular wave above the waters that would take us, however thrilled, home to Him? It is not easy to say what is beyond the chaos and nothingness of this world's primordial rage and emptiness that is for us. It is not by principles that govern how things are what they are that we may mount up, as if upon the wings of eagles, to go to the places he has prepared for us. This is not and cannot be a 'how-to' book. We do not wear upon our sleeves answers to the questions that ask 'why!'

His paths belong to an arrow of time only His light can draw into the boundaries of space as this world. They seem to belong to waves of energies whose direction spirals up against a perishing world, my world. They lead, I believe, to His new creation, but they take unimagined space and time out of the dark abyss of the past into a becoming that is not merely new but truly new, truly new for you and me. I have felt again and again on these paths a certain progress in which I am becoming for the first time more the human being that I ought to be. I hope to become that man who was meant to be, even before the Creation, and this progress occurs, again and again, because he is the Great I-AM He is, the Lord and God of whom we read in the Bible. (In those nights I spent right after my healing, I used to sleep with the Bible. I used to keep it under my pillow so that, when I would wake in the middle of the night from some nightmare, I could take it up quickly and read the words!) From the depths of the dark abyss and the dreaded emptiness of a nothingness twisted into a threat in a perishing world, the Great I-AM can seem like a long way off from us. But because he had crossed the chasm of that evil dream for us, I could be comforted in the midst of my fear and trembling and tormented times. He is the Lord and God, and in His freedom our Savior. He is the One who is who He is as the King of the universe, the Prophet of the Cosmos, the Priest of its Peoples, the Sage of its Beginning and Ending. Learning to confess him as this Great I-AM He is requires an AMEN that we cannot speak out of ourselves, but one He has spoken for us. What we cannot say, He has said for us. He has spoken for us with the Truth of His Grace and the Grace of His Truth. So we say that we write freely of Him who is free to speak for us. We write with a freedom that belongs to His Freedom. We have to do with time and times whose unimagined ways create a path for our paths in this world, where we are made to learn of His Love for our loves and hates, the Light of His Word as a light for our paths. We do say that we know him who knows us better than we know ourselves. We do say that He is as this Great I-AM the AMEN of the Lord God for us. He is all that truly matters for us with His New Creation. We do say that we hope and pray our readers will catch a glimpse of Him in this way of His Freedom for us.

I will attempt to frame an argument that would witness to the Revelation of the Lord God as His Grace and Truth with us. I will attempt to argue that He is who He claims to be, the Great I-AM of the Bible. As such, He is the Lord of His Covenant with His People among the nations and the God of a world that is His Creation. The movements in this argument have developed over decades of teaching in seminaries and universities. They form my best efforts to understand the One who healed and saved me from the pits of San Francisco. They form what I would call a Biblical Theology. I hope to show my readers that an integrated approach towards reading the Bible and apprehending the Light and Life of the Word of God become flesh in this world takes place at a cognitive interface between His revelations and our reason. I hope to help those who hear to seek that wholeness of being which belongs to the gift of His truth and grace for us. I hope to help people pray for their unbelief. I hope to help people in our weaknesses to hear a power that is not higher than we are, but in fact more near to us than we are to ourselves. I seek to lay hold of within the structures I find in the Biblical World a framework that

An Explanation

belongs to the Bible's witness to His Being who He is in His Revelation to us, a Self-Revelation that occurs in real space and time in a real world we may understand as His Creation. To make this argument has taken me years of healing along a very awesome adventure. I am not satisfied with my articulation of it, but it is the best that I can do now. It is done in any case to honor His gift and I offer it not in my own name but in His. I hope my reader will forgive me, hear its secret, and enjoy the mystery and freedom of this One for us. It is His righteousness with which we all have to do, believe or enjoy it or not.

Yet I find telling strangers that I am a theologian makes me even stranger to them. The strangest people seem to think that I am strange as soon as they know that I am a 'religious' man. They seem to think that being a theologian or religious man makes one something that they are not. Mention the Gospel of God and the category of 'human being' goes out the window, and perhaps into a black hole nearby somewhere. Even though I would attempt to say as a human being words that tell of our Father, I am a stranger more strange than the strangers I meet. Fathom that! For more than thirty-five years now I have stood astonished before stranger after stranger, watching their faces turn me into something less than a human being whenever I would introduce them to our Lord and God. People look at you as if you were worse than a stranger among them, but an alien, from Mars perhaps, come to invade the world they cherish or not. The kindness of strangers is important in our lives!

It is the stuff upon which the disenchanted depend! Yet are we not in some sense all strangers? We are all mariners on a sea of troubles, sailors who sail a tremendously fearsome world together. We must and we do depend upon the kindness of the strangers we are for one another. We are creatures then falling strangely into the vast void of a dark abyss where screams are heard echoing in the silence of our tormented generations onto the horizons of our existences in this world. No one really wants to come face to face with the other, with another stranger once more, let alone with the Face of God speaking with us more loudly than all of our vaunted screams. We may want to fear him or not, but no one wants to come face to Face with this One, without knowing the kindness of a stranger in our lives.

Mostly, it means, does it not, a fight—His Face in ours! Even if we turn to run, even when we run as fast as we can, we know our desperate flights shall not dismay him. He is there! Even when we think we are safely hidden, He appears there, a stranger with us. A poet has characterized him as the 'hound of heaven.' He pursues us. He smells us out. He hounds us. He traps us. He corners us and points us out. He makes His face shine upon us. He gives us peace. He is the surprise of surprises. He saves us from our twisted selves. He saves us from the torments of others and ourselves. He delivers us from the demons and from Satan himself. He gives us the mercy of His Might, His Love, and His Light. He makes us over again for the sake of His Righteousness, His enemies into His Children. Because of it, I am a theologian. How strange! How strangely I am become among the strangers a child of God! How strange it all is! How alien it is to all that we know and can anticipate. What an invasion into the bent places and twisted times and tortured hours in which we spend our dreadful existences! Here is the Great I-AM, a stranger in our midst, with whom we must come face to Face. Who can bear His assaults?

This primordial fact alone gives us to pause from time to time, rather unknowingly, in one place or another. Why are we here? What is elsewhere? Where do we go? In these rather long years of questions, in our sometimes very short times, we may experience the angel of His Being without even noticing Him, until He insists that He is with us, when we are stopped in our tracks, like Moses before the Burning Bush. Thank God for His strange traps! I am not now what I once was because of them. I am not what I wanted to be but what I never wanted to be. I am, I am aware, more nearly now what I ought to be than anything I was then. We become human very slowly. We know ourselves as He knows us, His children, reluctantly. The People of God are not His People readily. They are His People because, with the clouds of their days and in the fires of their nights, He leads them, year after dreadful year, to know Him for who He truly is with them. He draws them into Himself, to know Him whose face belongs to the Mighty and Tender One. He reaches down into our deepest dreads, and where we most need he takes us up to Himself. He takes our warped worlds and twisted lives and turns them to Himself, heals them, and delivers them as the grace and truth He is for them. It is right to say that he loves them more than he loves himself, for he goes into pits of our personal hells for us and there makes us into His children, children of God. There is no other One than this One, Great I-AM who is who He is as His Grace and Truth for us in this world. A stranger? Yes! But a very kind stranger among the strangers we are.

An Explanation

I have already mentioned meeting Professor Thomas F. Torrance at Fuller Theological Seminary, that he became a mentor and friend to me. When I completed my PhD at Fuller, while working as an Adjunct Professor and Special Assistant to its President David Allan Hubbard, Professor Torrance sought to gain recognition for me at various academic centers. He hoped I would become a fellow at the Center for Theological Inquiry in Princeton, New Jersey. He thought that much of me, more than I did of myself. He thought more of me than his colleagues could. In my last conversation with the Director of the Princeton Center I was refused fellowship with these scholars. I was told that I should write my book in California. "If you write your book here at the Center," he said to me, "it would not be a book that many people would read." The Center was conceived to witness to the Institute of Advanced Study at Princeton. Its publications do not, indeed, enjoy a wide range of readers. Surely the Director's point was well made. In any case, I am writing this book as my California book then—no footnotes, no bibliography, no index, no scholarly quotes, no critical comments and discussions, just waves, lots of waves—wave after wave of assertions that my reader might ride and hear this One who speaks to us in them. I hope to make some pretty good ones in this book, and I hope my readers will catch some of them and ride them all the way into the presence of God, where we are given real knowledge of Him. A very good professor once told me that my problem was I did not do what was expected of me. I suppose in a certain sense he was dead right, yet I have found the unexpected provides the best of waves and a real hearing of the Word of God. I hope my readers will find in my California book some waves to ride an energy that will land them upon a ground where real knowledge of God must obtain, the offer we cannot refuse.

I myself will seek in my book to hear a symphony played by the Word of God with a world that is our world. It is in this way, I believe, that His Word takes us from where we wait, lifts us up, gives us to ride, and out of our nothingness in His Creation transforms us into the something for which we were meant to be, into what only He can make, the children of His Kingdom, the children of His Word and Light, when we are known and given life that only He can give to the creatures in His Creation. *Sin ti, yo soy nada*, 'Without you, I am nothing!' I want to say that, beyond the 'Nothingness' that is thought to threaten our existence in the world, is made according to His Word a new creature, one that belongs to His New

Creation. I want to struggle against the perception that the 'Nothingness' of this world is sheer evil, that the chaos and emptiness of God's Creation is meant to negate life. I would seek to ride a wave above those evil dreams for the world's 'Nothingness,' and restore our perception of it as a part of God's 'Very Good' Creation ... When we suffer this world's calamities in the impersonal silence of the vast universe we know, we do not suffer meaninglessly. We are "not nothing" with good reason, the reason of His Revelation. We are not utterly insignificant creatures in a vastly indifferent space of time that cares nothing about us. I would argue that we are somebody, made out of the 'Nothingness' of God's Good Creation to be His children. Before Him we are not nothing, but somebody, somebody that we need to know as He knows us. Out of the 'Nothingness' of His Creation, He makes space and time for His children with Himself, when in this place we come to know Him who knows us, and because of this relationship for us we may understand that we have been fearfully and wonderfully made to image who He truly is in this world. Our sense of beauty and truth and grace comes from the fact that the One who has made us what we are possesses these qualities, and because He is who He is He is able and willing to make out of our 'Nothingness' a world He calls His Creation with His People. Even in the midst of our perishing and our suffering with our perceptions, with all the aberrations and phantoms and blind alleys we encounter in time, our human 'Nothingness' is meaningful and significant to God. It belongs to His 'Very Good' Creation, not to haunt our existences with purposelessness and emptiness, as our evil dreams about the 'Nothingness' would have it, but to give us a dignity and purpose that belongs to the power of His Word to make in His way the world His Kingdom. I will seek to ride perhaps a somewhat solitary wave on into freedom the experience of which makes days seem hours, hours but a moment, time with an Eternity only He governs. That is to say, upon a boundary where divine and human freedoms have been made to meet, where we may know and understand the meaning of our freedom in His own, even in our time with His time, even in our loves and hates with His love and hate. Because of this Lord and God, I would say, we are 'Not Nothing,' a potential made to serve an actuality that belongs to those new dimensions of being in existence where and when we are indeed to be known as children of God, children of Light, children with our Father. Only joy, a grateful joy, can be experienced riding this wave to Him. I hope my book will somehow bear the energies of the sounds of His Voice, the true Voice of Freedom in this

An Explanation

world. I hope my reader will be able to catch this solitary wave and ride it home to the blessed satisfaction, even in the midst of a turbulent and storming world. I hope you taste and see that the Lord's Life is the only Good Life, Good, I say, not over against the bad but beyond with an Eternity that He Himself is for us.

I believe that the Great I-AM the Lord God is with and for us, even in the midst of our dreams and nightmares about solidarity and our solitariness, has shaped and formed the substance and content of a Great AMEN for us that we can and do actually experience with our lives. I believe He has spoken this AMEN to us as the Person of the Lord Jesus Christ. I believe He spoke this AMEN even with and in and at *the* Beginning and that He speaks this AMEN to us 'today,' if only we will rightly count our days as individuals and as communities. I believe He speaks in His Divine Freedom and Holy Love now as He did then, and that He will speak of it with us forever. Just as He once spoke light into existence in the midst of the chaos and void of the dark depths of the primordial world, just as He once spoke stars and sun and moon and earth into existence, where He once made Man in His Image, He speaks with our world in our times even 'today.' Because He is the One who He is with us, the dusts of death and the world's perishing times, time past, present, and future, shall never be the last word upon human and created existences. He possesses a book of life in which He has written His Great AMEN for us as the Great I-AM He is. To hear His great 'Yes' is to know the secret of Man and the Universe. It is to possess a treasure of a wisdom that is more satisfying than any myth we might like to make up about our world or ourselves. It is to know your name is written there, even surrounded by the many waters of a world that has fallen from Him. I would write a book to bear witness to this speaking of this One and His AMEN in the waters and the words we experience in this world. I would speak of the tender might of this AMEN among us. I would know the comfort of who He is in this world. I would believe in Him. I would believe that you will believe in Him. I would believe that the Great I-AM He is has spoken and still speaks His Great AMEN to us in our times.

To attempt to begin anything is to face always a certain kind 'Nothingness.' To make a real beginning is not to make a false start. When we read, '*Call me Ishmael!*' we know we are in for a good read. We know a great story has been begun. When I write, 'I was born in Cleveland, Ohio,' it is just not the same kind of beginning. No great start has been made.

Perhaps even a useless one has been begun. Who really cares about a book written by a drunk from Cleveland, Ohio? The city is known in jokes that are made, like the jokes about the Polish one can find almost everywhere all the time. Cleveland, Ohio is certainly no Ishmael. But I would argue that both Ahab and the Clevelanders are plagued by a certain perception of the 'Nothingness' of this world. I would argue that both cannot be what they are without some expectation that they are more than dusts, more than ashes upon the seas of their troubles. I will argue that there is something and somebody that truly matters in time, and that out of the 'Nothingness' of which this world is made, a threat to many, comes and shall come that which truly matters. I would tell of things that here and now belong to a ride that would take us beyond ourselves, beyond the black holes of our imaginations, beyond the unknown mysteries that captivate our attention today, to the City on the Hill, to David's Town, to a center where forever is what forever ought to be—the City of God. Here all that matters is His Light, the Word of His Light, the Life of His Word. Here all that matters are that which knows Him, knows Him for who He truly is, knows that He truly is who He is here in time and space. I must plunge my hands into the midst of such time and times as these, born in Cleveland, Ohio, and try to speak of something that truly matters now and then, because He truly is.

I remember then that not even Moses began at *the* Beginning. He began at the Burning Bush. He began when he heard the Voice coming from within the flames in a desert out to where he was keeping a flock for his father-in-law in Midian—the Voice from a bush that remained unconsumed even as the flames burned. Moses began far away from where he began, as far from his reputation in Egypt as he could get. He began with a dialogue, listening to a Voice that could persuade him, over his many objections to it, to accept a mission in his life with Him. He is started onto a trip back into his past, but with a very different goal than that which he once had in mind there. He is begun as a leader of the People of God. He is meant to deliver Israel from her afflictions in the land of the Nile. He is begun with a call to bring Israel to her worship of her Lord God. He is brought with the People of God to the Holy Mountain. He begins in earnest at Sinai. He began in the midst of these things, not before or after them, but in the midst of their histories in the cities of the world.

We never begin at *the* Beginning. We begin in the middle of it all. We begin with a past. We begin in a present that is not the same as time past.

An Explanation

We begin for the sake of a future time, about which we can only prophesy. We begin with a Voice, His Voice, the Voice of the Other One, the Voice of the Great I-AM the Lord God is in the Bush. We begin with the One who calls us with His Name and not another. We begin on His Holy Ground or nowhere. We begin with bare feet. We begin on our knees. We begin learning to listen to what we cannot tell ourselves. We begin with our deliverance, as Moses began with his Exodus. We begin with fear and trembling, with a new-made freedom to do what we do not want to do. We begin with the Voice of the One who tells us that He is who He is. We begin with the Voice of the One who says He is our Lord and God. We begin with the One who has come to deliver us from our slaveries to His Divine Freedom to be present and known in the world. We begin as People of God in this way or we go on making our many false starts in this world. Thus, we belong to the history of God's Creation. We belong to time primordial, to ancestral times, to this present time, and to times to come. We belong to freedom. We belong to no idol. We belong to no idol making. We belong to Him whose Voice names and who thus gives Himself to us. If He were not free with His Divine Freedom to give us this beginning, we shall all of us remain committed to the false starts we know all too well. Time past, time present, time future will remain time that we have on our hands unable to rejoice in Him. We would remain with our hand in the hands of idols, deaf and dumb figments of our imaginations, myths about the way they crowd the world with the caprice and condemnations of our race. We would remain in their loveless grip, imprisoned in their times, victims of their vanities. Our theories and our experiences would never know any real beginning, just false starts, were it not for the kind of beginning Moses was able to make in his time. We would never know *the* Beginning as Moses knew *the* Beginning without his beginning. Only with the Voice he heard may we make any real beginning. Only with His Freedom may we make a free and true beginning. When this no Other One speaks, when we listen to Him, we make no false starts, but new and real beginnings that truly matter, because with them we are put on those paths that lead us from *the* Beginning to the I-AM the Lord God is for us all.

We say then that we are baptized right in the midst of things. I would jump into the chaos and emptiness of things, plunge my hands into the depths of my times, hope to grasp what it means to hold what resonates with these things that come from elsewhere. We do well to jump right into the middle of them. We do well to listen as they, with help from the Spirit of God, come to resonate for us with the beginnings of the Mighty One, the Tender One, commanding us like Moses to go where we do not want to go and do what we do not want to do and learn to confess, like Moses again, the Voice speaking to us from the flames of the Burning Bush in the wilderness of our lives.

My dad kept in his bedroom an old wooden trunk. He had preserved in mothballs in that trunk his uniform and medals from the First World War. I can remember the smell in the room when once a year, around Memorial Day I believe it was, he brought my brother and me there to show us his souvenirs. It was all so very wonderful, the smell of the mothballs, the stories of the gas mask and the grenades, the medals surrounded by the soft light in the room. He would tell us the tales of going to war. For our dad it was like going on a vacation. He was an Irishman whose father had immigrated to Ellis Island from the great potato famine in Ireland. His father had fought in the Civil War for his citizenship and then worked in the mines. My dad, fresh out of grammar school in Western Pennsylvania also became a coal miner. He went to work in the mines at thirteen, whistling to a mule while he worked. He was a small man and quick and he could run and whistle like a bird and from driving mules in the mines he was able to enlist, under age, in the Army. He became a runner and the bugler for the 1st Column of Company E in the Sixteenth Infantry of the 1st Division in the United States Army and fought in the battles against the Germans at the Muesse-Argonne, less than 18 years of age. I heard him say many times that the war in Europe was like a vacation for him. After the war, he could not return to work the mines. He took his bride and left Latrobe, Pennsylvania, where he was born, for Cleveland, Ohio. It does not seem a very easy way to begin.

He had gone AWOL to marry our mom, Margaret Elizabeth Hyde, just before he left for the war. After the war he took her to Cleveland, where he worked the steel mills, went to night school until he could take a job as a bookkeeper in the plumbing supply industry of the city. He told me he dreamed of becoming an engineer, but he became an office manager with the Cleveland Plumbing Supply Company a successful firm on the Eastside of the city. He worked his job there for the rest of his life. He was always grateful for it. Perhaps no one born after the 'Great Depression' can understand his kind of thankfulness. Mom had five children that lived, two that did not. They are buried, side-by-side, in Solomon's Cemetery near Brookside Park in a community on the Westside of Cleveland,

An Explanation

named Brooklyn. I knelt there beside their gravestones and wept not so long ago.

Mom died in 1958 of complications from untreated diabetes, just shortly after my graduation from Princeton University. My sisters said that she had hung on until then. Dad lived some fifteen years after her death, a confirmed widower. They had a very rough and tough, sometimes violent, marriage. Dad drank too much some nights and they fought violently, until the police arrived. For us children, it was a fearsome experience. Yet for our sakes they managed in Brooklyn to remain husband and wife together. But it was a terrible time, as my older sister once told my dad, and all of us kids grew up to live pretty self-destructive lives. I suppose we would be classified today as a dysfunctional family. In all the fear and confusion, we tended to live miserably and to die young. Everyone is dead now, except me.

My older brother, Quentin, was named after President Franklin Delano Roosevelt's son, who was killed in Europe during the Second World War. Quentin was a radio-gunner on a B-24 in the Pacific War against Japan. He once earned an air medal when his plane was shot down and the crew managed to bail out and find their way back to our lines. After the war, I remember that he liked to make model airplanes and set them on fire and fly them and watch them crash to the ground and burn. I did not understand him. I think he lived like that too.

My oldest sister, Peggy, born two years after Quentin and my younger sister, Patty, one year later, seemed at times like our parents. Tommy and I were ten years younger than they, respectively. We grew up pretty close to one another, mostly under the care of our sisters. I remember we kept a flag with a blue star on it in the window of our home for Quentin. I could walk the neighborhood and watch the blue stars change to gold. That meant the person had been killed. I hoped we did not have to change Quentin's blue star into gold. We did not. My older sisters and brother were all able to marry, but unhappily, and I have little to do with their families today, sadly.

Tommy left his college under rather dark circumstances and struck out for California, where he hoped to become an actor. He became a bartender. He hardly knew two children he had with a woman he married in Tijuana. They were man and wife for a very short time. He died of lung cancer. I saw him the day before he died. He did not much like my conversion to Christ. But he let me pray for him that day, his last upon this earth. His last words to me were, "*I'll see you at the end of the tunnel.*"

I had somehow managed to graduate from Princeton, to serve three years in the U.S. Army Security Agency, one year in Sinope, Turkey, one year in Bad Aibling, Germany, and afterwards to return to Cleveland to attempt to live with my dad, then a widower. It only took a few months to prove to be a disastrous attempt. I was drinking and carousing, and my dad hated it and he complained finally that I would give him a heart attack if I kept it up. I hitchhiked across the country to Laguna Beach. Tommy had taken up studying acting and working as a bartender there, and Laguna was a nice little artist's colony with a great beach beside the wonderfully soothing waters of the Pacific Ocean. For five years, I drank in that town, moving to San Francisco in the late 60s when the little artist's colony by the sea finally tired of my act and nudged me to go forth. I hitchhiked then to San Francisco.

I was just in time for the Flower Children and the Haight-Ashbury experiment. I met some Army buddies, was introduced to San Francisco State College, and decided to stay. In those days, drugs were so omnipresent that I had little trouble adding them to my daily alcohol. There I was, a graduate in Physical Chemistry from Princeton University, honorably discharged from the ASA, carousing and drinking among the Flower Children, among the Beat and Silent Generations, hoping for something about which I was totally inarticulate. My friends with the others wanted to assure me that, whatever the drugs were, I could prolong my life by taking them. Thus, I caroused with old Beats in North Beach, with Hippies in the Haight-Ashbury, the Flower Children of desperate families in our nation, with hope that this new movement and its creative energies might carve out a new kind of life in the nation, a life for which no one had words yet. It seemed worth the effort. I did try to write at the college. There was some real excitement about the possibilities; night and day enthusiasms dangling like participles under the spell of the Nazi holocaust, the bombs over Hiroshima and Nagasaki, unable to rejoice with the conflicts of the Age raging on our very own rage, when it seemed that eons were spent without foundation in a direction we called with great apprehension the future.

The call was '*Go West young man!*' Once there, however, with the Pacific Ocean conquered, there was nowhere to go but up. The Establishment rode its aircraft; the Subcultures drugs. Both sought to go up as high and as fast as they could. Those in the aircraft flew like eagles

An Explanation

to see the enemy and kill it, even in the face of a black sky, where they had to learn to think, all over again, about it all. Those who took the drugs, LSD and so forth, faced a multicolored sky unbelievably gorgeous at first, but then become filled with poisonous snakes, the rainbows turned into self-destructive death. Both existed in the Atomic Age. The pioneers of the aviation sought victory. The flowers of the desperate children in an abortive attempt to expand human consciousness sought their mortality. I do not know if we can yet explain them as one people we can call Americans. I think we need still to penetrate the depths of what happened in California then. Shall it be avionics or drugs? Shall it be victory or self-destruction? We need more than answers to our questions now. We need a place to go, a space we can call home. We need a certain freedom not easily defined today. I am not sure that anyone can explain the way we move in our time.

In Cleveland, Ohio, at James Ford Rhodes High School, I was an eagle among my fellow student. I loved my teachers. I got good grades from them. I was elected to membership in the National Honor Society. Twice I was elected president of my class. I loved to play sports. I loved to sing. I was good at mathematics, but I, unfortunately, hated history. I was disliked for certain haughtiness, a certain pride in achieving, a certain belief that my breathing in this world was all the history I really needed to know. I had unusual problems over a girlfriend, about whom I remained broken hearted for a longer time than can considered normal. I remember reading F. Scott Fitzgerald's *Tender is the Night* and being terribly moved by its story. I remember reading J. P. Sartre's *Nausea* and feeling more gripped by the antihero's sickness. The anti-hero, Quentin, with his nausea seemed to possess the very fiber of my existence. I could not think to tell anyone about it. I was a good student and a sick man. I do not know how to account for the fact that I was given a scholarship to Princeton University. A stranger, whose name I do not even remember, came to Rhodes High School the year I was to graduate and determined to help me become the second student in the history of the school to go to Princeton. He took me by the hand and before I knew it I was a member of the Class of 1957. I do not now know how to explain him except with some reference to the providence of God, to a freedom I did not understand.

When I spoke to my dad about Princeton, he told me, "*McKenna's don't go to college; we go to work.*" Later, however, in the fall of 1953, he drove me towards Princeton on the Pennsylvania Turnpike, a road we had driven together for summer visits to mom's relatives in Norvelt and dad's in Latrobe. He was driving a brand new Dodge automobile, when he offered me one of his cigarettes. It was a Lucky Strike, from a package that had on it a red bull's eye. He smiled approvingly at me and I took the Lucky Strike and we marked together my passage into manhood. My dad would become very proud of my graduation from Princeton. But I can still hear him pleading on the Princeton campus with my new Princeton roommate, *"Look after him, will you, this is his first time away from home."* I had been smoking secretly for years, but my new friend took seriously my dad's plea. Julian Hume Clark did try for four years at Princeton to look after me.

Julian had prepared for Princeton at a military school. He was the son of an American diplomat, who served in Batiste's Cuba. Raised with the son of the Cuban Dictator, Ruben, Julian was a diligent student, a young man of great integrity, who knew how to keep house. He looked after me in my bouts with drinking and roomed with me all four years at Princeton. Because of him, we were invited to Cuba just before the success of Fidel Castro, a red carpet visit there. Julian showed me how to study, something I did not learn at Rhodes High. I had to learn quickly the rigors of a Princeton education. Those years were filled for me with great despairs and failed prides. I enjoyed a bitter rate against the system of class prejudice on the campus. If I were an eagle at Rhodes, I was a crow at Princeton, or better yet a broken-winged sparrow. I know I would not have made it to graduation without people like Julian, Phil Sullivan, Bruce Bringgold, Dave Browning, Clive Chandler, and Jimmie Shea. With them, I was able to graduate with a Bachelor of Arts in Physical Chemistry in 1957. That was the year Life Magazine named us 'The Silent Generation.' I once in a drunken rage punched out in my room an old stained glass window, with its lead panels. I was fined for my rage and suspended for one weekend. There were other screams in the silence, I knew. On the day of my graduation, my whole family, except for my dying mom, came to celebrate with me. It is frightening for me to remember their photographs. I was such an unhappy, haunted, confused, and proud young man. My dad and sisters and Tommy appear in the pictures happy enough—but not me. As I said, we were a very tormented and self-destructive family.

Like the rest of the world, Princeton suffered in the spell of an abyss that had been fashioned by the photographs of the bombs. The great chasm that had developed between scientific culture, moral impera-

An Explanation

tives, and the humanities was sensible. John Archibald Wheeler, my physics teacher, had contributed to the Manhattan Project, lead by J. Robert Oppenheimer. Wheeler was proud of the bombs, Oppenheimer unusually sad about them. For me, Princeton in the nation's service was not a straightforward proposition. The student body was evidently bent on more romantic notions about this world. In some sense, Scott Fitzgerald's university, where the rich were very different from the poor, was still in evidence, in spite of any questions about the Atomic Age. The followers of Einstein's Relativity Theory moved on towards the discoveries of 'singularities', Black Holes, and the Big Bang Beginning of a new cosmology for the universe. The romantics moved on as 'The Silent Generation' in the common eye. There was a popular existentialism being embraced, of which Walter Kaufman was the master. I left the university then, unable to grasp any reason why we ought to think that life was meaningfully real in any sense, romantic, scientific, or otherwise. It was this view of the 'Nothingness' that I took with me into the world with my Princeton degree.

My brothers used to call it a jungle. I remember reading Joyce's *Dubliners* and *Ulysses*, instead of doing my chemistry lessons, soothing my pain with the beer I learned to drink in Cleveland and the Scotch whiskey I learned to drink at Princeton. Words did hold a certain wonder for me. I spent more time with Joyce than I did with Schrödinger's Wave Equation. It was years before I became aware that Joyce's 'quarks' would someday become a part of our everyday quantum mechanics, that bridges of some kind insisted on being built between the split cultures I could recognize Joyce's world as more my own. I wondered about poetry with the same sense of wonderment that mathematics sometimes gave to me. If it were not for '*The Nothingness*,' I can imagine I could have done something about all that wondering. Why the square root of minus one? Why was Bloom searching so incessantly in Dublin for a father? Why could we turn the Atomic Age into a movie entitled, *Doctor Strangelove*? I can remember seeing that film in San Francisco's North Beach, after an afternoon sitting with brandy and the silent Evan S. Connell . . . who has so un-splendidly found his way from portraying the life of a family the hard way to Jerusalem with his *Deus Lo Volt!* . . . with Norman Mailer trolling under the bridges ever since the war into the depths of Hitler's problem and finally God's . . . writers writing with a rage to understand in the nothingness of the world the horrible and the terrible and the brave and the noble . . . in our tears and in our laughters . . . our laughters and our tears . . . . rolling on the existential table the world is without the dawn of God, with Samuel Beckett's Godot, belly up, going down, falling to an elsewhere . . . where John Wheeler was naming it Black Hole time . . . something that we had to do with curved infinities of space and warped infinities of time in a singular instance of a universal pathos . . . something moving out there to where nobody had ever been or could go . . . standing in the way of . . . The Silent Generation . . . the Screams in the Sound of the Silence . . . *The Nothingness* of anyone, the race confined to gazing our a window at . . . fragments of ourselves . . . alienation in our loves . . . outsiders longing to see through the glass has long it is upon which the ages are shattered . . . watching out for what? . . . weeping over how it is? . . . why it is? . . . where it is and where it is going? . . . and who knows what we may mean at last? I have never heard anyone explain it all.

I did make an attempt, right after Princeton, to teach freshman chemistry at the University of Southern California. But I was drinking so hard by then that, with the death of my mom, I returned to Cleveland for her funeral and never tried to return to my position. I was soon drafted and then enlisted in the Army Security Agency in order to go to a language school in California. But I served as a Morse Intercept Operator in Sinope, Turkey and Bad Aibling, Germany. I did meet during those years a real disciple of Sartre in Sinope, learned first hand existentialism's real discipline, straight from the horse's mouth so to speak, but I drank heavily between duties and knew very well that in Sinope Diogenes had been centuries a failure there. Aldo, the existentialist, worked as a cook under contract to the U. S. Government and was saving money for his next journey to study the Japanese. He was from Trieste, a friend of Ezra Pound, and he actually came to visit me in Bad Aibling. We spent a night in Munich, when he tried to persuade me to come to Trieste upon my discharge. He would introduce me to Pound and I could find out what existentialism was really all about. It was a temptation. But I felt that I was an American; that I needed to return to Cleveland, spend some time with my dad, now widowed there. I sailed on a troop ship, got seasick, landed at the harbor in New York a terribly lonely man. I spent one night, feeling very much alone, in a hotel room, made my airline arrangements, and the next day flew to Cleveland. I had spent some weekends in the Big Apple while at Princeton, and knew Fifth Avenue and was surprised at my determination. Honorably discharged from the U.S. Army, without bands in the harbor of New York, unsure of everything, I flew home to Cleveland.

An Explanation

Joseph Heller's book, entitled *Catch 22*, became popular for the way it unraveled the dialectical knots we learn to tie as boy scouts. Cleveland, like the Army, were knots for me I had to learn to untie, from which I had to escape. But in my confusion, everything seemed to get all twisted up very quickly. I could never say anything about my desperation in my home. My dad, sober as a judge, saw me as a very bad son. Who can say how he hated my drinking and carousing because it reminded him of his own? He begged me to stay home to drink, to go to sleep at night at home, his home, where I had known so much violence. He told me finally that I would give him a heart attack if I kept up living the way that I lived. When my Army benefits ran out, I stuffed Jack Kerouac's *On the Road* in my back pocket and left. I hitchhiked the Mother Road to California. My dad drove me to the edge of the city, dropped me off one morning near an empty field, where I slept off my hangover. I was awakened by a police officer. The officer sent me kindly on my way. I stuck out my thumb and immediately got a ride. I was on Route 66, headed for California. Only when my dad died did I set foot back in Cleveland again.

For five years, Laguna Beach's bars were my new home. I suppose some people in those days actually believed that I was some kind of drunken genius. Laguna was home to all kinds of artists and so forth. There was a bar where they hung out named 'The White House,' a very old café that can be viewed in a 1938 picture of FDR's motorcade in the seaside town. This bar possessed legendary and mythical powers associated with the secrets for which writers and artists live. They drank there together with a common hope. It was a kind of church for the disenchanted. They congregated, believed, and hoped something good could happen to them. They believed in their creativity. People still talked back then about the great American novel. Writers laughed with cartoonists and con men about the world. Painters sought to move their hands on the canvas to go beyond Picasso. All kinds of secrets could be picked up in the 'White House,' as well as women, women who were generally too kind. I believe the saying is true: "God takes care of fools and drunks!" In spite of the many evident sins against Him, no one was immediately killed off. Hardly anyone went to jail. For my part, I could keep up with it only for about five years. Eventually, I wore thin on the little town. I left Laguna to see what was happening in San Francisco.

In the City by the Bay I met some 'old army buddies' from Sinope and Bad Aibling, when I decided to stay. I rented a cheap room in the Haight-

Ashbury. It was an old world neighborhood near a nice park. You could buy '*Piroshki*' there and talk with people dressed in black, drink black coffee with them, find out from where they had come to America, mostly from somewhere in Europe. The shops sold old hardware materials beside some tailoring. The talk compared America to home. Nostalgia came with the black clothes and coffee. But San Francisco is a city that you can easily walk. You don't need a car. I liked walking it and I liked the neighborhoods and being able to go all the way to the bay, sometimes grabbing a trolley. On the GI Bill, I was able to enroll at San Francisco State College. I lived as if I was a student learning to write in the Haight-Ashbury then.

 Very soon, the Flower Children began to appear. Then no one cared about where anyone was from. Breathing was all that mattered. A kaleidoscope of colors on young people invaded the old Slavs and Greeks. The shops were transformed almost overnight, paraphernalia for hardware. Old 'Beats' swaggered into the Haight alongside the 'Hippies,' and the movement of the Flower Children was in full swing. The times began to hum with guitars, psychedelic motions and notions, nude phantoms under the strange light of a moon under which the spirits freely moved. Song after song was composed there, trying to remember what no one had ever yet known. The nights became more alive than the days. Everybody was looking for something new. One could sense all around this energy longing and spreading out to some infinite space where no one had ever been before, as if everyone believed in some elsewhere. The effort was made steadily to cross the abyss of our times, sense then the vibrations of a new world in the old district. No one had every yet imagined what could be, but this becoming seemed better than the spell of mushroom clouds that hovered over the possibilities of the race now. Could the human imagination really undo and overcome that to which our technology appeared to have doomed us? Could anything really come out of the emptiness one feels while suffocating in the smog of industrial success now so easily questionable? Did the American Revolution lose its way in the world? Of what was the new nation capable in our times? The flowers shot up, bloomed beautifully awhile, but soon withered. I am afraid we were like that, too much like that!

 We were seeking to free ourselves from a certain desolation, to fill the emptiness we knew in our pasts, to find those prophetic powers that could shape a new world. We thought we could somehow remove ourselves from the smog and the spell of the Atomic Age, from abstractions

An Explanation

and existential despairs, and enter into a new aeon for the ages. We probably attempted to reach infinities beyond the mathematical and sensible. We sought with our imaginations a freedom for a new will upon the earth, beyond the evident death throes seemingly inherent in the march of the progress civilization was for us. We wanted a new shape for our lives. We wanted to discover new forms free from the inertial energies of our pasts, from the auto-technocratic powers by which the race seemed trapped, cornered by dead ends whose gloom could be seen everywhere one might want to look. We wanted to trade in our centers of commerce for centers of cosmic consciousness. We wanted with naked passions our lives to be free to breathe a fresh air. We wanted to transform the parochial self-centered worlds of Kansas and Michigan and Ohio into a center expansive, a cosmic center the past did not and could not and would not understand. The Flower Children were young. They were hopeful. They believed in this new freedom, and they were willing to put their lives on the line for it. The past belonged to mere slogans. The flowers wanted new words for a new freedom for a new nation. They wanted a new birth for this new nation. They were foolish historians with their breathing desires, but they soaked up the sun and the psychedelic air with an energy at which many gawked. Then they were soon gone.

 The Haight-Ashbury was in this way a kind of no-man's-land for me. It was as dangerous as the jungles of Vietnam. No one could last for very long under those conditions. Wounded generations would pay a price on those terrains that was every bit as costly for humanity as the Korean ground. They died there quickly in those wars. I remember a very great painter I knew in those days (He could paint like a Rembrandt!), saying to me on one of my visits from the Haight to Laguna, "*It's getting so that if you want to see anybody you know, you have to go either to the slammer, the loony bin, or the morgue.*" I remember being taken up short by his remark. It was too true. I believe it suddenly took my imagination away from the utopian prophecy of the flowers and into the sober country of the dying. It was unbelievable the way the world could turn so quickly into a desolate land. With no words for it, the phantoms of the imaginations whose drugged energies soon turned red-blooded children into homeless and estranged creatures, unrecognizable to their parents, members now of *Desolation Row*. I remember Bob Dylan sang his rather prophetic account of this rapidly changing time. The children as flowers, withered into forms of nightmares, were to be found at last strewn along the edges of the strange abyss of those lively nights, far from anywhere anyone ever intended to get. That was the Haight-Ashbury to me.

For my part, I read and struggled with steadily the English poet William Blake, and then the Irishman William Butler Yeats. I could rage back then with the best of them against Sir Isaac Newton's Mechanical Universe, against the denigration of the human will and the human imagination the determinism of this Cosmos spelled out for mankind. I could embrace the sexual revolution with an explosive energy that matched the bombs over Japan. I could bemoan the spasms and the phantasms of a culture split apart by a loss of meaning few wanted to say out loud. What was the cause of all these causes—Revolutionary War, a Civil War, of World Wars? What was the cause of these causes, of the Age of the Bomb, of the Korean and Vietnamese wars, of the war between America and the Communists? What was the cause of the causes of the Beat and the Hippies and the Flower Children? What was the cause of the causes of Czars in Russia, the cause of the Bolsheviks, the Revolutionaries? What was the cause of the causes of Marx and then Lenin and Stalin? What was the cause of the cause of the Nazi, of Adolph Hitler, and the murder of millions, especially Jews? What was the cause of the cause of the Allies, the cause of the freedom with which Imperial Japan struck so brutally into China, and then attacked our Pearl Harbor? To what causes did Sir Winston Churchill and his United Kingdom belong? What were the causes of President Franklin D. Roosevelt and the triumph of the United States in the cause of our Western Civilization? What is the real cause of all these causes for freedom? What was the cause of the freedom with which the existentialists sought from Europe to know who they were in this world? What is the real cause of the freedom with which the citizens of the United States seek to know who they are? What is the cause of the democracy of freedom? What are the causes, left and right, that makes our democracy what it is in the world? What is the cause of the individual? What is the cause of the community? What is the cause that needs the freedom to go to the moon? What is the cause that needs to kill Jews in Palestine? What is the cause of the Jews in their new homeland, the cause of their fight for their right to exist? What are these causes of the freedom of the fanatic in Islam who seeks to murder his way to heaven? What lies at the bottom of all these causes? What is the meaning of these freedoms? Who truly lives in real freedom? Why do all these causes seem to become so entangled at times? Who can untie the knots with which their dilemmas tie up the nations? Who is free to swim the river that runs through it all? Surely, the Flower Children and the veterans of Vietnam both needed answers to such questions, and perhaps all of us still today need them.

There is in our time a kind of nostalgia about the Sixties. If the flowers wilted too soon in the barrels of the guns of war, and if they are gone just as our will to obtain the unconditional surrender from our enemies, if we are so weary, if we are so fragmented, if we are so alienated, if our minds suffer in ways that make us seem like outsiders looking in through a window of a home that is not a home, then how indeed shall we live? I know now what I did not know back then—God is not merely watching all of these times. He is interacting with us in them. He is acting as the Lord He is in His time for us. We need to learn to hear Him. It is not easy to explain. But we can learn to hear Him. I must speak that, in the Name of the Person of the Lord Jesus Christ, He works steadily in our times for us, that we might become free to hear Him in time and times and time again. I must say this: *Where the Spirit of the Lord is, there is freedom*! His is a freedom we must learn, else go without the answers we need in our time.

The Corpus Callosum

The 'corpus callosum' is dead.
The mind's eye is ruined,
Human imagination is groaning
Beside the moaning sea.
On the waters the clocks are grieving,
Along the sands the waves are falling
In the hours kept along the shores,
People killing time and time killing them,
Their lamentations sent with tears in a bottle
Sailing on the storms of the world,
Their messages torn, unreadably divided.

The lily is wilting in his hands,
His sea-sick mouth like the mariners
Falling like happiness into the depths,
His brain on fire, his body crushed
Against the harbor rock.
The 'corpus callosum' is dead.

We longed for the cause of the causes of our years, even as we despise our God. Nostalgia helps us live the past again, invention the future, but the present does not readily or necessarily mark out the path to which our God has called us to take. Everything is, of course, at stake. Who can explain these things? Whatever was moving those flowered children, whatever was moving the warrior in the jungles, moves in the world still. Whether we believe it or not, our God also is moving. He moves within our souls. He moves within the world. He takes them to their destiny with Him.

> *From the belly that bid us stay,*
> *The invitation spread at home*
> *Across the table of the world,*
> *We sought to fly,*
> *Like eagles in the sky.*
> *We could not stay,*
> *We had to go,*
> *We had to go,*
> *We thought mankind must be our aim.*
> *You were fair to say*
> *We missed the mark.*
> *You are right to say*
> *We missed the mark.*
> *We missed the mark.*
> *What did you miss then?*

Those times marked the end to the world for me. Chain-smoking two or more packs of cigarettes a day, too often drunk, too much tormented, too driven, too desperate with rage, too many drug-filled hours with a creeping sexuality loosed onto the nothingness of the world, despairing down to the bone and somehow fearfully surviving, with enough of the gift of gab to carry onto the howling streets of the city the torrents of haunted footfalls with a heart broken to walking day or night among the phantoms of faces masked by the voices of demons for falling into the abyss the Haight became for the children of flowers, poised for their deaths. I will not bother my reader with all the specifics, only a survey.

    I did get a job in Berkeley for a time, a year or so, first as a janitor, then a technician, and finally, when my Princeton background became known, as a research assistant in an aerospace company. I did learn about the longing of the design engineers for what they called 'optimum core,' their search for a high strength to weight materials with which all the better to conquer space. I watched them place Ping-Pong balls in an aquarium, fill it with water, heat the whole thing up, and then look to

An Explanation

see if the expanding surfaces would produce a geometry that would lead them to some optimal configuration for the best strength to weight ratio in the honeycomb business. It is impossible to explain to a reader that, when I quit that job and later met a sculptor who saw spheres when he took LSD back in the Haight, we started looking for this thing in free space, and when we found it there—infinite geometrical fields generated by spheres in processes with themselves—I had to name the polyhedrons of one of the fields. I found that one of the fields was made up of polyhedral forms undefined in the literature. I named them the 'iso-icosahedron' and the 'endo-anneahedron,' a structural system that I patented in 1972, as a building and as the 'optimum core' the engineers sought. How can I explain without Princeton such lingering crossings of my interests in those times? How can I bother my reader with them? Poetry and mathematics! No, I will not bother a reader with them. Nor need I seek to tell of the Tenderloin of San Francisco, the racetracks and pool tables of her bars, and the terribly desperate souls we meet there. I will tell of Yeats and Blake, because they were in some sense right there with me at the end my world was then, when I seemed compelled to become interested in what one poet said were *'the relationships between things that tend to escape our attention.'* Perhaps this is what the human imagination is after on such new frontiers with which those times seemed concerned.

William Butler Yeats was a common uncommon man. He suffered the loss of his first love, Maude Gonne, because he lacked any faith in Irish politics. He married a woman then who was a medium. He became one himself, actually heard the 'voices of the dead' at séances to which his wife had introduced him, where and when he obtained the metaphors and visions for much of his poetry. He envisioned the whole history of the world with a rather esoteric geometrical picture gained from such 'voices.' His craft gave a powerful lyrical quality to his poems whose aesthetic reach pretended a universal grasp of things, including the meaning of mankind in times, past, present, and future. For his work, he was awarded a Nobel Prize.

When Yeats longed out loud for the city of Byzantium, his imagination was tuned into these 'voices,' far from the dirt of Ireland's political struggles. I remember feeling somewhat astonished to learn these things about him. He was certainly a great poet with words whose lyrical quality formed aesthetic lines now cherished with fame. But to learn their content came from these 'voices,' more than the green land that Ireland is, was a bit of a shock. Until Yeats, I had no taste for the supernatural. I reckoned it a curse upon Irish consciousness. It was the stuff that plagues the poor with leprechaun stories, filled with ghosts and ghouls that inhabit folktales told around the fires and at the pubs that ought to be put out, ancestral superstitions that grip a people with their poor pasts. To rid this tormented land of these characters with their cold superstitions would be a better cause than the dramatic visions Yeats produced for them. As far as Maude Gonne was concerned, the poet was perhaps a little crazy and out of touch. Yeats accused her in his work of marrying a man who knew no Dante. I could know his pains, but felt amazed at his supernatural interests and the reality of his muse.

William Blake turned out to be a song of a similar metaphysical wing. Blake's father was steeped in the works of Emanuel Swedenborg, and William, an ex-chemist became filled with those wonderful travels that could land him, not merely on the moon, but among the planets with a top grade messianic consciousness, following in his father's footsteps with its powers. Swedenborg was the name he chose when he moved from Sweden to live, with a pension from the Swedish Government, in London, where he spent nights in which he would leave his bed and travel to the distant *heavenlies*, homes of the angels. He would encounter the managing angels of those worlds and, after returning to his bed in London's foggy dawn, he would write down what he had learned. Long before the United States ever made its giant step for mankind and became a leader in looking for intelligent life in the universe, Emanuel had already been there and done that. He gathered up this very heady information about the world and the world's destiny with his god in a commentary on the Book of Genesis. He wrote profusely about God's Creation, His plans for the heavens and the earth, what he claimed that the human imagination was duty bound to become, as Christ's Mind, perfect and in this way to fulfill on earth Christ's direction of us. No wonder Blake could rage against the Newtonians. Sir Isaac was a 'sleepwalker' to the poet's mind. His mechanical universe had denigrated utterly the human imagination. The determinism implicit in the laws was the very enemy of the meaning of the race upon the planet. The poetry of his vision attempted to show us a god capable of being against the deism of Newtonians and the industrialization of civilization. Blake thus bore his father's influence upon him with a very heavy mantle indeed. He created a vision that painted in poetic terms a gravity that was beyond the gravity of the industrial

An Explanation

revolution of the Western World. He saw deism and determinism as the enemy of our civilization. For the artist, the progress of the industrial revolution was all smoke and smog and belching up the dusts of death over the race. It was stuff against the angels and the voices with whom he trafficked each night when he left his body on his bed and visited them in their homes, travels arranged throughout the solar system of our universe by a very active god, indeed. Is this not the source of what C. P. Snow labeled the split between cultures in the West? How much does this have to do with the split between the artist and his humanity and the scientists of the Bomb? How much does this have to do with the split between the flowers and the soldiers?

My studies into these two poets opened my eyes to worlds that had certainly escaped my attention. In the abyss of 'The Nothingness,' I knew the struggle to want to survive in this world. I knew my Sartre's *Nausea*. I knew Camus' *The Stranger*. *Le Neant* was my home. No one less than Walther Kaufman, Princeton's authority on *Das Nichtige*, had taught me the basics. Beckett had given me some great laughs. Ernest Hemingway, a bull of a prose writer, helped me with his *Nada*. Steinbeck wrote a Californian American pathos with people not surfers but fishers of the waves, and Faulkner with a view from the deep South gazed upon the tenacity of the human race. Joyce, going blind in Paris, writing masterfully down in the City of Light of a lost father left in Dublin far behind him. I had taken all that in. I had heard John Archibald Wheeler teach Einstein's General Relativity Theory. I had wondered about Schrödinger's wave equation. I was not an innocent Flower Child. But there was nothing in any of this that had prepared me for Blake's travels or for the 'voices' that gave metaphor to the lyric poetry of Yeats. I knew too Bertrand Russell's fist of a face, the stoic mask with which he faced '*The Nothingness*' of his world. I knew Eliot's wasteland, the bang and the whimper hollow men hear when sipping tea beside their universes. But what kind of a trip was it that Yeats longed to take when dreaming of sailing towards Byzantium? What kind of trip was it to travel with Blake's Swedenborg to the planet Venus, and there speak with master angels in the long silent night, his body resting alone in bed at home in London upon the earth? Under the spell of Hitler's holocaust in Europe, of the Age of the Bomb then, in the grip of the Cold War, the assassinations of John F. Kennedy, Pastor Martin Luther King, and Robert Kennedy, Korea, in the throes of bunker mentalities, guerilla warriors, run-away technologies, Dr. Strangelove and the

Tambourine Man, with the Sound of the Silence ringing in our ears upon *The Nothingness* of the world, we listened among the Flower Children in the Haight-Ashbury, when supernatural carousing surrounded us with desolation and death, to the end of the movement. What had these to do with our scientific culture and humanity's vaunted progress and the reason we are given to know the mysteries of the universe? When you add LSD to such volcanic lives, you may get a slight glimpse into the existence as it was at the end of the world for me in San Francisco's Mission District.

What if there was something from elsewhere beyond '*The Nothingness*' of this world? What if, beyond our vaunted sensibilities, beyond our abstract genius, from beyond all our great experiences, there is something metaphysical to the being of the universe? Perhaps there exist dimensions to this world that have escaped our mind's eye. Perhaps the magnitude of the human thought is not enough to measure what actually exists even beyond all the infinities to which we seek correspondence for our truly expansive world. Perhaps where the world is going no one truly knows. Such possibilities became questions for me. They seemed to bring me closer to my real fears than I wanted to get. To die and become nothing was something I thought I could train myself to do. But to die in this world's 'Nothingness' with the thought that this world possessed dimensions of being that belonged as home to such invisible creatures as angels and demons, good gods and evil ones, well, that was too much for me to gaze upon with a completely straight face. I began to tremble deep inside of myself. The possibilities frightened me in a place that was strange to me. I was too tired to live, too afraid to die, like the old Negro song says beside the river. I found myself crying out, as if in a wilderness of fear and trembling, to God. "*God, if you are there, please help me!*" It was as simple as that for me.

I remember an old lady handing me a tract on a street in downtown San Francisco. She told me that Jesus loved me. She said that he was coming back very soon. I told her, head down, hung over; weary as hell in a night of unseen stars, "*The sooner the better.*" I did have a few friends with whom I could talk about God. I started talking about Him with them more than ever. At a bar, in the middle of a night of drinking, among perfect strangers, I would begin to dare to speak of Him. Nobody, I assure you, wants to talk about Him in the middle of his or her night out drinking. I had one friend in Laguna who had once challenged me to read the Bible. He had taken a course on the Bible in college. To be an intellectual one needed to read the Bible, he argued. I had another friend, who like myself had gone from Laguna to San Francisco to live, and we talked about the Bible. He was raised in Chicago a Catholic, and remembered it at times with some fondness. I took up reading it then. I read through the whole thing. But it seemed to me to be a history of one damn war after another, until you got to the New Testament perhaps, when a man of peace, Jesus, declared a final war. I could hardly distinguish it from reading the newspapers. I had to admit that, when I came to reading the pages about Christ, a more lyrical mood seemed to be introduced, but with a pathos that told of the murder of the most perfect man who had ever lived upon the earth. There was something about His life that was different from all the rest. His killing seemed par for the course, knowing the world as I thought I did. His resurrection simply escaped the attention of my imagination altogether. I escaped utterly any grip it might gain upon the eye of my mind. That is the way I read the Bible in those days.

To feel you are alone in this world, to know your hours tormented and tortured with an emptiness and the pain of an utterly meaninglessness existence, to know you cannot shake it no matter how much you drink and so forth, means you are a soul arrested and imprisoned in a time cut off from whatever eternity is. During those times, I was once actually arrested for public rowdiness and once for being drunk in public and once again for running with a friend who was running naked in his neighborhood on a public street, disturbing the peace. I was only jailed once, for one night. The morning after, a judge lectured me on sobriety and rehabilitating my life, and then released me. I will say that the sound of iron bars slamming shut in your face does tend to sober you, all right, but when the judge suggested I enroll in a program, I argued that the State of California should not waste its hard earned money on the likes of me. There existed in this world no good reason for attempting to prolong my life. The judge finally agreed. He waived my probation and, that same afternoon, I was back walking the streets of San Francisco once more, with the desolation of the Haight-Ashbury and the fear of the invisible dimensions deeply settled onto my psyche. I thought I was, indeed, at the end of my world.

Once moved from the desolate Haight-Ashbury, I rented a room in the Mission District and gazed upon the skid row of the city. I felt isolated from even the few people who still knew me. When I would return at night to this room, having spent the day with a relentless loneliness, my nights were haunted with the phantoms, strange fires of a brain plagued by chemistry and the invisible world. I experienced an assortment of otherworldly phenomena, but no pink elephants. My sleep was inhabited with otherworldly creatures crossing like demons a landscape aching with sexual fantasies, so that it seemed to me that I belonged more to the myths of this world, to some old hag laughing live at the center of a universe made up of the stuff of the imagination rather than solid things. She heckled there over the lusts of my humanity, as my body was being crushed down into the dusts of death. I felt that I was at the very gates of hell. The metal of my soul was now a liquid fired burning down into the core of a Godforsaken world. The Steppenwolf was no longer at my door or in the mirror. He was what I had become. I was a 'wolf man' in the mirror. Why should I try to continue to exist?

It was only a matter of fear. I was a creature lost in the infinity of aberrations, delusions and allusions screaming out across the primordial abyss of a vastly wounded consciousness in the black silence of my God-forsaken world. I felt condemned to judgments of some unknown God made too long ago to remember, some God of this invisible world in which I could or would not believe. During those days and nights, I found myself crying out again and again, as I have said: "*Lord, if you are there, if you are really there, please help me!*" That He was listening, that He would actually help me, came as a complete surprise. Being hunted down by such a God can be a painful, I know, a very painful process.

I recount only a few of the events: 1) I had spent the better part of a day reading at the downtown public library. (I am still grateful for public libraries!) As I was checking out a book, a stranger spoke to me and offered to give me a ride home. I was weary enough to accept his offer. When we got to my rented room, he asked me if he could pray for me. Oddly enough, I accepted. He parked the car and there on a hill beside the room in the Mission District of San Francisco, the stranger said a prayer for me. I had never had anything like that happen to me before in my life. He prayed in the name of Jesus Christ. He wished me well. I felt astonished. 2) A young man who was the son of an old friend asked me to drive him in his father's car to meet some people he had met at the beach that day. I agreed to do it and drove that evening from City by the Bay to somewhere in Oakland, to a small garage where a small gathering of people had congregated. We sat while they worshipped and prayed together. We listened to a man preach, very passionately. From the garage that night, these people took us to a nearby stream, baptized us in the cold waters, two naked men in the moonlight, in the name of Jesus Christ, and I felt, coming up out of the water, strangely clean. When I looked up then in the night sky, I thought I could see among the clouds the figure of a man standing above us. With a surprising sense of wellbeing, from that time on I could not get him off my mind. Even when I went out drinking, even in the middle of my binge, I would not be able to get Jesus Christ off my mind. I began talking about him with perfect strangers I met in the bars. I am afraid I made quite a pest of myself then. 3) I walked into a church one morning, unable to bear what had been happening to me any longer. In the church, I asked three rather large men to pray for me, because of the strange things that had been happening to me. They were Swedes in the Mission District of San Francisco, with big hands, and when they prayed for me, it seemed to me that they knew everything about my trials. I was astonished, but I felt comforted. I promised to come to the church the next Sunday. Later, some young people in this church took me three Saturday nights to a motel bar in Berkeley, California. We listened there to a man by the name of Mario Murillo. Above the bar, he preached about the Resurrection of Jesus Christ. He called his organization Resurrection City. I had listened to the likes of Eldridge Cleaver and the Black Panthers in Berkeley, but I had never heard anything like I heard during those Saturday nights with Mario Murillo. He spoke of the way that God in Christ was alive. He was here in our time and in our space. He was alive and here to heal us. The way that he would point to someone in his audience and tell them that God had healed them of this or that disease was unforgettable to me. Yeats and Blake should have heard this Jesus among the voices of the angels that they did hear. It was all very strange, indeed, but I was so impressed that I took one of my old Army buddies with me to see and hear it the very next Saturday night. My buddy was a Catholic and I do not think he was much impressed with Mario.

But the third Saturday night, when I had returned from listening to his preaching to my room, while I was lying there in my bed, perhaps trying to remember what I heard, suddenly I thought a thunderclap struck down out of the window of the room. I went to sit up in the bed to see what the thunder may have hit, but before I was even upright, I realized that the thunder was not outside my window at all. It was indeed inside the room and, yes, it was even inside of myself. I felt my mouth gently open. I said some words I did not know. I felt no fear, but rather overcome by a peace or a strange sense of love. I lay back down. I slept like a baby. I had not slept like that for a very long time. (Addicts do not sleep; they pass out!) I say I slept like a baby that night for the first time in my life, and in the morning when I woke, all I could think was that I had been healed and that I had to find out about Jesus Christ. I had to learn who he is among us.

I was healed then from my most deadly habits, two packs or more a day, booze of all kinds, drugs of all sorts, carousing and all its twisted pleasure seeking. I knew I had been forgiven. I felt a deep sense of great joy. God had healed me. God had forgiven me. He had given me a new life. I felt a great sense of deep joy down in the depths of my being. I got up and went from that room to walk the streets of San Francisco to tell everyone what had happened to me. I began making up songs, singing them out loud (I had not sung since I had sung in high school and at Princeton!), stopping to tell anyone I could along those streets that Jesus was alive. Jesus Christ was alive and He would help them. All they had to do was cry out to Him! I remember meeting an old black man who had once been himself a preacher. He was drunk, and when I told him about Jesus, he tried to persuade me that he was a 'backslider,' far beyond the pale of God's reach now. I laughed at him. I told him again that Jesus had just the other night forgiven and healed me. If that were so, surely he would forgive him too. I never saw that preacher again, but I wondered how many like him there must be in this world. We do not know the power and scope of God's forgiveness in our lives. Like the black man, most that I met along those streets, like most of my few friends, simply thought they had met a mad man. I have always prayed since that time for people like that.

At night, I would read a King James Bible someone had given me. I took to copying down the words printed in red. They were the words of Jesus and, copying them down like that, helped my powers of concentration, always suspect in an addict's life. The truth of these words seemed to fill my body up with light, lovingly healing my being. They tasted in my mouth as sweet as honey. They flooded my soul with a river of the truth of His Life. I would read the words and copy them down in those nights until I felt that I could stand it no longer, and I would have to ask Him to stop—I could take no more. I thought that, if He kept it up, I would come right out of my skin. And the Lord would stop. I would go to bed, slip the Bible under my pillow, in case I woke in the middle of those nights, and sleep, again like a baby. I knew then, right from the beginning, the great and tender mercies of the Almighty. It was like that for me for five or six days and nights. And each morning, after thanking Him, I got up to walk the streets of San Francisco again, making up songs and singing them out loud in public. I wanted everyone to know what had happened. Jesus Christ was alive and he had pity on us. Most thought I had flipped out in those days. But each night, I felt His Presence with me. Each night, I read the Bible with great joy, in a rented room among the strangers in the Mission District in the City of San Francisco, early in 1972. For the first time in my life, I knew I was not alone in this world, and I was extremely glad.

The strange thing was that, just when I felt I had found my right mind, people thought I had lost it. Both friends and strangers thought I had finally taken too much LSD, and I discovered that many have no room for a Jesus Freak in their space! Yes, my life was wonderfully turned upside down. Yes, it was suddenly full of joy. Yes, I was un-alone. Yes, I was a forgiven man. Because he is, I was happy as a songbird in my own skin. I would return to my rented room at night in the Mission District, unafraid, un-alone, wonderfully joyful. The tormented hours had become time for Him. The Lord was with me. He had given me a whole new life. I slept deeply in those nights, with my head on a pillow under which I had placed my Bible, just in case. If I woke from some nightmare now, I could read myself to sleep again, like a baby. But nobody I had known believed me. What was I supposed to do?

I soon decided to hitchhike back to Laguna Beach. My brothers were still living there and I wanted to tell them what had happened to me. I got a ride that took me once more along the Pacific Coast Highway, beside the great waters of the Pacific Ocean, on a day that was all blue sky and white clouds and wondrous. I was indeed a happy man at last. I must say that I do not think that my friends ever enjoyed very much any of my happiness. In Laguna, both Tommy and Quentin thought like the others that I had gone off the deep end. They gave me, in fact, a bad time and hated my confession of Jesus Christ. I ended up sleeping on the beach. I spent a week of nights under the stars on the sand beside the wonderful sounds of the waves sometimes lapping, sometimes crashing onto my new home. With nothing to my name but the clothes on my back and the Bible, I was happy under those stars, happier than I had ever been in my life. I was 37 years old, a broken but happy man. I was grateful to God to be alive in His world. I thanked Him morning and evening for His Salvation. I thanked my new Lord day and night for his tender mercies. It was a grand time to be with Him under those stars on the beach of Laguna.

But it was not too long before an old acquaintance, a Christian man, helped me to find some fellowship. He introduced me to a group of Christians meeting on Sundays in a park alongside of Laguna's golf course. I was happy to tell them that Christ had healed and saved me in San Francisco. They embraced me as their brother, and gave me their fellowship. The pastor was a man named J. Michael Montgomery, a graduate of Dallas Theological Seminary, who had tired of playing church, gone to India for Christianity there, quit the Evangelical Free Church, and was seeking more spiritual challenges in the Jesus Movement in Southern California. He and his associates sought to embrace the testimonies of those homeless and estranged people we called the Hippies and Flower Children, to help us to begin to gain some knowledge of the Bible. What kind of courage did it take to drive up Laguna Canyon Road and minister to the wounded generations of the subculture of the Sixties? I will always be grateful that they had it, whatever it was.

One of the men among those Christians gave me a couch in his apartment to sleep on. But very soon, I was given an apartment of my own. I soon was living above an abandoned warehouse of a defunct lumber business at the end of the Laguna Canyon Road. The abandoned space had been turned into nothing less than the Laguna Outreach House. We took in the wounded from the experiments championed by the likes of Timothy Leary, Psychology Professor from Harvard University turned LSD Guru. Young people of all sorts and types would emerge from out of the caves in the surrounding hills. They would stagger in too from off the beaches along the Pacific or from the highways. They had hitchhiked to our shelter, and we would try to help them for a while. We would take them in, feed them, and attempt to lead them to Jesus. He was alive and He was what they truly needed in their lives. It was an amazing experience for me.

Six months into that ministry, I met Nancy Ann McVicker, and surprisingly I was married for the first time in my life just three months later. She lived with her son, Paul Drew, among the people in the Canyon. We had met one night at the White House Cafe in Laguna, where I attempted to tell old drinking buddies there about Jesus, much to their dismay. It was not much of a ministry, but it was what I knew to do. None of my old friends liked me as a Jesus Freak at all. But Mickey, my wife's nickname, was there that one night when she took my side against my mocking buddies, and

An Explanation

then she soon came to live with me at the Outreach House. She took up praying with me and helped us feed our drug-crazed guests. Her son, Paul Linden Drew, also eventually joined our efforts, himself out of the crazed, and he too began to help us, believing in Jesus among the disenchanted.

We lived at the Outreach House for about two years. We studied the Bible with Mike Montgomery and his friends, held regular church meetings, and sought to help the wounded generation we were. One of Mike's friends, a man named Ron Whitson, also a graduate of Dallas, eventually helped Mickey, Paul, and me to leave Laguna. We left for the Jesus Christ Light & Power House located near the UCLA campus in Los Angeles. I needed to study the Bible more deeply. I was regaining some of my powers of concentration and a systematic study of it to me seemed imperative. We moved to the Echo Park district and the gangs of Los Angeles. We spent two years learning prophecy from Hal Lindsey, practical theology from Bill Counts, a Princeton University and Dallas Seminary graduate, and Francis Schaeffer, the Midwestern Presbyterian gone to L'Abris, Switzerland, from Tom Brewer. Two years later, I felt ready to return to academic life. I was admitted on a probationary status to Fuller Theological Seminary in Pasadena in1975. Mickey and I moved to Hollywood, ministered to the street people there, no different from what we had known in Laguna, and I began to attend Fuller. We spent more than ten years at Fuller, from 1976 until 1987. I earned a Master of Divinity in 1979, a Doctor of Philosophy in Historical Theology in 1987, and became an Adjunct Professor in Hebrew and the Old Testament as well as a special assistant to Fuller's President David Allan Hubbard for two years. When President Hubbard retired I was dismissed from Fuller, but with their credentials, I found some work as an Adjunct with Azusa Pacific University, not far from Pasadena. Since then, I have taught at a number of universities and seminaries in California, much of the time with Koreans. The Koreans sent me to Lima, Peru, to Sao Paula, Brazil, in Ryzan and Moscow, Russia, as a part of their deep commitment to send missionaries to evangelize around the world. Eventually, the Worldwide Church of God employed me and with this church I have also taught in England, Scotland, and across the United States. I love to teach the Bible and Christian Theology. I no longer keep one under my pillow at night, but I love the Holy Scriptures of the Church of the Person of the Lord Jesus Christ. I love learning to know Him for who He truly is. This book could not be written without these experiences. My old friends may not want to know me as the Jesus Freak anymore, but I do not mind meeting strangers and I am, because of Jesus Christ, a happy man.

I was very fortunate to meet at Fuller in 1981 Professor Thomas F. Torrance of Edinburgh. This distinguished professor did not mind making a friend of me. He seemed at ease speaking about my walking wounded generation. He soon became a mentor and a friend as well. For me, he was like an angel of God. I will write in this book about a man named John Philoponus, a sixth century Alexandrian, whose work is not very familiar to most Christians. The Church roundly condemned him, East and West, and a formal Anathema in 680 AD kept him from history's credit. Because of Professor Torrance's willingness to guide my studies, Philoponus became the subject of my Ph.D. dissertation. He would help me revive my interests at Princeton in science, and I began to learn to relate the Word of God I had heard as Christ to our modern scientific culture. I have said this book must be a California book. There will be no footnotes, no technical arguments with scholarly opinions, no bibliography, just lots of waves, wave after wave; wave upon waves of thoughtful energies that I hope my readers shall be able to catch and ride with some real satisfaction. I hope that on the pages of my book a number of concepts will appear whose energies will resonate with some of our deepest needs. I hope you will learn to hear the Light as I have been taught to hear Him even upon the waters of this world. I hope you will be able to ride with some cosmic satisfaction these energies from the sea, like flying the winds in the sky with the seabirds and eagles. I hope you will glimpse the power of His Glory with us, the Almighty Creator acting for us in our times and in our spaces. I hope that my Christian Theology will be found to be formed on a real ground where our Natural Sciences must be understood as friends of His movements in the world, a space where Eternity and Time have been made to meet on our behalf. I hope you will become able to discover ways that will lead you to new integration of things that have, in the past, perhaps escaped our attention.

Some new friends, Pastors Edgar and Marta Mohorko, whose twin daughters, nicknamed Sisy and Eca, sing a song they wrote in the churches of Oxnard, California: *Sin ti, yo soy nada*, 'Without you, I am nothing,' have inspired me to write this book. I hope my readers will find upon these pages the way the Lord God is willing to makes us all out of the nothingness of our creations into His Children, Children of God taken up from pasts of twisting in the chaos and emptiness of our pasts, now destined

An Explanation

to be with Him and His Love forever. It is a wave no one should miss. It is a solitary wave whose solidity everyone should get to ride. It is upon this water that we are made to belong to an arrow of time whose mark is nothing less than the Glory of God Himself, the Lord of this Universe made solid by the promise of His Creation. We believe it is this movement in the world that is all that finally truly matters, both now and for as long as forever is with His Eternity. It is this energy that I hope the message of my book will bring to you.

Rough Beast

2

The Great I-AM

... I am who I am. Thus you shall say to the sons of Israel: I-AM has sent you.

Exodus 3:14

IN THE MIDST OF his years, Moses began his new life for Israel. A Voice speaking to him from the flames of a bush burning unconsumed beside Horeb, the mountain of God, in the desert of the Sinai, called out his name, "Moses, Moses." "Here I am," said Moses. Thus, with this event a dialogue was established between God and Moses. We call this meeting revelation. It occurred thousands of years after *the* Beginning. It posited a new beginning for the life of Israel among the nations, but it belonged to an old struggle between God and His People.

No one actually begins at *the* Beginning except God. We begin where we are, in the midst of our times, even when the Voice speaks and gives us to dialogue with who God is. While tending the flocks of Jethro his father-in-law, priest of Midian, Moses is met by the Angel of Yahweh speaking to him from the flames of the burning bush, that is the fugitive Moses from the land of the Pharaohs who has received a revelation compelling him into his new life, a life that knows God as the Lord from the Voice of the Great I-AM. We need to apprehend the significance of this new life as best we can.

Moses is a man on the run from the tribes of his birthright, the seed of Abraham, driven into Egypt by sin and famines. Moses is caused to stand on holy ground and to listen to the command of this Voice, for the Angel of Yahweh has heard the cries of the People of God and with His Voice has determined to make this new beginning with Moses for Israel. Moses will become the Leader and the Prophet of these tribes of events Israel shall never forget. He will be led by God to free Israel from her afflictions in Egypt and to make her free to worship Him. Moses' life, once God has thus spoken, would never be the same. Israel's life would never again be the same. The revelation of this God marks a new beginning in the history of the world, one that belongs to God's promise to Abraham and to *the* Beginning of His Creation. Time past, time present, and time future belonged to this Voice with the People of God. Long after *the* Beginning had begun, God makes this new beginning in the history of Israel among the nations for the sake of His covenanted relationship with His People in His Creation. It is a beginning that belongs to the power of God's revelation, to the command of His Voice. If He spoke in *the* Beginning, He speaks once more here from the burning bush with Moses of a new beginning. His purpose and intentions in His covenanted relationship with His People and His Creation shall not be denied. A new epoch is begun in the history of Israel and the Creation. We too must begin here, with the speaking of this Voice, with the revelation of God. We begin where we must, or not.

The determination of this Voice is commanding. This Voice wills to deliver His People from their afflictions under their bondage to Pharaoh in the land of Egypt. This Voice wills to keep an ancient promise made to Israel's ancestors. We begin with the command of this Voice for Moses. We begin with a Moses who would stay if he could. We begin with a Moses who must go. He must go where he does not want to go. He must do what he does not want to do. We begin with the gift of this Voice's command. We begin with the Torah of Moses for Israel, Moses sent from the holy ground created by the Voice of the Burning Bush to Egypt and then with the People of God to the Holy Mountain. We begin with the gifts of this Voice for Israel, with His Tabernacle, with His ways to worship and to fellowship with Him, with the gifts for a great journey across the desert wilderness to a Promised Land. We begin with the keeping in time and times of a great promise made to His People, with the Voice in Israel's nights and days and her destiny with this God, this Lord and God. We must begin where we will end, with this Voice for Moses at Horeb in the Sinai.

Here is the Voice of the Self-Revealing, Self-Naming, Self-Defining, and Self-Giving God as the Lord of His People. Here is the Voice of the Great I-AM He is as the Lord and God with Moses for His People among the nations. We must begin here with Moses on this holy ground, or stay elsewhere. We must begin and end with this Voice of the Great I-AM the Lord God is as Israel's Redeemer, even the Creator of the heavens and the earth in *the* Beginning. We must begin in a new world for Israel begun by the Voice of the Lord God with Moses. There is no other place to begin. Here is confession that is new in the history of the world, a confession Moses must make as he is compelled to follow the speaking of this Voice. Moses' confession establishes a new beginning for Israel, irreversible in the times of the world, made by the Voice of the Great I-AM He is with Israel, His People. This old man, a fugitive and murderer in the eyes of his generation, shall thus become the great leader and prophet of the history of Israel among the nations in the world. A new life in His covenanted relationship has been given Israel among the nations with this Voice.

We do not begin with a mystery of the mysticisms, the cryptic and magical sayings of other-worldly oracles in our times. We begin in dialogue with this Voice whose command will in fact deny such idol making among the peoples of the world. Moses must remove his sandals and stand on the holy ground this Voice makes for him, where the mysteries of the world are turned into a solid history Moses must live in spite of his past times. We begin with a dialogue that will last for as long as forever is between God and His People, the Voice that will remove the idols of the nations from the face of His Creation. When Moses learns to confess this Voice as the Prophet of Israel's existence in the world, he is a maker of history, not magic oracles. When he confesses the revelation of this Voice in dialogue on holy ground with him, he must become a man only the Redeemer and Creator of the world can make. He must become a man in time for the times of Israel's opposition to her Lord and God, a man who, face to face with this Voice of the God of his ancestors, commands him to be the great prophet of Israel's history in God's Creation. We would learn to hear the speaking of this Lord and God even in our study of Him with Moses.

We begin then with the Voice of the Great I-AM speaking as the Lord God He is with His People in His Creation, however difficult that is for us. We need to learn to stand in space and time on a holy ground created by this Voice for us. We would understand the command of such a Voice, the will of this Lord and God. We would hear the very same Voice that commanded Moses' confession for Israel's new beginning in *the* Beginning of the Creator and the Redeemer of Abraham, Isaac, and Jacob, the ancestors of the People of God in the context of their primordial beginnings rooted in the ground that is the history of the Creation itself. If we will not begin here, we would stay where we are, clinging to the idols of our making far from the Voice's place. For the confession of Moses, this matter of staying or going is a matter of life of death.

The Great I-AM

We must hear Him speaking, the One He truly is the One He is, who is who He is in His Divine Freedom the One who wills to be heard and known for who He is. No one knows this Lord and God against His Will. If we know Him, we know Him in His Divine Freedom to make Himself present and then known in this world to His Chosen Servant, to Moses in the case of the history of Israel. It is to this Voice with His Divine Freedom that we must learn to listen in to them. Without the will and command of this Voice, we will remain content to live with Moses, to stay where we are, beside the mountains along the edges of the desert wilderness, content to be a fugitive in a world indifferent to our flight, a murderer hiding out beside the concerns of God with the peoples of this world and their great civilizations. But with this Voice a great leader is made to arise in the world. The great Deliverer of Israel from Egyptian gods is given to emerge. The humanity of the tribes of Israel shall not remain enslaved by the grip of mythical authorities.

With this Voice, Israel is to know who she is in the world. With her redemption from Egypt, she is given to her Redeemer in His Divine Freedom. She is given to know her Redeemer in fact as the Creator He is among the nations of the world. With Moses' willingness in his dialogue with this Voice is born anew the Prophet of Israel's new beginning. The Divine Freedom of this Voice to command this man in the history of Israel among the nations creates a history that belongs to the covenanted relationship in which His Promise to Israel's ancestors is to be kept. History belongs to this Voice as surely as Moses belongs to this Voice. Moses shall become the deliverer of Israel. Israel shall become a free people, a people from bondage in Egypt, a people free to know this Voice. She is freed of the Egyptian pantheon so that she can worship the One this Voice is in His Command of her. That which had been begun with her ancestors is not a beginning begun in vain, but a beginning that is bound up with who He is even in *the Beginning*. Israel is free to know Him as the Great I-AM He is, as the Lord and God He is. She is to be free to know Him in His Divine Freedom as the One He is.

On the ground of this Voice, Moses is made to begin a confession that is to him absolutely commanding. With this Voice, Moses' life as Israel's great Leader is begun. Under the command of the Divine Freedom of His Voice, Moses shall become the Deliverer and Prophet of the People of God and their history among the nations in God's 'Very Good' Creation. It is a new beginning in the world. It is a new beginning for God for Man, for

Israel among the nations of the world, for God's Creation. Moses' confession possesses with this beginning an argument the thrust of which resonates this Voice from the Burning Bush with a beginning that affirms in fact *the Beginning*. This dialogue is created upon a ground upon which we are meant to stand and to hear this Voice of the Great I-AM the Lord God is in His covenanted relationship with His People. Here we may stand and see the meaning and significance of this One, this One who seeks with His Divine Freedom to be the Only One with His People in His Creation. If we believe Moses, we will hear this Voice, this Voice speaking to us from beyond the world with which we are so familiar in this world with His Divine Freedom commanding us as the One who is our Redeemer and our Creator. We need to hear Him even today, because His Voice is the Voice for the Ages.

THE DIVINE FREEDOM OF THE GREAT I-AM THE LORD GOD IS

With Divine Freedom the Voice, creating holy ground for Moses, names Himself with Israel, His People. He is the Self-Naming Lord God. In this freedom, He makes Himself present. In this freedom, He makes Himself known. In this freedom, He enters into a dialogue with Moses in order to renew His covenanted promise to Moses' ancestors. Revelation is given in this freedom He possesses in order to act for His chosen people. With this Revelation, the naming of the things occurs meaningfully. With this Revelation, events in time occur significantly. Words are given meanings that bear witness to Him. Without the meaning and significance of this Revelation, no one could ever truthfully say they know God. This Revelation is the will of this Voice's freedom to speak with us of the Truth of His Being. If anyone does know God, she knows God with His Divine Freedom. In His Divine Freedom, He is free to act to make Himself present and known to us upon this created and holy ground of His commanding will. Inherent in His Name lives this freedom to will and to do what only He can will to do in this world. Like Moses, He turns us aside to make for us a new beginning with our lives. Beside the mountains along the edges of the desert wilderness of our lives, He makes Himself known to us. He calls to us and He commands us with the Voice of His Divine Freedom. It is with this Freedom that He names Himself for us. With His naming of Himself, Moses is commanded, made free to go, unable to stay.

The Great I-AM

With His naming of Himself, Israel must become a people He has called to Himself, '*My People*' among the nations in the history of a world that is His Creation. The text is read very famously, right at the heart of Moses' confession (I have a picture hanging on the wall above my bed, made from the set of Cecil B. De Mille's film on the Exodus of Israel from Egypt, in which Charlton Heston became famous for his portrayal of Moses!):

Exodus 3:14–15

'And God said to Moses,
"I am who I am."
He went on to say,
"Thus you shall say to the sons of Israel,
I-AM has sent me to you."
And again God said to Moses,
"Thus you shall say to the sons of Israel,
Yahweh Elohim of your fathers,
Elohim of Abraham,
Elohim of Isaac,
Elohim of Jacob, has sent me to you.
This is My Name forever,
By which all generations shall remember me."

What's in a name, we may ask. To whom does the '*My Name*' in the text refer? Is it to the *Elohim* of Jacob, the *Elohim* of Isaac and the *Elohim* of Abraham? Does '*My Name*' refer to the *Yahweh Elohim* of the fathers? Or does it refer to the Great *I-AM*, the One who is who He is as the Great '*I am who I am*'? What do we hear when we hear this Self-Naming of this Self-Revealing One with Moses? May not '*My Name*' refer to all these names as this One? What, indeed, is in the name that is '*My Name*'? Is '*My Name*' all of the names that signify this *Great I-AM*? In the Self-Revelation of this Self-Naming Voice, how are we to understand the dynamic relations of all these names? The substance and content of '*My Name*' must belong to the life of this Voice who is this Great I-AM as the Lord and God who is the One of this Revelation. He is the Self-Revealing and Self-Naming One. His Revelation is made in His Divine Freedom. We must hear this Voice in this very new and real beginning with Moses for Israel. Without hearing Him, we shall remain fugitives beside the mountains on the edges of the desert, content to live and let history be whatever it will be. But when we hear His Name proclaimed in His Divine Freedom, we are certainly turned aside to see what this great phenomenon may be. We are called and sent to make history in the history of the world. This is the beginning of the Biblical World for us.

To understand the Great '*I-AM*' of the Exodus Tradition as the *Yahweh* of Israel's deliverance from Egypt and the *Elohim* of the fathers is to hear His Name in His Divine Freedom as this Lord and this God in the Biblical Covenanted Relationship (BCR) He has posited with Israel as His People among the nations in His Creation. His People and His Creation cannot be divorced from who He truly is with His Name for Moses. The meaning and significance of this Name is fundamental to the thrust of Moses' confession. To hear the Name of the Creator (*Elohim*) for whom He truly is, to hear the Name of the Redeemer (*Yahweh*) for whom He truly is as this One *Great I-AM* is to hear the Revelation, to be commanded by His Voice. It is to hear this Voice in His Divine Freedom as the Redeemer of His People that delivers His People from the gods and idols of the nations. It is to hear this Voice as the One who is the Creator of the history of the Creation. It is to hear the Voice of the Great I-AM WHO I AM. This is the One and no other whose power it is that compels the Exodus of Israel from Egypt. This is the Voice creating of God acting anew as the Lord to keep His Promise in His BCR with the history of Israel in the history of the world. This is the Voice of new beginnings that belong to old tradition of the Revelation. This is the Voice we must hear if we are to follow in His Divine Freedom the Being of this One in His interaction with His People among the nations. It is the command of this Voice as the Great I-AM that sends Moses to become the Leader and the Prophet of His new beginning in His covenanted relationship with Israel. For this reason, no translation of the Semitic idiom '*I am who I am*' has ever been resolved or could resolve exhaustively the meaning and significance of the '*My Name*' that we read in these more than famous texts in Israel's history in the world. It is *the* Name, beside which there is no other name. It is in this Name that all who do know God have been given real knowledge of Him as the Great I-AM He is.

This is the Voice that speaks with Moses from the flames in the unconsumed and Burning Bush. He is God acting with Moses to become the Lord of Israel's history in the world. In His Divine Freedom, He is this Great I-AM of His Name. It is this Voice that forms the basis of the theological thrust we must read as Moses' confession. The Lord God is free as this Great I-AM to interact with who He is within His Creation. In this freedom He makes Himself present and known with purposes among His covenanted people. Once we have heard Him for who He truly is in this freedom, we know Him as the God who is free to act with Himself within the structures of His Creation for His People, without consuming them. In this way, he commands His People. He is in this way the Great I-AM that He is, and He is this I-AM as the Lord and God of Israel among the nations in His Creation. '*My Name*' must never be employed in vain among the vanities of the gods. From the new beginning, marked by the Exodus Tradition in Israel's history and her development of her Holy Scriptures, to the new ending all the names of her Savior and her Creator must refer to this One Great I-AM He is with this Voice. The meaning of the Nature and Being of this Lord God belongs in His Name with His Divine Freedom to be who He truly is with His People in His Creation. For this reason, we do not seek to define its significance with better translations or expect to look its reality up in a dictionary or find its meaning in a journal article about the Name. We may translate the famous phrase in any number of ways, all of which must intend to point us towards apprehending Him for who He truly is. What's in this Name? In the case of the Semitic idiom, there lives more in the Name than we can define. When we invoke His Name we declare the One who speaks of Himself with us.

In His Divine Freedom, then, the Great I-AM is the One He truly is in His Act to reveal Himself freely and meaningfully in the history of the world even from His Eternity. Time becomes understood as much His servant as Moses and so forth. When we know Him in the Self-Revelation of this Voice, we know that we stand on holy ground to hear Him and that we cannot go to another to enter into dialogue with Him. He is who He is as this Lord and this God from His Eternity in this space and this time. There is no other ground to which we may go to gain some other perspective upon Him. As the Great I-AM He is with Moses, He is the Lord of His People and He is the God of His Creation as the Lord God of His Eternity. As this Great I-AM, He is the Lord God of all created reality, and He will have no others before Him. He is Lord and God of time, of times past, time present, time future, of the created space of His Creation, of all the history that has happened within them. In this Divine Freedom to be present and known, He is who He is both from within Himself and even outside of Himself. It does not matter how we translate the Semitic idiom. He is the '*I am who I am.*' He is the One who is what '*I have been* who I have been' or 'I am being who I am being' or 'I will be who or what I will be' or 'I am the Only One who is' or 'I am being the One that I am,' and so forth and so on. It is the reality to which His Voice would refer that is all that matters. It is the reality of the Living Lord and God who is who He is as this Great I-AM in His Divine Freedom to be present and to speak with us and to give us knowledge of who He is in the way of His Being in this world. It is this Voice upon which the nature of the BCR rests with the Lord God He is for the People of God in His Creation. We cannot subject the Bible to ourselves, but we must learn to hear Him with our understanding of it.

One of my teachers at Fuller Seminary, Professor Frederick W. Bush taught me perhaps best a good translation for this Name. He argued that the Semitic idiom in the world of the Semitic languages was a superlative, *'I am and I have been and I will be superabundantly present with and for you here in My world.'* On this ground and with this assurance, Moses may become persuaded, over his many objections, that the Voice who commands him is the Voice none can ultimately deny. We deny Him with a freedom that is not divine. He will overcome our denials of Him. Moses will not stay. Moses will go where he has been called to go. In His dialogue with the future Leader and Prophet of the tribes of Israel, the Lord God in His Divine Freedom will overcome all of the fugitive's objections to His Command. The Voice will send him to deliver His People from their bondage in Egypt, their service to the gods of the Pharaoh. The Voice from the Burning Bush with His '*superabundant presence*' will not fail to be with Moses who He promises to be. Moses must and can go. Thus, the naming of '*My Name*' with Moses would reassure the reluctant fugitive's call about his mission with His Presence. In His Divine Freedom, the presence of the Lord God will command through Moses deliverance for Israel. He will free His People of the Egyptian gods and, in spite of Moses' objections, in spite of Pharaoh's objections, the Great I-AM the Lord God is will make His new beginning the history of the world with His Israel. The new world will occur. If we take notice of these things in this way, we may seek to appreciate what is actually in the Name of God in the Biblical World. History is an object only this Voice can make. We shall attempt to hear the meaning of His Name then, as Moses was compelled to do. We shall seek to hear it across the history of centuries of a tradition whose times are marked by the renewals of His BCR, where we must learn to hear the heartbeat of the Great I-AM in covenanted relationship with His

People among the nations of His Creation. As we make this effort, it is worth taking some time to notice Moses' objections to the Command of this Voice. It is not a Voice Moses hoped or wanted to hear. It is the Voice of the Great I-AM the Lord God heard anew upon the pages of history. In His dialogue with Moses, Moses stands on ground with which he is not familiar, on created ground meant for him to listen to the One who is who He truly is. No doubt he preferred to be elsewhere.

But the reality of the nature of God's Being as the Great I-AM He is in His Divine Freedom with us, in His Holy Love to be present with His People as the One He is, must be understood as a reality that wills to shape the very substance of Moses' mission and confession. Argue across the centuries as we will, we must hear that what the Name means belongs to the Mission of His Being in covenanted relationship with His People in His Creation, and the Mission in His Name is not abstract philosophy, but down to earth holiness and freedom for what He has caused to exist. For this reason, it is valuable to seek to understand the use of the names of the Name who is the I-AM about which we must read in the texts. The significance of these names is never lost from the history of Israel. However much His People will not understand their meaning, His is not an act that is made in vain. They will understand. The names employed with the Voice in the Self-Revealing and Self-Naming Lord and God for Moses, recorded in the Exodus 3 passage, are also explained in Exodus 6. We need to observe them in both contexts.

Exodus 3 marks uniquely the new beginning the Old One is making with Himself in becoming this Revelation for His People at this time, in this place, on this created and creative ground. The names *Yahweh* and *Elohim, the Elohim* of the fathers and their ancestral faith, are the names employed to bear the reality of the Voice of this One Great I-AM, who is who He truly is with Moses and against the idols of the nations. We do not hear the name *Yahweh* without hearing the name of the Great I-AM as Israel's Redeemer. We cannot hear the names of *Elohim* without hearing the Great I-AM as the Creation's Creator. We cannot hear the name *Yahweh Elohim* without hearing the Voice of the Great I-AM in the Burning Bush commanding His new beginning with a work on behalf of His People in the history of the world that is unheard of across the centuries in the Ancient Near East. With the commanding presence of this Voice, with who He is in His Divine Freedom, and upon His Holy Ground this Voice enters into dialogue with Moses. Moses must hear the command of this

One as the One who is who He truly is both then and now and not yet. He must learn to do what this One wills to command for His People in the history of a world. He must learn that the One who commands is no local deity, but the Creator of all that is. With His names His Being in time and eternity is revealed. Thus, '*My Name*' is a personal Name of the Lord and God of His People among the nations and His Creation. There exists no generation that could or can afford to forget what is in this Name. This is the Name by which Israel must come to worship Him. This is the Name by which Israel may learn to follow Him. The gods of Mesopotamia, the gods of Egypt, the gods of Canaan, and the gods of everywhere and elsewhere all now belong to a past in God's Creation that is vanishing away. Something new has been begun. Something new has occurred in the history of the world. The relationship between this Redeemer-Creator and those gods of times gone by is changed forever. These are the gods that belong to the vanquished in God's Creation. This Lord God as this One and Only Great I-AM in His Divine Freedom is free to do this new thing with Himself among His People in His Creation. We do well to seek to understand these names of the Name. We do well to know this self-naming and great I-AM as He has named Himself with Moses for Israel. History is not and will not be what it is to be without Him. All pretenders with their idols shall be vanquished upon the earth. The tyranny of the idol maker is to be destroyed in this world. The Revelation of the Lord God has occurred. The future belongs to Him. His People belong to Him. His Creation belongs to Him.

Exodus 6:3 reads: '*I appeared to Abraham, to Isaac, and to Jacob as **El-Shaddai*** (usually translated as 'God Almighty'), *but by my name **Yahweh** I did not make myself known to them*.' The name of **Yahweh** is the new name for **Elohim**, and was not known to the fathers of the faith. It is a new name. It is given with an unveiling by His Voice of the Great I-AM commanding Moses and the Exodus tradition for Israel's history in the world. The new name stands for the Great I-AM in His Divine Freedom to choose to act with in the deliverance of His People from slavery to other gods. It is this deliverance that shall mark forever Israel as the People of God in the world: **Yahweh**! **Yahweh** is the name of the Great I-AM in His Divine Freedom to act to make history what it is for Israel as His People in His BCR in His Creation. As this Great I-AM and in this Name, the Lord (**Yahweh**) God (**Elohim**) is to be present to deliver His People, now known among the pantheon of the gods of Egypt as the Victor over all the powers of the dynasties of the Pharaohs. With this I-AM, Israel's afflictions in the Land of the Nile are ended. As this I-AM, with this new Name, **Yahweh**, Israel begins a new epoch in her history in the world. Before the time of this Name, no one had ever heard or ever seen anything like the times to come because of Him. No community of slaves had ever before, since *the* Beginning of the Creation, quit their jobs and left their king in the great civilizations of the ancient world. Throughout all recorded history, escape from the mastery and the tyranny that belonged to the kings and their gods was impossible. Slaves never announced their resignation from the royal rules and rulers of the times. They served with their lifetimes those ancient deities in a world whose forever was ordered by these rules and rulers. Israel's Exodus from Egypt was something utterly new in the history of the world, absolutely new in time. With the Exodus, the ancient deities belong now but to the past. The future belonged alone to this new beginning, even as it is bound up in *the* Beginning. It belonged to **Yahweh** with His People among the nations.

We translate this name as 'Lord' in our English Bibles. We read the name *Elohim* as 'God.' Whenever we read the title Lord God, we are reading about the Great I-AM in action for His People in His Creation. But the name 'Lord' identified with this 'God' was an utterly new designation in the history of Israel. No more could their *Elohim* be worshiped alongside of the 'other Elohim' among the nations. As the People of this Lord and God among the nations, Israel bore witness to a new world. The Name *Yahweh* marked for her an impossibly new thing that *Elohim* did with her Exodus. None other than the Creator of the world could have freed her in this way. Israel becomes a free people in this Name, free from the gods of the past, free for the Lord God of the future. She becomes a people free to worship in her times this Lord (*Yahweh*), this God (*Elohim*) in this Name, a people made free to introduce something new in the history of the world. Free from the idols of the gods in her past among the nations, now her Redeemer and Creator had called her a new life in the history of the world. It is with this newness of God and Israel in this history that gives His People their significance in this Name in His Creation. Israel is who she is because the Great I-AM is who He is. He is *the Yahweh Elohim* of His People and His Creation. His Voice spoke light into existence in *the Beginning* and His Voice spoke Israel into her existence. The speaking of the Great I-AM is this Voice making Himself heard as the Redeemer-Creator, to be heard in *the Beginning* and heard in the Exodus of His People. He who was once known as the *El-Elohim* of the fathers among the nations and the *El-Shaddai* of Abraham and his sons a long while ago, is to be known as the Great I-AM He is. Now He is to be known and shall ever be known as this One—*Yahweh Elohim*, the Lord God, the Redeemer-Creator, the Free God in His Freedom with His People in His Creation. There is no other like Him. There is no analogy for His Being except that which He creates with Himself. His Being is in His Act and His Act is in His Being as the One who is the One He is in His Divine Freedom with His People and His Creation.

The name *Yahweh* (translated as *Kurios* of the New Testament) is the Name by which the Redeemer of Israel is remembered by the history of Israel. Because of Israel's reverence for this Name, it is read more than 6800 times in the Old Testament. It is employed fundamentally and foundationally in Moses' confession with a rhetoric whose theological thrust we may not allow escape our attention. Israel did not pronounce it out loud. She was afraid of profaning it. To put the Name upon her dirty lips was to profane it in such a way that it meant her certain death. To honor His Name, then, is a matter of life and death for her. Instead of pronouncing it out loud, His Name was read by the scribal traditions as '*Adonai*.' Even today in the synagogues, the Jews do not pronounce it out loud. They say '*ha-Shem*,' which simply means 'the Name.' 'The Name' was read as 'Jehovah' in the King James Bible, a translation that had come to conflate the vowels from '*Adonai*' with the four consonants (the *Tetragrammaton*) of His Name. Thus, the Name that no one would pronounce in the traditions of her history became read as 'Jehovah,' a nonsense word for pious Jews. 'Jehovah' is a term that is a combination of the vowels from a word Israel pronounced out loud in order not to pronounce out loud His Name who is her Redeemer according to the Revelation with Moses. Scholars today pronounce His Name as '*Yahweh*,' but no one really knows precisely the correct pronunciation. His Name was never pronounced out loud and the vowels of the *Tetragrammaton* were never written down. Speculation about its pronunciation has led a consensus of scholars today to say *Yahweh* when referring to the *Tetragrammaton*. But we know that no one knows precisely how it would have been pronounced had it ever been sounded out loud, which it was not. We are fortunate that English translators have consistently translated the *Tetragrammaton* (the four consonants) of the scribal tradition as 'Lord,' a practice followed consistently by the translator's of the Septuagint's with *Kurios*. The point is that,

The Great I-AM

whenever you read the term 'Lord' in the Old Testament, you are reading His Name, the Name with which He names Himself as the Redeemer of Israel, who is the Great I-AM of the Revelation with Moses. The People of God remember forever this Self-Naming Revelation in which the history of the Exodus Tradition is celebrated across the world even today.

The name *Elohim* (God), on the other hand, is the name by which the Redeemer of Israel is to be understood as none other than the Creator of the heavens and the earth. As such, this name is used some 3500 times in the Old Testament. The name *El-Shaddai* (Almighty God), invoked in Exodus 6 as one of the *El* names of God among the ancestral fathers of Israel, has been given a very new significance in the Exodus. The assurance of His divine providence and provision with His promises to Abraham and his sons in the ancestral history in the ancient world is to be understood anew. Like at a mother's breast, Israel as the child of God's promise to Abraham, experiences the Redeemer-Creator of her Exodus from Egypt. Abraham's faith in this promise has gained him the reputation for being the father of her faith. The *El* names of God are common throughout the Ancient Near East in the ancient world, and the Old Testament transformed with Abraham's faith these names, when God called the father of Israel's faith out of his home in Babylon. The plural of *El*, *Elohim*, is thought to be a plural of majesty, also very common among the ancient peoples. The ancient cults proclaimed him commonly. This name is translated consistently into English as 'God,' and signifies God as the Creator, the One who made the heavens and the earth, the One understood by Moses with new and compelling force to be the Great I-AM of the Exodus, a theological polemic Israel as the People of God must not forget.

The Great I-AM with His Name, entailing the meaning of the names *Yahweh* and *Elohim* and the names of *El or Elohim*, is deeply and profoundly and freely bound up by the new name with the old names for God. The new name, *Yahweh* or Lord, and the old name, *Elohim* or God, stand now together as this One who is who He is in His Divine Freedom with His People among the nations in His Creation. With His Divine Freedom, He has acted freely to name Himself for His deliverance of His People from their bondage to the other gods. In this sense, all the names taken together possess that rhetorical thrust the theological significance of which is vital to the authorization of Moses' confession. The People of God are to know that the Great I-AM of the Burning Bush is not merely their Redeemer, but also *the* Creator of all things created with *the Beginning*. He may not be worshipped alongside of the other gods among the ancient peoples. The Redeemer of Israel is the Creator. The Creator is the Redeemer of Israel. Beside this One God there are no other gods. The Creator of the heavens and the earth and the Redeemer of Israel is this Self-Revealing I-AM, beside whom no other gods can exist. If we fail to hear the polemic in the naming of '*My Name*' invoked in the texts of Moses' confession, we let crumble the very foundation that is fundamental to its argument. The confession of Moses in the Five Books we know as the Pentateuch is what it is according to this Revelation of the Redeemer-Creator named in its tradition. We do well to hear its theological thrust.

When we read the names invoked of the *Name* of the Great I-AM of the Exodus Tradition, we are reading a theological thrust whose dimensions, implicitly and explicitly, are lost upon Biblical interpretation of Moses' confession with life and death consequences then. The use of the names of the *Name* that refers us to the Great I-AM truly is as the Lord and God of Israel's history and the history of the Creation stands now anew in the world against all idols and idol making, old and new in the time and times of the world. The confession is in this way fundamentally polemical, moving beyond the old and pointing to the new history of the People of God among the nations in covenanted relationship with the Lord God. We must be able to hear Moses as this Servant of God and this Witness to this Lord God. This is Israel's Lord. This is the God of the Creation. This is the God of all beginnings, old and new. There is no other One. If we will not understand this One, we will not hear Moses' confession of Him. We will keep our idols about God. But with this One, we may understand all beginnings, including *the Beginning*. With the same freedom that He freed Israel from Egypt, He created the world and made a new beginning that resonates with His Beginning. We must learn to hear this new beginning resonating with *the Beginning*, if we are to understand the Voice of the Great I-AM. Unless the theological *tour de force* that the Pentateuch is can be grasped in the light of this Voice, we will fail to stand upon His holy and created ground with Moses, and we will not grasp the dynamic reality of the dialogue made there. When we do apprehend the polemical nature of the argument of the confession, we may penetrate into the depths of the significance of His Divine Freedom and His Holy Love in His Name. He is the One who is free to be this One with us. He is the Great I-AM for the ancient promise, the renewal of this Promise in His BCR with Israel, His People. He is the One who is faithful to His Promise in His covenanted relationship with His Chosen People in His Creation. To make this history of Israel rest upon some other than this One is to deny Him His Divine Freedom, His Holy Love, and His True Willingness to be the Great I-AM He is in the confession, the Lord God of Eternity in His Time for His People.

THE HOLY GROUND AND THE APPREHENDING OF THE GREAT I-AM THE LORD GOD IS

We will have much more to say about the Holy One that the Great I-AM is as the Lord God when we consider Israel's worship of *Yahweh Elohim* as the People of God. Israel's development of her Levitical Torah is accomplished for the purpose of her communion with this Lord and God. For now, we only remind ourselves that Moses removed his sandals when entering into dialogue with this I-AM of the Revelation, with the Voice of the Lord God speaking to him from the flames of the unconsumed bush beside the mountains in the Sinai desert. Moses may know this Great I-AM for who He is and not another on this ground. This ground is created space and time. It is created specifically. It is created as the unique ground of the Revelation. It is not everywhere. It is not anywhere. It is a chosen space. It is chosen time. It is ground that belongs to the Divine Freedom of God's creative power, when He chooses to call and command Moses as the Leader and Prophet of His People in the renewal of His BCR to free them from Pharaoh's grip upon them and take them from Egypt to the Promised Land. It is ground upon which Moses is to become the Servant of this Great I-AM of Israel's destiny with Him. The Voice that speaks with Moses from the Burning Bush and gives him his mission is to be proclaimed as *Yahweh Elohim*, the One who is the God of the fathers, and the One who will not be confused with other gods and who will not in any case be denied His Being in His Divine Freedom. It is important to understand here that this Act of this Lord and this God cannot be divorced from who He truly is as this Great I-AM, the Redeemer-Creator who in His Divine Freedom is free to be who He is in His Acts in the history of His People. Who He is in His acts for His People cannot be divorced from who He is in Himself. Who He is in His Eternal Being cannot be divorced from who He is with His Being in His Acts throughout the history of Israel or the Creation. He is the Only One, the Universal One, and King of the Universe commanding Moses.

The Great AMEN of the Great I-AM
MOSES' OBJECTIONS IN THE DIALOGUE

Who am I? Moses asks *Elohim* how such a one as he should go to Pharaoh in Egypt and seek to deliver the Israelites from their afflictions under the reign of the Egyptian Pantheon. The Lord's response seeks to reassure Moses of His Presence and the success of the mission. '*I will be with you*,' He tells Moses the important thing is that He will be with him, and the proof of it will be that he will be victorious over Pharaoh. Moses shall return with the People of God to Horeb, a free people, a people free to worship Him who is their Redeemer, the Great I-AM. He is the Lord and no other and on His Holy Mountain at Horeb in the desert wilderness, Israel shall worship Him. That is who Moses and Israel are (Exodus 3:11–12).

Then, in the form of a hypothetical obedience, Moses asks the Voice for His Name, that he may give it to the Israelites when they ask him for it. Israel will want the God of their fathers to have a name for this time of their deliverance from Egypt. It is in the context of this hypothetical question of the name that the new history for Israel is announced: *I am who I am. This is what you are to say to the Israelites. I-AM has sent me to you.* At this time a new name is declared: *Yahweh*. This is the name of the Great I-AM as the Redeemer of His People. This is the name of the Great I-AM who is the God of the fathers. This is the '*My Name*' to be proclaimed by Moses and the People of God forever (Exodus 3: 13–15). It is also in this context that the great signs and wonders of the deliverance are to be done, that the tribes of Israel in Egypt might know that *Yahweh* is *Elohim* and *Elohim* is *Yahweh* as the Great I-AM who has sent Moses to lead Israel to the Land of the ancient promise. Thus, the People of God are to know of the power of this Name of the Great I-AM who is who He is as the Redeemer-Creator He is acting with His Divine Freedom in His Creation for His People (Exodus 3:16–22).

But Moses possesses some further objections to the Voice. He contends that Israel in Egypt will not believe him when he tells the people who sent him. They will deny him his testimony. What then could the new Leader and Prophet of Israel do? To this possibility the Lord God responds with more sign and more wonder. Moses' staff and the phenomenon of the snake will persuade the tribes, and they shall believe that the One who sent Moses is indeed the God of their fathers. Even the sign of the command of leprosy and then the sign of turning water into blood are to be given, that they might believe (Exodus 4:1–9).

Yet Moses can continue to object. He claims that he possesses not the ability to lead such a movement. '*I am not eloquent,*' he explains to the Voice. The Voice claims to be the Creator of all speech and all hearing provides Aaron, Moses' brother, who is surely not slow of speech. He will speak for Moses then. Moses cannot stay. He must go (Exodus 4:10–12).

And finally, what lies behind all the objections is made explicit. Moses begs the Voice to send somebody else. He simply does not want to go, no matter who he is, no matter what he can and cannot do. The Voice becomes angry with Moses, having given him Aaron to assist him on the mission. Moses can and must and will go. We can read this Divine Anger with His Divine Freedom for Moses and Israel throughout the confession of this mission in the history of the world.

At last, when all the objections of Moses against the command of the Voice have been made loud and clear, the Lord God sends Moses with the 'superabundant presence' of His power and freedom to Egypt. The new Leader and Prophet shall fulfill the purpose of the I-AM the Lord God is with His People in His Creation. Moses will accomplish all that he has been sent to do. This Lord and God has heard the cry of His People in Egypt, and He will answer Israel, for she is His People. He will deliver her. They are the Seed of Abraham. He shall be able to call them '*My People.*' He will be victorious over every objection to Him and the Israel of Moses shall call Him '*Our Yahweh*'!

Moses is able then to seek from Jethro, his father-in-law, permission to return with his wife to Egypt. He will go back to the land from which he has been a fugitive and a murderer. He will go back for Israel there. He will seek to deliver God's People from Pharaoh and the Egyptian gods. The Voice of the Lord God as the I-AM He is in the Burning Bush has conquered His Moses. He will with this Moses accomplish all of His Purpose with His People. The Voice of the One who says He is who He is in His superabundant, free, and powerful presence shall make Israel's history what it is among the nations now rings loudly in the ears of the great Prophet and Leader. This is a bell that tolls compellingly throughout the long life Moses knows as this Prophet of the People of God among the nations in God's Creation.

There are some who do not hear the 'superabundance' of the *I*-AM's presence as revealing the essence or substance of the Lord God. They believe that we can hear only the Lord God's insistence from the flames upon Moses' going. They do not believe the Bible is concerned with the ontology of Being or the Essence of this Voice. The *'I am who I am'* of the Revelation is a Self-Revealing and Self-Naming Voice that is saying to Moses that he should just go ahead and get on with it. Never mind musing about who or what He is. Just go as He commands and experience what He does with him. He is who He is and He is who will be with Moses as the commander in His Freedom, and does not seek that Moses and Israel shall know Him as He is in His own Eternal Being and Substance. His Presence simply works to command with His Will, without giving them to be concerned with who He is in Himself. He is incomprehensible. The Voice does not call Moses to some philosophy about the nature His Being. He calls to act in history freely so that Moses shall go on the mission He has appointed for him. It is enough for him to know that He will be with him in this way. Moses needs only to go and do what he is told, and in the obedience of this duty he will see what this One is with him. He is and will at all times be who He is with him, and that is all Moses needs to know. He does not need to know Him as He is in Himself and knows Himself. According to these interpreters, we need not exert any effort to understand who God is in His Essence. Ours is to obey. In this case, these interpreters can say that who God is in Himself cannot be identified with who He is in Himself in His acts in history and in His dialogue with Moses and Israel. His Being in His Acts and His Acts in His Being are confined to the history of Israel among the nations of the world. One can safely divorce His Being in Himself from His Being in His Acts in time and times. The Essence of God thus becomes the Unknown God. God is known only in His Acts. This is the One who is who He is as the commander of the Exodus and thus the whole of the Old Testament. He is not after us to know Him as He is in Himself, in the essential nature or substance of His Being, for He far transcends all that we may know. Even in His Self-Revelation and His Self-Naming, His Transcendent Being remains hidden from us. We remain ignorant of Him who lives in His own Eternity, without His Creation. We know only who He is in the immanence of His Acts in time. In this way, hearing the Name of His Voice from the flames belongs at last to the Great Unknown God, His immutability and impassibility beyond all that we know, who are given to know Him as God in His Acts towards us under the heavens and upon the earth. Biblical humility is, according to this understanding, a condition of being ignorant of God. Humility is finally a confession that we do not know Him, not as He truly is in own Being, outside of His relationship to history. The Transcendent Being of this Lord God, in spite of His Self-Revelation forever must escape our grasp of Him and His Eternity. He is who He is beyond the limits of human knowing, beyond the senses of human being, beyond the creativity of human imagination and will.

When the Being of the Transcendent One becomes lost in His Transcendence in this way, when His Immanence in His Acts in history becomes separated in our kind's knowledge of Him, then we tend to split apart His Being from His Revelation. We tend to make absolute our independence away from Him then. We tend to perceive our lives with an absolute autonomy free from the *I-AM* He actually is in Himself. We create the ground upon which we would think to explain our independence and autonomy in this world. We tend towards Deism with our Monotheisms. The One He actually is becomes divorced from who He is in His Revelation and His Salvation for His People. We tend to split up the One He is as the Creator from the One He is as the Redeemer, and fail to grasp the wholeness of His Being, both in Himself and in His Acts in history. It is this interpretation that has shaped much of the modern or postmodern world of thought. The so-called 'Age of Enlightenment,' when Revelation and Reason are torn apart from one another is the result. The Rights of Man with his Reason would become the master of his Fate. Religions and Secular Man become logically entangled. Wars and the establishment of powers to protect his Rights become Common Sense, while the Unknown God, it is believed, is up there somewhere above the heavens in His Elsewhere watching the human race upon the earth explore the world with its mastery. Notions about human freedom are produced, the theologies of which are at best but abstract conceptual systems of thought unable to find any real correspondence with the actual Essence or Substance or Nature of the Being of the Great I-AM the Lord God is. God at best is turned into an idea we possess about Him, like a premise or axiom in a rational system of knowledge, when good minds of free and well-intended wills belonging to common ordinary individuals are free to seek to create autonomously a Utopia for their dreamy ideals. Worldviews are championed that no one ever actually experiences, and so forth. We can characterize such developments with the problems of the dualistic split, its deism and its determinisms implicit in the loss associated with both abstract essentialism and positivistic instrumentalism prevalent in our time. We become divorced with our beings from the Being of the Transcendent and Eternal Living One.

The Great AMEN of the Great I-AM

We are familiar with the Essence of the God in theologies that claim to know God in His 'omniscience,' 'omnipotence,' 'omnipresence,' His divine attributes, and so forth. It is as if our ideas about Him could be thought of as possessing the same authority as He does with His Being. It is as if God had become the best of our ideas for the best of all possible worlds and our knowledge, our powers, our concepts of infinity, etc., reflected directly upon the One He truly is. Such theologies produce what we may call a 'reductionism' of human thought, when our understanding of God's Being, Essence, and Nature becomes confined to systems of thought that are related to Him with notions about an authority that comes either 'from above' or 'from below,' when a dialectical dynamic becomes the tension in a game making civilization a kind of chess board on which the mastering of mankind can play with an autonomy utterly lost from meaning and real responsibility. Any universal consistency or thoroughness of purpose and intention becomes impossible, divorced as they are from the reality of the Revelation. We apprehend Him as the best of our ideas in the best of all possible worlds watching our mastering with helpful eyes, like a sun shining with a smile on its face for us. The messy matters of real world experience faced us with an evil nothingness with which real historical events had to be given meaning by abstract means surrounded by the absolute authority of the race in the absolute space and time of these developments. In this way, it is easy to confuse God with ourselves, to compare Him to ourselves, and to create the religion after and out of our own ideas about Him. In this way, many can confuse the cleverness of their minds with the Mind of God. Prisons and asylums prove necessary because people cannot tell the difference between their being and the Being of God. The Revelation of the Great I-AM the Lord God is has become utterly lost upon them.

Gasping for the breath of God in the rare atmospheres of such abstract idealism and subjectivist existentialism upheld by any autonomous freedom, Biblical theologians rebelled against the 'Essence' of the God of the Enlightenment. They began to insist that this abstract God was not at all the God of the Bible. They insisted that what we know of God, as a matter of fact, comes from who He is in His Acts in our history and that the Bible was not concerned to teach us His Essence. God is the Lord who acts in the real history of His People, His Israel and His Church, among the nations of the world. We cannot and we do not know God as He is in Himself, in His Eternal Life. If we are given to know Him with the Bible, it is in His interaction with us that we know Him. It is in the real history of the world that we know of Him. The God of the Bible is the God of history. The Bible becomes a book about the history of a religion, of the religion of Israel and the Church. The cry went out that we needed to rid our reading and interpretation of Holy Scriptures of the imposition of the abstract doctrines with which the Church had read and interpreted the Bible. We needed to learn them afresh, without concern for the Essence of God and with a new appreciation for the God of our histories. The Dogmatic Theology of the Church's past, understood as some abstract imposition upon real critical thinking, became otiose to modern analytical methods for understanding the Bible or the world. A new movement, a Biblical Theological Movement was made among scholars, in which human thought could think to master even the book the Bible was among our books. We could know God as He is in His Acts in our history in this way, not as some distant deity abstracted from time and space and the people of this world, but as the God of history. Existentialism's lost generations belong to such movements in this world.

A methodological split or chasm between the 'Essence' of the Being of God as He is in Himself and who He is in His Acts with Israel and the Church among the nations, as recorded in the texts of the Bible, became firmly established. Romantic idealisms or existentialisms were embraced. I have called these 'reductionisms' reductionism upwards and downwards of human thought. They are reflected in phrases that claim to be thinking 'from above' or 'from below,' both lost to the I-AM He is. Yet with these methods scholars sought to grasp with some scientific precision their very pragmatic intentions and purposes about what we may learn when we read the Bible, about God, about the world, and about our mankind. The Bible contained, for all that it contained no 'ontology' with the Essence of the Being of God as He is in Himself. It recorded in a Biblical World the history of a People who thought they were special in the eyes of their watching God. His Essence might be the stuff on which the philosopher could feed. But any knowledge of God that we may gain from reading the Bible is to be confined to who He is in His Acts in real history. Revelation cannot mean that we are to be given to know Him as He is in Himself, but in the histories of autonomous men and women whose rights possessed as much authority as any Other. The God of Eternity remained the Transcendent One, the Unknown God of these histories. A deep and profound abyss was posited whose chasms provided the space in which

Revelation and Reason could battle it out with one another. Who God is in Himself in His Eternity and who He is in His acts in time and times in the history of Israel and the Church is not the same. Many readers of the Bible today still live in this nothingness that haunts our world, where the Lord God in Himself remains for many the Great Unknown God rather than the Great I-AM He is.

Both kinds of 'reductionisms' however, up or down, from above or from below, abstract idealisms or romantic existentialisms, can be shown to lead to the dead ends we face with our modern or postmodern critical scholarship. The Revelation of the God of the Bible in the history of the world cannot be understood based upon these kinds of reductionisms in human thought. The Revelation of the God of the Bible is the Revelation of the Lord of the world and all of its history. He would give us to know Him in the fullness and wholeness of His Being, both in Himself and in His Acts within His Creation and for His People. The Being of God in His Acts and the Acts of God in His Being are to be integrated in our knowing of Him according to the One Word we are to hear when we read the Bible. We may with this kind of integration think by thinking what cannot be thought. Some scholars have felt these dead ends and they believe that today we are in a crises of thought, one in which the identity of the God we worship is given new and fresh and open structured thinking that can think what is impossible by thinking to think—the Being of the Great I-AM with us. We need to overcome the reductionisms of the past and we need to believe afresh in the power of the Revelation of His Word for us. Here, I believe we possess the kind of theological nose a scholar needs to smell the rats in the dead ends and for deliverance from the alleys of our absolute autonomies, whether they come 'from above' or 'from below.' We can call today for a truly fresh reading and interpretation of the Holy Scriptures. We can seek afresh to understand and integrate what we read with the real world that belongs to the Subject of the Bible. We may seek to overcome the abyss we have created for ourselves, leave behind us the chasms we have created between Revelation and Reason, and with our thought learn to think that which is impossible to think—the true Being of the Great I-AM for us.

In this way, we may hope to produce a Biblical Theology faithful to the God of the Bible and the reality of this world. Clearly, we cannot continue in the divorce between the Dogma of the Church and our diverse interpretations of the Biblical texts in any time or space. We need to penetrate afresh with the powers of our attention to grasp anew the making of our reasons in the Light of the Revelation of His Word for us. The meaning and significance of what the Bible is saying to us cannot be divorced from His Eternal Life. What may have escaped our attention in the past must be apprehended today. Such reflections could provide a way to understand both who He is as the God of Eternity and the Lord of Time and Space. The Transcendent One is who He is precisely in His Acts immanently in the history of Israel and the Church among the nations of the world with the same Word He once had for Moses. With this kind of resonance and integration in our hearing, we will leave behind us the fragmented and alienated modes of existence and become more believing and faithful to the faithfulness of who He is in the nature of His Revelation with the Bible and the history of the human race upon the earth under the heavens where He would make Himself known to us in the mystery of His Being the I-AM He is.

This kind of reflection would help us appreciate the role of the Canonical Traditions in the history of Israel's faith and the Church's faithfulness. We might clear a way for a new and steady grasp of the role of the Canonical tradition with the Biblical texts in His actual Inspiration of the Bible. The Canon belongs to what His Revelation is with the human race. Historical-critical methodologies are to be responsible to His Revelation and Inspiration and not against the Dogma of His Being who He is for His People in His Creation. Revelation recorded by the Canon of Biblical Faith cannot be conceived in any abstract idealistic or romantic existential manners. What informed the early Church is to be understood as that which informs the Church today. Progress is only real when it is not cut off from the past. Revelation is not revolution either from above or from below, but transformations in time and times that call us quite beyond the splits and disorder of our fallen from Him world. We must learn to become critical of our assumptions about our theories of history, so that some new understanding is apprehended in such a way that both the reality of history and the reality of God's Revelation are known in the actual dynamics of a wholeness that belongs to the very nature of the BCR we read in the Bible. From beginning to end our knowledge of God and the world is to be told from within the actualities of the covenanted relationship He renews steadily with His People. We need to produce a Biblical Theology that would recover the Dogma of the early Church and its Prophetic Vision of the One God made known in Christ, and then go on to see what kind of integrations and progress we can make as believers in the Bible and the Bible's God towards understanding time and space and the Redeemer-Creator even in our times and in our places. Our understanding of His covenanted relations must be able to resonate with the realities that belong to the reconciliation inherent in His BCR for us, intrinsic to His Revelation with us. Thus, we may learn to grasp with new depths the nature of the poles inherently and dynamically active in His BCR with us in our histories. We may apprehend that faith that has to do with His faithfulness to this BCR in His Creation. We need to know that what we have been given to know is not just something about Him, but Himself in His Divine Freedom, and that our freedom depends vitally upon His.

This argument will form in any case the fundamental explication of the waves we seek to ride in my book. We need a new and more profound grasp of the reality of the nature of Israel and the Church among the nations as the People of God in a world that is indeed His Creation. We need a fresh and more profound grasp of them in the depths of His Being as the Mighty Creator-Redeemer He is, the Transcendent One in whose transcendence for us mankind sees itself as reconciled to who He is as this Lord and this God, to this Great I-AM in His Self-Revealing and Self-Naming nature in the history of Mankind and the Creation. To remove the various impasses that the academy faces, with all its commitments to the diversity of thought about Him today, and to seek afresh for a real ontology and epistemology whose hearing of the Great I-AM speaking '*I am who I am*' superabundantly for you and your freedom as '*My People*' in the Creation would go a long way towards overcoming the various forms of 'reductionism,' and to direct our attention away from its fragmentation and alienation marking so much of our past efforts, producing a more positive way of listening to His Speaking of the Word of His Being in our history. It is after all not with ourselves alone that we have to do but with Him. The Bible is *the* Book it is among the many books in the world because it belongs to the Revelation of God who gives us in this way His Reason to believe. It is a history in which millions have been made to bear witness to that knowledge He only can give to people. He is the only comfort these millions had in their histories and the reason that they are able to confess who He is as their Lord and God among the nations. Because He has given Himself to be apprehended in this way, millions have been given to know Him in the Incomprehensibility of His Being the Great I-AM He is.

THE INCOMPREHENSIBILITY OF THE GREAT I-AM THE LORD GOD IS

Karl Barth has championed in our time the integration of the Eternity of the Great I-AM the Lord God is in Himself and in His Acts as the Word of God for His People in His Creation. Revelation and Reason cannot be divorced from one another, however much we must be able to distinguish them. Thomas F. Torrance, perhaps Barth's best interpreter, has argued throughout the many works of his lifetime for a reformation of the Reformation Tradition with this integration in mind. These great theologians have sought to take us quite beyond past ways of carving up reality and point us in a direction that would accomplish a new grasp of the dynamics of the Word of God with the world in the Light of His Revelation. Here the point must be that Biblical humility is not a confession of our ignorance of God, but one rather of our knowledge of God given in the Light of His Word for us. All this must mean that humility is bound with a confession of the knowledge of the Incomprehensibility of God with His Divine Freedom to give us to apprehend Him for who He truly is. Divine Freedom, the gift of apprehending God and His Incomprehensibility all belong to the confession of Moses' knowing of the Lord God as the I-AM He is.

If knowledge of God is given in the Light of His Being in this way, human reasoning of this Revelation possesses definite knowledge of God in the Light of His Incomprehensibility. Revelation comes with its own Reason. There is no 'Unknown' God of this Word. There is only the Mystery of the Incomprehensible One made known in His Self-Revealing and Self-Naming covenanted interaction with His People Himself in Himself and in His Acts. We cannot divorce who God is in Himself in the Divine Freedom of His Eternity from who He is in time and times and space and places in the making of the history in His People in His Creation. We cannot divorce who He is in His acts in history from Himself in His Eternity. He is not One who is in one in His acts in history and another One in Himself. He possesses an integrity that commands our integration of Him with Himself and with His Acts in the history of the world. However difficult it is for us to grasp with our understanding the kind of integration that is 'essential' to the nature of His Being in our knowing of Him, it is not a difficulty to which we can object. It belongs to the Mystery of His Being with us in His Freedom. Given to apprehend Him in His Speaking, we possess permission to accept the challenge of the Revelation.

We are free to seek to learn of Him as the One He is in the Mystery of His Being both apprehended as the Incomprehensible One and in His Divine Freedom for us. The People of God are given to know Him both in His Being in His Acts and in the Acts in His Being—in a wholeness where and when we learn to confess with a positive knowledge of His Word. It is this One with whom we are faced, when we turn with Moses aside to witness in the Burning Bush, unconsumed beside the mountains in the desert wilderness at Horeb, the Voice from the flames, His Word for our lives. In the Mystery of His Being, all levels of the wholeness of the Great I-AM the Lord God is, His Divine Freedom, His Holy Ground, His Apprehensibility, and His Incomprehensibility are confessed as belonging to the Reason of His Revelation. Those who cannot confess this knowledge of Him cannot confess the Incomprehensibility He is known to be. They may confess something beyond the limits of our senses or our imaginations, but their unknown One will never be the I-AM the Lord God is of the Bible, the Word that as the Voice of God would speak for us in the Holy Scriptures.

Though, we may and must distinguish who God is in His Acts in history from the One He is in His Eternity, nevertheless in His Name of His Self-Revelation, we may not separate and divorce this One from some Other, as if behind what He has given us to know of Him is not who He truly is in Himself. Though we may differentiate this One from the Other He is, we may not create for ourselves an abyss or chasm between them. They belong to a Unity of Being whose dynamic life must not escape our attention. There exists wholeness to the nature of this Being whose business it is with us enlightens us as His People. The Speaking of this Great I-AM as His Word speaks in time and times in this world with a certain power we ignore not without consequence. God is this One Sovereign God who is the Lord of all space and time, and when we know Him, we know Him in His Divine Freedom to be this One for us, this One and Only One with us, beside whom there is no other One. We are given to apprehend this One Lord and this One God as the One Lord God who is the Great I-AM the Lord God is with the Bible, with His Holy Scriptures, for the People of God, on His Holy Ground and with His Divine Freedom. Thus, when we claim that we have been given real knowledge of Him, both as He is in Himself and as He is in acts in history, we are confessing that we know Him as the Incomprehensible One He is. Real knowledge of God gives us the freedom to know Him as the One who is truly Other than who and what we are in this world. When we are given to know the

Lord God in His Divine Freedom and on His Holy Ground, we are given to know Him then in His Own Incomprehensibility.

In this case, no ratio of any kind or sort may be posited between human ignorance of God and God's Incomprehensibility. If we have been given to know Him in His Freedom, we are given to know Him on the Holy Ground of the Mystery of His Being, His Incomprehensibility. It is because of this Self-Revealing and Self-Naming movement of the I-AM in the BCR that we truly confess Him for who He truly is. He gives us to know Him in the actuality of His Being who He is in His Divine Freedom and on His Holy Ground, so that we may apprehend Him as the One He is utterly Other than ourselves. This is what belongs to the confession of His Name. It is vital to grasp the dynamics of this kind of relational truth.

Many today think that they are being humble when they confess their ignorance of God, their Unknown God. This is never the Biblical confession the Lord God commands us to make in our meekness and humility before Him. We tend to insist that human humbleness means not knowing Him as the I-AM He is, accepting each other's opinions about Him with tolerance and human dignity and a civil sense of getting along with all opinions about Him. We are as human beings full of deep humility when we confess that we do not and cannot know God for who He truly is in Himself, that one opinion of Him is as good as any. With this terrible pride in our humility, we confess the Great Unknown God, perhaps as the Unmoved Mover of the world or the Moved Unmover of our world processes, as if such humility obtains to some natural correspondence with the command of Moses' confession, when in fact we are merely worshipping our own views, ideas, images, and so forth about Him, meeting one another in our ignorance of Him. It is in fact kind of fashionable to worship Him as the Unknown God in our time. The Unmoved Mover of abstract theology and the Moved Unmover of process theology are steadily worshipped in the terrible fragmentation and alienation our society and cultures experience today with our Lord and God, the Great I-AM who is who He is.

For such people, His Incomprehensibility and their ignorance go hand in glove together to define humility and human nature. In their ignorance of Him, they may bow down to Him. They bow down to what lies beyond all human knowing, beyond all human limitation, beyond all human sense, beyond all human imagination, with their opinions about Him, all meek and humble in their ignorance of who He truly is. But this of course is a long way from Biblical humility. It is still further away from the Truth of His Revelation. It is an empty confession about His Name.

The Bible teaches us that true humility lies with the freedom that possesses the knowledge of Him that compels our confessions of Him. His Self-Revelation as the One He is, as the Great I-AM He is, as the Lord and God He is in His BCR with His People in His Creation must not be denied. Not even the great Albert Einstein understood human humility as something other than what belongs to this kind of confession. Humility had to do with knowing the truth of the nature of the physical Universe, and for the Legend of Science, even this kind of knowledge could not be divorced from the 'Old One.' Thus, he often made reference with his General Relativity Theory and its gravity to God. His famous sayings about the Lord, and the 'humble attitude of mind towards the grandeur of reason incarnate in existence' that is implicit between the world and the Transcendent One, upon which his thought ultimately sought to rest, cannot be ignored. If the Lord is subtle but not malicious, if imagination is more important than knowledge about Him, then we must be able to grasp this 'Old One' as the One who created the world in *the* Beginning. We must be able to understand that He is free to share His Mind with us in this world. This is not a confession that seeks to find in human ignorance of God any real humility. It is a confession made in all humility that the One who created in *the* Beginning is free to interact with us even beyond our times. He is free to give us the gift of His Reason, the gift of His Word in this world. This is a meekness that belongs to a confession that belongs to the great traditions of Moses, Abraham before him, David after him, and the freedom of the Lord God to become the Other as the One He is in the form of Israel's Messiah, the person of Jesus Christ who cannot be passed off as some '*bon mot*' in the history of the world, but must be taken for who He truly is in resonance with the Great I-AM as the Great I-AM He is. This is the kind of dynamics whose relationships we cannot afford to allow escaping our attention, if we are going to confess Him as the One He truly is for us in the Name of His Self-Revelation and His Incomprehensibility.

This is the One the fugitive from Egypt met in the Burning Bush. This is a fugitive chosen by this One to know Him as the Redeemer-Creator He truly is with the world. This is the One that leads His People from the grip of the gods in the Egyptian pantheon towards His Worship at His Holy Mountain in the Sinai. It is this God and Lord who delivers His People

The Great I-AM

with the words of His Command, with His great signs and wonders, with His victories over Pharaoh towards the Land promised their fathers of this faith. This is the Incomprehensible One, the Sovereign Redeemer of Israel, the Sovereign Creator of the heavens and the earth commanding into existence a new history in the histories of the world. When His 'incomprehensibility' is thought of as the great Unknown God and merely associated with human ignorance and opinion about Him, rather than as the confession that has been made of His I-AM, then the true meekness of the confession is utterly lost upon us. But when His Incomprehensibility is understood to belong by the nature of His Being in His Revelation, then mankind's knowledge of Him belongs to the Voice in the Burning Bush. Humility finds its real purpose in the world—to confess the Great I-AM the Lord God is. It is this One who gives meaning to what is or is not.

This is the Lord and God (*Yahweh and Elohim*) who is the Great I-AM of Israel's history in the world. This is the One who, acting with His Divine Freedom, creates the Holy Ground upon which we may know Him for who He truly is. It is this knowing that characterized the nature of the covenanted relationship He has posited between Himself and His People among the nations of the world. With His Freedom, we may know Him as the Incomprehensible One as the ground His Voice makes for Himself in His Creation. He is free to be One with His People. He is free to be this One with His Creation. He is the Redeemer-Creator of the confession. In this freedom, we are given to know Him in the mystery and holiness of His Being and Nature. In this way, He is free to be and become who He is and will be, against all the paths of all the gods of all the peoples of the world. He is free to speak of Himself and to voice a path for the history of the world, against all the idol making that would make of history mere mythological journeys across the plains of times that belong to the unknown gods. In this way, He is free to bear, with the pathos of His Divine Freedom for His People in His Creation, all the opposition to Him the world and His People will give Him. It is this pathos of His Divine Freedom to be with us that we must learn to hear what we read when we read the Self-Naming of the Great I-AM in His Revelation. With Himself, His Name is given to bear the One who commands Israel's Exodus Tradition, her *Yahweh-Elohim*, fundamental and foundational to Moses' confession and the theological thrust of the Five Book of Moses. This Great I-AM is no unknown god, no god who leaves us as orphans in His Creation, but He is truly the Lord God of the world's salvation. He is not some idol projected up onto some unknown deity from out of the pathos of human idol making and human mythologies about the world, but He is in His Divine Freedom the One who is and will be with Israel with a prophetic pathos by which His Voice will be heard in His covenanted relationship with His People. In spite of any and every objection to Him, in spite of all of Israel's preferences for another, He is and will be the Great I-AM He is who will not be without Israel among the nations in His Creation.

Yet even within the Exodus Tradition of Moses' confession, we must read that Israel prefers another to the Great I-AM He is. When we read of Moses' objections to being sent to Egypt, we also anticipated Israel's objections to her deliverance. Disobedience will mark the freed People of God in His BCR with them. After her deliverance from her afflictions under Pharaoh and the Egyptian gods, we read that soon enough Israel become anxious to return to Egypt and to her idol making there. Even after she has been given the Torah of His Command at the Holy Mountain, even after she has been given instructions in Sinai in order to prepare her for her life in covenanted relationship with this One and her journey towards the Promised Land, we read that she prefers another to this Great I-AM this One is. Better to be back under Pharaoh and Egyptian gods in Egypt, she believes, than to live under His Command. The confession of Moses' Lord and God in Exodus 32–34 speaks to us of Israel's preference for another One. We read that she makes for herself a Golden Calf to dance around. She carves out of her own imagination that which she shall worship under the Holy Mountain.

It appears astonishingly enough—the Golden Calf of her preference. We remain astonished about her, in fact, throughout her record of her history among the nations, because of such preferences. To have been given so much in order to give her so great a future and yet to be seen as preferring another to this Giver is almost as incomprehensible as He is. It is like desiring to return to the past that belongs to the time of God's chaos and emptiness, to a time before light was spoken into existence. It is an irrational desire. It is to ask to experience the primordial curse all over again. In this astonishing context, we read what I have called '*The Little Credo of the Great I-AM*.' The holy mutability of God and the divine faithfulness of the Lord possess a passion whose freedom is self-defining with His People in His Creation. This is His 'Credo' for His People, for Israel, who prefers her Golden Calf to who He truly is. What we need to

The Great I-AM

learn in reading the terms of this 'Little Credo' will be the subject of the next chapter. The terms of the 'Credo' provide us with the Self-Defining of the Lord and God who is in His Self-Revealing and Self-Naming Being and Nature the Great I-AM Israel refuses to worship, in spite of the gift of her Torah, her Tabernacle, her Worship of Him. In this way, the Lord God defines who He will be in His BCR with His People in spite of opposition to Him. In spite of their '*stiff-necked*' opposition to Him, He will in His Divine Freedom choose to be who He is not without her in the history of the world. We have apprehended on Holy Ground and in His Divine Freedom this Incomprehensible One who, in spite of His People, will define Himself in His BCR in such a way that He will be who He is as the Great I-AM with Israel among the nations of the world. The Mystery of His Being is in full bloom in this Self-Defining of Himself with her. This is the way He will give Himself to her in the world. His Divine Perfections with her signify, not the static attributes of an abstract first cause or unmoved mover in God's Eternity, but the way He has chosen to be present and known with His Divine Freedom as Great I-AM He is in His BCR with His People in His Creation, in spite of Israel's '*stiff-necked*' opposition as the People of God to their Lord.

The Great AMEN of the Great I-AM

Cosmic Pen

3

The 'Little Credo' of the Great I-AM

*... Lord, Lord, the God of compassion and favor,
long-suffering, and of great grace and truth ...*

Exodus 34:6

WE NEED TO GRASP the significance of His Name in the 'Little Credo' of the actual I-AM He is. He is to be known as this Lord God in His Divine Freedom with His Self-Revealing, Self-Naming, Self-Defining being and nature in His BCR with Israel in His Creation. His freedom to define Himself in this covenanted relationship in this way is vital for the '*stiff-necked*' idol making of His People. When we are able to read His Freedom in this way, a freedom to define Himself with the tribes delivered from slavery in Egypt, we then can see Him acting with Himself for Israel even across the record of their history that we read as Holy Scriptures. For this reason, I have called Exodus 34:6–7 '*the Little Credo of the Great I-AM.*' With the same freedom that He spoke with Moses in the Burning Bush, He speaks here with His Leader and Prophet for His People. In this context of the making of their Golden Calf, we can understand why Israel continues to exist, when she ought to have been punished and killed under His Command for her idol making. In this context, we read that He gives Himself ever to be known by His '*stiff-necked*' People among the nations. We need to be able to glimpse His Divine Freedom to define Himself in this way with us. We need to be able to know Him as the One who is who He is with Israel with a freedom His People shall not finally deny or betray. In the 'Little Credo' we hear the Voice with Moses once again speaking of the embrace of the Great I-AM with Israel's time and times. It is an embrace that ought not to escape, that must not escape our attention.

In this context the famous event of the Golden Calf seems shocking to us (Exodus 32–34). It seems irrational for the tribes to deny the One who has delivered them from Egypt and given them Torah, Tabernacle, and His Glory in their worship there. It seems impossible that they could so readily sin against who He is. But it is even more shocking that the Great I-AM He is would with Moses be an atoning Lord and God in the face of their sin and define Himself for His People with His Divine Perfections. In spite of Israel's willingness to join the nations as an idol maker against Him, the Lord God wills to give Himself in His BCR with His People in this way. Here with this Credo the Self-Defining Lord God of the Self-Revealing and Self-Naming I-AM has voiced His Being with Moses even in the midst of Israel's sin among the nations. Although He ought to kill His People in the covenanted relationship of their lives with Him, because of the Golden Calf, He wills to continue on with them in His BCR. We may understand the 'Little Credo' as His way of renewing covenanted relationship in Israel's history. It is His response to Moses' intercession for Israel.

In this way, we learn to read the divine perfections of His Being and Nature as the 'Little Credo' of the Great I-AM. We learn to hear the terms with which He defines Himself with Moses as His way of overcoming His People's idol making and working to atone for their sin and give their life in His freedom the meaning and significance that only His Voice can give created reality. With His Divine Freedom in this Self-Defining and Self-Giving way, we are given to understand the dynamic nature of His Being both in Himself and in His interaction with Israel's experience of her time and times, of her history in the world. Israel, in her covenanted relationship with who He truly is, lives, whether she believes or not. In this way, we may come to grasp the way He chooses to relate Himself across the centuries with and for His People. I will seek to interpret Exodus 34:6 as the 'Little Credo' of the 'Great I-AM' as a dynamic explication of the nature of His Being the Lord God who is with His compassion, His favor, His patient wisdom, and His great grace and faithfulness the I-AM that is for His '*stiff-necked*' People in His Creation.

I translate the Hebrew names *Yahweh* and *Elohim* into English as 'Lord' and 'God' consistently, as does the various translations of the New Testament. They are names that bear theological significance of the Voice speaking at the foundation and formation of the renewal of Israel as the People of God in the history of the world with the Redeemer-Creator, so that what he whispered once here at the Holy Mountain in Sinai will be remembered throughout Israel's history. What is spoken in the face of the

The 'Little Credo' of the Great I-AM

preference of the People of God for their Golden Calf, these words will be rehearsed throughout the centuries of Israel's renewal of her BCR among the nations of the history of the world. What was whispered in the ears of Moses, shall be proclaimed loudly and forever, where His People are to know Him as the Great I-AM He is:

Exodus 34:6–7
> 'And Yahweh passed before him and declared:
> "Yahweh, Yahweh, El of **compassion** and **favor**,
> **Long-suffering**,
> And of **great grace** and **faithfulness**;
> Keeping grace with thousands,
> Forgiving iniquities and transgressions and sins,
> Yet surely not leaving unpunished
> The iniquity of the fathers
> Upon the sons and the sons of the sons
> To the third and fourth (generations)."'

With these words, the Lord God defines Himself with Moses that Israel's tribes may live. Moses can continue as Leader and Prophet of His '*stiff-necked*' People because of this Voice. In spite of her evil opposition to Him, in spite of her preference for the Calf, and in spite of her desires to return to Egypt, He will be who He truly is with her. Thus, the 'Little Credo' of the Great I-AM becomes the Self-Defining giving of the Great I-AM to His BCR with Israel. The terms of this 'Little Credo' need to be heard as the power of the Voice acting with atoning perfections for Moses in time and times from His Eternity. Here is the same Voice as the Voice of the Exodus, the Voice of the Torah and the Tabernacle, and the Voice that speaks to Israel in her worship of Him. The terms of the 'Little Credo' are then understood as His 'Divine Perfections.' They announce the will of His Voice as the Great I-AM He is in His Divine Freedom to be who He is with Israel throughout her history in the world. These are not merely ideas about God. They do not inform us as to the attributes of some abstract God we may want to conceive with our minds. Their significance is who He is and who He chooses to be among makers of idols. They sign a meaning for us that belong to the reality of the nature of His Being the Self-Revealing and Self-Naming One He is in time and times and the time of His Eternity with us. They are the way He has chosen to be with Himself in His Divine Freedom for Israel in His BCR with her. They are who He is in the dynamics of chosen interaction and dialogue with His People. They define the way that He will provide with Himself for His People. They say the way He will be in His BCR with His Divine Perfections on the ground His Self-Revealing, Self-Naming, and Self-Defining Being creates. It is because of this freedom's power to define this One He is with her that the purposes in His BCR with Israel will be sustained and realized in the time and space of this world. Upon this ground the renewal of the covenanted relationship with the '*stiff-necked*' can and will occur. Israel shall become what He has purposed for her, the object of His attention forever. This is the Great I-AM the Transcendent One is, who will be superabundantly present in this way for His People for as long as forever is made to be.

Understood in this way, the dynamics of the perfections of the Divine Freedom as the acts of His Being, the terms of the 'Little Credo,' are to be read as the will and command of the Great I-AM embodied in His BCR in order to accomplish its purpose in the history of His Creation. This means that we need to learn to hear the Transcendent One for who He is as the Living Voice in His transcendence in the BCR, living through all the sin and evil He experiences against Him in the idol making of Israel's history among the nations. Who He is in His Eternity and who He is in the history of Israel among the nations in His Creation cannot be divorced from one another. We shall have to come to apprehend the meaning of this One in the world. Yes, we need to distinguish His Eternity from who He is in acts with Israel, but we may not divorce Him from who He is in His Acts on behalf of His People in His Creation. Thus, it becomes clear why no dictionary definition of the terms read in the 'Little Credo' can ever prove adequate to state their meaning and significance. They are to be understood as signs that refer to the creative power of the Voice to give Himself that His People might live. They are signs that signify that, in spite of His '*stiff-necked*' People, this Lord and God has chosen out of His own freedom to be even in Israel's history the Great I-AM of the Promise. We want to study these terms then as the power of this Voice for her history. I hope my reader, because I would present the Hebrew terms as His Divine Perfections and not merely words with which we are already too familiar, will be reminded that we cannot simply look these words up in a lexicon or concordance or dictionary and read them for what they are intended to mean. I believe we need ultimately to hear them become embodied in the David of the Latter Days of Israel's prophetic vision of the Word of God, when new personal definition is given to their significance among the realities of world history. I hope my reader will understand my effort in this book in this way.

RACHUM: 'COMPASSIONATE, MERCIFUL'

The first term of the 'Little Credo,' *rachum*, is cognate with the Hebrew '*rechem*,' the word for 'womb.' It is often translated with English 'compassion,' but also with 'mercy.' '*Remember your **rachum**, O Yahweh, and your **chesed**, for they are from long ago*' (Psalm 25:6). The Septuagint uses five different Greek words to translate Hebrew *rachum*. It is German's *Baumherzigkeit*, and it is good to remember that the words or terms do not come first, but the reality to which they would refer that gives any language its meanings. We may think for *rachum* of God's care in beginnings. He makes His beginnings with great care. He conceives things with His Holy Love. The term bears conceptual significance in analogy with the way a mother's womb cares for her fetus. God cares for what He conceives and begins like a mother wombs her child for life. It is this love that gives beginnings their meanings, with this love that we may conceive of the significance of 'compassion or mercy.' It marks the beginning of life with Divine Care, life as God has made life to begin. As such, the Lord God is understood to act with deep and profound mothering love for His People. Just as He provides for His Creation in *the Beginning*, He provides for the beginnings of His People. His covenanted relationship with Israel is this provision, a real beginning, a beginning that resonates with *the Beginning*, because of who He is. His power to create is not another from His Power to give birth and to shape the life of His People among the nations. Everything that does not appreciate the way He mothers with His 'compassion' or 'mercy' Israel's history, does not understand the beginning she has been given by the life of the Lord God Himself, the Redeemer-Creator of the entire Creation.

Perhaps there is no better insight into the significance of this term for the history of Israel in her BCR with her Lord and God than that which we may read in the Book of Hosea. The second child of the marriage between Gomer, a temple priestess, and the prophet Hosea is named '*Lo-Ruchamah*' ('Not-Pitied' or 'Not-Cared-For!'). This child signifies the terrible judgment Yahweh has made against His People for the idol they would make out of Him. It is the reversal of this just judgment that is at the heart of the prophet's message. At the heart of the Word of God with

Hosea and his marriage to Gomer is the Divine Freedom with which God is free to define Himself in His BCR with Israel in spite of Israel's steady disobedience to Him. Here we may read the term of the 'Little Credo' as one of the divine perfections of the Great I-AM in the dynamics of His life with His faithless People. We may understand the significance of *rachum* as belonging to His Divine Freedom to act with His People, just as He acted in *the* Beginning, but now to restore the fortunes of His People in His Creation. We obtain here a glimpse of the way His Word with Hosea is rooted in His Eternal Being as the Great I-AM He is. In the Book of Hosea, the Lord God He is of the 'Little Credo' is free to interact with what He has caused to exist with a mothering care capable of reversing His judgment, announced in the form of the children, against His People. Just as Gomer is with Hosea, Israel is with *Yahweh* as His Wife. He has given her His Word in such a way that the prophet may re-envision Israel's future, even after the judgment is executed. In her Latter Days with Him, as her husband, He will prove His Care for her.

We understand this '*care*,' this '*compassion*,' this '*mercy*,' yes, even this '*holy love*' in her beginnings as belonging to the light of who He truly is for her. If she can make of Him the 'Not-I-AM,' He will make of her '*My People*.' With this love or care or compassion or mercy, Israel shall know her Great I-AM, and that He is who He truly has said He is with His Blessing of her. Quite beyond His judgment against her and His curse upon her, her 'latter days' will be filled with joy and salvation. In Hosea 11:8–9, we read that, because God is God and not man, Israel, in spite of her sin against Him, shall be saved. In her future lies His Blessing for her, when she will know Him as the Great I-AM He is. The Lord God, because He is who He is in her beginning, will not be without her in the end. Israel's existence among the nations in His Creation depends utterly upon His *rachum*. Here is the power of the reversal of the fortunes as the People of God in the world. Israel shall know that her conception was not a beginning that was created in vain. She is a beginning that, with His compassion, shall achieve all she was meant to be. The notes that Moses strikes between the 'Little Credo' of the Great I-AM and the prophet Hosea's Vision of the Word of God can be heard resonating also with Exodus 33:17–20, where we are able to read both *Rachum* and *Chanun* as the interaction in Divine Freedom of the Great I-AM the Lord God is in His BCR with His People in the time and times of Israel's history among the nations. Thus, He is who He truly is.

The 'Little Credo' of the Great I-AM

CHANUN: 'FAVOR, MERCY'

This term, often translated 'favor,' is cognate with Hebrew '*chen*,' a willingness to affirm and confirm the existence of things that have been begun and are. It is sometimes translated with English 'grace,' but I prefer translating the forth term of the 'Little Credo' (*chesed*) by the English 'grace.' Again, the Septuagint translation employed four or five Greek terms for this one term. I avoid translating it as 'grace' because of the vital importance of 'grace' for understanding the restored fortunes of Israel as the 'grace of the Lord' or the *chesed Yahweh* in action in the 'Latter Days.'

Chanun may be associated with 'charm' and 'beauty' in action. There is this display with the 'favor' of God in its significance. In Exodus 33:19, we read that the Lord God will have *compassion* and *favor* upon whoever He wills to have *compassion* and *favor*. The idiom belongs to this subject with Divine Freedom. It is precisely the same idiom as that which we read in the articulation of His Name in Exodus 3:14. 'I am who I am.' 'I will favor who I will favor.' In this freedom is His Name understood as 'My Name,' the Name that signifies His actual Presence to be known as the Lord God He is, the Great I-AM He is with His Command for Moses and Israel. This is the One who is who He is in the superabundant presence of His promise of life for His People. He is present as this One, the Other who sustains what He has conceived in Himself and with His Freedom in His Eternity from *the Beginning*. The terms '*compassion*' and '*favor*' together signify who He is with His People in His care to cause with Himself the subsistence of His People. What He has caused to exist in the first place, with His '*favor*' will be sustained. That which He cared to create with its beginning, He will favor and continue to give life. Just as He acted with Himself in Israel's beginnings, He shall act with Himself to sustain her, and this with a purpose to which He is utterly committed.

I like to think of the two first terms of the 'Little Credo' as together possessing primordial and existential significance. The renewal of the BCR in post-exilic Israel that we can read in Nehemiah 9 depends upon the 'compassion' and 'favor' of the Lord God for her. The meaning of Israel's history is significance that cannot fail in the history of the world, because of the One He is as His People's Redeemer and Creator. Even in the face of her opposition to Him and in the face of His punishment in her history, her time and times, time past and time future belong to Him in this way. With His Divine Freedom and Holy Passion, the pathos of Israel in her covenanted relationship with this One is utterly supported by the I-AM He is. Without His 'care' (*rahum*) and 'sustaining power' (*chanun*) in His BCR for her, Israel long ago would have perished from this earth.

'ERK 'APAYIM: 'LONG-SUFFERING, SLOW TO ANGER'

This term is the most vivid and the most difficult to abstract from real experience in time than any of the five terms signifying the Divine Perfections of the Great I-AM read in the 'Little Credo.' It forms the center and apex of the confession's perfections in time's service to the Transcendent One. It marks Israel's present with His superabundant presence. The term literally means '*wide of nostrils.*' It pictures for us a bull's readiness to strike. Its anger is ready to strike when the nostrils of the bull's nose are as far apart as they can get, when the animal will strike. Because God's nostrils are able to spread so wide apart, there is a very long time before He fills up with anger and, at the end of His patience, is ready to strike. We can read this term often in Israel's Wisdom Literature (Proverbs 14:29; 15:18; 16:32; 25:15). Patience belongs to what the Wisdom of God actually is. He minister's His Judgment with great patience, patience only His Wisdom possesses. He does not strike unfairly, and when He does He strikes with His wrath the unrighteous. With great patience and wisdom His Judgment is to be experienced by His People. Yet when His patience has reached His limits, when His enemies have become so evil against Him, He will and does strike them down decidedly. This term is often translated with English '*long-suffering*' or '*slow to anger.*' Because I think of this term as bound up with the Divine Freedom and Patient Wisdom of the Lord God, who is who He is as the Great I-AM He is in His BCR with His People, I hear the term resonating with significance that is bound up with a Wisdom that we can read even in the Book of James, the Wisdom of the New Testament that comes from above for the good of His People and not their destruction. Wisdom in time in interaction with God's Eternity makes the meaning of this term what it is at the center or apex of who He is in His BCR for Israel among the nations. In this sense, it is the key for understanding time as His servant with Israel. The history of Israel among the nations in His Creation belongs to His Wisdom in *the Beginning* as well as to who He is in her redemption. The history of the world cannot be written without this patient wisdom, His 'long-suffering,' His 'slowness to anger.'

The 'Little Credo' of the Great I-AM

In Habakkuk 3:18–19, we read the culmination of this prophet's burden and prayer for Israel. A younger contemporary of Jeremiah working in the shadow of the rising powers of Babylon, he announces the Lord's anger or wrath in this wisdom. He surveys Israel's times in her covenanted relationship with Him, when finally the prophet offers his song of thanksgiving for her salvation. Israel shall experience quite beyond any experience of her judgment under this wrath or anger of God her salvation with her Lord. Here I think that God's *compassion* for what He has conceived, His *favor* in sustaining what He has begun, and His *'long-suffering'* are all bound up together with one another in His Divine Wisdom with His Divine Freedom to make Himself present with her among the nations. A supra-abundant Eternity makes for a superabundant presence in time and times that give Israel's history the shape and form she takes within the orders of His Wisdom with His Creation. With this Wisdom we find the secret not only of the Creation's Beginning, but the beginning of Israel as His People in His BCR for her. Wisdom and covenanted relationship cannot be divorced from one another, however much we may want to distinguish blood, sweat, and tears, from the joy we experience in our salvation of Him. This means that a dynamical and personal freedom with divine perfections together must be apprehended in the very nature of the covenanted relationship between the Great I-AM and Israel as His Wife. Israel as the People of God cannot understand herself with her Mother Wisdom. A very rocky marriage no doubt it is in history, but one that shall not fail. He is who He is with her, time past, time present, and time future in the way of this patience, this long-suffering, this slowness to anger in the part of her Lord and God. The Lord God is no bulking, quick to strike, but He is wise and patient in His Divine Freedom.

RAV CHESED: 'GREAT GRACE'

The term, *'great of chesed'* is certainly one of the most significant and vital theological terms to be found in the Old Testament. I hesitate to translate this term into English for my students. I do not want them to believe that it means what they think it means. It does not signify something with which they are already very familiar. Even the Septuagint translators employ diverse terms to cope with its meaning. The term is invoked in Moses' Song celebrating the Triumph of the Lord God over the Egyptian gods in the Exodus (Exodus 15:13). It is at the heart of the matter in the ascension of David to the Throne of Israel in the Land, when the Lord God promises His Grace to His House forever. The lack of His Grace so far as the prophecy of Moses is concerned is the condition for the punishment Israel must endure. Psalm 136 celebrates the Grace of the Lord throughout the history of Israel in her covenanted relationship with Her God. Even among the Babylonian exiles, the Sage Daniel can invoke its meaning in his prayer for Israel's renewal. It appears about 245 times in the Old Testament. There have been numerous monographs written on its significance for Israel (E. Sakenfeld, N. Gleuck, and N. H. Smith). I have tried to hold before as steadily as possible its meaning in my interpretation of the Bible. Sixteen times it is coupled as parallel with the last term of the Credo, 'Great Faithfulness.' We cannot fail to understand that it bears witness to the significance of God with Israel's future times in the world.

It is often translated '*abounding in love*' or '*loyal covenant love*' or '*loving kindness*' and sometimes as '*grace*.' What it signifies is the divine perfection of the One who is who He is as the Lord God in His command in the nature of the BCR He has posited with His People, a command that shall not fail. It possesses significance that we need to study again and again in the Bible. It abounds with the meaning of covenanted love in time and times for Israel as the People of God. It is a term that is bound up with Israel's future in the history of God's Creation. Only the Lord God with His '*great grace*' for His People among the nations in the orders of His Creation can give it meaning in its ultimate definition. It belongs to who He truly is with Israel as His People. It is a fact of history that we can easily lose its significance in our midst.

Thousands of pages have been written wrestling with its meaning and significance in times and time. No less than five different Greek words were employed to translate its significance by the writers of the Septuagint, a translation made by Alexandrian Jews into Greek two centuries before Christ. In order to attempt to appreciate the various nuances of the meaning of the term found throughout the Old Testament, Greek speaking Jews in Alexandria had to struggle to translate, in the context of the BCR, the real significance of the term as understood in the third century before Christ. We cannot survey here all the complexities found at this interface of language and culture. When we read the Hebrew and Greek Bibles, we can glimpse the moving feast inherent in the meaning of the term. Suffice it to say that the entanglement of the two cultures was profound and is no doubt with us still today. But suffice it also to say that the word grows steadily in significance across the centuries and cannot be understood as a static term. We would say here that the profound depths and breadths and heights of the meaning of this term in the BCR create a glimpse of the way that in space and time the theology of the Old Testament must be understood as shaped and formed. The dynamic nature of the term will then become extended into the New Testament. In this way, a trajectory in space and time must be found if we are to grasp the Grace of the Lord God with His People in His Creation in His Divine Freedom. The trajectory belongs both to the Divine Perfections of His Being in Divine Freedom with His Eternity and His Divine Freedom to choose to be who He is with His Wisdom and Patience, a freedom that allows Him to go outside of Himself and become in time and times what shall fulfill His purposes in the BCR, a development that in the latter days shall be seen to belong to no other than His Glory. Without some grasp of the dimensions of such a trajectory, implicit in the significance of the term as a Divine Perfection of the Great I-AM in His BCR, we easily miss its meaning in time. The Great Grace of the Great I-AM the Lord God is with His People demands our steady attention.

The term *Chesed* appears some 245 times in the Hebrew Bible. The development as the People of God into her Monarchy with the House of David and her ultimate vision with her Messianic Hope is rooted in the ground of the significance of the *chesed Yahweh* with Israel. This hope is celebrated most eloquently in Psalm 89, when we can read sixteen times the *Chesed* along with His *'Emet* that nurtures Israel's Messianic Vision. In Micah 7:18–20 we read: *'Who is a God like Yourself, forgiving iniquity, passing over transgression for the remnant of His inheritance. He does not strengthen His anger forever, because He desires '**chesed**' and He turns and has '**compassion**' on us and covers over our sins—You give "**emet**' to Jacob and '**chesed**' to Abraham and to our fathers you long ago swore the oath.'* We cannot fail to realize the dynamic aspects of its significance in the nature of the BCR between Israel and the Lord God. It is as such that these perfections are bound up with the actual nature of His Being as the Great I–AM He is in His Divine Freedom as the Lord and God of Israel and the Creation. God is in His Divine Freedom defines with His Being the significance of His *chesed and 'emet* for His People among the nations. Here is the heart of Israel's hope shaped and formed in the world. Here her renewal of her covenanted relationship with Him gives the substance and content of His Grace for her, and Israel must know that her redemption is rooted in the ground of His Grace, the One, the Transcendent One who is in His Divine Freedom 'gracious' with her. The way that 'grace' in fact is given to her, with the I-AM the Lord God is, provides the power of her future's existence. If *compassion and favor* mark Israel's beginnings, then under the reign of His patient wisdom, His *grace and faithfulness* marks her future with Himself.

We would argue that the nature of the dynamical ministry of His Grace provides the actual means by which He makes Himself present and known as the Great I-AM He is with Israel in this world. Manifestly, His Grace in His Divine Freedom and Wisdom has found its mark with His Freedom to Incarnate His Word or Speaking in the BCR, witnessed by the New Testament writers as the final renewal of this covenanted relationship in the form and being of the Person of the Lord Jesus Christ. In this way, both time and space become something they have never been in their service to Him. When God becomes a man in this New Covenant, he becomes something He has never been and Israel then becomes something she has never been, both because of the Grace and Truth He is with His Being and Becoming for His New Creation with His People. God has in this way embodied His *grace and faithfulness* for the sake of His promise in Israel's future. The point that we must be able to make is that His Grace or *Chesed* cannot be conceived as defined merely by any form of static metaphysical or physical rationalisms. We understand here that the Great I-AM the Lord God is, embodied as His Grace and Truth, is the Freedom of His personal Being and Nature to become the Person of the New Covenant who commands the history of His People towards the New Creation. In this way, we may see who He truly is as the One He actually is with Moses, Israel, and the Church as His People in this Creation. The dynamic Being of this Self-Defining and Self-Giving I-AM as the Lord God He is with Israel marks the whole history we read as the Biblical World. But this world is the real world, not a mythical world or a dream, but the world that is what it is as His Creation. But this world is only clear to all who, by the Self-Defining and Giving of this One, have been called to know and follow Him for who He actually is in freedom with the real space and time of His Creation. There is no other book that we might read that would give us to understand the dynamical nature of this Grace and Truth. His great passion to be who He is with us in His Divine Freedom ministers Himself to His People in His Creation. We cannot fail to grasp the personal power this Person possesses for this world. We need to be able to follow Him in this personal freedom and power.

This is the significance of the claim made by the Person of the Lord Jesus Christ that we are called to read as the 'Light of the World.' He is as such the Great I-AM He lives, even before Abraham was born (John 8:12, 58), as the Redeemer-Creator He is. He is the Great I-AM of the Old Testament, the Great I-AM of New Testament, the One Voice we are called to hear as His People. What God once spoke to Moses, He speaks with us in His Church today as this Lord and God, this Messiah—Jesus of Nazareth. He is Himself the definition in His Divine Freedom and Holy Love as God's Grace and Truth in His BCR with His People. Here with Him both time and eternity have been given union at once together with one another as this One Person. As this One Person, He is both the Transcendent One in His Transcendence as the One who is the One He is as His Grace with His People and with the Great I-AM He is. In spite of her '*stiff-necked*' sin against Him, in spite of Israel's faithlessness towards Him and her steady opposition to the purpose of His Being with her, His Grace in His BCR prevails over her according to His Command of her. He will not be the Lord and God He is without her in His Creation. She may and she must live in the hope of His Redemption for her. She is His People. He will in time call His People '*My People*'—even the heavens and the earth themselves wait for this trajectory of His Word in time and space to reach its mark. With some final defining meaning of the *Chesed Yahweh with His People* shall be realized to His Glory the Promise He has made to her. He is the *Grace as the Great I-AM as the Redeemer-Creator He is acting for her in this world*. There is no time that has not and will not know the meaning of this Grace. Thus, it is good to remember that, in the Song of Moses, the *Chesed* and *Strength* of the Redeemer and Holy One, who once gave Israel the victory over armies of her enemies, has given the People of God victory in the Person of the Lord Jesus, Israel's Messiah.

RAV 'EMET: 'GREAT FAITHFULNESS OR TRUTH'

This term, '*great of faithfulness*' (the adjective 'great' in the syntax of the 'Little Credo' governs both '*grace*' and '*truth*' or '*faithfulness*'), marks the ultimate boundary of God's Self-Defining purposes in His covenanted relationship in the time and times of Israel's history in the world. If '*compassion*' and '*favor*' are ways He relates Himself to times past, if '*long-suffering*' or '*patient wisdom*' marks what we may call the present, then *grace and truth* mark time future for the People of God. The divine perfections read in the 'Little Credo' signify the relationship of the Eternity of the Great I-AM to time past, time present, and time future. '*Emet* is cognate with the Hebrew '*Amen*,' a term so common that we can easily overlook its real significance in the Biblical World. It means an affirmation, a confirmation, a justification, a sanctification of who God truly is in His covenanted relationship with His People in His Creation. It must signify the keeping of His Promise to Israel among the nations in His Creation. It is used about 125 times in the Hebrew Bible.

Genesis 15:6 is quoted by St. Paul in the New Testament. The apostle understands this term as bound up with that '*righteousness*' which belongs to the Lord God in His covenanted relationship with Abraham and his sons. It is God's '*Amen*' to Abraham's call. He associates it with the Righteousness of God. This One, who is reliable, truthful, and faithful to what He has promised Israel, in spite of Israel's opposition to Him and her preference for her Golden Calf, has proclaimed His AMEN with His People of God in this way. He has kept the promise He made in His Covenant with Israel with His Righteousness. If '*compassion*' and '*favor*' and '*slowness to anger*' are heard to resonate together with '*grace and truth*,' with the Divine Freedom of the Great I-AM the Lord God is, then I believe we have come to apprehend in the context of His Divine Freedom the Self-Revealing, Self-Naming, Self-Defining, and Self-Giving Lord and God of Israel and the Church in time and times and all time. What the Lord God has promised as I-AM He is, He has kept for the sake of His Name with Israel as the Redeemer He is and the Creator of the heavens and the earth that He is, the One True Revealing of the One True Lord and God of all that is created reality. His *faithfulness* makes with His righteousness for all time and times the affirmation and confirmation of what has been from the Beginning made good.

Because the *Yahweh Elohim* of His 'Little Credo' is the Lord God who as the Great I-AM is jealous or zealous (*El-Qanah*—Exodus 34:14) His personal dynamics with His Divine Perfections in His BCR with His People continues to command Israel against her idol making. She is not to cast idols and she must keep the Festivals that remember the Revelation and her Exodus from Egypt. With this command, Israel is steadily made to confess and affirm her Lord and God in her relationship with Him, even across the centuries of her history in the BCR with Him. The point I believe we need to appreciate here is that, when we allow Exodus 3:14–15 to resonate with 34:6–7, we may hear the Great I-AM the Lord God is in His Divine Freedom to define and give Himself in the covenanted relationship, always in spite of Israel's opposition to Him, struggling with His People to give them freedom to worship who He truly is with the People of God among the nations. The God of *compassion* with Israel is not ever some One different from this Great I-AM. The God of *favor* that has been given Israel comes from the God of Eternity. The Lord God with His *long-suffering* is the Creator. The Lord God of *great grace and truth or faithfulness* in His Covenant with her is the God of the Beginning. We do not, when we can hear this resonance, divide and divorce the Great I-AM from the Lord God of the Covenant in Israel's history. He is who He is in His Acts with her just as surely as He is who He is in Himself without her or the Creation. We may distinguish who He is in His acts in Israel's history from who He is in Himself (recall the apprehensibility and incomprehensibility of the Great I-AM the Lord God is for us!), but we cannot believe that He is some One in His acts and some Other in Himself. It is the dynamics of this kind of relational veracity that is important to hearing the Voice speaking to Moses in the Burning Bush and in Israel's history with Him, the Voice of the Being and Becoming of the Redeemer-Creator confessed by the great prophet of Israel as the People of God.

If she will not hear this Lord and God as the Great I-AM He actually is in His Self-Revealing, Self-Naming, Self-Defining, and Self-Giving interactions with her in this way, she will not confirm Him in His relationship with her. She will not '*amen*' what He has '*Amened*.' She will not know Him for who He truly is. The point then becomes that we must learn to understand Him on His terms, the five terms of the 'Little Credo' of the Self-Defining Great I-AM He actually is, the Lord God is in His Divine Perfections, who belongs both to time and the times right across the history of Israel among the nations in His Creation. In this way, we may follow Him who is who He is even before He became the Creator and created the Creation and then became the Redeemer of Israel. The covenanted relationship posited by Him with His People belongs, from all beginnings to every end, to His Eternity and Eternal Will and Holy Love for His People and His Creation.

We may read, then, the many contexts and the various ways in which Israel is made to experience Himself in His Divine Perfections with her. She finds Him again and again to be true in His Divine Freedom with

His Perfections to be who He truly is with her. The dynamics of this Self-Giving One as this Self-Defining One belongs to His passionate struggle with her across the centuries of her history in the world. It is this passion and effort that gives her history meaning among the nations. This 'Little Credo' of the Great I-AM, once whispered in the ears of Moses at the Holy Mountain, is forever remembered as the power of this Lord and God in His Freedom to name and reveal Himself with His People. In this way, the nature of the covenanted relationship between the *Yahweh Elohim* (Lord God) and the People of God bears the secret of who He is with her in time and times for her, a secret that cannot be divorced from His Eternity and His Divine Freedom to define who He is with Israel in the BCR. There is no page of Moses' confession that does not possess this secret of His *apprehensibility*, His *incomprehensibility*, and His *willingness to make known* with His Name the Personal Nature of His Being. A short survey of the invocation of the 'Little Credo' throughout the Old Testament will suffice to help us grasp or apprehend the way that the incomprehensible One is free to continue to struggle with His People in His BCR for them in His Creation. What was once whispered in the ears of Moses becomes the constant in Israel's history in her relationship with this Voice. The very ground upon which she is given, as the People of God, to understand her Lord and God as the Great I-AM He is belongs to the way His Voice is free to minister His Divine Perfections as His 'Little Credo' with her among the nations.

After establishing the Torah with the Tabernacle and the Orders of Worship at Mount Sinai, Israel is made ready to journey into the Wilderness towards the Promised Land. The eyewitnesses of the Exodus as nomadic tribes organized about this center of God's Revelation now caravan into the desert. Their story in this wilderness is the story of the passing of a generation, the old generation, and the preparation of the new generation for entry into the Promised Land. The destruction in this wilderness of the eyewitnesses to the Exodus is the story of a 'murmuring' or 'complaining' generation, a 'stiff-necked' generation unable to rejoice in all that the Lord God has given them and done for them. Thus, it becomes necessary to establish a new generation of Israel's tribes as the People of God. It is this new generation who will take and occupy the Land of Canaan, the Land of the Promise. In the narrative of this movement from one generation to another, the 'Little Credo' of the Great I-AM is significantly invoked. We read the account in Numbers 14:17–18. In the face of the rebellion of the old 'murmuring' generation and its trepid spying on

The 'Little Credo' of the Great I-AM

the giants in the Land, Moses asserts that the Great I-AM, who is who He is as the Lord and God of the Exodus with His People, shall be with a new generation of the Promise, even as He was with her at Sinai:

> *And now! May the Lord's strength be magnified,*
> *Just as when you spoke—the Lord, long-suffering,*
> *And of great grace, forgiving iniquity and transgression . . .*

In this way, even beyond her Wilderness experience, Israel continues to invoke the presence of her Lord and God with her in His Self-Giving power to be with her in spite of her failures in the covenanted relationship He has established for her among the nations. We may read the strength of this Divine Freedom both in Israel's Psalter and among the prophets of her Prophetic Tradition.

The People of God did learn to celebrate the way that this Lord God had given Himself to be present and known with His People through Israel's priestly tradition. The 'Little Credo' of the Great I-AM is invoked explicitly in Psalms 86:15; 103:8; and 145:8. Psalm 86 is a petition bound up with the 'Little Credo.' David can invoke it against his enemies—*but you O Adonai are the God of compassion and favor, long-suffering, and of great grace and truth*. Because of this One with His perfections in her history, Israel's king can plead that His Presence (His Face) might always be the source of her comfort. Psalm 103 is a wonderful song that celebrates with memory all the benefits Israel has been given in His Name. With the celebration of the names of His Name, His People may rehearse, with great forgiveness and healing, the Blessing of the Promise of Israel's Lord and God. Thus, the song commemorates the way the Lord God had made Himself known to Moses and the history of Israel. The 'Little Credo' of the Great I-AM is invoked in verse 8: '*the compassionate and favoring Yahweh, long-suffering, and of great grace*.' Thanksgiving in this way is the proper response to His Blessing. Again, what was whispered to Moses at Sinai comes to be invoked in David's Jerusalem. Psalm 145 is an acrostic poem, devoted by King David from 'A to Z' ('Aleph to Tav'), to the praise of God as the King of the Blessing in His Name. Verse 8, or the *chet* verse of the acrostic, invokes the 'Little Credo'—'*favoring and compassionate Yahweh, long-suffering, and of great grace*.' The practice in Israel of beginning each verse with a letter of her Alphabet effected a complete devotion of the poem and the poet to the celebration of the subject or theme of the song.

It provides here the basis for honoring the King of the People of God. In this way, He is understood as the throne of a Monarchy whose origin is the Great I-AM. At the heart of King David's relation to King Yahweh or King Elohim beats the significance of the words *Yahweh Elohim* once whispered at Horeb into the ears of Moses.

Beyond the priestly tradition of an atoning love, the 'Little Credo' is also well known among Israel's prophets. After Judah's exile to Babylon, it is well known among those who return to the devastated city of Jerusalem. Among the ruins of the Temple, once the proud possession of Israel's Monarchy, we can read in the midst of the prophetic vision of God's judgment upon Israel's fallen Kings and People (Joel 2:13): '. . . *Rend your hearts and not your garments and turn to Yahweh, your Elohim, for He is favoring and compassionate, long-suffering, abounding with grace, and comforting against the evil . . . .*' Even in the midst of the great Day of the Lord, when He will judge the whole world with His People, Israel must look to Him as He has defined Himself to them in the 'Little Credo' of the Great I-AM. There is no Other who is her Redeemer and Creator in this world. Jonah 4:2b reads: '. . . *O Lord (Yahweh), is this not what I said when I was yet in my land and I was determined to flee to Tarshish, for I knew that you are the favoring and compassionate God (El), long-suffering, abounding in grace and comforting against the evil . . . .*' Jonah, because he knows the way of the Lord God in His Divine Freedom and Self-Giving in the 'Little Credo,' has good reason not to go to Nineveh. If anyone knew the Assyrians the way that Jonah knew the Assyrians, that one would not want to go to Nineveh, but anywhere else—even to Tarshish. Jonah would have hated to see Nineveh saved from the judgment and calamity that was her due. And he knew very well that *Yahweh Elohim* might, with the message he had from Him, repent and escape the judgment upon her. This despised city and its notoriously cruel people might also find the *grace and truth of God* and, if you are Jonah, that is the last thing you want to see happen to the Assyrians. The Lord God might be with them, as He had been with Israel. Jonah would rather die than see Nineveh saved. Of course, Nahum 1:3, a part of an acrostic poem devoted to the Lord's judgment and wrath against the Assyrian evil, teaches us that Jonah's fears were in any case ill-founded. Timing is the issue here. The God who is *long-suffering* and of great patience does indeed relent from punishing the evil that opposes Him in His world, but He ministers Himself with His wrath in a Divine Freedom that belongs only to who He truly is and

The 'Little Credo' of the Great I-AM

not according to the judgments of men and even prophets. We need to observe, for instance in Isaiah's invocation of the *chesed Yahweh* with the Servant of God of His Vision (Isaiah 55:3), that, fundamental to the 'Latter Days' of the Word of God, Israel as the Prophet envisions a proclamation of the Light of His Grace with the House of David in both the mode of judgment and the mode of salvation. Judgment and salvation belong to the Freedom and Grace of who He truly as the Great I-AM He truly is, and not in any sort of timing. Thus, His wisdom is inherently involved in any real understanding of the time and times of the ministry of the obedient Servant, who is both the fulfillment of the covenanted relationship between God and Israel as well as the Light of God among the nations of His Creation. The *long-suffering* in the ministries of His Divine Love in Grace and Wrath belongs to this One, the One who is who He is as the Great I-AM of the prophetic Vision of the Word of God. Divine Wisdom is inherent in the Light of this Word, the prophecy of which shall not fail either in Jerusalem or with the People of God in the latter days of the future of the world as God's New Creation.

Finally, we may see the meaning of the 'Little Credo' of the Great I-AM extended even beyond the Exile and into the period of the Return. From Babylon under Nehemiah the Exiles can return to remember and invoke once more the reality of their Lord and God and His Promise among them. In the midst of the rebuilding of Jerusalem, the Temple, and the People, under Persian command, Nehemiah looks in the tradition of covenant renewal to the 'Little Credo' of Moses' confession. Ezra, the skilled scribe of Israel's Return, reads the Book of the Law of Moses for the regathering of Israel in the Land. At the center of his desire for renewal, the whole history of the People of God is once again rehearsed in their hearing. First, the sin history of the People of God is laid out in no uncertain terms before them. Then, once they are reminded of their 'stiff-necked' opposition to Him, they can remember who He truly is with them in the way of Himself with this 'Little Credo' of the Great I-AM He is. Nehemiah 9:17b reads: '... *But you are the Eloah (El) of forgivenesses, favoring and compassionate, long-suffering, and of great graciousness, never abandoning them ....*'

Throughout the centuries of Israel's history, in the time the Great I-AM the Lord God has made for Himself with His People, the nature of His covenanted relationship with her has been made to bear the meaning of His intent and purpose with her. The 'Little Credo' of the Great I-AM serves to quicken at the center of His Promise with His People among the nations the way of the life of God with Israel. In this way, the covenanted relationship is renewed and established again and again across the centuries with the Divine Freedom of the Great I-AM He is as the Lord and God He truly is for '*My* People.' In this way, He Himself is the ground and grammar for every renewal in time and times and all time in the Divine Freedom of His Being and Nature. His 'Apprehensibility' and His 'Incomprehensibility' is intrinsic in all knowledge of this One. He is who He truly is with and for His People in His Creation in the way of this Freedom, Grace and Truth, Long-Suffering, Favor, and Compassion. What Moses learned of Him that night at Horeb, even among His '*stiff-necked*' People, with their preference for their Golden Calf, is remembered and invoked across centuries of struggles with the passion of this work with Israel's kings, prophets, priests, and scribes. When we learn to appreciate this renewal tradition at its heart and in its actual center at the very real nature of His BCR in the history of the world, we cannot but help to grasp the depths of the significance of His Divine Freedom as the Great I-AM He is for us. We may find ourselves able to follow Him then, freely, in that relationship in which meaning and significance is actually given to the history of His People in His Creation. When we read the terms of the 'Little Credo' as His Divine Perfections working in time and times and all time to give His People real knowledge of who He truly is, and thus knowledge of who Israel is as His People, then we can appreciate the terms not as static definitions of His attributes, but as Self-Defining Being in places and at times where and when His People are commanded to throw away their idols and their idol making and to worship Him for who He truly is with them. This is the One who is who He truly is in His Self-Revealing, Self-Naming, Self-Defining, Self-Giving commitment to the history of Israel, in spite of His People's 'stiff-necked' opposition to Him in His Creation. In this way, we may apprehend the Incomprehensible One in His Divine Freedom as the One Being whose Nature is such that He will not be without His People and He will be known by His People in this world. World existence and mankind's existence must bear witness to this One who is this Great I-AM.

If we understand the Great I-AM as the Lord God He actually is in His BCR with His People in His Creation in this way, then I believe we are in a position to understand the foundations and the steady passion for the formation of the People of God from Israel's Exodus tradition onwards according to the pathos of His Divine Freedom and Holy Love for His Elect in the world. He is Israel's Redeemer-Creator in this Self-Defining power, to be read in the 'Little Credo', across centuries of time and times in all of Israel's experience of Him. It is the transparency of who this One is both Himself and who this One is in His acts in Israel's history that allows us to see the dynamic pathos and passion of His interaction with her among the nations in His Creation. Both His Transcendence and His Immanence are creatively posited in the history of the People of God in this way. It is this Self-Defining and this Self-Giving that we may understand as His Divine Freedom in the acts of this One who is at the heart of Moses' confession and the formation of the People of God. Between the events of the Burning Bush and the Golden Calf, Moses understands this Lord God as the One who delivers Israel from Egypt's Pharaoh and gods as the Creator He is, the triumph of the Great I-AM He is in the world over the idols among the nations. In Exodus 19:4–7a, we read the account thusly:

> 'You have seen what I did to the Egyptians,
> When I lifted you upon the wings of eagles
> And I have brought you to Myself.
> So now, if you will indeed hear My Voice
> And keep My Covenant,
> You will become for Me
> A singular people among all peoples,
> For the whole earth belongs to Me.
> You will become with me a kingdom of priests
> And a holy nation.'

Moses is able to confess the formation in this Light, in the light that the Great I-AM is with His People. The confession is certainly not merely the result of an eyewitness, of TV cameras or tape recorders or satellite tracking systems or journalistic speculations about origins, and so forth. The phrase *'upon the wings of eagles'* is a metaphor whose literary value is not to be denied, but whose meaning belongs to the acts of the Great I-AM Himself with Israel among the nations. The *'wings'* give meaning to the events of the Exodus—they give to the mind's eye an understanding of what it sees as brute facts. They call for a hearing of what is plainly to be seen as this Lord acting in this world's history. The reader is given to understand, then, the Majesty of His Truth in the world, the theological thrust of this Lord and this God in these events that would shape the formation of the People of God among the nations. The significance of the phrase belongs with the inner power of God's Being and Nature to be who He is in this way in Israel's history. The meaning of the texts belongs to His Divine Freedom to be this Lord and God and to remove His People from their slavery under the tyranny of Egyptian Pharaohs and Egyptian gods. The '*wings*' thus belong to the will of the Lord God to make His People free to come to Him and to worship Him rather than the gods among the nations. It is, indeed, something very new in the history of the world. It marks truly a new epoch in world history. It does not belong to the endless cycles and fates of the ancient peoples with their idols and idol makers. It marks the age of the Great I-AM, who will have none of these 'no gods' beside Him in this world. The Lord God as the Great I-AM who is who He is, makes these events mean what they mean, even as something new occurring in world history. Something unheard of before is now happening and it will shape history with a Majestic and Divine Freedom that belongs only to the Truth of Faithfulness of the Creator God and the Redeemer to be the Righteous Lord of His People among the nations. TV cameras and journalists could not have seen these events in the way that they were understood by Moses—events that took place in a sky he sailed '*upon wings of eagles*,' a sky that belonged to I-AM the Lord God is.

They belong to the Revelation of the Great I-AM the Lord God is in His covenanted relationship with Israel in His Creation, where with Divine Freedom He gives history its meaning and significance, its arrow and its mark. In this majestic freedom His People are called to Himself to worship Him in a freedom that only He can give to those He has called. The struggle of a band of slaves to caravan out of Egypt and into the face of the hot winds upon desert sands and the desolation of the Wilderness of Sinai, in order to come to God's Holy Mountain and there to worship Him for who He truly is as their Creator and Deliverer, cannot be told by the brute facts of bare events in history. A poetry that belongs to God as the Eagle of this history is necessary to grasp the significance of the events. In this way, the Divine Freedom of the Great I-AM to be who He truly is with His People in His Covenant in His Creation can be read upon the pages of the confession.

It is important that we understand the logic of this Being of God and His freedom to employ human language to speak to us of who He is with and for us in this world. The Bible is a book produced by the history of the People of God, a confession that demands from beginning to end a theological interpretation that is witness on its pages to the Subject of all subjects. The prose and poetry of the Bible is to be read with reference in this way to this One, the One who is both Lord and God of His People in His Creation as the Great I-AM that He truly *is*. The Bible is not merely the product of people seeking with their history in the world to create for themselves their favorite heroes or heroines. It is a record of the personal reality of this One Great I-AM the Lord God is with His People in spite of the fact that His People prefer their Idol to Himself. The formation of the People of God depends from beginning to end, at all times, upon this confession's prophetic power. In spite of Israel's disobedience to His Voice, He will not fail. He will not fail because of His Majestic and Divine Freedom to act for them. The formation of the People of God belongs to a confession that, in spite of every 'stiff-necked' opposition to Him, records the ways of this *compassionate, favoring, long-suffering* God, of *great grace and truth* as the Great I-AM He truly is. With His Divine Perfections and in His Divine Freedom He is and will be who He truly is with every renewal of His relationship in a world history where the People of God shall be His People. The majesty of the power with which He does these things is told '*upon the wings of eagles*.' With this power, Israel has received her Torah, her Tabernacle, and her Festival Life with this One. It is with His Self-Giving power that she may journey towards the Land He has promised her ancestors, Abraham, Isaac, and Jacob.

Thus, Israel's heart is uniquely shaped and formed as a People for God among the nations. She possesses a new knowledge of Him in His new revelation of Himself as the Great I-AM He is in His Creation. She is given to know His New Name, her Lord, her *Yahweh*, her Redeemer, and as this One, who both keeps His Promise to her and is the Creator of the entire world, she is to know Him for who He truly is. When we read the Book of Leviticus, we must be able to come face to face with this One. The One who speaks with Israel in the Tabernacle, through the Levitical priesthood appointed for her Festival Services, is none other than the One who spoke with Moses in the Burning Bush. He is the One who delivered Israel from Egypt. His Voice is the One that is vital to hear with the Book of Leviticus. We are to read a book about the way the Lord God has chosen in the Majesty of His Divine Freedom to provide for His '*stiff-necked*' a union and communion with Himself.

We read the way He has chosen to continue His dialogue even with disobedient Israel. We read the way His People might come in covenanted relationship with Himself and experience His Blessing, in real union and communion with Him who is as the Great I-AM the Holy One with His People. In this way, He has chosen to lead her with His Glory to her destiny in the world with Him. Leviticus is not a book about the laws and rules of life with God, but a way that Israel might live and not die in communion with this One. It is a book about His provision for her who will not obey. It is a book of Holy Love, about the Divine Freedom to be who He is and to provide for Israel, in spite of her 'stiff-necked' condition, a fellowship in His Covenant with her. It is a book about the way that the Great I-AM the Lord God is provides for the 'profane' and the 'unclean' to become before Him 'holy' and 'clean' and blessed. It is a book of His Atonement for her who sins against Him, who would prefer another to Himself in her life. It is a book about union and blessing with Him, about the Glory of who He is as Israel's Holy One. The burden of the Book of Leviticus is to teach Israel His Holy Love for her. Would that more people might read it as such!

You shall be holy as I am holy' (Leviticus 19:2) ought to be heard in the way the prophetic power of His Voice as both the Creator of the heavens and the earth and the Redeemer of His People among the nations is to be heard in Israel's worship. The Voice of Israel's existence in the world is heard with His willing and atoning love for her among the nations. It is this Voice that we cannot make a voice of the ghetto. The same Voice that spoke with Moses in the Burning Bush and the Voice that speaks in the Tabernacle with Israel's tribes delivered from Egypt, given a freedom to worship Him in sacred space and time, possesses a prophetic purpose among all nations in God's Good Creation. That the People of God are the 'stiff-necked' people they are, that they can prefer to worship a Golden Calf rather than the I-AM He is, that Israel can oppose her Lord and God in His Divine Freedom to be who He is in her history in the world—these historical facts and experiences cannot be the basis of her union and communion with this One. It means that He must take the 'profane' and the 'unclean' and convert them into the 'holy' and the 'clean,' so that He may accomplish with her the prophecy He has given of Himself for her. His Command must be the last word on her relationship with Him. Because He is always who He truly is, His People shall be blessed and not cursed with the Holy One that He is. The purpose of the atoning sacrifices is to convert Israel from the profanation of Him and His Name into a communion with Him that would honor Him, His Name, and His Glory with her in the world. Thus, a 'stiff-necked' People are made to worship Him.

The 'Little Credo' of the Great I-AM

She shall be 'holy' as He is 'Holy.' The unclean must become clean. The Lord God must be worshipped for who He truly is. He will not be another than He is with her. His People must possess no idols before Him. The way of His Atonement in the Tabernacle Service thus provides an imperative that must be understood with prophetic power, the power of the Holy Love of the Great I-AM as the Redeemer-Creator that He is. Israel may live under the Blessing of His Glory in this union and communion with Him, outside of which is experienced His Curse of death upon evil and sin in the world. This is the burden that we must learn to read in the Book of Leviticus.

For the People of God, becoming holy as He is Holy was never a matter of keeping rules or laws. Leviticus recounts the way the Lord God has, in His Divine Freedom and with His Holy Will, chosen to provide for His People, even in their 'stiff-necked' opposition to Him. In spite of His People's sins and transgressions and iniquities against Him, He has provided a way for them to continue in fellowship with Him. The Levitical priesthood records the ways He has chosen to forgive Israel her 'transgressions' and to create her in fellowship with His Blessing. This real union and communion with who He actually is, where Israel may choose fellowship under His Blessing, is the purpose of the atoning sacrificial system we read in the Book of Leviticus. It records the provision for His People of the Great I-AM that He is for Israel. In this way, the Self-Revealing, Self-Naming, Self-Defining, Self-Giving Great I-AM the Lord God as this Holy One for His People among the nations, against all the idols of all the nations surrounding the People of God, will not be without those He has chosen for Himself. In this way, His Chosen are called, with the same freedom He exercised in the Exodus, to come before His Presence and know the Blessing.

We may rightly come to understand the Book of Leviticus as an account of the way that the Great I-AM has chosen in His Divine Freedom to be, with His Holy Will, who He is for His People among the nations in His Creation. His is the power to make Himself present and known for who He truly is, according to His 'Little Credo,' with His People. It is a Self-Giving whose Divine Freedom is exercised to this very day as His Holy Love. In fact, the very meaning of '*today*' must be understood as bound up with the Will of this Divine Freedom and Holy Love. I believe we would read the Book of Leviticus much differently if we could understand it as an historical record of this determination that only the Lord and God of

Israel's history in the world could and does possess as the Great I-AM He is. We would grasp the prophetic power of the speaking of the Lord God with His People. We would understand that His speaking with their priesthood provides the ground upon which His People can stand before Him and live. We would better learn the lessons of the conversion of the old priesthood into the new priesthood that is prophesied in this way. We would better learn the lessons of the conversion of the old sacrifices into the new sacrifice of the Great I-AM in this way. The transformation of the old communion into the new communion with which He has provided a new union for His People with Himself would become more sensible to us. The power of His atoning love in this way would be heard as a prophetic power. His speaking in this way would never become divorced from who He is and the prophetic power of this speaking would better be heard in the time He has provided for Himself with His People in this way. We would know Him for the Lord God of space and time that He is. It is with this prophetic power and this divine freedom of the Word of His Being that creates this space and time for His People, that forms the shape of the ground where we must learn to stand in time to hear His Voice as the Great I-AM He is, the object and subject of Israel's worship in her history with who He truly is.

This kind of listening would go a long way towards helping us understand the Holiness of His Holiness. He is not something or someone that we may define with or by or for ourselves, in and of or for ourselves. Worship of the Holy One, on the contrary, would take us quite out of ourselves. It would take us into a real relationship with our Lord and God. Without His chosen sacrifices and without His will to act with His atoning love for us in this way, His People must remain unable to define His Holiness, the Holy Love of the Holy One for His Holy People. If He does not define Himself in this way on this ground, where He wills created with His Divine Freedom a communion in which His People become sanctified with Him, then His People are set free to be present with Him and live. Where He has chosen to interact with His People and in the time and times when He has chosen to communicate His Blessing His People, there and then they must become, free from the Curse in His BCR, those whom He would name '*My People.*' The One who is the Lord and God of *compassion and favor, long-suffering, great grace and truth* is the One whose Voice gives to His People the freedom to worship Him in His Presence and to live and not die before Him. It is a definition of space and time and people

The 'Little Credo' of the Great I-AM

and places that belongs to His Glory. The Glory of His atoning love and work for His People is His BCR fulfilled with His People in this way. This is where and when His People may learn that He will not be who He truly is without them. Again, the One who spoke with Moses in the Burning Bush is the One who speaks again and again with Israel in the Book of Leviticus. Worship becomes the place and time of the free gift to a free People given from the free Lord and free God for Israel. If it is given in appointed times at sacred places, it is for the sake of freedom that it is always and everywhere given. In this way, Israel may have union and communion with Him, be blessed in the nature of His BCR, rather than cursed, among the nations in His Creation. It is far from a legalistic system that we must hear in this way, but a free and freely speaking God. His Blessings and His Curses are both ministered in this free way in these places and at these times. He is who He is in this way with His atoning love creating space and time for Himself with Israel. His will to define with this atoning love such time and space and people is vital for understanding the prophetic power that is His Word spoken in the Book of Leviticus.

If we read the Levitical Worship of Israel's worship of the Speaking of the Great I-AM the Lord God is in this way, perhaps we would better understand the tendencies of His *'stiff-necked'* people to become *'high-handed'* with their 'strange fire' in the system. Perhaps we would better understand Israel's sin history under the Curse of the Great I-AM. We would better understand the boundaries of the 'sacred' over against the 'profane' that belongs to who He is with His Name in Israel's worship. Perhaps then we would better understand the Divine Freedom of this Holy One in His passionate struggle to be present and to make Himself known for who He truly is with His People. The *'sacred'* world and His Blessing and the *'profane'* world and His Curse would become more vivid in our understanding of this Holy One. We do know that the Book of Leviticus teaches us that, unless the *'profane'* is converted to this Holy One and becomes holy as He is Holy, no one shall ever see and live the Glory of God with His Blessing. We must not miss this prophetic power of His Speaking in His Holiness.

In our time definitions of 'holiness' and the Holy One are legion. Most seem to me a long way from what has been set forth as the Speaking Lord and God to be read with Israel's worship tradition. Rudolph Otto once wrote a book about 'holiness' that claimed to understand the Holy One as a mysteriously silent one, who was quite other than we are, to whom we must bow in a tremendous silence that entails utterly the world and its peoples. Holiness had to do with what is other than we are in tremendous mystery whose silence we can hear if only we would listen hard enough. This is a long way from the teaching of the Holy One in the Book of Leviticus, but quite common among us just the same. As far as it is away from the speaking we are to hear, it is at least an effort to establish some appreciation for the mystery of this speaking Lord and God, something all definitions of 'holiness' that would reduce it down to one system of behavior or another are without. No form of legalism can touch the speaking we are to hear in the prophetic speaking which is to be found in the Levitical priesthood of Israel's history with the nature of the BCR.

If we understand the Levitical sacrificial system as constituted with His atoning will as a work the Great I-AM is willing to do on behalf of His People, then the sovereignty of His Divine Freedom is grasped in the full exercise of His Speaking as the Lord God He is. Because of this speaking, His People may worship and know Him and live under His Blessing. Because He is willing in this way, in spite of His People's transgressions and sin against Him, to provide a place and time in His atoning love for their union and communion with Him. His People may live without His Curse upon their sin and the evil of their relationships against Him. There is no sense of appeasing an angry deity in this system. There is only the creation of this fellowship, a fellowship for which His People are taught that they are forgiven and must be grateful for their life. Atonement is meant to provide life, fellowship, union and communion, blessing with the Living One, in His Holy Love and Will for that which belongs to Him in any case. In this way, His People may learn of His desire to bless them who are people He is free to name '*My People*,' for it is that He will not be who He is without this People. These are the sacrifices that can only mean God is willing to provide for His People. These are the sacrifices He will to honor and give meaning and significance that leads to Life, Life in His BCR with His People in His Creation. These are the sacrifices that are the praise of Life. We must not fail to hear the prophetic dimension of this Speaking of the Great I-AM He is. Atonement cannot be appreciated for what it actually is unless this compelling love and faithful will are heard holily and understood for Life!

Otherwise, we can readily reduce the meaning of this system down to a worship where rules of behavior are broken and punished, when we turn upside down the significance of the Blessing and the Glory of the

The 'Little Credo' of the Great I-AM

Almighty. A priesthood can easily become a vaunted display of mankind's willingness to obey, rather than a real recognition of His Divine Dialogue with His People in His Tabernacle in His appointed times and places. A priesthood can easily become '*high-handed*' and offer '*strange and alien fires*' to some tremendous mystery, turning on its head the Speaking of the Great I-AM the Lord God is. A priesthood can easily take upon itself what only God Himself can say and do. Israel's priesthood was not to be compared to those in Egypt or Mesopotamia or Canaan, etc. Israel's worship was not to be confused with the worship of the gods of the nations. In the lands that stretched from Mesopotamia to Egypt around her, the Lord God has posited with His People, a very unique way of worship that was bound up with who He actually is in the world, beside whom there is no other, not in times past, not in the present, and not in times future. We need to grasp the meaning of the power of this Speaking in all times and all time, as it comes from the Eternal Life and Will of the Holy One He is who will not be without '*My People*' in His Creation. Here in this place and at this time with His People, He has chosen to speak and create for Himself this Israel of God, this People of God among the nations. We cannot miss the new dimensions of this utterly new way of life He has created with His People among the ancient peoples of the world's nations.

We understand atonement then, not as something defined by the priesthood of the People of God, but the way of service to the Voice of the Great I-AM the Lord God is with speaking in His Chosen Tabernacle with us. We know that this Voice is the same Voice that spoke with Moses in the Burning Bush and that delivered His People from Egypt. Atonement possesses a meaning and significance that only this Voice can give it as His Act upon His People in His covenanted relationship with Israel. It is the Speaking of this Voice that commands the appointed times of the Tabernacle and Israel's worship of Him. Atonement is a gift to His People from the God who is free to define and give Himself as He is to a people whose uncleanness and profanity cannot prevent Him from providing His Blessing for them. It is a gift for which His People may be grateful because it is the provision of the Lord God for their transgressions and sins against Him. We do well to remember this gift of His atoning love and His holy will as it comes to us from the Hand of this Great I-AM. He is no Golden Calf that men so love to kiss. We do well to receive it with thanksgiving, for we are assured that He is who He truly is with His chosen '*stiff-necked*' People who He wills to convert from being 'unclean' and 'profane' and 'cursed' into a people He names 'My People,' a people cleansed and made holy and blessed in fellowship with Himself, free from their 'high-handed' worship of idols invented for themselves. It is against the ungrateful condition a 'high-handed,' willing to offer Him their 'strange fire' that His Curse in His BCR is leveled against Israel. The blessing of His atoning love is denied this 'alien fire,' such blasphemous sacrifices. When this atoning love is rejected by Israel, His People can only experience all over again the Curse upon sin and evil she has known from the very beginning of her history in the world. When this work, found so deeply and profoundly in the heart of the Nature of His BCR, the very Voice of His Being and Becoming is refused, then this 'high-handed' People of God must suffer the punishment for their idol making against Him. Redemption, Reconciliation, Renewal, all the great theological concepts we are taught in this way, belong to the Mystery and Freedom and Righteousness of this One Speaking Being. How can Israel prefer another Voice to this One? 'He Declares,' is the title of the Book of Leviticus. Thus He speaks to His People with a Voice, the Voice whose prophetic power is such that He promises with it that He will not be who He truly is without His People in His Glory with His Righteous and Holy Judgment across the whole of His 'clean' Creation. We do not do well to regard the Book of Leviticus as a system of rules or laws. When we cannot read it as the proclamation it is with Israel of the actual Will of God to be present and known for who He is as the Lord God of all space and time, we are unable to rejoice with Him. When we are unwilling to know His Will for us, we are unable to rejoice with Him as He takes His People and His Creation to their destiny with Himself.

It is this Glory of this Self-Giving Lord God, this Speaking One that moves Israel then from Sinai out across the Wilderness towards the Land He once promised Israel's ancestors. It is this Glory that is manifestly experienced on her journey across the desert between Horeb and Canaan. It is times such as these times in Israel's history that she comes to understand herself as marked, even though she has been an eyewitness to the Exodus, with a certain 'murmuring,' for which she will pay dearly. A whole generation of eyewitnesses 'stiff-necked,' 'profane,' and 'highhanded' shall die in this Wilderness with its 'murmuring' people in its dusts against the Great I-AM. This complaining of these eyewitnesses about their deliverance from Egypt brings down upon the head of this whole generation the curse of God in His covenanted relationship with Israel. It is because of this 'murmuring'

The 'Little Credo' of the Great I-AM

generation that a whole new generation of Israelites must be formed. It is as this new generation that Israel shall enter as the People of God into the Promised Land, to the Glory of God. The Book of Numbers is an account of these '*generations*,' the old wounded generation that perished in the Wilderness and the new generation to be prepared for Israel's entrance into the Land of the Promise.

The eyewitnesses that formed the first census (Numbers 1) are those doomed by their '*murmuring*' to die in the Wilderness. They are replaced by the new generation of the second census (Numbers 26). This generation marks the connection of the Book of Numbers and its pointing to the future of the People of God with Israel's past and the generations, primordial and ancestral, that we read in the Book of Genesis. This new generation is the generation that will be readied to enter the land promised their ancestors. The old generations/new generations of the narrative that is the Book of Numbers may, in the light of the Great I-AM, be understood to resonate with 'the generations' that give shape and form to the Book of Genesis. The new generation is a generation renewed in the nature of the covenanted relationship in which the Lord God struggles to renew for His Purposes His People. They are made ready to go beyond the '*stiff-necked*,' '*highhanded*,' and '*murmuring*' condition of the old generation to possess the Land as a new generation called to obedience in the Name of their Lord and God. We have already observed the use of the 'Little Credo' of the Great I-AM in this narrative. In Numbers 14, the Lord God determines to end the history of the generation of eyewitnesses because of their rebellion in the Wilderness (Numbers 14), when once again, as he did in the incident of Israel's making of her Golden Calf, Moses intercedes for the tribes of Israel with Him, and at this time invokes the 'Little Credo' (Numbers 14:18–19): '*The Lord is slow to anger, abounding in love and forgiving sin*,' so that the purpose of the covenanted relationship with the People of God may continue. The death of the '*stiff-necked*,' '*high-handed*,' '*murmuring*' generation may very well be required of the seed of Abraham, but a renewal of a whole new generation will be provided. This Lord as this God will continue to be who He is with Israel in the history of the world.

We may note here that, in the light of this renewal of the relationship, even foreign kings are made to hear the Voice of this Holy One. In Numbers 22–24, we read the wonderful narrative of His Sovereign Power even over Mesopotamian prophets and Moabite kings. The account of King Balak in Moab, seeking to buy the prophet Balaam's words in order to curse and war against the tribes of Israel passing through his territory, teaches us about the Sovereignty of this Lord and God. He has determined to bless Israel and not to curse her, and in this way controls even the Moabite's plans for her. Though Moab is willing to spend its wealth to curse the ancestors of Abraham, the Great I-AM is not. If He reigns even over the People of God, He also reigns over Mesopotamian peoples, and what He has blessed, no one can curse. What He has cursed, no one can bless. He reigns as King over His Blessing and His Curse. Blessing and cursing belongs to Him who has called Abraham from Ur (Genesis 12:1–3). The prophet Balaam of Aram and his donkey must both know that this One is sovereign over all the words that are by all the peoples of the world over the tribes of Israel. The Great I-AM is free as the Lord God He is in His sovereign determination to bless and to curse His People among the nations of the world. It is, in fact, on the heels of this confession that Israel is seen to indulge in that sexual immorality with Moabite women that leads her finally to her destruction as the old generation in the Wilderness, that leads to the solid need for a whole new generation of Israel's presence in the world. Thus, we read in Numbers 26 the census of this 'New Generation,' who is the tribes that shall prepare to enter into the Land of the Lord's Promise with His People.

We would argue that the nature of these generations in the renewal of the covenanted relationship taught us in Israel's history is a confession made to resonate with the narrative of the stories of the People of God explained by the primordial and ancestral possessions of Israel's beginnings. The context of covenant renewal shapes a domain for Israel's history that is defined for us by the force of this theological thrust inherent in Moses' confession. To explain the People of God, Moses must gather up his understanding of the times past and there grasp the Divine Freedom of the Great I-AM to be the Lord and God with His People in His Creation. We can and we will say that learning who He is in this Divine Freedom and with this Holy Love and Will for His People enables us to apprehend the meaning of all these events. They mark Israel's times, her time past, her time present, and her future with His time for her. They are lights that sign the passion and pathos of His Being her Creator and Redeemer with her. They are to be read accordingly. Without this resonance, we will hear another voice, give them other significance, and understand them in other ways even in our own times. Is it not true that we thus have trouble hearing the way the Great I-AM gives meaning to history?

The 'Little Credo' of the Great I-AM

I believe we need to learn afresh to hear and see these things in the actual light of who He truly is in His Time for Israel's times among the nations. It is the Voice of this One that gives meaning and significance to the nature of the covenanted relationship and its renewals within Israel's history in His Creation. It is the *compassion and favor, patient wisdom,* and *great grace and truth* of this Voice that provides the power to revive His People for His Holy Love and Promise in His BCR with Israel in His Creation. It is this power that lies behind His seeking to free this People from their sin against Him, to silence their disobedience of Him, and put away their deafness to His Speaking, their preferences for their idols and their idol making. It is the Divine Freedom of this One Voice that is at the heart of all true freedoms in this world. I believe that Moses, the Servant of this Lord and God, with his confession sought to explain this renewal tradition of God and His time for His People in His Creation. He had learned to see and hear things in the way of this Divine Freedom's power, love, and will that beats in the heart of the Self-Revelation of this Great I-AM that he was called to face in the Burning Bush in the desert wilderness. I believe that it is in the light of this power's freedom that Moses shaped his confession's explanations and articulated with theological force the passion and pathos of the Lord God in His covenanted relationship with His Chosen Israel among the nations. It is for this reason that his witness employs the possession of primordial and ancestral beginnings as the background to the generations of the Exodus and the Wilderness.

Moses lived in a present that belonged to a past whose future was bound up with the very beginning of God with His People in the Creation. He lived in a present that belonged to a vision for this future, to a prophecy whose significance was creatively commanded by the very Being and Word and Act of this Lord God. In these times the very power that forms the history of times, time and time again, even with such a reluctant Servant of God, is able to create what must be to guide His People to Himself in His BCR among the nations. With a faith given to him by the Great I-AM Lord God is in His Self-Revelation and Self-Naming and Self-Defining and Self-Giving Moses is enabled to confess Him as the One True God He is. As thus One He is the Lord God of *the Beginning*, the heavens and the earth, the mankind made as His Image and Likeness, the Speaking God who creates His Sabbath relationship with what He has begun and blesses it as His very own *Begnning*. All the beginnings experienced by Israel as the People of God are to be understood as bound up with *the Beginning*. This is what history is, what time and space are according to this faith, the holy ground upon which one may stand, rooted in His atoning love and prophetic command of the prophet Moses is with his words. Moses can confess this Lord God as the Lord of the Primordial Ancestors and the God of *the Beginning*. He can confess this One as the Lord of Abraham and his sons, the Lord of Israel, who has heard the cry of His People's afflictions in Egypt and who will answer them. This is the history that belongs to the faith that belongs to the Divine Freedom of this Lord and God of all history, the history of the Creation and the history of the Ancestors of this People. In the Light of the Great I-AM the Lord God is as the Sovereign over the Exodus and the Wilderness experiences of Israel's history among the nations, Moses is given to apprehend this incomprehensible One in His Divine Freedom and Will and Power to be present with and known by this People among the nations. Moses can confess that the Great I-AM of the Burning Bush is indeed the Creator of the universe, the Creator of mankind, and the source of their meaning and significance as His Creation. From *the Beginning*, from Adam to Seth, from Noah and his sons to Abram and his sons, these people mark the times with the will of the Lord God with Israel in the history of the Creation and the Ancestors. It is the Command of His Voice, this Great I-AM, which lies behind the secret of the history we read with Moses. In the Light of this Voice of the Great I-AM the Lord God is, we may learn to see and to hear and to follow His freedom and passion and pathos in the divine perfections we understand as personal *compassion and favor, long-suffering*, and *great grace and truth* for His People, for Israel in time and times among the nations in His Creation, in spite of the great making of idols He faces with His People. In Him, we may learn to understand, because He is this Redeemer and not another, because He is this Creator and not another, and because He will not be this I-AM He is without Israel in His Creation.

Bull in Snow

4

The Beginning of the Generations

In the beginning God created (bara' Elohim)
the heavens and the earth . . .

Genesis 1:1a

THE GREAT PRINCETON PHYSICIST John Archibald Wheeler used to tell his students that every man and woman in this world ought to wake up each morning and spend the first twenty minutes of their new day reflecting on *the* Beginning. He claimed that it would change one's life, especially the lives of scientists. He would have people think about the inertia of particles, the motion of the planets, the constitution of the stars, the fall of a sparrow, the buzzing of star clusters, the earth in the Milky Way, the power of Quasars, the expansion of the universe, the primordial process that manufactured the study of which we have been made each morning of their lives. His exhortation, I believe, applies as well to theologians. How much time do we actually spend reflecting upon the times *the* Beginning, especially as confessed by the prophet Moses? God's Time for our time and times in relationship with His Freedom to be present with His Creation makes for a challenging subject to contemplate. The confession of Moses is made in the light of the Great I-AM's past, primordial and ancestral, with His People delivered from her bondage in Egypt for a freedom that belongs to His ancient promise to her ancestors. It is a confession made in the light of the speaking of this Great I-AM that the Lord God has revealed Himself to be. It is a confession made against all pretenders to the Throne. It is a confession whose seeing and hearing belongs to a revelation of the Lord God who seeks to reconcile His People with Himself. Israel with this confession is challenged by a faith made solid with Moses by the Voice that spoke with Him from the Burning

The Beginning of the Generations

Bush. It is this Voice that we must hear in the Speaking and Act of God in *the* Beginning.

The history of Biblical interpretation by Christian theologians tends to show that we do not take as seriously as we need the doctrines Creation out of nothing in *the* Beginning as understood in the Light the Great I-AM has become as the Person of the Lord Jesus Christ, the Incarnate Word of God, who is the Redeemer-Creator, the One and Only and Incomparable God. We tend not to understand the Creator of the world as the Father of the Lord Jesus Christ. We tend to split apart the One God from the Triune Lord. We work with assumptions that posit an abyss between the Creator of the heavens and the earth, according to Moses' confession of *the* Beginning, and the Father of the Son and the Son of the Father who is the Redeemer of Israel's Messianic prophecy as the Davidic King of Israel's future. The Man Jesus is, as the Creator of the world, in spite of the Creeds of the early Church, tends to escape our attention. In the history of exegesis, there has been created, for reasons good and bad, a deep and profound chasm between the Old Testament's Creator and the Creator as the Creator is confessed to have revealed Himself in the New Testament. We need to overcome these splits. *The* Beginning confessed by Moses and the New Beginning Christ has made with His Incarnation and Resurrection cannot be divorced from one another in the Biblical World.

Moses confessed the power of the Wisdom of God's Being in *the* Beginning as the One whom he had encountered in the flames of the Burning Bush in the desert wilderness. This pre-Iincarnate form of the Word of the Lord God has not readily been understood as the Great I-AM. His becoming as this Word with His Incarnation is an ultimate Light upon His Being and Becoming. The Incarnate Word is in fact the Light of the Becoming of God's Being in Eternity in relationship with the created time and space of His Creation. It is in the Light of this Word that Moses confesses the Creator against all the idols of the peoples of the ancient world. The same God who created out of nothing in *the* Beginning, who then spoke light into existence in the midst of the chaos and emptiness of His Creation, is the One with His Divine Freedom that Moses is charged to obey. He is as this God, the Creator, the Redeemer of Israel, Lord of His Creation. In this way, the Great I-AM as the Creator acts with His Being to create *the* Beginning out of nothing and to speak into existence with His created light the orders of time and space we experience on the earth under the lights of our days and nights. The impetus that belongs to the

Wisdom of the Divine Freedom of God in *the* Beginning is a two-fold power. It creates the existence of the chaos and emptiness and so forth of *the* Beginning as His Creation and then in the midst of it all the light by which the orders of time and space are established on earth under the heavens. The Redeemer-Creator thus shines as the Word and Power of the Lord God in *the* Beginning from the Beginning of the confession. We need to be able to grasp this impetus right from the start of our thinking about God and His Creation. In this way, in the Light He has become as His Incarnate Word, we may hear the confession of His Word and Power in His primordial reality with the Creation as well as the prophecy inherent in its intention. Moses' confession provides the background for the generations that are recorded as the history of the People of God. We must learn to see and hear this God as the Lord the Great I-AM is with His Being in becoming the Creator and in His Becoming the Eternal Being of His Word over and with and in His Creation. It does take some meditation perhaps each morning of our lives to hear and see Him rightly. The silent power of His creating out of nothing and the power of His Speaking as the One Voice who is the Light of all created light must inform the very assumptions of our reflections, when we seek to exegete Moses' confession as Genesis 1. The confession provides the ground on which we may stand to hear and see not only in *the* Beginning but also with Israel among the nations in His Creation. Right from the start we make each morning with our lives in this world, we spend in His Creation. John Archibald Wheeler in this respect was certainly right to exhort his students about meditating on *the* Beginning.

The Great I-AM the Lord God is, who chose freely to speak with Moses from the flames of the famous Burning Bush, would fulfill His Promise in His BCR to His People in the Creation. That the Incarnation is an event that will occur centuries after the event of *the* Beginning cannot and does not mean the two beginnings are not made to resonate with one another in the Biblical World. It means that time has a Lord who is able with His Divine Power and Freedom to become who He was not while remaining who He is as the Redeemer-Creator of Man in His Creation. The times of the light of the heavens and the earth serve the Light He has become, in the fullness of time, from before *the* Beginning. The Voice He is in His Incarnation is the same Voice Moses heard to confess this Beginning. No mere admirer may define the Nature of God's Being and Becoming in this way. He is and will be, as we have seen, Self-Defining and

The Beginning of the Generations

Self-Giving in His BCR with His People. He defines Himself within the history of His Creation as the One who is who He is before His Creation, with His People among the nations in His Creation. The dynamical nature of such definition ought not to escape our attention. The dimensionality of the 'nothingness' of the chaos and emptiness as well as the light of the heavens and the earth cannot be defined by some other means than by the Wisdom of this Lord God, who is free with Himself in this way for His People in His Creation. What is and what it means in time to belong to both created time and the uncreated time of His Eternal Being and Becoming. It is a dynamical reality worth our attention every morning. The Creation's history is not a proposition that we are able to lay down with our concepts and ideas about the Creator and His Relationship to the world. As God and this Lord, He is the Lord of all time and each time, of time's orders in the light of His Creation. This assertion is fundamental for understanding Moses' confession of *the* Beginning. Free to become the Creator, the Great I-AM as this Lord God is free to move outside of Himself and become even a man in time, while remaining who He truly is with His Eternity. We need to sense the power of this freedom with our understanding of *the* Beginning, right at the start of our contemplations of these first verses of the Bible.

Many view such an attempt as reading back into Israel's history the later development marked with the event of the Incarnate Word, as seeing the Old from the perspective of the New and therefore intruding upon the past with an imposition of a present or a future period upon the time of an earlier era. This view is commonly taught in our schools today. We ought to attempt, it is regularly laid down, to read the confession of Moses in the Book of Genesis without reference to the time and times of this Light of God's Speaking with us, as if His Speaking in the Redemption that we find in Jesus Christ is another kind of speaking from the speaking He did in the Beginning. The God of the Beginning is not the God of Jesus Christ. The New Beginning we read with Him does not resonate with the Beginning. To view the witness of the Old and the New Testaments as a whole under the Speaking of the One God the Lord is and the One Lord that God is as the Great I-AM is to impose upon the past an understanding that has nothing really to do with the original intentions and purposes of the authors of belief in the Beginning. I can appreciate the concerns that belong to such suppositions, but not with their resolutions. Without the present and the future, there is no past to consider.

Without Jesus Christ, the history of the Creation cannot be told, and thus the Burning Bush and the Incarnation mark vividly the presence of the Voice that we are asked at all times to hear in the Biblical World. I would argue that the real world is this Creation; that the Universe we study is this Creation, however much we would like to suppose a chasm between the Incarnation of this Voice and our sciences.

    I see the big mistake here, the steady confusion, and therefore the great tragedies in our interpretation of the Beginning belong to a belief that the "Nothingness" of the Creation exists only to threaten the existence and significance of the human race upon the earth, that the 'Nothingness' exists merely to deny Man his or her meaning in the world, to annihilate an existence come from the Voice of God. It is to betray this Voice of God, the Creator, for another voice. The Word of God in the Beginning spoke to give light in the midst of the 'Nothingness,' the chaos and emptiness, the darkness upon the deep, the primordial waters over which His Spirit watched, like an eagle her eaglets. When this light is spoken into existence in the midst of this 'Nothingness,' time and space are given shape and form to make a home for Man upon the earth, a mankind, male and female, made in the Image and after the Likeness of God. This 'Nothingness' then served as the potential whose environs light is caused to appear, when the heavens and the earth become the home for Man that can be blessed by God, their Creator. It is in relationship with Him and His Work, His finished and beautiful and 'Very Good' Creation that we are to understand the confession of Moses. That this 'Nothingness' can be thought to be evil, merely something with which to threaten the existence and meaning of Man upon the earth is a betrayal of God, His heavens and earth, His First Man, His Blessed Creation. It is a lie about the Voice. It is the voice of another, the Nachash (the serpent) of whom we can learn nothing until he appears in the Paradise of God according to the account we read in Genesis 3. Here the 'liar' about the Beginning sounds to persuade the First Parents to betray the good and the beautiful and the true of a universe of light and the home for mankind in space and time. It is true that, once light has been spoken into existence, the 'Nothingness' of the Creation becomes a thing of the past. It is also true that the Word of God can use this past time to punish His People in His BCR with Israel (cf. Isaiah 34:11, Jeremiah 4:23), allowing time before the light was caused to exist to become again the world of idolaters. This is the tragedy. They live in a past that belongs to time before the free Creator had finished His free Creation. They live without the freedom of Mankind called and made to live both meaningful and significant existences with a future that is the 'Very Good' Creation the world is. It is easy to find the first reflection of this betrayal in the Paradise of God reiterated over and over, again and again, throughout the literature of the world, as if people prefer to live in the past than the future of the universe of light as God's creation. The freedom and beauty and good, that marks with light the Creation in the Beginning, with its 'Nothingness,' is denied the Creator, when all of their potential is betrayed and people fall tragically away from their Creator and His relationship with their history in the history of the Creation. It is a tragedy that can be told again and again in the theaters of our own making. Yet with the resurrection we discover that the potential the 'Nothingness' possesses as His Creation has not been made 'Very Good' in vain. God may very well reject the lie about the 'Nothingness,' but not what He has caused to exist in the Beginning. The New Man, in whom we are to see the fullness of God dwelling bodily in His New Creation, has rather justified it. The 'Nothingness' of the Creation is made to serve and not to threaten the existence of Man.

Thus, God creates time for Himself with and for our time and times. The stories of the generations are to be told in the Light and with the Voice of this Divine Freedom of His Eternity to be with and involved in the history of His People in His Creation. Such created times mark irreversibly an arrow of time and times that belong to His aim with them. Any theory of history that bans such events from the way it links up by cause and effect, the significance of history in our consciousness, is committed to idol making according to Moses and Jesus. To assume that the intent and purpose of the confession as the Great I-AM the Lord God is, according to Moses or Jesus, is empty of significance in our times is an assumption in possession of a secret that belongs strictly to the unknown. One could not discern in this case a liar from a well-intended idea man. No one would want to wake up in the morning and contemplate a case. Perhaps this is why few actually do wake up and seek to reflect upon *the* Beginning?

The Creator of the Creation with all of its times and spaces, potentials and possibilities, as the Redeemer of the world seems preposterous for a theory of history that has no room for the transcendence and immanence of the Great I-AM of all time and space. When Jesus Christ confesses He is the Great I-AM the Lord God is, His claims belong to Moses and the Self-Revelation of His Father, even as the Lord of the past. Without this

Divine Freedom to be who He truly is, His claims must appear as blasphemy. How can an individual Jew in Palestine claim to be the Creator in *the* Beginning? It is a question we keep asking just because it seems so impossible. But not for the Great I-AM the Lord God is, says Moses, says Jesus. The Old belongs to the New. The New belongs to the Old. The two are one, however impossible that may seem to many. I believe the appearance of blasphemy belongs to a perspective on the Being and Nature of the Lord God that, mistakenly, would define Him and His relationship with time and space with a theory of time and space that are inadequate even to grasp what we do discover about the nature of the world as a created reality. How can we imagine, with any real meditation upon the kind of beginning that is *the* Beginning according to Moses and Jesus that Eternity has nothing to do with time and space? The 'beginning' upon which Professor Wheeler exhorted his students to mediate each morning may have been in his mind a Big Bang Beginning, but I doubt that the great physicist himself reflects there upon *the* Beginning of which Moses and his followers wrote. In any case, I would read with the fathers of the early Church, the Book of Genesis in the Light of the Gospel of St. John and other New Testament writings. I believe that the Bible contains a better theory of history than we can read with our many historians, even on the subject of God and the world of men and women. With the fathers of the early Church I would read Moses' confession of the Creation Week, not as a philosophical treatise, but as an inspired confession, written with a faith that belongs directly to the Word of God the Redeemer-Creator is of His Creation with its peoples.

An illustration of this kind of reading of *the* Beginning may be found with the work of John Philoponus, the sixth century Alexandrian Grammarian living in the Empire of Justinian. In his time (529 AD), he attempted to read the Genesis account while taking seriously the Light of the Incarnation. In this effort he followed the fathers before him such as Athanasius of Alexandria and Basil the Great. But he also anticipates the efforts of Karl Barth, the great Swiss theologian, to read the Creation accounts, when he has attempted in our time to read Moses' confession in the same Light the Creator is as the Person of the Lord Jesus Christ. I would argue that reading Genesis 1 in the Light of John 1 is indeed not merely the best way to interpret Genesis but the intended way that it is to be read. I believe the Voice we hear in the Incarnation is the Voice we need to hear in the Creation, the Voice Moses heard coming from the

The Beginning of the Generations

flames of the Burning Bush. Without the Blessing of this Voice, we will not interpret *the* Beginning in the way that Moses and Jesus intend *the* Beginning to become known among us as mankind made in His Image. It is thus, I believe, a very fruitful way of meditating upon Moses' confession of the Creator and His Creation of the First Week with the First Man of His 'Very Good' Creation. Some kind of hubris is involved when modern critical commentators refuse to consider this possibility for our reading. Any theory of history must belong to beginnings made with and by the Divine Freedom the Great I-AM the Lord God is as our Redeemer and Creator with and in this world for us.

We need to allow both the transcendence and the immanence of God their full implications in relationship with the history of the Creation, with time and times and our times, with the space and spaces of these times. We need to allow the full explication of His interaction for us without and within the reality of the Creation. Only in the way of this full implication and explication of His Being with and for us in this world may we contemplate any full and solid justification of the original intention we must discern in the 'Very Good' and 'Blessed' Creation that is His from *the* Beginning. The Creation is not the best of all possible worlds or the most perfect world, but it is a world consecrated by His holy love with Himself. To interpret the nature of the Creation without this consecration, without this Blessing, without this Voice that calls the whole of this world 'Very Good' is to make an idol out of it, something from which both Moses and Jesus sought to free us. We cannot obtain an understanding of the nature of Moses' confession, its time and times, its histories, and its witness to God except in the freedom of this Redeemer-Creator the Great I-AM is, pre-incarnate and incarnate, to speak for Himself with His Creation and with His People. But in hearing this One, we may come to apprehend how Genesis 1 confesses the Creation in such a way as to be valuable for all time, from one time to another, and grasp the way in freedom its significance ever points us away from our idol making and to this world as God's Creation, with all of its particulars. In this way, we may become free from our idols about it, from our myths about it, delivered from them in order that we may actually worship the reality the wondrous Creator of His Creation as the world where we have been given our beings and natures. We may participate with Him in this way that alone may give meaning and significance to the nature of our created reality with Himself. We may honor Him as the Lord of light and space and time that He is.

Moses' confession of the Creator with His Creation Week posits the heavens and the earth as the whole, a Creation 'out of nothing' by the only God, who has made mankind as His Image and Likeness within the orders of its light and the Sabbath Relationship with its blessing in relationship with Himself for that which is not Himself. Genesis 1 proclaims a beginning of a 'Very Good' Creation against the mythmaking and idol making of the peoples among the nations. It is a confession written down against all pretenders, against all that opposes His Being the One He is and His Freedom to do what He does with Himself. It is in the Light of this Great I-AM that Lord God is we are challenged to seek to understand Him in His Divine Freedom and with His Holy Love in *the Beginning*. The Being and Becoming of God is involved with the world, with the world's mankind in this *Beginning* and not in any false or mythical start posited against *the Beginning*. We need to understand that, without the new beginning made with His People in the Exodus, *the Beginning* cannot properly be confessed. In this way, the Being and Becoming of the Creator in His Incarnation provides us with the Light that allows us to see His Speaking in *the Beginning* that is *the Beginning begun out of nothing but His Will and Wisdom*. The Revelation involved with Israel's Redemption is not merely an event at a particular point in time, but a point made to serve the point of all time and time's relation with God's Eternity. It is an event the whole of which, including its meaning and significance, is to give us an understanding of the embrace this One possesses of all time and space. The Creator is this One Lord God with His People in His Creation and not another.

The Bible teaches us that the kind of time God has created possesses 'fullness' as well as 'sequence,' not merely a linear trajectory in space, but a topology that belongs to Him. It is in the *'fullness of time'* that the Becoming of the Being of God is realized with the new beginning begun in the Incarnation. It is in this way that time and times are bound up with the Eternal 'Time' of the Creator-Redeemer. This uncreated 'Time' marks time with the entry of the Great I-AM the Lord God is as the Son of His Father with an Eternity that gives meaning and significance to time and times, that fills created time up with meaning and significance from the Eternity of the Redeemer-Creator. The whole of time belongs to His Time for all times. I suggest, with Barth and Philoponus, that we find this time in order to contemplate Moses' confession. I believe that fruit, far from forbidden, is indeed commanded here. We will be fruitful with such contemplations.

The Beginning of the Generations

In this way, the testimony of the *'fullness of time'* that belongs to the life of the Person the Lord Jesus as the Christ of Israel, the Word of God sent by His Father from beyond all beginnings, will shine upon the salvation of the world and our salvation with a radiance whose heat shall bear fruit upon the earth. He is in this way the Great I-AM who is the Creator of the world. He is the Lord of all world histories, of all spaces and all times that truly belong to His Creation. We need to believe that Philoponus and Barth were right to seek to understand Genesis 1 in the Light of the Gospel of St. John and its resonance with the confession of Moses.

The dynamical relations of the old and new generations of the People of God in Biblical covenanted relations, read throughout the record of the Exodus-Leviticus-Numbers Traditions in the history of Israel, can never be lost from our considerations because of who He is. At the very foundations in the formation of the People of God, we can read the commitment of the Lord God to renew what His People have ruined in His BCR with Israel. This forms the content and theological thrust of the Pentateuch as the Witness it is to Him. Under the command of the Voice of the Great I-AM that the Lord God is, first from the Burning Bush with Moses, then at Mt. Sinai, and then in the Wilderness with Moses and Israel's tribes, the divine passion and pathos of this One is there to be read. He shapes with Himself Israel's times even from His Beginning as the Creator in *the Beginning*. These traditions all belong to a confession whose theological thrust is understood by faith, says Moses, in the Redeemer-Creator. The Creator is the Redeemer. The Redeemer is the Creator. He is the only and majestic One, who is the origin of all that is created reality, space and time. His is a speaking that reaches back in time and times, even beyond Israel's ancestral past, back into a primordial past beyond the records of history, as far back to the very 'Beginning' of all beginnings bound up with Israel's existence in a world that is His 'Very Good' Creation. Because of the speaking of this One, against all pretenders and every myth, Israel is the sign she is among the nations. Her beginning is bound up then with *the* Beginning of this Great I-AM He is as the Lord of the deliverance of His People from Egypt and as the Creator God of the Creation. Moses' confession is in this way a theological argument from beginning to end. It is inspired by a faith given with the Revelation of God. It is an inspiration that proclaims knowledge of the Creator who has come against all idols and idol makers in the world. He who 'created' (***bara'***) the heavens and the earth out of nothing in *the Beginning* will have no others beside Him.

He is the King of all kings. He will have no pretenders beside His throne. He who is truly Israel's Redeemer is this Creator and not another. This is the One with whom Israel and all created reality have to do. Moses understands that this I-AM, who defeated the gods of Egypt in His Deliverance of His People, is none other than the Creator God who is over all the gods of all the nations of the entire world. He is the true Creator and as such to be worshipped as the One He is. The worship of any other is to bow the knee to the idols He has condemned among the nations.

The Creation's *Beginning*, then, *the heavens and the earth* of this *Beginning* and no other, all its created chaos and orders, all of its lights and times spoken into existence after *the Beginning*, the time past of the primordial 'waste and emptiness' in the 'dark' that surrounds the primordial waters, the time and times of the days and nights of the light of the heavens, this is the 'Very Good' Creation where *Mankind*, '*created*' in *the Image after the Likeness* of this One Creator God. This is the object that stands against all the various creation epics we can find to read among the kings and priests and peoples of the ancient world as blessed with His Sabbath Blessing, a total work of very good proportions, indeed. He is the Only One to justify this work. It is the light of His Divine Freedom to be and to reveal Himself as the One He truly is that we must read Him acting in *the Beginning*. It is in the light of the actuality of this Divine Freedom, that we are commanded to hear Moses' confession of His creating and speaking as the One He is, with His Being and His Becoming, even as the Great I-AM He is, that we may understand Him as the Lord of Israel's history and the God of the world's creation. When we hear the Voice of the Creator as the Voice of the Redeemer that He is, we are enabled to hear and to see the solidity about the world that distinguishes the world from dreams and myths. It is an object made to reflect His Being, His Being the One He is. It is an object that will be justified by the Only One the Redeemer-Creator is as the Great I-AM of the Bible.

When we learn to read the Book of Genesis in this way, we may understand it as the theological 'tour de force' that it is—the confession of Moses, the prophet, with the Lord God for Israel, His People, the Great I-AM of the Being and Becoming of Him among the nations in His Creation. He is Himself as the authority that frees His People from their afflictions in Egypt. The freedom of His People belongs to His Freedom as the Creator He is. Genesis is confessed in this divine and human freedom. The primordial and ancestral beginnings serve in this way to give

The Beginning of the Generations

meaning and significance to Israel's future in the world. Her presence in Egypt, her deliverance from the gods of the Pharaohs, her journey across the Sinai and into the Wilderness, the journey of her new generation into the Promised Land—these are all bound up with this Redeemer-Creator. The God of *the Beginning* is none other than the Lord of this history. The Voice that spoke with Moses in the Burning Bush is the Voice that spoke in *the Beginning*. This Voice of the Great *I-AM* the Lord God is possesses within Himself the secret of *the Beginning* of the heavens and the earth, the beginning of Mankind made in *His Image* and after *His Likeness*, the beginning of His *Sabbath* relationship with His 'Very Good' Creation. When we can hear this Voice for who He truly is in His Creation, created out of nothing in this way, it is with some astonishment that we read only to discover that, out of this *Beginning*, the very first generations (Genesis 2:4—*Toledoth*) of the heavens and the earth and out of the very first marriage of man and woman, the First Adam in this Creation preferred to listen to another voice than the Voice of the confession. Who can fathom how and why it happened then that Adam and Eve could listen to a talking creature rather than to their Creator?

But this question is asked of every generation in Moses' confession. All generations face this Voice, are shaped and formed, according to Moses' narratives by this Voice. Moses' argument would confess with the sagas and stories we read as the Book of Genesis the real history, primordial and ancestral, that explains Israel among the nations. Israel is an object the subject of which must be the Great I-AM the Lord God is with her. Israel's faith belongs to Him. With this faith, she must understand her history and we must read and understand these sagas and stories, primordial and ancestral beginnings of Israel among the nations. She is the reason for the Book. She belongs to the Creator Himself. Her beginnings belong to *the Beginning* and then to the generations that follow. All the ten generations of these narratives are told to be read as background to the Israel of the Lord God. They provide the explanation for Israel's history as the People of this Lord and God who is the God in all Creation (2:4; 5:1; 6:9; 10:1; 11:10; 11:27; 25:12; 25:19; 36:1; 37:2—*The Ten Toledoth*). These *Toledoth* or 'generations', to read in the Light of the Creation Week, provide the framework that gives shape and substance, form and content, to the narratives that we read in the Book of Genesis. It is with this framework that the confession of the Five Books of Moses speaks of the heart that beats in the theological thrust that belongs to Moses' argument.

From *the Beginning* to the 'Promised Land,' Israel belongs to the God of the Creation's history and not to the idol making that prevails among the peoples of the ancient world. The Book of Genesis is a record then that provides its reader with the background to the meaning of the epoch-making events, founded with the Exodus and completed with Israel's readiness for her entrance into the Land of His Promise, which cannot be understood without Adam, Abel and Cain, Noah, Abraham, Isaac, and Jacob. Who can interpret these stories but as the sign that God as Lord is with Israel? Who can better hear them than the One who fulfills their meaning in the world? It is their Messiah as the 'Light of the World' who can see and hear them in time and times for their real significance, the Christ of the Covenant, the Lord Jesus as this Great I-AM who can claim they are written about Him. When we will not listen to Him, we listen to another. This is the One who has claimed that Moses wrote of Him. We will argue that, with the Divine Freedom the Great I-AM exercised in *the Beginning*, He commands history, that the very nature of His BCR forms the content of this history, the very shape of the substance of His covenanted relationships with His Creation and His People. This is the basis for Jesus' claim of Being as the I-AM that spoke with Moses, that lived even before Abraham, and who has revealed the Father of all time and times in His *'fullness of time.'* This is the way that God has made time for Himself with His People as the Great I-AM He truly is in the space and time of our world. Without His eyes and ears, time and history remain merely a troublesome series of events, epoch and eras, a sequence of disasters that can speak only with despair over a race that prefers another voice than the Voice of the Great I-AM.

We are fortunate to be living when a new vitality for a whole new exploration of the nature of the universe now inspires our scientific communities. Because of the way these communities are free today to search for a new window for our understanding of the world, we find ourselves compelled again and again to learn afresh the foundation upon which we may stand to experience our world. Here the questions we seek to form and answer about the relationship between our scientific cosmologies and theological science call again and again for new listeners to the light of the universe. We would hear what the light is saying to us in our time. We would hear with this light's speaking the Word of God, the Speaking of God. In this new way, a new and deeper grasp of the nature of truth itself is demanded. In our time, the nature of the universe and its God faces us

The Beginning of the Generations

with the possibilities of relationship that have indeed escaped in the past our attention. God and the potential in this relationship between Himself and the world's mechanics compels our attention as perhaps never before in the history of the world. Enemies of past developments, past controversies and conflicts, weary of carving up reality in opposition to one another, now may seek new integrations that excite the human imagination with new potentials not dreamed in time past. Modern developments hold out between Science and Theology a much friendlier relationship. Theologians and scientists can find today ground that creates new discussions on the nature of light, energy and matter, time and space, in motion in a world whose mysteries cannot be divorced from our questions. We do well when science and theology are able to discover a time for a deeper understanding of the created reality of the world and the uncreated reality of God in relationships with one another that belong actually to God Himself. Our world will be a better place when we can find this kind of understanding in it.

When the early fathers of the Church, faced with the worldviews they found among the people of the Graeco-Roman Empire, were compelled to seek to root the Gospel of the Lord Jesus Christ as a Judeo-Christian tradition there, a clash of epoch-making proportions occurred. An entanglement of perspectives eventuated that required a most creative outpouring of explanation and articulation of a Truth the majesty of which belonged to the Great I-AM of the Gospel. The Church's proclamation of the Gospel demanded the very soil of the Empire's ground be ploughed up and new grounds for this Truth nourished, where the Church could establish herself and grow in her knowledge of God. The worldview of the Gospel and the worldviews found within the Empire met with thundering demands of revolutionary proportion, with the majestic and surprising triumph of a once much persecuted minority. The Gospel demanded that the Church must seek to rethink all of the Empire's notions about light, energy, matter, space, time, and motion in the Cosmos that had now been lit up by the 'Light of the World.' A profound transformation of prevailing assumptions and presuppositions about the nature of the Cosmos in which the Empire existed was called for. Because of the Incarnation, belief in the nature of this Cosmos had to be changed. God's nature was not what we thought Him to be. The nature of the Cosmos was not what the race necessarily thought it to be. The nature of Man in the Cosmos was not what we thought it to be. Because of the Act of God with His

Word speaking in Christ anew in the world, a new understanding of God, the world, and man had to be achieved. His creating out of nothing in *the* Beginning and His *New* Beginning with His Incarnation had to be tuned into one another if we were to understand afresh the whole of these concepts. The contingency of the created world had been justified with surprising powers and they demanded a new understanding of the significance and potential that was inherent in the created reality of the world. When the Word He had always been became flesh in this Cosmos He had made, the 'Good News' could not be properly announced while divorcing itself from realities of the space, time, light, energy, matter, and so forth that came from Hand and Speaking of the Creator God, who was indeed the Redeemer of the 'All.' The Gospel is an invasion of Greek thought and rationality and intelligence, a transforming invasion, a tremendous challenge for the Church, but one she knew with tumultuous promises. It is imperative that the Church today faces its own challenges with as much discipline and courage that we read in the early Church.

The early fathers of the Church thought that, if the Gospel was to take root in the soil of the Empire, the foundations of human knowledge had to be transformed. Ways of carving up the relationship between God and the world, between the reality of the *Logos* and the reality of the *Cosmos*, much debated in Graeco-Roman thought, had to be questioned and explained anew. New questions had to be found whose answers would discover those shapes of substances that truly obtained in the Light of the Word's Incarnation. The new answers to such questions were, indeed, forthcoming. Whole new resolutions to the question of the relationship of God and God's *Logos* to the *Cosmos*, and to its Mankind, were posited at the foundations of human thought. The fact that the nature of the realities of the Biblical World clashed with the prevailing Graeco-Roman worldviews formed an encounter like lightening in a night sky, the thunder of which has marked the experience of the nations across the whole range of human thought and desire, a lightening and thunder that has given us our Western Civilization. Genesis 1—2:3, the confession of Moses about the Creation and the Creator, is written against all mythical relations between the Divine and Human natures, against all idols and idol making legions among the creation epics in the ancient world. Genesis 1—2:3 proclaimed these the superstitious things that belonged to the past. In the Light of Incarnate God, new light now shines upon the objects time and space are, a new understanding of Moses' confession is gained in the dynamics of

The Beginning of the Generations

the relationship between Creator and Creation. The Creator has become what He has never been. Mankind has become what mankind has never been. The world as His Creation has become what it has never been. The idols and idol making of the past, confronted with this free Creator, are things that definitely belong to times that are vanishing. The God who created *the* Beginning out of nothing is truly the Lord of all space and time and He has called Israel out of Egypt for His purpose among the nations of His Creation. 'Time' itself has been made to serve His Presence in this way in the history of His Creation. The Being and Nature of this free Lord and God, this Great I-AM, who is who He is as this One, reigns over the entire Creation as the 'The Light of the World.' It is the speaking of this Voice within the out of nothing Creation that we are called to hear.

Moses' confession, then, that the Lord of the Exodus is none other than the God of *the* Beginning possesses a theological thrust that belongs to the structures of light, space and time. It is open and dynamically free to be ever involved with the actual Divine Freedom the Lord God possesses to make Himself present and known in His Creation. It is a confession that provides God's People with a whole new way of seeing their world, hearing Him speak as this Lord and God in relationship to the world. The two creation accounts as understood by modern scholars are to be heard in these freedoms as one account. They are bound up together with one another by a rhetoric whose argument is theological in form and content from beginning to end. It is an argument whose significance has gripped the imagination of the human race across centuries of the development of human thought. It belongs to the Revelation that belongs to the Being of God Himself. It belongs to a faith whose God is Lord of His People in His Creation. It belongs to a people become reconciled to who He truly is in His Revelation in His Creation. It belongs to a purpose that would at once rid the race of its idols and give shape and substance, form and content, to its life in the world. It belongs to a confession made so that the People of God might know and live in the presence of their Redeemer and Creator, might hear the Truth of His Voice in time and space. The history of Creation, the history of Israel among the nations—this is the Biblical World—the history of their relationship to the Great I-AM the Lord God is with them in His Divine Freedom belongs to this covenanted relationship with them, to His passion and purpose in His BCR in the world.

With this faith, the confession of Moses posits a creative confrontation of the Holy One that the Great I-AM is with His Voice in the Burning

Bush. It was a Voice to which the ancient peoples, with their many myths, had grown deaf. Now the Voice of Israel's deliverer is heard commanding the deliverance of His People from Egypt's Pharaoh with an authority that only the Creator of the heavens and the earth actually possessed. It is this faith that knows the One who spoke light and time and space and mankind into existence in *the* Beginning as the One who also spoke with Moses in the Burning Bush. It is this faith that knows no dualistic divorce of Redemption from Creation, of Redeemer from Creator. It is this faith that knows Him as One Lord and God. We need to feel the full weight of this argument in our time—the *Elohim* who created in *the* Beginning is the *Yahweh* who delivered Israel from slavery in Egypt. Without a real appreciation for the gravity of this argument, the confession's purpose will not be found in the Name whose many names must refer us to the Great I-AM is. We will use his Self-Naming with His names even as His Being escapes our attention. We will with Israel prefer a Golden Calf to His Self. We will with our hands try to make something do what only He can. We will create a chasm between Creator and Creation, between Creation and Redemption, in whose abyss only alienation from this One is known. Alienated from this One, we will not will what He has willed in His Divine Freedom for us. We will render our selves dear to His Word, dumb to His Being, blind to His Acts in the world, lost from the authority of His Command as the Redeemer-Creator of all that is His Creation. We will miss the Sabbath of His relationship with us, the Blessing of His Love and Wisdom for what He has created and made. We will miss, as they say, the mark of His Glory upon the earth under the heavens. We will continue to make myths and idols out of a reality whose existence possesses the secret of who He truly is with us, pre-incarnate and incarnate Lord God.

But when we attempt to understand the Creation Week, the First Marriage of the Adam as male and female in His Image after the Likeness of God, with the heavens and the earth and all the orders of light spoken into existence by the Creator, including His Sabbath relationship and His Blessing for Man in His Creation, then we belong to the future and not the past of the race in the history of the Creation. We exist on the planet named earth with a solid hope that dispels the world as a dream or a myth. We are commanded to throw away our idols in this world, and to grasp of God the powerful movement of time with the race. It is into this future that we may hear Him as the Great I-AM He is, that we may follow Him to that which He has prepared with us. This is a faith that understands the phenomenal realities experienced by humanity in the world as bound up freely with the mysteries of the Creator's Being and Acts. This is a faith that understands what it means that all things created have been created not only out of something of the past, but also out of nothing whose future is in the light a 'Very Good' Creation. This is a faith whose origins belong to the very Freedom of the Being and Nature of this One Lord God, who as the Great I-AM reigns transcendently and immanently over and with all Creation. When we read Moses with such faith, his confession is understood to assert no separation between theory and experience in the human world, and the Voice we are to hear belongs to this One who is faithful to what He has made. No divorce of the phenomenological realities of the events the world is may be posited here.

The rationality of the world belongs in this way to the Word of this Voice. Theoretical realities within this world are to be heard in concert with our experience of the world as His Creation. Our experience in this world is to be seen as the gift it is, a created existence given to us from the Voice of God in wholeness that is His Image in His Creation. It is existence that cannot be and subsist without Him, without His Being the Great I-AM He is. What is found in the everyday experience is experienced as rooted in the mystery of His Being who He is with Man in His Creation. The Creation is what it is because it belongs, in theory and in experience, to who He is. The orders and mysteries of created freedom found in this world of light are to be understood in the Light of His Being and Nature, in the Light of His Mystery, and the Freedom with which His Righteousness justifies what He has made and spoken into being. It is this One who speaks and because He speaks the world is filled with light and time and space and matter and motion that is moved with His Future for it. This is Moses' confession of the *Elohim* who acted *(bara')* and then spoke *('amar)* against all idols in *the* very Beginning and who spoke with this one Beginning an existence of a universe of light that is what it is because it is His Creation. With His Being and with this free will, they are what they are and what they will be. His Becoming and their becoming are bound up with one another. This is the One who is who He is and who sent Moses for His People to deliver them from Egypt and thus to know Him as this One, and in knowing Him as her Lord and God Israel might look to Him in her times for her destiny with Him in the ages to come. This being and becoming is at the heart of why Christ can claim that Moses wrote of Him.

The translation of the Hebrew *bara'* with the English 'create' can be inadequate. In the English language every Tom, Dick, and Jane can 'create.' The verb 'create' can be employed as a predicate with a legion of subjects. Men create machines. Women create sensations. Dogs create messes. Storms create havoc, and so forth. In the Hebrew Bible, however, only *Elohim* is capable of the act that is signified by the verb '*bara'.*' The verb *bara'* has only ever for its subject, throughout the Biblical World, *the Elohim* of the confession. This *Elohim* alone can act in such a way that a world is made which is the object of His unique divine action—'*bara'.*' The Beginning of the Biblical World belongs to a Divine Freedom that belongs only to *Elohim*. Only the Creator can exercise this freedom in order to *bara'* the heavens and the earth out of nothing into their existence. Only God can 'create' this Beginning—*the* Beginning. Only God is free in this way to act to make a beginning that is this Beginning, *the* Beginning of His Creation. Because only this God is free to be this Creator and to choose to act in this way, to become with the Nature of His Being the Creator He is, we must understand that the Creator Moses confesses is the One who is who He is in His Divine Freedom, who named Himself as the Great I-AM He is in His speaking from the flames of the Burning Bush. The One who rescued His People from Egypt is the One who in the beginning created and made reality what it is. Thus, the great Exodus Tradition in the history of Israel among the nations in His Creation is to be remembered in time and times and all that time may be.

The doctrine of creation out of nothing is rooted, then, in the ground of this understanding of the I-AM of the Divine Freedom and His unique willingness to act in order to bring into existence something that He is not. This is fundamental to the signification of the verb '*bara'.*' The Creation is what the Creation is because of His Divine Freedom to become this Creator and to act in this way for *the* Beginning, against every pretender in the ancient world. The verb *bara'* is without analogy in this world then. We need to hear the power of the action it signifies, a silent power with transcendent dimensions in relations that form what created reality is. Upon this power rests the very meaning of the Judeo-Christian doctrine of Creation. Creation out of nothing in **the Beginning** signifies an absolutely unique act that God alone in His freedom can take with Himself to become what He has never been to make what He is not. This doctrine of *creatio ex Nihilo*, as it is named in the Latin world, Moses lays down in opposition to the mythologies and pathologies and superstitions legion in the ancient world. With his confession, they are rendered things of the past. It is important that we appreciate this about the doctrine. It is something new in the world, like the Exodus is for the People of God, and the new knowledge of this faith becomes fundamental not only to the Judeo-Christian tradition, but also to the science of Western Civilization. The Divine Freedom of God to be as Lord the One who truly is the One He is, the Great I-AM become this Creator and Redeemer of Israel, beside whom there is no other, is the same freedom that we meet everywhere in the nature of the BCR between Him and His People. This One informs the compelling reality of Moses' confession. Without the Burning Bush, there is no confession of this beginning—**the Beginning**. When we hear God speaking in this beginning, we are listening to the Voice of the Redeemer of Israel. The Redeemer of Israel is the Creator of the Universe. The Creator of the Universe is the Redeemer of Israel, and there is no other I-AM who is the One who is who He is. It is this One who alone can act as this One across time and times as the Lord God of His covenanted relationship in the history of the world. He alone is capable to *bara'* **the Beginning** into existence. This One is the Lord God (*Yahweh-Elohim*) of Moses' confession.

The verb *bara'* must signify then a divinely free act of God in **the Beginning** whose uniqueness entails both the Transcendent One and the Immanent One in action for His Creation. At least four other verbs in the confession, all of which are vital for establishing of the nature of 'Day One' in the Creation Week, must be considered as dimensions in the fullness of the act that is 'bara',' The verbs 'brooding,' 'speaking,' 'differentiating,' or 'dividing,' and 'naming' are all employed to render the confession of the Day One what it is.

The verb '*brooding*' in Genesis appears only one other time in the Scriptures. In Deuteronomy 32:11 it signifies an action that a mother eagle will take while hovering over and caring for her young. If we are allowed to hear some resonance here, then we may say that God cares with His *brooding* for the 'chaos' and 'emptiness' ('*tohu* and *bhohu*' or waste and void) in the dark that covers the waters of His Creation. He is like a mother eagle *brooding* over her eaglets. Such care is vital for subsistence of the world. But it is a care with a great purpose—for life! It is essential to the 'Very Good' Creation that His Creation is. This verb belongs to time past, once light has been spoken into existence.

The *'speaking'* of God is fundamental to light and light's time and times in the space of the Biblical World. It is that Word of God whose action gives orders to make the entire Creation Week what it is. Light created with this *speaking* and all the orders of time and space belong to a present that takes the world beyond its *creatio ex nihilo* and into future with the *Speaking of God*. The heavens and the earth, the whole of the Creation's order, are made to depend upon this Speaking. In the midst of His care for His Creation out of nothing, even as He *'broods'* over His *'chaos and emptiness'* in the deep dark of the waters of His Creation, He *speaks* and causes to appear the light of the universe. In this way, the time and space of a new order Creation is posited as His Creation. *Brooding* over the chaos and emptiness of the waters of His Creation alone becomes a thing of the past. Now He *speaks*, in the context of this old space and time, the light and lights of the heavens and the earth into their existences. With this Word of the Creator, a new order is given the space and time of the Creation. The nature of His light marks the boundaries of this Creation. The time and times of the dark past served the time of this light. *The* Beginning of the heavens and the earth entails this past and this present for a definite future. This time-space is inherent in Moses' confession of the Creation Week. The time of this *bara'* belongs in this way to the Transcendent and Immanent One of this Divine Freedom that the Creator possesses in this beginning. Each of the days of this Week is confessed as belonging to the speaking of this Speaking One.

That the *'brooding'* and *'speaking'* of God belongs to the freedom of this One to *'differentiate'* or *'distinguish'* between light and dark and so forth forms the boundaries whose names are essential to the confession. Differentiation is vital to the orders of the world. The heavens are the heavens and not the earth. The earth is the earth and not the heavens. Yet they form one Creation out of nothing whose orders belong to His Freedom. We can never generalize these laws of differentiation and boundaries in this universe of light. Yet we must integrate them as one created reality whose created nature is what it is because of His Uncreated Nature and Being. Both differentiation and integration are essential to the order of space and time in this Creation. We must be able to distinguish one thing from another in order to grasp the order of the light of the Creation and we must be able to understand this differentiation in the one light that gives shape and form to the substance and content of the created reality the Creation is.

The Beginning of the Generations

Thus, to '*name*' light 'day' and to '*name*' the dark 'night' is to give significance to this differentiation in an integrated Creation. *Naming* a thing gives meaning to that thing in the space and time and light of the Creation. It is a vital concept in the confession of the Creation. It is to call our home a world that has been created out of nothing and given the time and space of light to define and mark with boundaries a world that is a home for God's People. **The Beginning** cannot be understood without this freedom to name things and to participate with them then in a world that is home to the Adam. The morning and the evening of 'Day One' are thus bound up with all five of these verbs—divine creating out of nothing, brooding, speaking, differentiating-integrating, and naming of the God of **the Beginning**. All nights and days of the Creation Week come from this beginning. It is this freedom's making that God sees again and again as '*good*' and finally when finished as '*very* good.' *In the Beginning the Creation in its entirety was named 'Very Good' and blessed in a relationship freely created by God, the Creator.* We ought to take seriously the exhortation of John Archibald Wheeler to his students. But I would also suggest that we take seriously that this confession does not end with the Creation Week, but that its confession belongs to an introduction that cannot bear intense scrutiny except with meditation also on the Adam of this Week. We ought to wake up every morning and spend some time contemplating **the Beginning**. The significance of *creatio ex nihilo* ought never to be lost upon us who live as men and women upon this earth and under these heavens. But we will better hear the meaning of the sentence *in the Beginning bara Elohim'* when we hear it along with the ears of the Adam under the heavens and upon the earth. The First Adam, the confession will tell us, made something other than 'Very Good' out of the Creation and the Creator. The faithfulness of the confession of Moses cannot be read without both accounts of the heavens and the earth, the Creation Week and the Fall of Mankind from its Blessing. Thus, we read this confession as belonging to the One who knows that, without deliverance, His People will not hear Him for the Great I-AM He truly is. We need to know Yahweh if we are to confess Elohim.

I believe we can gain in this kind of reading a deeper understanding of *the* Beginning, of the speaking of God in the Beginning and the relationship of His Voice to the light of His Creation, of 'Mankind' made to exist in *the Image and Likeness of the Elohim*, and of the Creator's *Sabbath Relationship with the Whole of His 'Very Good' Creation*. In the Light the

Voice of the Great I-AM is in this way, according to Moses' confession the Creator, we would better gain insight into the primordial realities of Israel's history among the nations. We would better hear and see Israel's Creator as the One He is with the fullness of His significance in His interaction with the world. We could better understand the Adam as the Immortal 'Male and Female' created in the Image and Likeness of God who is Israel's Lord and His Sabbath relationship embedded in her understanding of who she is in His Creation. We would be able better to see in the Light of His Being the universe of light that the Creation is, out of nothing, purposed for a home in which the human race is made to live. We would better be able to hear Him speaking as the One He is and to follow His Command of His Creation. We would better understand the orders of created freedom as they are rooted in the speaking of His Being—the Divine Freedom of the Great I-AM the Lord God is as He truly is with us and for us in time and space. It is this Creating and Speaking God that commands with prophetic and providential power the confession of Moses' faith. We would be able to read the confession in its original intention and purpose—to point to the prophetic and providential power of the Becoming of His Being and the Being of His Becoming with who He truly is with us in His Divine Freedom.

With such faith, I believe, we are commanded to hear Him speaking in the time and space where and when the Light of the Person of the Lord Jesus shines and speaks. This Great I-AM, the Redeemer-Creator is among us in the uniqueness of His freedom as this Creator-Redeemer. Reading Genesis 1 in the Light of His Speaking compels us to see as men and women His Creation for what it is and has been made to be and what it will become. The phenomena of the events in Moses' confession are not naïve and mythical times. Neither are they scientific explanations of the experience of the race upon the planet. But the freedom of the Word of God to be who He truly is as the Creator and Redeemer in His Self-Revealing, Self-Naming, Self-Giving Person is confessed. I would argue that the Christ who claims to be in the New Testament 'The Light of the World' and the Great I-AM of the Bible (John 8:12, 58) is the One who is with the prophetic and providential power of the faith who He is for us (cf. the 'Light of the Lord' in the Vision of Isaiah). We need to be sure He does not escape our attention in our interpretation of Moses' confession of Him. We need to give the Being and Becoming of this Great I-AM the full freedom He actually possesses with the space and time and light of

The Beginning of the Generations

His Creation, in all of our meditations upon *the Beginning and its meaning for us in His Beginning*. The Redeemer is the Creator as this Great I-AM. The Creator is the Redeemer as this Lord and God for us, this One who was sent to give us access to His Father, the Maker of the heavens and the earth. I believe we ought to seek to understand Moses' confession in this Light. It will help us meditate upon the real beginning. It will help our faith as well as our science. The Biblical World of this Faith is the real world, no matter how difficult that claim is for our beliefs and faiths. The light of the heavens and the earth belongs to the speaking of this God. The light that enlightens mankind belongs to this God. This is the God Moses has confessed in the light of the Lord's deliverance of His People from Egyptian idols. I do not believe we shall get right the relationship of Genesis 1 to our sciences until we are able to hear it significance as taught us by the 'Light of the World' the Great I-AM has become as the Redeemer of the world.

Moses confession then is of the real time and space, old and new, that belongs to the Beginning as created realities, as the heavens and the earth. The early fathers of the Church can be found defending its significance again and again. It shook the foundations of the ancient world and it goes on shaking the foundations of the new worlds. The dynamics of its meaning as seen and heard in the Divine Freedom of the Great I-AM to be the Lord and God He is as this One Being among the nations provides a ground upon which the People of God may be formed and their understanding of the world explained in terms that attack the myths and idols of the peoples of the world. They are the fundamentals of the Judeo-Christian confession in the world. These fundamentals saw the nature of the world, made out of nothing, and its relationship with God with new force, and the force of this Revelation went right on shaking the foundations in time and times. A great clash with the idols and with the idol makers among the peoples was established. Even the power of the Graeco-Roman Empire felt this shaking, and eventually we can read its success in the world as the making of our Western Civilization. The Incarnation and the Creation resonating together in the minds of the People of God mark the advance we know as Copernicus, Galileo, Newton, and Einstein. The very foundation and formation of the technological world we enjoy today cannot be divorced from this shaking.

The Doctrine of Creation out of nothing, the brooding, the speaking, the differentiating, and the naming read in the confession of the *Elohim* in *the Beginning*, is posited then to explain that the heavens and the earth are what they are as the only Creation of the only Creator. As such, the Creation is an object whose created reality is to be known in its wholeness as bound up with the Divine Freedom of the Creator to be who He is, the One who is who He is in His Freedom to become the Creator and create His Creation. This doctrine of the Creator in *the Beginning*, to be known in His Divine Freedom as the Creating-Speaking God He has revealed Himself to be, is a doctrine that demands transcendence and immanence of this freedom of God. The 'Being' of God in His 'Becoming' and the 'Becoming' of God in His 'Being' is implicit in its confession. Both dimensions of freedom belong to what the Creation is as an object of His creative power. In this way, we are compelled to acknowledge that God is God with or without His Creation. He does not need His Creation in order to be the God who is who He is. Then, we have room in our thought to contemplate the fact that God with His Being and Becoming in His Freedom chooses to be the Creator with His *bara'* in His 'Very Good' Creation. This is the source for our understanding that all created reality is what it is, independent of God's Being and Nature, a contingent rationality, absolutely dependent upon the Wisdom of His Will for its purpose and meaning, its being and nature. *Bara' is a verb that signifies that the Lord God only can do with Divine Freedom what makes the whole of created reality a free reality utterly bound up with His noncontingent Being and Nature.* The doctrine of creation out of nothing and the doctrine of the contingency of the creation go hand in glove together in the power of God's freedom to choose to be the Creator He is with what His Creation is. The freedom of God to act in this way, to *bara'* His Creation, must mean that the freedom of the Creation must reflect the power for His Divine Freedom. The world did not have to be the Creation that it is. It could have been some other creation than the Creation it is. The world in and of itself possesses no necessary existence. It could have not existed. But the world is the Creation that it is, out of nothing, because of the wonderful freedom God has exercised with the Will of His Wisdom to become who He is in His *bara'* to give the heavens and the earth existence as His 'Very Good' Creation. The fullness of these doctrines needs to be fully appreciated. We must not read Genesis 1 in the dark, so to speak, and expect to grasp the real nature of the world, its God and its Mankind without the Light of His Revelation.

The Beginning of the Generations

Across centuries of time, we can trace throughout the development of human thought and civilization the debates about the doctrines belonging to the confession of the Creation Week. If the prophet Moses' confession is known to Israel's prophets, it is also known to Socrates, Plato, and Aristotle, and so forth. No time has been without some effort to understand the Creator of the world and the world as His Creation. The concept of the contingency of the Creation, as taught by Moses, has never had smooth going in the history of interpretation. It is difficult for us to grasp and define the concept. What the Creation is in its independence of God, while at the same time being utterly dependent upon His Will has never been a question easily answered. What is the Creation's dependence upon God? What is the Creation as independent of God? How is it that the Creation can be both independent of God's Nature and yet utterly dependent upon His Wisdom and Freedom for its existence? Such questions challenge logical analysis. They appear to demand the integration of opposites. Timeless dialectics are posited to produce rationality in relationships that readily escape our attention. We would like to make timeless a logic the rationality of which must be filled with time. Is the Creation an Eternal World in its dependence upon God? Is the Creation a perishing world in its independence of God? Such questions have been the stuff of many dreams about the Creation or a world without God. Whole centuries of human experience are filled with them. The rational contingency of the world, its substantial form and content before God, often suffers from one form of reductionism or another when we read the history of the exegesis of Genesis 1.

I believe that it is only in the Light of the Great I-AM the Lord God is that we have been given the freedom to learn to think rightly about the truth of the contingency of the Creation. What is out of nothing what it is from the wisdom of the will of this Creator can cause confusion. I believe that the Incarnation possesses the ultimate secret to such confusion. If we will seek to see the Creation in the Light of the Incarnation, and so forth, we will become able to integrate things, naturally differentiated from one another on their own level of reality, participating in an order whose beginning belongs to *the* Beginning. The whole of a created reality here is found to belong to the uncreated reality of God's life for us. I would argue that the Incarnation is a confirmation and an affirmation of God's Very Good Creation in *the* Beginning, made out of nothing, and that in this way the Great I-AM has given us to know Him as the Father He is, the

Father of the heavens and the earth as well as the Father of Jesus Christ. As such, the Creator of the Creation's nothingness and its *something-ness* is to be known. In this way, I believe, we may indeed avoid making out of this Creator an idol of our choosing, a 'Golden Calf' for our histories, one more version of the '*stiff-necked*' People of God, as Moses confessed them in the Exodus, Levitical, and Wilderness traditions of Israel's history. That is, the Incarnation's affirmation of what God was able to *bara'* in *the* Beginning, what He called 'Very Good' then, is what He has been established with an Ending in view, a view He alone can see for us, when all idols and idol making shall be utterly vanquished in the New Creation, our opposition to Him overcome, and we will know Him as we have been known by the Great I-AM He actually is, the idols of our making gone. I believe that, only in this way, may we come to appreciate Moses' confession. I believe that, only in this way, can we apprehend in all of its depths the inspiration of this confession, its prophetic power and providential weight among the peoples on the earth. Only in this way will we seek to hear the Speaking of this Great I-AM in our time. Only in this shall His willingness to make Himself known as the Redeemer of Israel's history and the Creator of the heavens and the earth be honored as it ought to be. The Creator is the Creator of the wholeness of our humanity; a being that it is what it ought to be as His Image and Likeness in His Heavens and Earth, in His New Creation. The Sabbath Blessing of the Old Creation has been established with this Incarnate Word, this Light of the World, this Great I-AM that He is with us. I believe that Professor Wheeler hoped we would be able to think about this One, and not another, with His Beginning each morning of our days upon the earth.

In any case, this kind of understanding of the world's created reality, as coming into being out of nothing and to be known as a contingent intelligibility with a contingent rationality belonging to the Speaking of the Creator God, belongs to, according to Moses' faith, a new enlightenment for the people of this world. It is a prophetic enlightenment that will find its promise ultimately kept through the Person of the Lord Jesus Christ, the Son of God with His Father as this Creator of God's 'Very Good' Creation. The development of our understanding of the relationship between theology and science in our time very much depends upon our understanding of the contingency of the world. If the Creation is uniquely a contingent reality in its wholeness and in its parts, out of nothing, with no necessary connection but itself and the Creator, then we may begin

The Beginning of the Generations

to understand it in our freedom with His Divine Freedom right from *the* Beginning. The relationship of Grace between the Creator and the Creation, right from *the* Beginning, is inherent in Moses' Confession. The uniqueness of the nature of the Creation is bound up with the uncreated and created freedoms at the poles of their relationship in *the* Beginning. The Divine Freedom the Great I-AM, as the Lord and God of His People and His Creation, possesses from *the* Beginning and throughout the existence and subsistence of the heavens and the earth with its mankind, is a wholeness and continuity only the Revelation of the Lord God can give us to grasp. As a contingent intelligibility, created out of nothing, which is very good in both its wholeness and its part, the substantial rationality of the Creation's reality may not be reduced down either to chance or to necessary relations of cause and effects. We say that the universe is neither necessary nor accidental, but an object whose created reality belongs to the freedom of God's wisdom to give existence to what He is not. It is neither an object from which we may abstract absolutes about it nor an arbitrary reality from which we may derive probabilities about it. God's Being, Nature, and Will are reflected in the freedom of the Creation freely. We say that it is what it is because of the Freedom of His Wisdom. We say that the very *bara'* in the Beginning signifies an action only He can take in the Beginning and with the Beginning. It is this object over which He broods, in which He speaks, whose orders are differentiated and divided in the context of a wholeness that is bound up in its freedom with Him. We need to recover this concept of the contingency of the universe and learn to relate its created nature and reality to the uncreated nature of His Being in His Acts right from the Beginning.

Thus, the wisdom of His free acts of creating and speaking must belong fundamentally to our understanding of the rational and intelligible contingency of all that is created reality. The concept of the Creation provides for a rational wholeness whose intelligibility is bound up freely with the Great I-AM the Lord God is. He is this I-AM as the Redeemer-Creator of His People in His Creation. With freedom and wisdom the Lord God establishes freely the origin of all contingent and created orders created out of nothing. All resolutions of the problems that arise between our contemplations of relationship between the infinite and the finite in our experience of the world are bound up with this wholeness. What is continuous and discontinuous, what is universal and particular, what is permanent and changing all and each belong to this world, where there exists no necessary connection between created reality and the uncreated reality of God. Neither may we claim that only randomness or an arbitrary relationship is all there is between the two. Contingent reality is a reality whose wholeness in its parts and whose parts in its wholeness are together dynamically bound up with one another according to the Free Will and Holy Love of a Wise Lord and God who has chosen to make Himself known in His Creation to His People. The *bara'* of the Creator in *the Beginning* signifies a divine action that is rooted in the ground of the very Being and Nature of God Himself, the God of all light, created and uncreated, where Wisdom is inherent in who He is as the Great I-AM He is. With this Wisdom He becomes known in the New Covenant of the New Creation as the 'Light of the World.' The God who created in *the* Beginning is the God who in His Divine Freedom in His BCR with His People is the Lord Jesus Christ of the whole of created reality. Thus, we may confess that He is indeed the Beginning and the End of all created realities, the fulfillment of all of Israel's prophecy about the Light that once constituted the House of David in the history of the People of God among the nations and is now embodied as Christ with His Creation.

If I ask most ordinary citizens how many mornings during their lifetimes they have spent contemplating *the* Beginning in this way, again and again I have seen common sense persons suddenly begin to gaze off into some far distant world, an infinity away in fact, perhaps rightly named the great unknown with them, and then back at me as if I were a man from Mars or even further out in outer space come to inquire about perfectly alien things. When I see them once again gazing away, I know that their days and nights, their mornings and evenings, have been spent elsewhere than with Moses' confession. The days and nights, the evenings and mornings, the calendars of these days and nights, the times of these evenings and morning, the clocks that track their hours across cycles of season and even centuries, go by for them without the Creation Week. Most modern people, so good at measuring time, let time itself escape their attention. They have trouble relating their times to the time of the Creation. In fact, for centuries the rational and intelligible contingency of the world's beginning and ending has not found an easy audience among us. In the Middle Ages, it was asserted that nothing can be established about the contingency of the world without the Revelation of God, as confessed by Moses and then found in Christ. No scientific view of the universe today takes contingent rationality seriously except as some form

The Beginning of the Generations

of accident, or as a plan B, behind which lays some form of necessity in dialectical tension with chance and randomness. Our scientific culture debates the determinism and indeterminism of the reality of the world and their relationship with one another. In our time the contingency of the world as God's Creation, the backbone of the history of our civilization, finds little enough notice. Champions of contingency have had to struggle hard to keep its cogency upon the minds of the general public. Though *the* Beginning is a concept which ought to be taught and contemplated throughout the mornings and evenings of our lives, it is a concept little known for what it actually means and signifies in our seeking to understand the potential of the physical and mathematical worlds and their correspondence with us in time and space. Somehow, the popular imagination, with all of its seeking, seeks to avoid facing the unique nature of the relational wholeness that belongs to God's covenanted relationship with His Creation and His People among the nations. Israel and the Creation! Here is the universe of Moses' confession.

We will try to take up some of the answers to this lost seeking in a later chapter, but now in the context of Moses' confession of the primordial and the ancestral worlds of Israel's history, we must seek to learn to hear the background that can explain Israel's 'stiff-necked,' 'high-handed,' and 'complaining' condition among the nations of the world. The source of this background is rooted in the ground of her very unique origins, an origin that belongs to the speaking of God with His Creation out of nothing, a speaking that requires a listening that is related to the Voice of God in the Paradise of God, where listening to another is an evil disaster for the People of God. Listening to this other voice is in fact the origin of the Fall of Mankind from its Creator. Listening to this other voice's commands belongs to the evil mystery of the betrayal and contradiction of God, the mystery of the attack of evil against His 'Very Good' Creation. This is that voice that stands behind the Fall of the Human Race, out of which Israel has been called into existence, as in *the* Beginning, for purposes that would redeem the Race from this betrayal and contradiction of the Lord God and give us a new beginning in the Creation. The Curse of God upon this fallen human race, with its expulsion of the Adam and Eve from the Garden of God, proclaims the primordial judgment upon evil and sin in the home that was made for Man as God's 'Very Good' Creation.

We do well to follow, as best we can along these lines, Moses' intentions and purposes with his confession. He evidently means for us to understand with this background that the Creator is both transcendent over its nature as well as free with Himself to enter into relationship with its existence, to be immanent for His Eternity with His created time and space. In this same freedom, He is confessed as the One who sustains as 'Very Good' His Creation. He is free to enter into a relationship with what He creates out of nothing and what He sustains in being what it is that belongs to who He truly is as the Creator. The Voice of the Great I-AM speaking out of the flames of the unconsumed Bush is heard as the Commander of Israel's Exodus by Moses, however reluctantly. This Voice is none other than the One who spoke in the Beginning the light of the world into existence. That we can read of the contradiction of this Voice by another voice coming from a very beautiful creature in the Garden of God with Adam and Eve cannot be explained by any power of our reasoning. It belongs to the mystery of evil in the 'Very Good' Creation, but it also belongs to the Curse of God upon it and His resolve to justify and sanctify what the Lord God made in the first place. The same power and wisdom with which the Lord God names Himself and commands Moses to lead Israel's Exodus from Egypt is the power and wisdom with which He willed to create the holy ground for the prophet Moses must become then to redeem Mankind as Israel from its opposition to Him. To will to listen to another voice than His Voice is a will that must be overcome. Mankind must be redeemed from its willingness to betray Him. Thus, from *the* very Beginning, we are to understand the Creator as the Redeemer and the Redeemer as the Creator with Israel, the People of God among the nations.

All the doctrines of this One's Creation Week, creation out of nothing in *the* Beginning, the heavens and the earth as a universe of light with its orders of time and space, its mankind, male and female, made in the image of the Creator, God's Sabbath relationship with His 'Very Good' Creation are all under attack when the voice of evil persuades the Image of God as Adam and Eve to disobey the Voice of the Creator. When the race would listen to the other voice, obey the voice of evil in the mystery of God's Good Creation and its Paradise, then the race is judged and driven from the Garden of God to live under the Curse of Death in the world, cherubim with swords flaming every which way and keeping the first parents of the race from their rebellion against the Voice of their God. When they choose in their freedom to obey this other voice, the voice of the *Nachash* (the Serpent) in the Garden of God's Paradise, they place themselves under the Curse of God with His covenanted relationship with them. We ought not to trivialize in any way this first disobedience of Man. Betrayal of the 'Very Good' Creation is more to the point of the Fall. Most of the rage we experience in this world belongs to the mystery of this attack upon who the Lord God is as our Redeemer-Creator. We need to hear afresh the doctrines of Moses' Creation Week, even in our modern scientific cultures. The Old One as the New One steadily brings to bear the Word of His Divine Freedom upon the freedom we enjoy to study our universe.

When a voice other than the Voice of God becomes the choice of the human race upon the earth, the whole of the Creation is ruined with our lives. Moses' confession understands the depths of this trouble. The whole of the heavens and the earth with its mankind, its invisible and its visible dimensions, made freely in the Beginning to belong to the Divine Freedom of the Creator, brings down from its center in Man the Curse of God upon itself. Choosing to hear another voice than the Voice of the Creator brings shame and guilt and deafness to the ears of Man. Ears deaf to God's Voice warp our mind's eye, and the whole of the race envisions what is not, an attack upon the One He is, the Creator of His 'Very Good' Creation. The opposition, an attack of the voice of evil, a betrayal of the Creator, spells the utter ruin and ultimate death for the Adam's race. We name this tragedy 'The Fall,' with which the race is marked from its primeval history. Made in the Image of God, our kind now images someone other than the God who made us. The mystery of evil has been posited within God's 'Very Good' Creation. Yet the One who moves the whole of the Creation moves the mind of men towards its confrontation with His Glory.

Thus, we may seek to understand the created contingent orders of God's Divine Freedom possess a freedom that, even in the evil use of the created independence away from the Creator, is yet sustained by Him for purposes that belong to His Being. The created orders belong with created freedom to His Divine and Uncreated Freedom and Order. The created orders and freedom are then to be thought of as under attack when mankind is listening to voice other than the Voice. We understand then that the fallen creature no longer is able to grasp the original intention and purpose of God's 'Very Good' Creation with its Mankind. Indeed, against that intention and purpose in *the Beginning*, and all that these entail in Moses' confession of the Creation Week and the Adam of God, the fallen human race becomes the listener of the other voice. Adam and Eve thus lose their meaning and significance as personal creatures with the Lord God and their home with Him. The freedom with which they are said to exist after their Fall is a created freedom unable to grasp why the world is the Creation it is. Mankind exists as a created freedom that is lost from its roots in the Divine Freedom, driven from the home God had made for its life upon the earth and under the heavens. They exist now under His Curse. With their sin, they learn death, the Voice of God against the other voice. With the other voice ringing in their ears then, they exist with great trouble hearing the command of their Creator. They exist lost from His Paradise for them. They live without the space and time that was once their home, guarded now by a Flaming Sword moving every which way in the hands of the Cherubim, in the service the Lord God. They are no more what they once were. They must seek a life lost from their original purpose and intention in the world, the Life of their Creator lost from their plans. Before this Fall, the Adam as male and female lived as the Image of God, after His Likeness, Blessed with His Sabbath Relation in the Paradise of His 'Very Good' Creation. After the Fall, Adam and Eve exist with cursed Mankind, along with the other voice in God's 'Very Good' Creation. They are driven out of the Garden into the wilderness of the world, where the care of the Lord God for their misery is the only real comfort they can know, their freedom and their beings haunted with death, sin, and evil. Having chosen against their Creator, they have chosen a life alienated from who they have been and their life with Him who created them out of nothing in their beginning and out of their dust breathed into them His Life for them. Their created freedom has become what it is not, an absolute freedom away from Him, without any real knowledge of their origins in Him. Before the Fall, their marriage was good. After the Fall, it was not. We are reading a narrative whose time dimensions are defined by the Lord God of all time, primordial time, ancestral time, and the prophetic time of the history of the People of God in the history of His Creation.

It is this wisdom in Moses' confession that provides the providential and prophetic thrust to his argument. The One who spoke to Him from within the flames of the burning but unconsumed bush is the One who speaks in the accounts we read in the Book of Genesis. It is vital to appreciate the fact that the Great I-AM the Lord God is in His Divine Freedom in Israel's Exodus Tradition is the same I-AM that God is as the Creator of this heavens and this earth. If we can hear Him for who He truly is in this way, then I believe we may hear the intention and purpose of the Lord

God with Moses' confession, over against the other voice and all the other gods that would inhabit the ancient world with the ancient peoples on the earth. We can hear then the 'great light' that marks the time of Day, not as the 'sun god,' but as the *Elohim*, the only Creator. We can hear the 'little light' that marks the time of Night, not as the 'moon god,' but as the *Elohim*, the one and only Creator. We can hear all these things and events that we experience in the phenomenal world, not as things and events in the gods, but as they are in existence from the hand and mouth of the Sovereign Creator. The light and lights of God's heavens, the lights upon God's earth, the time and times of God's Creation, His Image as Man in the light of the orders of the universe is God's 'Very Good' Creation. We can hear them as the contingent intelligibility they are, with the contingent rationality they possess as being made out of the nothing, with the nature of their independence utterly dependent upon the freedom and faithfulness of this Creator, over against all other pretenders. We can hear the meaning of the First Marriage of the first man and the first woman of God's Creation, at home under the heavens and upon the earth in their significance as servants of their Creator, His Image after His Likeness in the great mystery and freedom and blessing of His Holy Love with them. Here is the Great I-AM He delivered His People from Egypt to be known as the Creator He is, against all idols and idol making of the peoples upon the earth. Without Moses' confession, no notice of such a beginning would have been taken in the ancient world. Israel's religion would be one among many in the history of the world. Without the Revelation of the Great I-AM the Lord God is with Moses and Israel, the world would remain in the grip of its old gods and goddesses, its old myths and phantoms of the divine that prevailed in the old world. But here with Moses and Israel, something new has been done to rid the world of its phantasms about God, the world, and mankind. The race may not be consumed by its projections about God onto the heavens and the earth, but shall be free to know the Lord God for who He truly is—the Great I-AM. Without His Revelation, the real meaning of *the* Beginning would have utterly escaped our attention. This is the wisdom of the prophetic power of Moses' Confession.

So the relationship of this world to this Only One who is truly the Creator of the nature and being of all created reality is to be read throughout Moses' confession. This confession belongs to the Revelation of the Great I-AM as the Redeemer-Creator of the history of Israel and the history of His Creation. The Creation of this Lord God is no more a self-substantiating, self-sustaining, or self-explaining reality than Israel is a self-substantiating nation among the nations. And no mythical god can explain it either. It is neither the nightmare of a bad dream or some eternal essence in the minds of philosophers. It is a truly created reality whose nature and being possesses a created freedom that is to be understood as utterly dependent upon the Divine Freedom of the Great I-AM the Lord God is both in Himself and with His Creation. It belongs to the wisdom of His free will even in the very nature and being of its independence of Him. It does not exist as an eternal necessity. It does not exist without His Will. It exists out of nothing as what it is independent in its nature from Him while absolutely dependent upon Him for its existence and subsistence. He is absolutely transcendent over His Creation and free dynamically to interact with His Creation. From the Beginning it is His Creation and it is His Creation in its Ending.

With this Divine Freedom, in the mystery of the Being of this Creator, there is to be found the way that He is free to make 'time' for Himself within His Creation, free to make 'time' for Himself with His Mankind, free to make 'time' serve His Sabbath Blessing of them, even as their Lord and God. Created time and Eternal Time in the Being of God from *the* Beginning cannot be divorced from one another, however much they cannot be confused with one another. However right it is to distinguish them, it is also right that, with their differentiation, they are found in integration with each other and this across time and times for as long as forever is with Him and His Eternity. The 'All' that is created reality must be understood relationally in this way, where time and times are made to serve the uncreated reality of that which has duration in God's Eternity, in God's before and after, in God's freedom to be who He is with us in real freedom and significance in time and Eternity. The 'All' that is utterly independent of Him is absolutely dependent upon the ways of His Freedom, the mystery of His Being in Divine Freedom for us, the Wisdom with which He began things in the Beginning out of nothing, the Wisdom with which He is free to become not only the Creator of the world but its Redeemer. The 'All' in this way is given meaning by the Lord God. Man's experience of time and times in all the places of created space within all the orders of the created universe of light and time and mankind is bound up with this free Creator who can joy over that which He has bara'-ed *in the Beginning*. This is His Creation. This is the Creation of His Holy Love and Wise Will. Eternity, light and time and space and mankind are inher-

The Beginning of the Generations

ently bound up together by *this Beginning*, a beginning whose meaning we ignore not without deep consequences in our time. I like to remember that John Archibald Wheeler was right in his exhortation to his students about contemplating *the* Beginning each morning of their waking in the days from their nights in the world.

If we will not or cannot grasp this confession about the contingency of the Creation, we will not rightly become able to contemplate the very first words of the Bible. If we fail to grasp these words in all the depths of their significance in the world, then we shall be committed to the many false starts we can make about it. Never shall there exist for us a mathematical reality that can reflect the actual created intelligibility of the heavens and the earth and mankind in relationships with the Redeemer-Creator. We will not reflect upon *the Beginning*, but upon our false starts. We will doubtlessly be unable to spend our mornings and evenings in any strong resonance in contemplation of a true Beginning. These words will exist in the language of our worlds as empty signs leading us to nowhere, rather than *the Beginning*. When *Elohim bara'*-ed the heavens and the earth into existence as a home for mankind's making in *the Beginning*, He acted freely from within Himself. He chose freely from within Himself to choose to become the Creator and *bara'* the world that the Creation actually is, where He chose freely to give life form and content in His 'Very Good' Creation with His Sabbath Blessing. We do well to hear Him speaking in this Divine Freedom in *the Beginning*. We do well to accept Him as the One He truly is in it. We do not do well when we would reduce the freedom and nature of His Being down to some impersonal principle, as if we may turn Him into an abstract principle from which we may derive logically and as it were timelessly knowledge of who He truly is. He is and was and will be the Living God, who is who He is as the Redeemer-Creator He actually is as the Great I-AM of the Revelation. We will not understand Him as the One who is, as this Lord God, *compassionate, favoring, patient in wisdom, and of great grace and faithfulness* as the Redeemer-Creator with His People. We will not take seriously His freedom to define Himself in covenant with Israel in the powers of His Divine Perfections. We will not be able to follow Him as He freely gives Himself in His BCR with what He has created and made and sustains with His Purposes to Bless and Glorify His Name among His People in His Creation.

To see and hear someone or something less than or other than the One He actually is in His Divine Freedom in *the Beginning* is to spend the first twenty minutes of your day on some other mystery than the mystery of the Creation, the mystery of the Creator, the mystery of His Being who He is with and in the world. It is to spend the mornings in vain. It is to spend the hours with mythmaking. It is to project up onto the Redeemer-Creator our ideas in this world, who is not merely an idea, let alone our idea. It is to sunder belief and faith from reason and knowledge. It is to make with our thinking and seeking a very false start, to paralyze the movement in all real beginnings. To make a true start is to be rooted in the actuality of *the* Beginning, to joy in the potential of the Creation, to know a world that is not a toy, especially our toy. It is to know a great joy that no toy can give us, even as the Children of God. It is to be able to joy in the creative power of His Holy Love for the world. Perhaps it needs to be said that we are much better at making false starts with our beginnings than we are at grasping the meaning of our beginnings in *the* Beginning. We need to know that our Creator is neither an abstract principle nor some arbitrary deity about which we may retain one romantic notion after another in our times. He is always the Subject of all subjects. He is the beginning of *the* Beginning, and He does not allow Himself to share His Glory with another. Thus, He makes Himself an object for our attention. He subjects the race with its phantoms and fantasies about Him to the judgment of His Holy Love, so that human beings might know Him for who He truly is. He will not be faithless with who He is. He will be who He is in His relations with us. He will be the One He is for His Creation and His People among the nations. This is the confession reluctant Moses had to learn. In this way, we may learn to grasp the theological thrust of the confession, the prophetic power of the confession. *In the Beginning bara' Elohim the heavens and the earth* are words that come from the mouth of Moses with the mystery and freedom and righteousness of the Great I-AM who called Him to be the great prophet of Israel's beginnings. He is to be confessed as the One He is in His Divine Freedom to be who He is with His Creation and with Israel. These are the first words of the Revelation of the Great I-AM whose Word we must learn to hear in this way.

It is in the domain of this one Beginning then that we may learn to read and hear the Voice of the Six Days of the Creation Week and the Voice of the Sabbath Blessing as the confession of Moses' faith. He is neither the Unmoved Mover nor First Cause of the Greek god, whose immutability and impassibility provided the transcendent power of the Cosmos, nor the Moved Unmover of modern processes found within this World.

The Beginning of the Generations

He is the Great I-AM who is the Lord God of Israel's Election and the heavens and earth's creation. Genesis 1 is a highly formalized and somewhat symmetrical account of these origins, origins confessed over against the myths and idols of the Ancient World. Its words, however similar to other perspectives on the Creation in the Ancient Near East, are not the words of an eyewitness over against other eyewitnesses, but the words of a prophet whose faith, formed within the Sabbath culture of Israel's history in the world, seeks to proclaim an understanding of the Creator as the Redeemer of His People. Most scholars today recognize the account as a priestly record of these ancient stories or sagas, an account perhaps not solidified until after the Return of Israel from her Exile in Babylon. The accounts surely go back to Moses' confession among the ancient traditions found in the nations, but its final form is reached only after the times of Ezra-Nehemiah and the Chronicles. The account reflects these ancient traditions with Moses' confession. But the canonical form that we read today is thought to have been shaped by post-exilic Israel, when the Scribes of Israel turned the Jews, in the light of their past with the Lord God, into a People of the Book, when attention to the Book received new purpose and commitment for Judaism as the People of God. The problems that we have understanding the origins, preservations, and interpretation of the traditions that may have in some sense influenced the confession remain very much with us today. We will not attempt here to resolve these problems. But we will argue that this one *Beginning* cannot be understood without the priestly work of the Great I-AM the Lord Jesus Christ is as the Incarnate Word of this God. We are faithful to Moses' confession when we are faithful to the Revelation of the Great I-AM, and any analysis of the texts that does not refer us to this Revelation in the history of Israel cannot throw light upon the power and significance of Genesis in the history of the world. Moses confessed the Sovereign Reign of this Lord God as the Creator and Great I-AM of Israel among the nations, and we need to understand that the existence of God is not in question here, but the nature of the independence of Mankind in God's Creation.

It is this creating, this brooding, this speaking, this differentiating, this naming, this seeing, and this giving that marks the acts of this God with Moses as polemically different from anything that has gone before it. This confession is the great prophecy of this Great I-AM, unknown for who He truly is before His Revelation with His Voice in the flames of the Burning Bush as the Living God of Israel's history in covenanted relationship with Him. This One in His Divine Freedom establishes Himself with His Blessed 'Very Good' Creation with His Sabbath Relationship to the whole of the Creation. The Seventh Day of the Creation Week celebrates the way that the Creator gives meaning to all that He has made and sustains and sees as 'Very Good' with Him. There is no mention of 'evil' anywhere in this initial account of *the Beginning*. All its days and nights are 'Good.' All its time and space and mankind are 'Very Good.' All created reality, invisible and visible, exists under this Blessing of this One God. It is in the context of this Blessing that we are told then the stories of the primordial and ancestral generations (*Toledoth*), whose contents form the account of Israel's primeval and legendary past. Ten *Toledoth* shape this narrative into a confession whose theological thrust is the prophetic past of the People of God. As such, the Book of Genesis serves as a very specific background to the history of Israel's Exodus, Worship, and Wilderness Traditions, just as the Book of Deuteronomy serves as the foreground of her life in the Promised Land among the nations. We do well to remind ourselves that this 'Very Good' Creation is conceived as a home for the First Marriage in the Paradise of God. The heavens and the earth are home to this Image of God as the Creation in *the Beginning*. It is with this 'Very Good' background that we read the background past of Israel's history in the world. The Very Good First Marriage is what goes very bad in the First Generation of the heavens and the earth whose story we read in the Book of Genesis.

The Adam of the Creation Week, made male and female as the Image and Likeness of God, becomes in the account of the First Marriage in the generation of the heavens and the earth the Adam and Eve whose beings are wed as one flesh. As such, they are naked and unashamed and at home in the Garden of God's Paradise for them. The First Generation then, the story of the heavens and the earth, narrates the relationship of the Image of God as the First Marriage in its primordial and immortal intention and purpose. The rhetoric of this account is most important. The theology of its argument insists that the *Elohim* of the Creation Week is none other than the *Yahweh* of the First Marriage. In Eden, God is none other than this Lord. This Lord is none other than this God. In Hebrew, *Elohim* is *Yahweh*. The Creator is the Redeemer. *Yahweh* is *Elohim*. The Redeemer is the Creator. With this use of the Names in the Revelation of the Great I-AM, Moses' confession can and does stand over against all myths and mythologies about the gods in the ancient world. All the pathos of the

The Beginning of the Generations

Lord God cannot be reduced up or down into the pathologies of the idols and idol makers. They are all condemned without any ultimate cogency. All the creation epics that we can find to read in the ancient world are thus rendered false by the confession. The *Elohim* who bara'-ed in *the Beginning*, the one who by His Spirit broods over the dark chaos and emptiness of His Creation out of nothing, the one who speaks into existence the orders of light within this Creation, the one who distinguishes with these orders the light from the dark, day from night, the One who gives to Creation the time of its space and the places of its times, this Creator-Redeemer and no other is the One Moses has been sent to confess. He is the One who is truly the One He is, the Lord God of the People of God, the Deliverer from all bondage to Egyptian or Mesopotamian gods, the Creator of the 'All' that is created reality.

We cannot read Moses without reading this polemical nature inherent in the rhetoric and theological thrust of this confession. Redemption and Creation that is of this Lord and God (*Yahweh-Elohim*) are to be understood in the light of the Great I-AM He is, the One who named Himself for Moses from the Burning Bush, the Living God who commanded the prophet of the Exodus on his mission for His People to Egypt and gave Moses His Torah at Sinai. Without understanding this Oneness, the theological thrust of Moses' confession in His Name is lost upon the reader. It is a rhetorical point that must not be missed. It is like the mathematical point whose vanishing means something in the world. The rationality of this Speaking One cannot be heard without this integration of who He is in Himself. His Name thus possesses a power prophetically to compel the theological thrust of its argument in the history of the Creation and the People of God. It is the real ground upon which we may know God as the Lord He is, the Lord as the God He is. It is the real ontological basis where Knowledge of God is provided for Moses, even over his objections to his commission. We cannot fail to argue for this fundamental polemic of the Name at the foundations of the formation of the People of God as taught us by the Five Books of Moses. It is at this dynamic and personal center of God's Being in His Acts and God's Acts with His Being in His Word where the prophet learns what he must know of this Lord God. He is who He is as the inspiration of Moses' confession of the Creator. It is this inspiration that shapes the background for the formation even of the canonical content we name the Pentateuch. It is this Canon of Israel's Scriptures that is the Canon of the Lord God's Majestic Truth in His Being and Acts in speaking with Israel in the history of the world. We cannot fail to learn this lesson if we are to interpret the confession for its original intent and purpose in the history of Israel as the People of God. If we become alienated at this point from the confession, we have lost everything it means. And how often has this loss sought to assert that it understands these texts of the Bible? The Bible with its Five Books of Moses has been read as a Pentateuch that in many ways has become alienated from this fundamentally polemical nature with Moses' confession. Why?

In Genesis 3 of the First Generation, we read as the narrative of the heavens and the earth with its mankind as Adam and Eve, the male and female made in the Image of the first and mysterious appearance of 'evil' in God's 'Very Good' Creation. Within this First Generation of the heavens and the earth, we read of Eve, the woman of Adam, willing to listen to another voice than the Voice of the Redeemer-Creator. We must also hear that Adam, along with his wonderful woman, with whom he has become 'one flesh' in the Image and Likeness of God, is willing to hear the wondrous speaking of 'the beautiful *Nachash*' in the Garden of God. 'Evil' appears suddenly and mysteriously to speak against God's Voice in the 'Very Good' and 'Blessed' Creation to which He has given its *Beginning*. Sometime after the First Marriage of the First Man with the First Woman as God's Image has been established, Adam and Eve freely choose to hear the voice of another rather than to obey the command of the Voice of their Lord and God. The Lord God, who is who He is both in *the* Beginning and in the Paradise of God, opposes the betrayal of Him with all that He is. They choose the voice of 'evil' over their Creator. The Creator chooses them.

Who has ever fathomed the mystery of this choice? Who can fail to understand its implications and its explicit consequences? Who can explain the first sin against the Lord God and who cannot fail to understand that with the First Man and Woman the whole world fell away in its freedom from the free God? The mystery of freedom, the mystery of order, the mystery of holiness and profanity all are to be faced just here, in the contradiction of God's Speaking by the listeners to another voice than His Voice. The First Man would hide himself from his Lord and God and from His 'Very Good' Creation. Who can read this saga without wondering about these primordial mysteries, without being touched by their meaning and significance for our race, without contemplating the wonders of this mystery of divine and human freedoms in a world made out of nothing and is sustained in existence for these freedoms? Who does not seek to hear the meaning of the Voice of freedom in our world? Who are we, indeed, in this freely falling world? Where are we then with our freedom in this world? Why then are we here?

The First Marriage of the First Adam, of Adam and Eve in Paradise is ruined. They are sundered from their Lord and God and driven in their ruin out of the Garden, compelled under the Curse of the Lord God to live in the fallen world. Instead of God, pandemonium and confusion reigns, and in it all their lives seeking in guilt and shame to hide themselves from their Creator, far from the Paradise they once knew. They can be asked the question about where they think they are. They can be asked the question why they think that they are the way they, naked, ashamed, covered with animal skin. But they must move into a world that will not answer such questions. Somewhere the real world has turned into a dream for them, a nightmare, a nowhere, their memories lost from the Garden. Their *Elohim* is not their Redeemer-Creator. They seem distant from the Great I-AM He is. Alone and ruined in a world lost from Him and His 'Very Good' Creation, now evil and sin reign in their lives, and the curse of death rests upon them. On this primeval canvas, they are painted forever as the immortal race become mortal because of its preference for another voice than the Voice of the Creator. We are all so familiar with this picture that, for most of us at least, it has lost all but some ancient mythological meaning. It is a picture that bears no longer any real significance for us. Of familiarity does breed contempt, then this case is perhaps the best of illustrations. We would argue that with Moses and his confession it was real background to explain the People of God of the history of Israel among the nations in the world.

Having eaten of the forbidden tree, sometime after *the* Beginning of the world, Eve brings into the First Marriage the first betrayal of, and thus disobedience of, Man with the Lord God. All of the problems of humanity are sourced in this first betrayal and disobedience. As such, Eve is the mother of all the living. Once made with Adam the Image and Likeness of God, very much to be at home in the First Generation, the generation of the heavens and the earth, at one with her husband, now she experiences alienation from their Creator and His Creation. She with Adam is driven out of the Garden of the Paradise of God. She with Adam must begin to experience life under His Curse in His relationship with them. Together, they must endure existence as a fallen marriage in a desolate world, a world that is not His 'Very Good' Creation. It is judged existence, judged by the Lord God in His relationship with *the Beginning*. It is existence lost from the 'Very Good' of God's *Beginning*. Poets, playwrights, and artists of all sorts and kinds across centuries of human thought have applied their minds, in many contexts and cultures, to the consequences of this Fall. Who can say that we have yet penetrated into the real significance of this Fall with us? Who can say what it took for the Lord God to overcome its effects upon us? Who has known the reason for the 'evil' in the speaking of the other voice with the First Marriage?

Lamentation defines the mood. A tragic pathos requires a lyrical sympathy. Here is tragedy so great that only the comedy of tragedy can deal with it—the First Disobedience of Mankind. The human race upon the planet earth endures a history in the world that cannot be told without the real event of the Fall. It has been painted, sculpted, sung, and analyzed across centuries of human thought. Here is stuff for storytelling that the human imagination cannot do without. The Primordial Parents in the mystery of time and all times lost from God is a mystery that never for very long escapes our attention. *The* Beginning of the Creation, the First Marriage, the Fall of Mankind from Paradise, the existence of men and women under the Creator's Curse, the inexplicable abyss into which existence has fallen and falls and will fall in a world that becomes a mountain the human imagination will seek to climb. Perhaps we do well to wake every morning from the evening of our lives to contemplate them. Perhaps spending the first twenty minutes of every morning of our days and nights is not a bad idea after all. Throughout all the seasons of our years, perhaps meditating upon *the* Beginning, the First Marriage of Fallen Man, and the way that the Lord God has chosen as the Great I-AM He is to deal with the primordial history of the race upon the planet is not such a bad idea at all. Lost and confused and desperate in the desolate emptiness and chaotic nightmare of our existence, one could begin in less fruitful ways. But who is allowed to pass by the Cherubim with their flaming-every-which-way-sword and enter once again into the Garden of the Paradise of God? No one without the permission of the Great I-AM!

It is within this first *Toledoth, the generations of the heavens and the earth*, where we read the primordial history unfolded as the tale of Cain and Abel and the events leading to the first murder found in the midst of a human race living under the Curse of the Lord God. The first children of the first parents reflect with murder what has been chosen by God and belongs to the first disobedience of their parents. We read then of the protection the Lord God provides for the First Murderer. With him, He is merciful. Even in this fallen and cursed world, the Lord God is merciful. This is the world that belongs to Him, and not to the other voice. Though He would punish under His Curse, even the first murderer is made to bear his punishment. While the race of Cain, Abel gone, must bear the punishment, still the race learns from this way to call upon the Name of its Redeemer and its Creator. The ancient curse upon Israel's existence among the nations will never be the last word upon her life in the world. Under the Curse, under His protection, even as a murderer she shall live to experience the merciful work of her Redeemer. The birth of Seth, brother to the dead Abel, speaks of his blood with her. Shield and new birthmark who He is in His acts with her even in this primordial world. Always with an ear on her redemption brought to her by her Great I-AM the Lord God is does Israel find herself among the nations. It is this Israel Moses confesses in *the Beginning* and in the generations of the heavens and the earth.

There follows four other generations in Moses' account of Israel's primordial history:

The book of *'the generation'* of Adam (Genesis 5:1) provides a genealogical record from the First Man to the times of Noah. It is of great theological significance. Noah's father experiences the comfort of the Lord even as His Curse covers the whole earth (Genesis 5:28). With the life of Noah, we read the account of the Great Flood. Rephidim had been born to the daughters of men in intercourse with the 'sons of the gods' in a world whose violence had filled the earth with its opposition to the Lord God, when the Lord determined to execute His Judgment against this cruel race of men. The Great Flood of Noah's generation is never lost from the memory of the race, and bears a significance that carries over even into our own times.

The story of *the generation* of Noah (Genesis 6:9) and his sons marks the new beginning made upon a punished earth. The Great Flood kills every breathing creature upon the land—the waters above and below the earth minister God's Curse upon the race. But with his famous Ark, Noah and his sons are chosen to survive the judgment and to make a new beginning for humanity. In this generation, the first use of the term covenant (*berith*) is read. This generation marks the relationship posited by the Lord God between Himself and Noah and his sons with a 'rainbow,' a memorial to the nature of His covenant with *the* Beginning, a form that marks with a new beginning God's faithfulness with His Creation. In spite of the human race upon the earth, the Lord God with this covenanted relationship for His Creation possesses the last word upon the Creation and its mankind. Both belong to His Elect and Sovereign and Divine Freedom. The 'favor' of the Lord God fills the skies of the heavens and the memory of His People with the divine purpose and intentions of the Great I-AM the Lord God is. The assurance is given to the reader with this wonderful 'rainbow.' It is to serve among the clouds in the sky as His sign, a sign that signifies the freedom He possesses and exercises over His judgments in the history of His Creation, its time and times, and especially the times of its future. Here is a sign that all peoples of all nations can see and remember with Him of His BCR. Thus, after the Flood, we read the table of the nations under the wondrous meaning of this sign.

Still, *the generations* of the sons of Noah (Genesis 10:1) remain gripped in a hubris that again leads the race upon the earth into further opposition to its Lord and God. The nations from Noah's sons spread throughout the world a hubris that leads to an exaltation at Shinar (Genesis 11:1) of its own life even into the heavens. The race's one language would exalt itself into the heavens. The race plans to build a Tower of Babel, filling the gate (*Bab*) of God (*El*) with the praise of mankind's wondrous pride. It is a pride only the Fall could explain. It is in opposition to its Creator. We read of the way the Lord God acts to confuse the race's one language, to scatter across the land of the earth the sons of Noah, and to render impossible the goals of the prideful reach. Yes, a man's reach should exceed his grasp, but not with this primordial hubris.

The story of the Fifth Generation, the narrative of the account of Noah's son, Shem, (Genesis 11:10) is to be read as a genealogy of a nation among the nations that has been chosen to provide the basis for the new world that belongs to the election of Terah and his son Abram. Even covering the whole earth, the hubris of the peoples of the nations does not possess the last word upon God's Creation. In this sense, we read the end of the Primordial history as the beginning of the Ancestral history of Israel among the nations in God's Creation. The fifth *Toledoth* accounts for the eight generations that form the background for the call of Terah, the father of Abram, the father of Israel's Faith.

The Beginning of the Generations

It is the story of this Sixth Generation (Genesis 11:27) that begins the Ancestral history. It is the history of the Great Promise of the Great I-AM the Lord God is with Israel. It is this promise in His relationship that becomes fundamental for understanding the call and command of Abram in the world. With the human race scattered everywhere in a confusion of human languages across the earth, the Lord turns to speak in Ur of the Chaldees to Abram. He speaks just as He had spoken in *the Beginning*, just as He had spoken with Moses from the flames in the Burning Bush. The Ancestral history provides a direct link between them as God's time for Israel among the nations. Abram is commanded here to leave the land of Ur and go to a land the Lord God Himself would show him. In the Land of the Promise, Abram will prosper and become, under the Great Blessing of the Great Promise, a Great Nation among the nations upon the earth. We read of the appearance of the Lord to Abram in Genesis 12:1–3:

> 'And Yahweh said to Abram,
> "Take yourself from your land, your clan,
> And the house of your father
> To the land that I will show you.
> There I will make you into a great nation
> And I will bless you and make great your name,
> And be a blessing;
> I will bless the one blessing you,
> But the one making light of you I will curse."'

Modern critics have rightly observed that the motifs read in these verses play a substantial and vital role throughout the whole of Moses' confession of Israel's ancestral past. We hear at least three notes of a chord struck again and again throughout the composition played of this Promise in Israel's history among the nations. We can trace these notes and their overtones, with their various nuances, points and counterpoints, throughout the narrative that is Moses' confession. These notes play out three aspects of the Great Promise the Lord God has determined, in His Divine Freedom, to keep in His Covenant with His People. Abram bears the character of their harmonies and disharmonies throughout his life. Israel's experience in her covenanted relationship with the Lord God cannot be told without them. The Great Promise of the Lord God to Abram is to Israel's ancestral past what *the* Beginning is to Israel's primordial past. Kings, prophets, priests, and sages of Israel's history all understand the chords of their melodies throughout the composition of Israel's life in the world. When Israel understands Abram/Abraham, she sees the father of her faith alive with the Living God. The three aspects of this Great Promise weave the contents of the Five Books of Moses into a theological argument the thrust of which must not escape our attention. We may identify them as follows: 1) The Land of the Great Promise 2) The Seed of Abram that is to become a Great Nation among the nations of the world, and 3) The Blessing of the Lord God in His covenanted relationship with Abraham and His Seed in the Land among the nations. It is because of this Great Promise that Abram becomes Abraham, the father of Israel's Faith. It is with his Seed planted in the Land that is the chosen place of the Lord God for His chosen people. It is the Seed in this land that is the object of the Blessing Lord God will give to His Elect. This is the call of Abram, the Elect of the Faith. This promise bears the purpose and intent of Abram's call in time and times in specific spaces, places that serve God's freedom to make time for Himself with His People among the nations in His Creation. These three dimensions are to be traced along the lines of those trajectories that shape Israel's history in place as God's Elect in God's Creation. They form an invasion of the Lord God in His freedom with His Creation in relations with His People that defines, in spite of all that is in opposition to Him, His Will to be for His Elect in His Creation. They participate in a service in a world of God against the 'evil' that would speak with another voice to His People.

The Land aspect of the Great Promise will not come into sharp focus until the renewal of the covenanted relationship with the new generation at Moab. Moses then and there will prepare a generation that was not eyewitness to the Exodus for its entrance into the land of Canaan. The Seed or descendants that are to be given a great name and made into a great nation among the nations on the earth is in question very emphatically throughout the ancestral accounts (Genesis 13:16; 15:5; 17:5f; 18:18; 22:17; 26:4; 28:14; 35:11). We cannot read these stories without grasping the Divine Freedom of the Great I-AM's passion in His BCR with Abraham and his sons. The Blessing steadily runs its course throughout the narrative. Blessing and curses are utterly significant in the modes of events experienced under the passion of the Lord God and the Promise with Israel. The Promise of land, seed, and blessing shapes a world whose significance means to establish Israel among the nations in God's 'Very Good' Creation. We cannot read the destiny of Israel in the history of the Creation without this Promise, its land, its seed, and its blessing. The generations of Terah and the sons of Abraham (Genesis 11:27; 25:12; 25:19; 36:1, 9; 37:1) tell the stories in a narrative that finds at last the Seed in Egypt, far from the Promised Land, Unblessed. To keep the Promise to Abraham, the Exodus is commanded. The Lord of the Covenant will not fail Himself or His People.

The concern for the Seed belongs steadily with the holy passion of the Lord God for His Great Promise in His Covenanted Relationship with His People in His Creation. In the *Toledoth* of Terah, we read how wondrously the Lord God would be Shield to the father of the faith (Genesis 15). Abram may worry about the Seed of the Promise. He may be anxious about his death and his inheritor and the Promise, but the Lord is his Protector and the One who provides for him. Perhaps real anger belongs to Abram in this encounter with this Lord of the Promise. The father of Israel's faith may very well accuse the Lord God about ignoring or being indifferent to His Promise in His relationship with him. But the Lord God is His Shield. He is the Shield and assurance to Abram about Himself and His Seed in His Promise. A very famous passage belongs to the encounter here between Abram and the Lord. Once the Lord has persuaded him about the Promise, we can read: '*And he believed in the Lord and he reckoned it to him as Righteousness*' (Genesis 15:6). The Righteousness of the Lord God in covenanted relationship with Abram is secured here. The Shield is believed. Abram's fears and angers about the Promise and his Seed are assuaged, and he is able to 'amen' what the promise of the Lord God would 'AMEN'. Just as surely as the Lord has brought Abram from Ur, the Lord shall plant the Seed in the Promised Land with His Blessing upon them. With this assurance, we then read the beautiful account of *Yahweh* cutting His Covenant with Abram in that night. While Abram sleeps the *Tardemah* that is the deep sleep of Adam, when God made a woman for the First Man, the Lord God promises to make out of His Elect a blessed nation among the nations blessed in him. It is important, I believe, to observe here that the Lord God makes His Creation bear witness with Him to Abram in covenanted relationship with his Redeemer-Creator. Here we see *Yahweh* walking alone in the midst of animals sacrificed for the purpose of the BCR and vowing on this ground to keep faith with His Chosen People. It is to this Covenanted Promise that the Father Almighty has chosen to be faithful.

In Genesis 17, the Promise in the covenanted relationship is confirmed and renewed with the sign of circumcision in Abram's flesh. The circumcision marks also the change of Abram's name to Abraham. The sign and change of name affirms the fact that the Seed shall come through Abraham's loins and not from another. The Promised Blessed Seed will come, indeed, through Sarai. It is Sarai's child who will be the Child of the Promise. With this assurance, the names of Abraham and Sarah become the parents of the Seed of Promise. Their laughter at the impossibility in such a development provides the child's name—Isaac. Because the parents laughed, the boy is named 'he laughed.' The will of the Lord God with them is thus affirmed. His vow is established for them afresh. Beyond their doubts, the Lord acts to keep faith with them. In His Divine Freedom, the Lord God thus deals with Abram's fears, anxieties, angers, and the nervous laughter of Isaac's parents, with a renewal of His relationship that belongs to His passion for them (Genesis 17:6–7). He will complete what He has determined to do with them (Genesis 18:10–11). For it is through them that He has chosen in His freedom to make Himself known to them and to all the world.

With the birth of Isaac, we learn that the Seed that comes through them shall not belong to their plans or the offspring of their plans (Genesis 21:12, 17). The Lord God Himself will keep faith with His Vow. In the pursuant struggle, the reader must come to terms with His Divine Freedom to love them in His relationship with them as the Self-Revealing, Naming, and Defining Great I-AM that He is. He perfects His powers in the BCR for His People with this Holy Love.

We may illustrate the pathos of this passion with reference to the terms of 'The Little Credo' of the Great I-AM that we have studied in the Exodus. With His *Grace and Truth*, the ancestors said to be made to bear the faith that belongs to the truth of His Glory with them. Making *Chesed* and being *'Emet* for Israel in the BCR is not merely perfections in the present, but also perfections in the past. It is in fact the very power to which history bears witness in time and times and times to come. The narratives of the ancestral generations contain the salt and light of these terms. They are the Lord God in His acts with His perfections in the history of Israel among the nations. Throughout Moses' confession, they signify the power of the divine perfections to work in His covenanted relationship with Israel to make her His People. They are the force that drives her flowering in the world as the Vine that she is. In Genesis 24:12, 14, 27, and 49, it is the perfections as the *Chesed and 'Emet* of the Lord God that makes for Abraham's servant the success in finding a wife for

The Beginning of the Generations

Isaac. Rebekah, because of the *chesed Yahweh*, becomes the wife of Isaac. Jacob, Isaac's son, knows well this *Chesed and 'Emet* (Genesis 32:10–11) in the relationship he has inherited with his election. In Genesis 39:21, Joseph, trapped by Potiphar, the wife of a court official of Pharaoh, and then put into an Egyptian prison because of her, knows the Lord's *'grace'* and *'favor'* as being given him because he belongs to the comfort of Israel in this world. In Genesis 40:14, Joseph can ask the chief cupbearer of the court, when he is restored to Pharaoh, to show *Chesed* towards him and ask the Pharaoh to deliver him from his imprisonment. In Genesis 47:29, in the account of Joseph, at the deathbed of his father Jacob, we read: *'When the days of Jacob drew near to death, he called for his son Joseph and he said to him, "If I have found 'favor' in your eyes, place your hand under my thigh and make chesed and 'emet with me—do not let me remain buried in Egypt."'*

If we are indeed made able to hear the Great I-AM for who He truly is, for who He truly is in defining Himself with His divine perfections in His covenanted relationship with His People, then we are surely free to understand that the One who is this One and no other is Himself what He is in His perfections for Israel, in spite of her troubles with Him. He is not something different in His acts from who He is in His Being for His People. We are free in His freedom when we are known in the passion of this Being, His Being with His passion in His Becoming. He is who He is in His acts with His Being and He is who He is in His Being in His acts with Divine Freedom of the wholeness of the I-AM He is. This is fundamental to the nature of the BCR in the Biblical World. He is in the narrative of these generations, with His 'Little Credo' understood as defining Him in time the One He is as the Eternal Lord and God, free to keep faith with His Vow to Israel. The Chosen Seed of His Promise in His Covenanted Relationship with His People in His Creation shall be blessed in His Chosen Land. With this Self-Defining wisdom and power, the Divine Freedom of the Self-Revealing, Naming, and Giving Lord and God is understood to be seen and heard throughout the history of Israel in this world. There is no hope for Israel without the Self-Giving of this Self-Communicating Great I-AM who is the Lord and God of Israel and His Eternity. We miss much of the richness of the dynamic Being of this Lord and God when we do not see and hear his interaction with Israel in these stories as possessing the real Grace (*Chesed*) and Truth *('Emet)* with which He has vowed to keep His

Promise. We surely miss Moses' point when we are unable to hear these notes in the symphony of his confession.

Perhaps a most sensitive account of the tender mercies and wise power of the Almighty with His Promise is to be read in Genesis 22, where the Lord chooses to minister Himself as the Provider He is with Abraham, a shocking narrative of the substitution for Abraham's Isaac of a ram from the thicket on a mountain in Moriah. The chapter recounts the *'testing'* of Abraham about the Promised Seed. The father of the faith has been brought to bear the Almighty Command with him, but in the process of making an offering for the relationship, the question that arises on the child's mind is *'Where is the lamb for the offering?'* The answer that Abraham gives his son, the Promised son, is *'Elohim will see to it!'*—Biblical faith in action with the Almighty. Only when Abraham raises on high in his hand with his knife poised to kill his son is the *testing* concluded. Only when the father's willingness to kill his only son has been proven does the *messenger of Yahweh* halt the sacrifice. From the heavens comes the message to stay the execution. Isaac is released from the altar of sacrifice. Surely the narrative emphasizes the Divine Freedom and Holy Will of this Lord and God that the Almighty Commander is. He will keep His Promise to His Chosen Seed in His way.

When Abraham passes this *'testing,'* his anxieties are replaced by a *fear of Yahweh* that becomes known in Israel as the beginning of Wisdom. He worships with new found depths the Almighty who has called him out of Babylon and commanded him with His Purpose: *'And Abraham called the name of that place "***Yahweh foresees***." So that it is said even to this day—"On the Mountain of Yahweh, it will be foreseen"'* (Genesis 22:24). This is the place where the Blessing of the Covenant is to be experienced. It is the Blessing given in the *Grace and Truth* made with His Divine Freedom as the Great I-AM He is to fulfill His Promise in the experience of His People. The Lord God of the Covenant, Moses tells us, will be in this way with His People. His People will in this way experience the blessing of their Redeemer-Creator. Thus, the great prophet is the great mediator between the Lord God and Israel. In the BCR, He will provide in His Divine Freedom the power that speaks of the way He will provide for His People and keep His Promise to them. This then is the ancestral past Moses confesses. This past with Israel's primordial history forms the background against which the prophet Moses understands Israel's Exodus, her Torah, her Tabernacle, her Worship of the Lord God, and her time in the Wilderness. We cannot understand the nature of the BCR that is taught us in the Bible except in this Divine Freedom of the Great I-AM as the Lord God He is in the freedom of the history of Israel among the nations in His Free Creation.

We need to learn the lessons of the time past in this confession. The promise to be kept from them is the promise that will be kept by the Great I-AM the Lord God is. God Himself with His *Grace and Faithfulness*, His *Grace and Truth* with His Chosen People shall see to it. He will provide for it. The nature of the BCR possesses always at both poles of the relationship, divine and human centers, where consciousness may be shaped and formed to prove the power that constitutes and reconstitutes again and again in time and times the way that He will keep His Promise with Israel, until it is realized in the fulfillment His purposes with the relationship to the magnificence of His inexplicable Glory. The reality of the nature of the BCR cannot be explained without both of these poles, divine and human, fully and freely substantiated in the places and times of God's free will. The transcendent, immanent, and empirical aspects or dimensions of the divine nature in this covenanted relationship are thus present in every epoch of the history of the BCR, as it is recorded for us in the Bible. We do well to take such time and space seriously with us.

All that the People of God in the BCR are to know the entire human destiny and very sinful human history of the human race as bound up with this Election. All opposition to Him is steadily to be overcome. All articulation of its meaning and significance within a framework of human thought is provided by God's Divine Freedom to be who He truly is with Israel among the nations in His Creation. In time and times and across one epoch after epoch, one event after another, from one place to another, at one time and to another, the history of Israel is made to tell the destiny of this relationship in the world. With both poles of the relationship in full and free sway the warp and woof of Israel's history, time past and time present and time future, is to be understood as belonging to this freedom of the Great I-AM that the Lord God is in the world. We must learn to grasp these times and these places as event where both freedoms mean something to God, the world, and to mankind. If we are going to understand the real significance of the movements entailed in the framework that belongs to the real nature of the BCR in the Biblical World, we need to apprehend the significance of Israel among the nations in this way. At all times and in each time, specifically as embedded in this time and that time, is the nature of the covenanted relationship a definition of the place where God struggles passionately and freely with His Chosen. With all its continuities, with all its discontinuities, with the unconditional and conditional dynamics of its true and false passions, with all its real and imagined pathos, the space and time of God's Self-Revelation with Israel is never to be abandoned. This is the history of the BCR with the history of the Creation that is be understood as the home of mankind. This is the beginning of the race upon the earth and the ending of humanity upon the planet. We are meant to know this Divine Lord God in His Divine Freedom as the Great I-AM He is as our Redeemer and our Creator. We must not remain alienated from Him if we would expect to face without His Curse upon the evil that so readily has overtaken and will overtake us without Him. This is the background of Moses' confession in the BCR with the Great I-AM.

Scientists may attempt in our time to understand the contingent relationship of the Lord God with His world and today seek with all the brilliance of our race to explain the invisible nature of the world by the visible phenomena we experience as human beings in a universe, but still the secret belongs to the Creator in and from *the* Beginning. In the science of very small things and in the science of very big things, there exist the secrets of the continuous energies and particular matters that make up the reciprocities inherent in the dynamical nature of the physics of the world. Both symmetrical and asymmetrical relations, linear and non-linear, are necessary to describe the nature of this universe with us. Mathematical realities associated with quantum field events in the physics of the micro cosmos and the invariance in the physics of the macro cosmos, when both indeterminate and determinate resolutions of the equations compel us to understand that a deep and profound secret remains with the universe, a secret we say belongs to this Great I-AM, this Lord God is. Both irreversible and reversible dimensions of the processes involved in these kinds of reciprocities compel our understanding of the nature and being of this world to develop in time. Space and time become redefined again and again in a profoundly relational creativity with what belongs to the power of the free Creator, whose acts we must understand as truly acts of a redemptive will and creative determination. In these reciprocities, we experience this world. But we say that this is the world of Moses' confession, with all that freedom must mean with it.

The Beginning of the Generations

We have seen that, the Great I-AM the Lord God is in His BCR with His People in His Creation shapes a framework of interpretation whose dynamical composition forms a grasp of His Divine Freedom to be who He truly is with His Creation, time past and time present. The nature His Divine Freedom found within this relationship also belongs to His I-AM and to the nature of human freedom as His Image in His Creation. His struggle to justify this choice is everywhere present in the narrative of the Book of Genesis. Between the Great I-AM the Lord God is and His People in His Covenant in His Creation, there exists a relationship whose dynamics cannot be explained except by His decision to keep a promise to His Elect in His Creation. This is the faith that is the backbone that belongs to Moses' confession. There is no time in the history of Israel when both Divine and human freedoms are not significantly involved in the dynamics of the exchanges and entanglements that we read theologically in the confession. Between the Great I-AM and Moses, the great prophet of Israel as the People of God there exists by His Will in His Divine Freedom a determination that teaches us that He will not be who He is without His Elect in His Creation. The nature of the BCR is such that its secret belongs to His *Chesed* and *'Emet* belonging to this relationship, where a real reciprocity, both symmetrical and asymmetrical, is established in time and times with a view towards the keeping of His Promise to Abraham and his sons. When Israel in Egypt blesses his sons, the prophecy of the Promise is being kept. We do well to grasp this relational view of God and Man in God's World.

In this way, Land, Seed, and Blessing are the realities with which the BCR binds His People to the I-AM He is. When we speak of divine passion, we speak of His willingness in His freedom to be who He is as committed to this relationship. Even when His People seek another and evilly will to oppose Him, He will not be who He truly is except with His Israel. His Freedom will make her freedom serve to His Glory. The relationship possesses with this end in mind a nature that provides with His great atoning love for Israel a vision of hope not otherwise found in the ancient literatures. It provides a way to teach her of His willingness, in spite of her unwillingness, to be her Redeemer-Creator. In this way, the Lord God has said His 'Yes' to her past. As this Lord God He remains always free within and without Himself to seek to reverse whatever 'evil' against Him has been conceived and done. He is free to contradict the contradiction of His People. He is free to accomplish, always with a new beginning, that which must be done in order to reverse the consequences of His judgment against His People and to deliver them from their evil among the nations. Without a deep and profound grasp the nature of this covenanted freedom and this willingness of the Lord God, the Great I-AM He is remains unknown to His People. This is what He has given of Himself to be known with His People in His BCR with Israel among the nations. We may remain continuously or discontinuously confused and alienated from who He is as our Creator-Redeemer, yet He remains absolutely committed with His Being in His Acts to His BCR in a world that is His Creation. Here we learn the significance of His *Grace and Truth* with us. Here is the secret of His relational life with us. Here is the secret of His love for us. Ultimately, it will take nothing less or other than His Incarnation to persuade us about Him. Yet even this Speaking of the Lord God is profoundly resisted because of evil in a world that is His Creation. Yet He is who He is and He will be whom He will be as the Almighty keeping His Promise to His People in His Creation. He will not be the I-AM He is without His People in the Land.

'You intended to harm me, but God intended it for good.' This is what Joseph knows of the wisdom of the providence of the Lord God in the prophecy with his brothers. They are far from the Promised Land. They live in the land of Egypt, the prophecy of the Promise with them. Joseph's generation can tell with his bones the certain wisdom inherent in the narrative of his life and death. His story shows its readers that prophecy and providence together work to bring about the fulfillment of this Promise to the fathers of Israel's faith. The Lord God the Great I-AM is in His Covenant with His People in His Creation is a relationship the poles of which are active in shaping what history is, what history is in time and space. Here is wisdom that would teach us of the way that God in His Divine Freedom is free to take the evil plans of humanity up and make them serve His Truth and Grace. He shall contradict him who would oppose Him and His Promise in this world, and out of their contradiction the I-AM He is will bring about the fulfillment of the Promise. This story teaches us some basic aspects of the fundamental nature of the BCR in the Biblical World. With Joseph's generation, the People of God learn their past, bound up as it is with His Divine Freedom, in spite of the Primordial and Ancestral sins against their Lord and God, belongs to a future that belongs to the Blessing. From Joseph's dreams—his brother's sheaves will bow to his sheaf and even the sun and moon with their 11 stars will bow

down to him—to his buried bones in an Egyptian coffin, Joseph's story would show us the wisdom of this Lord and God in action in the world in spite of all that lives in opposition to Him. From the life and death of this 'dreamer,' this possessor of his father's special favor, this young man in his special coat, in spite of the murderous treatment by his brothers, Joseph's bones know the Blessing of the Seed for the Land promised Abraham and his son. Even in the form of his bones, this Promise is to be carried back to the Land, where they shall bear a meaning only his dreams can tell Israel. They are the objects or subjects now of the speaking of the Lord God with Israel's past. Like the speaking of God with the blood of Abel, they speak of a Primordial and Ancestral past of a faith that belongs to the People of God in God's Creation. They form right from *the Beginning*, through the lives of the Adam, Cain, Noah, Abraham and his sons and down to Joseph's dreams, what the People of God are in the world. This is the Israel of Moses' confession. This is time past of his prophecy. When a Pharaoh rose up to reign in Egypt who knew nothing of Joseph and his dreams, when only the gods of Egypt's Nile were known, the afflictions of Israel were increased. Her troubles as stranger in an alien land were intensified. With only the orders of 'Ma'at,' with only the orders of the Egyptian pantheon in sway along side the rhythms of the River once again, where the Egyptian civilization flourished on her banks and the backs of the Hebrews, Israel as the People of God were compelled to begin to cry out to her Lord and God. The dreams of Joseph in Moses' confession, under the afflictions of Egypt's Pharaoh, are shaped into loud cries. They are cries the Lord God determined not to ignore, and after 480 years of bondage, the People of God in BCR with her Great I-AM is delivered. The Seed of the Promise in Egypt shall be delivered to the Promised Land. The Exodus is then in the hands of the Great I-AM.

We cannot read the Book of Genesis without hearing the cry of the People of God as the Seed of the Promise far from the Land of Promise. In the power of the Divine Freedom of Lord God, the Five *Toledoth* of her Primordial Past and the Five *Toledoth* of her Ancestral Past, come from the Creation Week of God's 'Very Good' *Beginning*, we read Moses' Confession and Prophecy among the nations. With the same Divine Freedom that He made Himself present and known with His Voice from the Flames of the Burning Bush for Moses, the Great I-AM the Lord God is has shaped with His Grace and Truth the time and times of Israel's history. In this Divine Freedom, she is to fulfill His Promise to His People in His Creation. The time past is understood in its service to Him as the background that explains Israel's present time in her BCR with the Almighty. Her future is thus bound up with Him in the very nature of the BCR in the eyes and ears of the great prophet and leader of Israel among the nations. If Israel has been freed from the Land of the Pharaohs, it is because His Promise to her shall be kept. The Promise that extends back to *the* Beginning, the primordial and ancestral beginnings of the generations of Creation and Israel's Fathers of her faith, has not been made in vain. It is this keeping of His Promise upon which Israel's existence steadily depends. The meaning of the BCR belongs buried with Joseph's bones. In spite of all evils, primordial and ancestral, Joseph's dreams are to be realized. Carried up by his brothers, in spite of their evil intentions against him, his bones bear the significance of intentions of the Great I-AM from the Blessing of Abraham and his sons in the Land. The meaning and significance of Israel in the BCR with Him is secure. The God who will do it is none other than the Creator Himself. It is the dreams of these bones that belong to the Divine Promise of the Almighty, to Abraham and to Abraham's Seed, to the Blessing in the Land, to the Lord God who has chosen Israel among the nations, that He might become known for who He truly is. These are Israel's dreams then, the Land, the Seed, the Blessing. They shall be realized. The Promise will be kept. Moses' prophecy and prophetic leadership shall be justified.

The righteousness of Moses' confession for Israel's past belongs to these dreams. Moses confession is not merely a confession of Israel's sin history, but one that belongs to the Divine Freedom and the Holy Love of this Great I-AM who is both Lord and God of Israel's history in the history of the world. The Great I-AM is her *Yahweh-Elohim*. He is the Redeemer-Creator. He is who He is as this Redeemer-Creator in His BCR with her as the People of God among the nations, under these heavens and on this earth. He is this as Creator of *the* Beginning and of all of world history. This is the Lord and the God whose interaction in His Divine Freedom with His People in His Creation has determined to keep this Promise with Israel in His Creation. The BCR is a covenanted relationship that possesses a nature the Grace and Truth of which belongs to this Promise of the Great I-AM. The Fathers of Israel's faith in the world belongs to the time and times of this BCR. The world as Creation belongs to this BCR. The meaning of the world and its people belong to this BCR. We need to hear Moses' confession as the prophecy of this BCR, of

The Beginning of the Generations

Israel's past understood as belonging to the righteousness of this Lord God. Real explanation of Israel's time is bound up with the wisdom of the providence in this prophecy with who He is. This is the Voice of the Great I-AM of Moses' confession. Time and times past and present and future are to be viewed as the ground upon which Moses can stand and gaze upon a future for Israel that belongs to this Lord, this God. The Primordial and Ancestral past of Israel's times in the world belong to this Redeemer-Creator. The Voice that speaks with Moses, the Voice of the Angel of the Lord is the Voice that spoke into the *bara'* of *the* Beginning the order of light where the Adam is what Adam ought to be. It is the Voice that spoke for the Ancestors to Israel's faith, and it is the Voice who will speak for her destiny among the nations in His Creation.

Cosmos

5

These Are the Words—A People for the Land

Hear, O Israel, the Lord, our God,
the Lord is the One ('echad—one)

Deuteronomy 6:4a

I F IN THE BOOK of Genesis Moses looked back upon Israel, in the Book of Deuteronomy he looks forward. The old generation, eyewitnesses to the Exodus, is dead. The new generation, the Seed of the Promise, is poised at Moab to enter the Promised Land. Afflicted in Egypt, the Seed is meant for the Blessing of the Promise in the Land of Canaan. Thus, at Moab, we read for the Seed another renewal of the BCR. The Lord God with Israel shall fulfill His purpose with His People in His Creation. The Hebrew Bible entitles this book *'These are the* words.' They are the words that bear Moses' last will and testament with Israel as she prepares to enter into the Promised Land.

The Seed is called together to hear His Name and to honor the Great I-AM for who He truly is with Israel. In this renewal of the covenanted relationship, Israel is to hear the *'echad* as the One with whom her future is bound up—that the prophecy of Moses shall be fulfilled. Here Moses writes his last will and testament to the People of God. The tribes of Israel shall inherit the Promised Land as they are destined to experience the Promise kept. The Seed will be blessed in this Land. The Lord God has chosen in His Divine Freedom to relate Himself to His People with His Righteousness in this way. We need to be able to read this transition as the establishment of the Great I-AM as the solid object He is as the One *'echad* who is who He truly is with His Elect People in His Land in His Creation. He is the One that His People are to love with all their hearts and strengths and greatness in the place where God chooses to set His Name and calls Israel to come and do *'what is Right'* (*yashar*) in His Eyes. This is the fundamental content of the prophetic renewal of the BCR through Moses and his death between Yahweh-Elohim and Israel.

The '*Lord God*' is not to be considered merely as a number among many numbers in this world. The *'echad* is not one of many, not merely a number, but the incomparable One whose Being and Becoming is unique absolutely both without and within His Creation. He is to be loved as the unique Being He is; the Great I-AM He is, even in His Becoming in His BCR with His People. Moses makes the number one (1) in his prophecy of the renewal of His covenanted relationship at Moab serve what is in the first place not numerable. No magnitude can be employed to create any image that is acceptable to the incomparable and unique One He is. The prophet calls the People of God to love this One as the unique Lord God of the BCR in God's Creation. He does not at Moab intend to develop a number theory for Israel's entrance into the Land of the Promise. To hear this One is to hear Israel's Redeemer-Creator as the Lord of time and times, the God of her history among the nations in the history of His Creation. It is to hear Him as the Great I-AM He truly is that with this renewal He makes His Presence appreciated for the solid One He is, a solid objectivity that commands Israel to love as He must be loved in her history with Him. It is to hear Him in the utter uniqueness and incomparableness of His Name in this way that His People can apprehend the nature of His Being and Becoming with her. This is the burden of the words of Deuteronomy.

It is with this renewal action that Israel as His Elect must become what Israel ought to be with Him. It is to hear Him war against all the idols of all the idol makers throughout all the world that He shall be known and loved as the Great I-AM He is with the world. It is to hear the Speaking of God as this Lord and God making time and space for His Presence with His Chosen in His Creation. It is to hear Him making Himself known as this solid object of His Love with His People. It is to hear the Redeemer for who He is as the Creator. It is to hear this Creator as the Redeemer. It is to hear this One speaking in His Divine Freedom in the Creation with them. It is to hear Him as the One who Israel may love. It is to hear Him as the Great I-AM Israel is meant to know and love as her Redeemer-Creator, as the *'echad* He is. It is to hear Him in the will of His Being, His Will to be the One He is as Great I-AM He is for Israel. It is to hear the Glory of His Name. It is to hear to worship Him and learn of Him with His Wisdom in a world that is His Creation with a people that are His People. It is to go to the space and time that He has chosen for Himself and there and then learn to do the Right Thing in His Eyes. It is to hear to be and become as His People what He can say is 'My People' as His Elect in His Promised Land. To hear the 'uniqueness' and 'incomparableness' of this free One Lord and God of the world and Israel's tribes is to hear Him as the I-AM He is. It is to hear Him with His Promise to her—in this world. To hear this One, we need prophetic ears and eyes, to learn to hear and see this One as the Great I-AM He is. This is the Lord God who speaks prophetically with Moses His Law or Torah for His Elect. We need to learn to know Him as this One, this *'echad,* and not another. We need to hear Him and see Him in this Becoming of His Being, the Great I-AM, as the Great *'echad*, One, is to be heard and loved for who He truly is with His Promise for His People in His Covenant with His Creation.

The primordial and ancestral pasts of the People of God, the tabernacle and the festivals of the worship of this One, belong to the renewal of the I-AM the Lord God is with His Promise in the history of Israel. He speaks that they may exist in places and at times where and when His Blessing is to be experienced as the prophetic meaning of the BCR in the nature of Israel's renewals in the world as 'My People.' It is renewal in chosen places and at appointed times of this Only Holy One, this Unique One beside whom there is no other, this Great I-AM the Lord God is to whom His People are to give their devoted attention and love. To His Place and at His Appointed Time in His Promised Land is the People of God to go to do the Right Thing in His Eyes. Here in this place and at these times, Israel is to receive His Blessing in the Land. In this way, His People are to live in the Promised Land. In this way, His People are to honor who He is in His Creation. In this way, Israel is to understand her future as the love of this I-AM. In this way, the renewal of the BCR at Moab is to be read as Moses' last will and testament as the Prophet of Israel's existence. In this way, we are to read the Book of Deuteronomy. Moses' confession sees Israel living under the prophetic power and thrust of this Revelation. He calls the Israel that is the new generation to hear this One speaking and to enter the Land of the Promise in love with Him. Thus, the 'Five Books of Moses' culminate the confession with the prophetic promise rehearsed in renewal of the People of God for the Promised Land.

With her primordial and ancestral past ringing in her ears, with the cry of her afflictions in Egypt and with her deliverance still singing in her heart, with what Israel at the Mountain of God saw and heard in her

These Are the Words—A People for the Land

memories, the meaning and significance of her existence and her future in the Promised Land is bound up with the renewal that belongs to the last will and testament of her great Prophet and Leader. She must stand as a New Generation of the Covenant of the Lord God in this Land. At Moab, she prepares to enter into this Promised Land, into this Promised Destiny, into the Blessing of the Great I-AM the Lord God as this One. But Canaan is a land that once belonged to peoples whose gods were mere idols. It is a land filled with the idol making whose evil the Lord God would remove from His Creation. What Israel once heard at Sinai, she must hear in Moab, but with assured eyes and ears that her Redeemer is indeed the Creator of all that is created reality, of all that is the heavens and the earth; this is the invisible and visible world. She may rehearse her past, but only for the sake of her future with this Voice. The Book of Deuteronomy is a call to hear this Voice of renewal in her relationship with who He is. It is a renewal of Israel's covenant as the People of God in relationship with the Great I-AM He is. It is renewal with the One who is and will be the One that He is, even in Israel's future. What the Exodus began, the renewal we read in the Book of Deuteronomy intends to finish. We ought to be able to read the prophetic thrust and the prophetic power in this last will and testament of Moses among His People. Moses is dead. Long live the Promise of the Lord God. Moses is in this way the great Prophet and Mediator of Israel's history with her Lord and God among the nations of the world. What the old generation would not hear, the new generation must learn to hear. The Name given for this renewal is the Great 'echad of the Great I-AM. He is the One that Israel as this new generation must love. He is the One to whom the People of God must listen and not another. This is His Name binding time past, time present, and time future together up with His Eternity. All that created time is, with Israel's history in the world, is bound up with His Life among them.

    I do not think the English title does justice to the form and contents of this book. The 'Book of the Second Law' or the 'Book of a Copy of the Law' does not indicate the significance of Moses' last will and testament in the BCR for Israel about to enter into the Promised Land. The title 'The Book of Deuteronomy' only describes very conventionally the intent and purpose of the renewal at Moab. The title of the book in Hebrew is 'These are the Words.' 'These are the Words' that Israel is to hear. 'These are the Words' that she is to take with her into Canaan. 'These are the Words' by which she can live under the Blessing of the Lord in the Land of the

Promise. '*These are the Words*' by which she is to live in the land her fathers only passed through. '*These are the Words*' of the Ten Words she heard codified at Sinai. '*These are the Words*' the Lord God has put into her mouth. '*These are the Words*' of her faith. '*These are the Words*' that shall determine her future in the world. '*These are the Words*' she must hear in order to love the solid truth of her Lord's Being and Will for her. '*These are the Words*' that belong to the Great I-AM the Lord God is with her and the *'echad* He will be for her. Israel belongs to the Blessing of these words. She belongs to the Glory of these words. There is a certain beauty to these words that every reader of them ought to be able to appreciate; we are to hear the Book of Deuteronomy as they ought to hear it. They bear a prophetic significance for Israel that is never lost, even across the centuries of her existence in the world. They belong to a certain wisdom that belongs to the One and Only Unique and Incomparable One who is the I-AM of the BCR. They are the last will and testament of a man who belongs to the power of the Living God, to the Prophet of Israel's history in the world. They belong to the One who is free to chose the space and time in which His Presence is given a solid reality where Israel can go and do what is right in His Eyes.

With these words, the exhortation of Moses' last will and testament for the People of God is put into the mouth of Israel in the Creation of the Lord God. The prophet calls Israel to renew her covenanted relationship with the Great I-AM the Lord God is that she may love Him and go to the place to do what is right in His Eyes (Deuteronomy 6:4–6; 12:1–7). We may read this renewal of the BCR in Moses' teachings as the words of the Redeemer-Creator, the *Yahweh Elohim,* of Israel's history among the nations in the world. With these words, the new generation of Israel's faith is established in the BCR. Nowhere else in the confession is the passion of the leader and prophet of the People of God more solidly adamant. The renewal of the BCR as his last will and testament makes him the Prophet of His People in Israel's history. He leads Israel's tribes into her purpose as no other. He may have disciples, but never an equal among the tribes of the People of God. These are not his words but words of the Lord God. They form the concrete basis for the new generation's hearing in the Promised Land. With these words, Israel may obey the Speaking of the Only Incomparable One Lord and God is as the Great I-AM of Israel's life in the world, of the Lord God's blessing of the Seed of Abraham in the land of Canaan. It is a wondrous speaking indeed. His Speaking in *the*

Beginning, His Speaking with Abel and Noah, His Speaking with Abraham and his sons, and His Speaking with Joseph is the Speaking of this *'echad* with His People. *'These are the Words'* the Lord God speaks as the Great I-AM He is in His Divine Freedom with the tribes of Israel as the new generation about to enter into the Promised Land.

As this last will and testament of the prophet Moses is with Israel, these words are not merely a repetition of the Sinai Torah. At Moab, Israel hears anew what she would not, as the 'stiff-necked,' 'high-handed,' and 'murmuring' people of the old generation, hear. What she would not hear from *the Beginning*, what Adam would not hear, what Cain would not hear, what Abraham and his sons had trouble hearing, what Israel with Joseph was willing to disobey, here she must learn afresh to hear. The beauty of the Book of Deuteronomy belongs to the prophetic power of its call to hear. With these words, Israel's deafness in the past shall be overcome. She will come to know that she truly belongs to the Lord and God who will not be who He is without her. The Command of the Lord God in the Book of Deuteronomy belongs to His Holy Will to bless His People. He will not be who He is without blessing Israel. Israel belongs to the pathos of His passionate promise to her. In Exodus 20:1 we read: '**Elohim spoke all these words: "I am Yahweh your Elohim, who brought you up from the land of Egypt, from the house of afflictions."**' At Moab, Moses seeks once more and anew with this heart for Israel. Once in the Land, His People shall go to the place where this Only Incomparable One shall choose to set His Name and there she shall learn to do what is right (*the Yashar*) in His Eyes. The People of God must learn to center their lives in the life of this Great I-AM, who in His Divine Freedom has chosen in this way to be present and known among them as the One He is for them in the Land. The imperative mood of Moses' exhortation thus is to be heard with the pathos of this prophetic passion of *'these words.'* The beauty of His Wisdom in His Providence with His Divine Will and Holy Love is brought to bear upon His People with these words. They bear the meaning of His determination to be known for who He truly is with Israel.

I have counted the times the combination of the names Lord and God, in one form or another, appears in Moses' testimony. We must not fail to appreciate the prophetic rhetoric of this use of the Names in Moses' exhortation. **Yahweh our Elohim** (the Lord our God), **Yahweh your Elohim** (The Lord your God), **Yahweh is Elohim** (the Lord is God) shape the movement of the beauty of these words. These names are found with these words in this testimony some 297 times in the Book of Deuteronomy. Again and again, the command of the Sinai Torah is rehearsed at Moab in this way. It is meant to hammer His Name into the heart of this new generation. These words are to be written even on the doors of their homes. They mark the lives of this People with His Name. The prophetic and providential power of His Name must never thought to be lost upon this People of God. The future of this Israel depends upon her hearing these words of her Lord God. She must go to the place where He has freely chosen to set this Name, and there call His People to come and do *the Yashar* in His Eyes. The rhetoric of this Name with *'these words'* argues for a significance whose meaning belongs to a future that belongs to all time. It belongs to the very nature of time in the BCR between the I-AM the Lord God is with His Command of His People among the nations in His Creation.

I have a friend who is an astrophysicist. His favorite verse in the Bible is Deuteronomy 29:29 (verse 28 in the Hebrew Bible): *'The secrets belong to **Yahweh your Elohim**, and what is revealed to us and to our sons forever, to do all the words of this Torah.'* He thought these words were most cogent for doing science as well as for Biblical Theology. The secret of the mystery that comes with the Revelation of the Redeemer-Creator defines a relationship between the Voice the Creator is and the universe His Creation is. The ultimate nature of this universe rests upon its relationship to this free Lord and God as the I-AM He is. All that is created reality belongs to the reality of His Uncreated Nature. The secret of the contingency of Mankind in the contingent order and freedom of the universe rests upon this relationship of the Only and Incomparable One as this Lord God, the Almighty Sovereign, who is who He is in His Divine Freedom over all that is created reality. The One who moves the whole of the Creation also moves the mind of mankind in His Sabbath Relationship with all that is created reality. We are to seek to hear Him, to understand Him with His secrets as the Great I-AM He is for us. We do well, my friend often said, to believe, to seek to understand the secrets, for often enough in the history of science we have made discoveries that witness to His Self-Revelation. We are given to know the Lord in this way with a universe that is His Creation. The very significance of the created freedom of the contingent orders we find in the world as a universe is bound up with the secrets of who He is for us. My friend studied the sun for his Ph.D. in physics. He worked most of his life with the equations of Einstein's Gravitational

Theory and the Dirac Equation for Quantum Physics, especially as they helped him to grasp a certain star complex named SS433. His studies led him to conceive of new resolutions for the Dirac Equation's relativistic form and the physics of the electrons of the hydrogen atom as the starlight we observe from the star with our instruments. The correspondence between our experience and our theory belonged to God's secrets and His willingness to share them with us. This astrophysicist understood that the correspondence always belonged to the secrets of the Creator with His Creation.

Everyone should be able to have a friend like Boris Kuharetz. For him, Einstein's famous saying was true, '*Science without religion is lame; religion without science is blind!*' It is a saying that may stick in the throats of both scientists and theologians, but the saying signifies the fact that some deep cognitive relationship exists between who God is and what Creation is meant to be with its Mankind. Man as a scientist was in this sense the Priest of Creation. He was a sign that seeking redemptive healing in the universe was empty of meaning and significance. In the secrets of this relationship with this Only and Incomparable One, the personal God who is both the Creator of the Universe as well as the Redeemer of Man, we can find within the Creation echoes or reflection of the Great I-AM He is. The secrets of the **Grace and Truth** of this Being are commanded and given to Man as both scientist and theologian. We do well to be open to such potential in this relationship. For my friend, the modern search for 'Unification' in our sciences is bound up with the secrets of the Lord who as this God may be subtle, but not malicious. It is with His secrets that we may be led beyond the geometrical invariance of General Relativity Theory and beyond the Quantum Geometries, beyond the dialectics of indeterminism and determinism, and into the new physics for which scientists seek today. He believed that this new physics will make us appreciate the potential in a world that is God's Creation, perhaps as never before in our times. Perhaps we will become open to the beauty of His Wisdom in time and space and the world of the human race and see clearly beyond the tragedy of our fallen times and spaces. In this way, theologian and scientist alike will grasp something deeper and more profound about the correspondence between them.

But such development belongs to the nature of the Great I-AM who is both Lord and God of His People and Creation. He both distinguishes Himself from all that is created reality with His Sovereign and Divine Freedom as well as makes Himself known to them within it. His is that solid personal reality of Being that will not be divorced for what His Redemption is with the world. Redemption is the answer to our questions about why the Creation is the world it is. Redemption gives ultimate meaning and significance to the history of the world as Creation. No divorce between the theology and science is ultimately possible, for both belong with His secrets to the One He is. What we have been given to know of Him we know in the Light of the Nature of this Being in the acts in and with His words for them. The actual Nature of His Being and Becoming as the Incomprehensible One He is, only understood as this Only and Incomparable and Wise God, who is this One Creator and One Redeemer for His People in His Creation. Deuteronomy 29:29 is a verse whose words my friend heard speaking to him of these secrets of the Lord God in science and theology: *'The secret things belong to **the Lord our God**, but the revealed things belong to us and to our children forever, to observe all the words of this law.'* These things belong to the Living One, to the Loving Lord, to the Commanding God, who with His Divine Freedom ministers at all times His secrets in the Name of the Great I-AM He is with His People in His Creation.

We may neither confuse knowledge of God with knowledge of the universe nor divorce them from one another. This is why the concept of contingent rationality and intelligibility of the objectivity of physical nature is so important for both scientist and theologian. The Only and Incomparable One in His Divine Freedom in His BCR creates a relationship with His Creation and His People. He makes all that is created reality what it is in space and time. The 'All' of created reality is sustained under the Sovereign power of His Command, His Judgment, and His Blessing. He Himself as the Great I-AM He is holds the secret of the significance of theology and science with the human race. We do well when we do not confuse the two subjects and when we do not alienate them from one another. We must hear them both respectively in Him, the Only and Incomparable One, zealous with His Transcendent Wisdom for the world He has caused to exist and sustains in existence. His Revelation belongs to His Divine Freedom to be present with Himself in the world He loves. We must learn to hear Him as this Creator, as this Redeemer, because He is this Lord God. In His Name we are given to know Him for who He truly is, as this Redeemer-Creator, and as this Great I-AM without and within the history of the Creation and His People. Ultimately, we are to know the Universe in His Name. Ultimately, we know the Creator in this Name, and in all of our knowing, the rest of His secrets with the One He truly is. Everyone should be so fortunate to have for a friend someone who can help us to understand these things.

I believe Moses most certainly understood this kind of relationship between the Great I-AM the Lord God is with His People in His Creation. His exhortation of the new generation to covenant renewal as the Israel of God at Moab asserts with providential and prophetic power the secret of this Name. The prophet and prophecy belong to the Glory and Righteousness of this Only and Incomparable One: '*I am Yahweh, your Elohim*' (Deuteronomy 29:6). *I am the Lord your God! I am* the One you must hear. *I am* the One who transcends time, time past, time present, and time future. *I am* the One who enters into the space of all time as I-AM that I-AM. *I am* beyond you and *I am* with you. With me, you know. With me, you shall know. *I am* the One who gives knowledge of me in time and space. To the place where I have chosen to set my Name, I call you, where you may come and do what is right in My Eyes. This is Moses' exhortation to the new generation at Moab. This is the Only and Incomparable One, Moses insists, that Israel must hear and must come to love because He is the One who is truly zealous for Israel. This is the imperative mode in which the Blessing is proclaimed. The secret of its roots belongs to the nature of the Being of this One in the Land of His Promise.

Many scholars believe Moses' exhortation was strongly revived in the period of Israel's Monarchy. They speculate that the scroll found in the reign of Judah's King Josiah (620 BC) may have been a scroll of '*These are the words.*' These words caused the renewal for which Josiah called in the days of the prophet Jeremiah. These are the words that fell in those desperate days for Israel's Monarchy upon the deaf ears of a very self-centered people. Even when the Babylonians were about to destroy all that had been sacred to the People of God, the exhortation is not heeded by Israel's generations. This is the setting, they say, when the exhortation to the place where the Name has been established was most vital. The urgency of the imperative is felt when Babylonian armies surrounded David's Jerusalem, the City of David, the Zion where God had chosen to set His Name and to keep His Promise to David's House and Throne. Yet I find no mention of Jerusalem in the imperative of Moses' exhortation. I find there only the command to go to the place the Lord God will choose to be present in His Name to bless His People. To this place His People must go to do what is right in His Eyes. I read a prophetic exhortation, one that never loses its value and vitality in the world. In all of time, in times past, time present, times future, the call to hear remains fundamental for life with God in the Land. *These are the words* that belong to all times in His Creation.

Yes, this centralization of worship is a new command for a new generation. Israel's tribal and nomadic history has known nothing of this new kind of worship. They are clans of people, delivered from their afflictions in Egypt and brought to Sinai to give them to worship Him as this Lord and God. They must learn that this is the way to hear the One who has chosen to teach them their worship of Him. The command in Deuteronomy 12:4–6a reads: '*Do not do so with* **Yahweh your Elohim** (as the peoples of the idols of the gods of Canaan do), *but only in the place among all your tribes where He shall set His Name—in his Tabernacle—there you shall seek to go, there you must go with your offerings and your sacrifices, your tithes and your gifts in your hands . . .*' Yes, this place becomes Jerusalem in Israel's history. But His Command speaks of a moveable feast. His chosen place speaks of His Freedom to provide for the People. It speaks of a chosen center, moveable in time, a dynamic center that waves across the waters of Israel's history with her Lord and God. Whether the place is Shiloh or Jerusalem, it is in every case a chosen center where in this world the People of God are commanded to go to do what is 'Right' in the eyes of the Lord God. To the chosen center Israel must go to worship the One, this *'echad*, who is the Lord God that is the Great I-AM in His BCR with Israel among the nations. It is a sacred space for sacred times that provide the ground when Israel might learn of who He truly is among her tribes. The Book of Deuteronomy is not about Jerusalem, but about the Divine Freedom of the Lord God the Great I-AM is to choose where He shall establish His Name, that there His People might go to do what is 'Right' in His Eyes.

Everyone should also visit a synagogue to hear the Cantor proclaim Israel's Great *Shema'* to this community of faith. Little necessity will be felt to go to the commentators after hearing the verse chanted from the Holy Scriptures. One can hear there those tones of times, those overtones of time itself, in such a way that their meaning seems to sing across the centuries, bearing the Command of Moses' exhortation to us, even yet today. The *Shema'* of Israel sounds loud and still in the synagogue even in our times with a force that does not allow our attention to escape its significance in the world. It is as if all time and space is made to hear the command of this Lord and God. Perhaps scholars would do well to learn to hear the *Shema'* with the intention and purpose for which the Command was recorded. It is meant to be heard. His Voice is meant to be adored. They are meant for the love, the love that God is. The Command of His Voice is not to be merely analyzed. Deuteronomy 6:4 keeps the beat of a heart whose energies and passions waved and continues to wave across the mansions of time we read as centuries upon our calendars. They mean for us to hear the Living One, the Great I-AM. The voice of the cantor today is not the voice of God, but across the abyss of the years His Presence still sounds in his chant. His voice still calls us to the place: '*Hear, O Israel, the Name* (Yahweh) *our Elohim, the Name* (Yahweh) *is 'echad.'* Still today the Cantor dare not pronounce out loud the *Tetragrammaton*, for these four consonants bear the holy significance of that Voice which is the Voice Moses heard coming from the flames of the unconsumed and Burning Bush, the Voice of the Lord God, the Voice of the Great I-AM speaking to His People. Still today the Name is a name no Jew dares to put upon his dirty lips, lest he should profane the Revelation in this Name. This is the Name that declares to Israel that the Only and Incomparable One is love and to be loved. This is the Name that is above all names. This is the Name with which the God of Eternity has named Himself for His People.

Israel's scribal traditions replaced any out loud reading of the *Tetragrammaton* with the word '*Adonai*,' a term often employed for a husband or a lord or a master, etc. The vowels from '*Adonai*' were placed with the four consonants of the *Tetragrammaton* in this tradition. This guaranteed that, when the Name of the Lord appeared in the texts, the Scribe would be reminded to read in place of the *Tetragrammaton* the personal noun '*Adonai*.' When the vowels of '*Adonai*' became conflated with the consonants of the *Tetragrammaton*, then a strict transliteration of the writing could not be rendered into English as 'Jehovah,' thus the famous name for Lord in the King James Bible. So far as the Rabbis are concerned, this is a nonsense word, merely a conflation of the vowels from '*Adonai*' with the consonants of the *Tetragrammaton*, the Name of the Lord that no one ever pronounced out loud in Israel's history and still do not today. The synagogue today simply employs the definite article with the noun for 'name' in the Hebrew language—the Name.' In this way the Jews express their reverence for the Name. The Name is modernly translated as 'Lord' and appears more than 6800 times in the Old Testament. The noun 'God' appears more than 3500 times in the Old Testament. The title Lord God, which we argue is fundamental and vital for Moses' confession, bears a significance as He is bound up with the Revelation of the Great I-AM, which name for the Lord God is told us only once in the Pentateuch (Exodus 3:14). It is the syncretism of the Name Lord God with the Baalim of the Canaanite gods, an act that turns the I-AM the Lord God is into a 'Not-I-AM' and marries the Lord God to Baal that brings down upon Israel's worship His Curse in His BCR with His People (cf. Hosea 1:9 and Psalm 50:21). This is the Only and Incomparable One whom Moses confesses in his exhortation in the book entitled '*These are the Words*' of this Great I-AM as the Only One. This is not a world in which the question 'What's in a name?' may be answered with mere conventions. In the Semitic world, a rose by another name would not be a rose and would not smell as sweet. This is a world in which a name is meant to signify the reality of that to which it would refer its reader. In the case of the Lord God, the Name must refer us to the I-AM He is as this One, this solid One in space and time in His Divine Freedom to make Himself present and known in His Chosen Center for worship.

What, indeed, must Israel hear when she hears the call of the Name *'echad*? She certainly is not merely to hear a number among the numbers. The Lord God is not to be conceived as a number among the many numbers. His simplicity among the ancient gods is not simply the first number or the number of all numbers known to what the ancient world thought they knew about numbers and infinities. She certainly was exhorted to hear not the number One as a number, but number defined by the nature of the Being and the Becoming of the Only and Incomparable One who has no equal in magnitude with the Creation. No image of this One was to be sought within the Creation. Israel was to hear a Being that was utterly unique. She was to Unique One, beside whom there is no other, without any analogy of the Being of His divine nature. She was to hear that this One was none other than the Great I-AM the Lord God is with her. He is the One who delivered her from Egypt. He is the One who has promised His People a Land. He is the One who is to be the object of her love, the chosen of His Holy Love acting in the world. Israel was chosen to hear that He had chosen her for the sake of His Name. The Book of Deuteronomy is prophecy because Israel is made to hear that she had been called to the place where He had freely chosen to be with her and to make Himself known to her. Here in this freedom, she was to hear and see and remember and know Him for who He truly is. This is the One who had taken up her life and given her a worship that did not belong to the gods of the past among the nations. '*And you shall love **Yahweh your Elohim** with all of your heart and with all of your being and with all of your much-ness*' (Deuteronomy 6:5). This concept of loving the _____ as the Great I-AM and Lord God He is, as the Only Unique and Incomparable One He is, belongs to the renewal in the world of Israel's call and history. The new generation as the object of His Love, unlike the old generation dead in the wilderness, is to bear witness to the nature of His Being with Israel and for her purpose in the world. This is the meaning of the Name, the Name above all names.

The command to love Him is without analogy in the ancient world. No other peoples could claim to have experienced this love's command. Both the transcendent mystery of God's Being and the immanent actuality of His Nature acting with His Divine Freedom for Israel among the nations were to be confessed in this love. Moses certainly knew very well that, according to the angers of times past, Israel would not love Him according to His Command. He knew very well the 'stiff-necked' People of God. He had seen their 'high-handed' worship. He had heard their 'murmuring' in the wilderness. How then could this new generation heed the command to love Him? Incomparably alive beside the idols of Israel's idol making, the command to love could easily be lost upon her. She could easily be more comfortable with her old gods, with her old ways, her old thoughts, with the life of her ancestors. To love Him as the One He truly is was no readily obeyed command, not for the 'stiff-necked,' 'high-handed,' 'murmuring' People of God. Perhaps even today, with all our definitions of love, we still do not know the significance of this command to love. When we read the 'Song of Moses' at the conclusion of his exhortation to the new generation at Moab, when we hear sung the deep and profound determination of this One in the nature of covenant renewal of this love, we clearly hear that the great Prophet's most forward look at a disobedience for which the Lord God alone in His Name must atone with His Elect People. To realize the consummation of this command to love will not be actualized without His atoning work. In this sense, the Law of Moses is the great prophecy of the Name. Every doctrine of love is rooted in the ground signified by what is in this Name. In this Name lives the source of all that is truly solid and concrete and holy of the love the Lord God commands His People in His Creation. It is this renewal of the BCR that makes the Prophet the Leader he is in Israel's history among the nations.

The secret that belongs to this Name may be heard and seen and remembered by the reader of the Book of Deuteronomy. The Divine Freedom to renew the BCR at Moab is expressed with words faithful to the free will and love of its commands. To gain some understanding of the love commanded in this Name, it is helpful to look at the use of names of the Lord God employed with these words of Moses for Israel. I think of the words in Deuteronomy 4:1–43 as the heart and soul of the relationship being renewed with the new generation. There we read the use of two names of the Lord God that vitally show us who He is in His BCR at Moab. Deuteronomy 4:1–24 is bound up with the Name as the '*El_Qanah* (often translated 'a jealous God'—in 4:24) in the relationship. In 4:25–40, the Name is named '*El_Rachum* (often translated as 'a merciful God'—in 4:31). We read the name '*El_Qanah* in the context of the Ten Words at Sinai (Exodus 20:4–6). We also read its cognate with Israel's Wisdom Tradition (Proverbs 8:22). The second name belongs to the 'Little Credo' of the Great I-AM (Exodus 34:6). '*El_Rachum*, we recall, is the first term of the Lord God with His Self-Definition for His 'stiff-necked' Chosen People. With an appreciation for the meaning of these names, we gain an understanding of what actually is in this Name—*Yahweh Elohim*—this Great I-AM who is the One He is in His covenanted relationship with His People among the nations in His Creation. These names signify two vital aspects of His freedom to be who He is in the nature of His interaction with Israel in the world. The secret of His covenant renewal of the new generation at Moab is in these names. What Israel must hear and see and remember with these names of the Name is vital for her future. Israel's future will know what it is that these names mean for her time and times with this One Lord God.

The name '*El-Qanah* with its resonance from the Exodus Torah (Exodus 20:4–6) and from the Wisdom of God's Word with Israel (Proverbs 8:22ff) refers to the Redeemer-Creator this One Lord God is. The Ten Words of the instruction Moses has delivered to Israel are to be remembered because He is '*El-Qanah*, the jealous or the zealous God in His Covenant with His People. He is to be known and loved without images and image-making. Because He is this Lord God, this Redeemer-Creator, '*El-Qanah* is to be heard with His Wisdom, action that binds His People among the nations in His Creation to His transcendence and His immanence with the tribes. There is no time or times when this Wisdom is not significant for Israel's knowledge of her Lord and God in her history with Him. Moses invokes the memory of Baal-Peor in this text (Numbers 25:1–5), when the Lord God smashed the idols of the Baalim and punished Israel's sexual immorality with Moabite women and His People's willingness to worship their idols. Moses reminds Israel that this is a sure way to bring down upon themselves the Curse of the Lord God in His Covenant with His People. The Lord God is a 'zealous' Lord and God, who will not be without what belongs to Him. He is a 'jealous' Lord and God, who will not pretend He is some other god than the One He is. He will prove to be this passionate One with what belongs to Him, with Israel, His People in His Creation. What belongs to Him cannot belong to another. He owns what He has made. He does not abandon what He has made. He sustains what He has made. His passion for Israel shall not fail in His BCR. He will never utterly forsake His People. He will not be without Israel, even if He punishes her, in His Creation. She belongs to Him.

The root '*Qanah*' is employed as a verb in Proverbs 8:22, where it signifies an action Yahweh takes with Himself even before He created His Creation, before the heavens and the earth are what they are, before man is what he is. It would refer us to an action that belongs to who He is in His Eternity. It would refer us to the secret Wisdom with which His Being in His Divine Freedom exercised His decision to become the Creator He is and to make with Her His Creation. The Creation is a reality made not without the Wisdom the Creator is. She is with Him 'begotten' in Eternity before the foundations of the heavens and the earth are laid down. The Creation is thus in its nature utterly dependent upon her. Wisdom and Divine Freedom are married in His Being and Becoming even the Creator He is. To *qanah* His Creation must mean for us an action that transcends anything that can be done, when the Creation must be understood as possessing immanent relations with the One He is. It would refer the reader to an utterly Divine Act of the Divine Being and Nature of God with His Wisdom. It is this Divine Freedom in Divine Action that must explain the existence of the Creation. Because of this Act, the Lord God with His Wisdom may be understood as the origin of all that is created reality. With His Wisdom, He *qanah*-ed, even before *the* Beginning, as the Creator He has chosen to become, the Creation that is what it is because of who He is. We cannot love this One without knowing the passionate power of His Being to be present and known in Israel as the One He is, transcendent over, immanent within, self-giving with His People.

This means that we must understand with the Lord God there exists what we may name 'eternal duration,' an uncreated duration that is echoed or reflected in the significance of created durations, times and times, and that these two durations may be experienced in the space of our times. The action of owning what belongs to Him in this relationship between *Yahweh Elohim* and His Creation must be considered as even more real than the reality of the world as the Creation of the Great I-AM. He Himself is the source of the meaning of the name '*El-Qanah*, a jealous God or a zealous Lord who will not be who He is without what He has made. It signifies in this way something that at once belongs to the nature of God's Being in Himself in His Eternity and the nature of His Freedom to Act with Himself in order to choose to become the Creator and as such to cause to exist what He is not. What He is not cannot possibly exist without Him. The Creation is a world that cannot subsist without Him with His Wisdom. '*El-Qanah* means that just as He will not be without Himself, He will not be without His People with His Wisdom. With His Divine Freedom, He possesses a covenanted relationship with His Creation and His People, and in this relationship His People must know that She is His Wisdom, Lady Wisdom against the woman of folly with the world. Israel is to know Him for who He truly is with His Wisdom. All idols and idol making is the prostitution of her. All the gods and myths of the ancient world are deaf and dumb to this 'zealous' or 'jealous' One. This Only and Incomparable One whose passion for what He has made exists with this Divine Wisdom, lifts us the reader of these words into the God of Eternity. We cannot believe we know Him for who He truly is without this knowledge. Mankind alienated from the Great I-AM He is does not exist.

The name '*El-Rachum* may be heard referring to the 'Little Credo' of the Great I-AM the Lord God is in the beginning of the formation of the People of God delivered from Egypt. It signifies His Self-Defining freedom with His People as that One who is the God of *the* Beginning and all other real beginnings. He is the Self-Giving Lord God in His BCR with Israel, even as this One Lord and God. We have studied in Exodus 34:6, in the context of the incident of the Golden Calf, that Israel faced His Presence with 'stiff-necked' preference for the Idol. She sought with her idol making to contradict the One He is. The Name of the Lord God in His Divine Perfections in such beginnings is to be known in her call to be the Israel of His Promise in the world. Now with this renewal of Moab, the 'compassion' He possessed for her in her beginning with Him is to be understood as the same compassion for her subsistence and renewal. Here with this new generation then, Moses confesses that the day will come when Israel, even scattered in punishment throughout the nations, will come to the day of her repentance, when her taste for idols and idol making will have ended, when the gods of the nations and their myths about the world shall no more exist in the Creation. She will know, because He is the Lord God He is as the One who is who He is in these names, *'El-Qanah* and *'El-Rachum*, active in His BCR with His People in the world. Moses' confession knows that Israel's Creator is *the Elohim* whose passion will not fail to fulfill His Promise in His Relationship with her. His passion is holy and shall not fail. This is the prophecy whose argument steadily and compellingly shapes the thrust of the exhortation with the People of God. *'You were given to see these things to know that* **Yahweh is the Elohim** *and there is nothing without Him'* (Deuteronomy 4:35). *'You will know in that day, when you turn with all your heart that* **Yahweh is the Elohim** *in the heavens above the earth, and there is no one like Him'* (Deuteronomy 4:39). Here is the heart of the self-defining and giving command of the One with His perfections in His covenanted relationship as the Lord God with Israel's new generation at Moab. No divorce is possible from this passion. Prefer idols as she may, she will repent before Him and His Day with her. The command of this Redeemer-Creator shall never fail. There is no possibility then of divorcing with this Only and Incomparable One His Creation from His Redemption. When we hear Israel's great *Shema'* sung in the synagogues, even today, we must hear the passion of this Holy One. His will commands us still, who are His People in His Creation. It is this One, whose passion and compassion for His People shapes and forms the substance and content with these words of history, prophecy, and the apocalypse of His Name in Moses' confession, that determines for us the Glory of His goal for our race in the world.

'These are the words' of the Lord our God, the Lord who is known as this Creator in the name of this Only One—the *'echad*—of the Name with Moses' confession at Moab. Here is the Great I-AM of her Exodus Tradition made concrete by His Love for her in His covenanted relationship with her. Here is the Only Unique One. Here is the Incomparable One. Here is the One who has chosen to be here and not somewhere else. Here is the One who acts with Himself to make Himself present with Israel at this time in His Name. Here is the truly free One, who is free to set down a holy place in the space of His Creation, who is free to appoint

holy times in the time of His Creation, so that His Name is among His People in His Creation. Here is the One who is free to call His People to come at appointed times to chosen places and do what is right (*the Yashar*) in His Eyes. The new generation at Moab must hear this One. The new generation must hear this One for who He truly is with them. This new generation must hear this One in His Divine Freedom to be with them in this chosen place and at these chosen times, where they might become His People truly. This is the way of His Blessing. This is the way of His Covenanted Blessing for Israel among the nations in His Creation. '*These are the words*' we must hear with Israel.

This One is the Redeemer-Creator of Israel. This One is the Creator of the heavens and the earth. This One is the Lord God of the entire world. This Unique and Only One is the One who Himself in His Divine Freedom is the One who speaks with His People in His Creation. The way to put it is this: The Creation without the *'echad* is mythology; the *'echad* without the Creation is an idol. The pathologies and mythologies of the idols and idol makers of the world shall not prevail. This Only One reigns over all that is created reality and His People. Though the phantoms of idols by their legions may inhabit the world with their dreams and aberrations, these delusions shall not triumph over this One. Israel must bear the significance of this One in the world. Israel must hear this Lord and this God, this Great I-AM as this Only One, who is who He is freely acting with Himself in His Covenant for His People in His Creation. This is the *'echad* that Israel with all that she is must learn to love. This is the Lord God who is the Wisdom and Care that shapes secretly and solidly the beginnings and endings of time and times—past, present, and future of Israel—with her God in this world. With His Divine Freedom, she is bound to realize that, because He makes time for Himself with her in His Creation, she is who she is among the nations. It is this One that gives prophetic muscle to the last will and testament of Moses with Israel at Moab, a universal muscle.

'*These are the words*' with which Moses exhorts Israel's new generation about to enter the Promised Land. In three speeches, chapters 1–4; 5–28; and 29–30, the renewal of the covenanted relationship commands the preparations of the tribes for entry into Canaan. Chapters 31–34 form then, a ratification once again of this covenanted relationship between Israel and the Lord God. It is this exhortation that is passed from Moses onto Joshua, his assistant in the Exodus and the Wilderness. Moses' Song (chapter 32) celebrates the renewal of the Blessing and Death inherent in this Covenant with the Redeemer-Creator. These speeches do not merely repeat the commands at Sinai, but they shape a passionate effort to move the new generation beyond the 'stiff-necked,' 'high-handed,' and 'murmuring' condition of her past opposition to Him, explained by her primordial past in Adam and her ancestral past in Abraham and his sons, into a new life in the new Land. Here Israel is to resolve anew in the place where He has chosen to set His Name to go and do what is right (*the Yashar*) in His Eyes. But this song's celebration knows well the failures in time past and the spell under which Israel shall fall in her future with Him. It is a question of centeredness. To be centered in Him in the space and time of His choosing removes His People from their self-centered interests in Him (Remember the boundaries of His Holy Love are well defined in His Command!) The question of self-centeredness is to be answered in Israel's history with Him. It is with this knowledge that Moses can sing his song over Israel's destiny. She is the Israel of the Divine Freedom of the Great I-AM the Lord God is as the Creator and Redeemer of the world. She can be no other just as He can be no other.

The confession tells us that Moses sang this Song in its entirety for the new generation. These are the words the new generation must hear as the prophecy of the Lord God for their life in the Land. We read its holy passion for Israel in Deuteronomy 32, as a thanksgiving celebration that understands the Only One, the Unique One, the Great I-AM the Lord God has become as Israel's Redeemer-Creator, shall prevail over His enemies. In this song, He is the Rock. In this song, the *'echad* that commands Israel's love is the Rock of the destiny of her life in the Land (32:4, 15, 18, 30, and 31). If we do not allow the Song's use of the names of the Lord God to escape our attention, we may gain a great insight into the nature of the renewal of the covenanted relationship that has been posited freely between Himself and His People. This nature possesses a significance that is envisioned with prophetic power in Israel's history. He is Himself the Only Unique One who is, in His covenanted relationship with Israel among the nations in His Creation, the *'echad* that is both the Great I-AM and the Rock for His People in His Creation. There is nothing more solid to celebrate in this world than the Being of this Stone with Israel.

Moses' Song begins with an invocation of the heavens and the earth (32:1–3): '*Listen, O heavens, for I am speaking; Hear, O earth, to the speaking of my mouth: Let what I know fall like the rain; let it descend like the dew—my speaking, like showers upon the green grass and the abundant mists upon the tender plants, for upon the Name of Yahweh I will call, ascribe greatness to our Elohim—* **the Rock**—*O perfection is His work and all of His ways are justice He is 'El-Emunah, without shamefulness; Righteous and Uprightness is He!'* The Song culminates with this ringing exhortation: '*Sing, O nations, with His People, for the blood of His servants shall be raised; vengeance shall turn upon the besiegers, atonement for His Land and His People.*' With the Divine Freedom of the Great I-AM the Lord God in His atoning act in His Covenant with His People in His Creation, the righteous fulfillment of His Promise to Israel shall be realized, in spite of Israel's rebellion against Him. He will be victorious over all of His enemies!

To hear the thrust of this song, its celebration of the Name, and the Being of the Rock, is to see the Divine Freedom and Faithfulness or Majestic Truth of Israel's Lord and God in the world. The *'El-'Emunah—* 'the God of faithfulness' is the *'Emet* the Great I-AM as proclaimed in His 'Little Credo.' With Moses' song we hear and see the Great I-AM defining His victory over all that would oppose Him in His Creation. The Creation itself is called to bear witness to this Speaking One. The heavens and the earth as all that is created reality shall see and hear of the victory of the Rock that He is with His People in His Creation. Even the great eighth century prophet, Isaiah of Jerusalem, knows well the speaking of this Lord and God. The vision of his prophecy also invokes in its beginning the witness of the Creation: '*Hear, O heavens, and give ear, O earth, for the Lord is speaking*' (Isaiah 1:2a), when Israel is invited to walk in the Light that hears the Word of God of Isaiah's Vision.

Scholars can hear in these calls a form whose context belongs to the culture of Israel's ancient society. The lawsuits conducted in the city gates by the elders of the towns are common customs with the jurisprudence in ancient Israel. The prophets have simply taken over these forms and given a prophetic meaning to their significance, where *Yahweh-Elohim* is pictured as bringing His Case against His People before God with the heavens and the earth as witnesses. It is these lawsuits adopted for prophetic use by the prophetic understanding of the covenant between *Yahweh* and Israel's history. It is case law employed against the People of God. It accuses Israel of breaking covenant with her Lord and God. Creation itself bears witness to the offenses. This prophetic lawsuit is thought to be fundamental to the prophetic movement envisioned in Israel. Across centuries of time her faith is tried by these accusations, and she is punished accordingly. Israel's redemption cannot be divorced from this Creation; Creation itself cannot be divorced from Israel's redemption. This is the Word the prophets envisioned. This is the speaking of the Lord God in the Biblical World. The Creation bears witness to what Israel must hear—the Truth and Grace of the Speaking Lord God. The poetry of Moses' Song is not then to be read merely as metaphorical language, language that can exist without real correspondence to the actualities of the Song's heavens and the Song's earth and the Speaking of its God. Unless we can make this point clearly and solidly, we shall not hear *Shema'*, the intention and purpose of the *'echad* the Great I-AM is as Israel's Rock and Lord and God and the Only Unique One who shall determine truly the destiny of His People in His Creation.

The Song accuses the People of God of corruption (32:5), asks the rhetorical question *'Is He not your Father, your Qanah, the One who made and established you?'* The crookedness of the generations is as sure a thing with Moses as his knowledge of the Fatherhood of the Rock. It is with the wisdom of this knowledge that Moses can rehearse the primordial and ancestral past of His People, remember the Exodus and the Wilderness, and accuse Israel of opposing with her own foolishness the Rock He is, of abandoning and forgetting Him who is the God of all beginnings, of Israel's very Beginning (32:7–18). His accusation is made with a finality that is appreciated with stunning poetic force. The Song is language to be remembered by all generations.

With His profound grief, Yahweh proclaims how He will deal (32:19–27) with His People as His Enemy. He will with the Blessing of His Presence (Numbers 6) reverse the punishment of His sons and daughters, who would turn Him into the *'No-god,'* and He will endure them and bring them to Himself as *'My People.'* He who judges them to be *'Not-a-people,'* who will punish and scatter them, who will exile them from the Land, who will curse with the wrath of His Wisdom His enemies, all those who oppose Him as the One that He is, will reverse in His Name their fortunes in the world. If Israel in opposition to the Great I-AM is cursed, Israel in union and communion with Him shall be blessed. (The Wisdom of the Prophecy, as we shall see, is to be especially apprehended in the eighth century of the prophet Hosea!) The Lord God will be known as the Only One He truly is—the Rock—this Rock that hates evil and punishes all that is evil among the nations, that brings down calamity and desolation upon those who hate Him (32:28–38), this Only One, this Rock shall gain His victory with His People among the nations.

In Deuteronomy 32:39–40, we hear the Great I-AM speaking: '*Look now, for I, I am He, and there is no Elohim beside me. I, kill and I make alive! I have wounded and I will heal, and no one can escape from My Hand, for I lift up to the heavens My Hand and I say* "*Life—I am forever*."' This is the Rock who is the Only and Incomparable One that, as Lord and God of Israel among the nations, will act in time to atone for His Land and His People. His Promise, He shall keep. The Song of Moses is remembered in Israel's history for these reasons. Its meanings resound again and again throughout the times of the People of God, time past, time present, time future, in her covenant with her Redeemer and the Creator. Does Moses know with this Song that His People will go into the Land and do something else besides what the Lord God had commanded Israel? Does he not know the 'stiff-necked,' 'high-handed,' and 'murmuring' generations, rooted in a primordial and ancestral past that we have come to name the Fallen World? What is to come? Surely, it is this Rock, who even by a 'self-centered' people will not be defeated. From this Rock comes the 'Blood of the Covenant.'

The Song is followed by a rehearsal of the Blessing of the Lord God. Moses' death is recorded with the assurances of this Blessing. From the great *Shema'*, with the boundaries of His Holy Love well defined, the Festivals of the Tabernacle well in place and times, the Levitical Blessing is taken with these words to establish the last will and testament of the great Prophet and Mediator of Israel's destiny in the world. Moses is buried outside of the Land, but with the Blessing of the Promise written in his heart. With the heart of this Prophet, the hope that belongs to the secrets of the Lord God in His Divine Freedom to act for the sake of His People, His 'self-centered' People, with His Holy and Atoning Love lives in the Land, where Abel's blood and Joseph's dreams live on. We do well not to allow this love to escape our attention. It is a love that embraces all time and times and meaning of time with the Lord God. It is in the Name of this Great I-AM that we may hear his Song. Because of it, I can insist with my many students that we can get blood from a rock—we do get blood from Israel's Rock! With the atoning love of this Lord God, all Israel among the nations has to do! Space and time have been made in which the Great I-AM, in the Light and Word He is with Israel, provided the blood that offers for the whole world redemption and reconciliation from sin and life with this Lord and God. It is this love that is the holy love with which we shall learn to love our Redeemer and Creator.

With the Divine Freedom of this Lord and God in His Self-Revelation and His Name, we are given Moses' prophecy for the People of God. With this Mediator, He has defined Himself for His People. From the Exodus Tradition of the Creator of the heavens and the earth, all mankind is to hear Him and to learn to love Him. He is in *the Beginning* and He will be in what is to come who He truly is with His People. To not hear Him is to forsake the prophecy, deny the meaning of His Divine Freedom to be with Israel and to make Mankind in His Image, after His Likeness. It is to deny the faith of Abraham and the faithfulness of the Great I-AM in His Covenant with His People in His Creation. For we have read a confession the power of which continues to compel the race upon this prodigal planet, continues to sing the *Shema'* and the Song among the nations. It is an imperative whose hope is rooted in the very Nature and Being of the Lord God Himself. It is the only ground upon which the speaking of the Great I-AM He is may be heard. Here Eternity in His Freedom has made and will continue to make Himself present and known in the world. As the People of God, Israel's hope is rooted in this ground.

It is with this that Israel as the People of God enters the Land to develop a nation of tribes that will form what we know as the Monarchy of God. This Monarchy shapes under the reign of the King the Great I-AM is the People of God for the Kingdom of God. Thus, Israel is made to give to the nations of the world a Messianic Hope, a hope that belongs to Moses buried outside of the Promised Land also to the Self-Revealing, Self-Naming, Self-Defining, Self-Giving Rock who is Moses' Lord and God. It is between them that the Great I-AM possesses the secret of His Promise. We must not go deaf to hearing this One. We must listen to this Only One speaking also in our world, speaking with His Freedom to our freedoms, speaking with His Voice among the many voices that are seeking from time to time our attention. Because of this Voice, the Torah of Israel, Moses' Five Books, the Pentateuch possess a Majestic Grace and Truth we must learn to hear. To seek to interpret these texts and the history of these texts without this Voice is to seek to replace His Revelation with our own imaginations, to subject ourselves to the abstract and romantic idealism that even now plague our world. It is to remain centered in ourselves, in our self-wills, unable to go to the place where He has set His Name to do what is right in His Eyes. It is to live without real hope in this world.

The Great AMEN of the Great I-AM

To overcome our tendency towards self-centeredness does not lie within our powers. Our lives are imprisoned in self-will. No one can escape with a will their will. We need to be delivered just as Israel was once delivered from her affliction under the Pharaoh. The Name of the Great I-AM *('Ehyeh)* must possess for us a significance that cannot be torn out of the actual Being and Nature of the One True God Himself. He is the Redeemer-Creator with whom we have to do and who we must hear if we are to love as we ought to love. It is the hope in this love that belongs to the Divine Freedom of the Transcendent and Immanent One in our times, our time past, our time present, and our time future by which we live. This is the secret of the nature of the covenanted relationship between God, the world, and its peoples.

Moses' confession has become for the world the Five Books of Moses (Torah). It belongs to a Canonical Tradition around which Israel still gathers for her witness to her Lord and God. It belongs to her TANAKH, what is well known as the Old Testament, Israel's Moses, Israel's Prophecies, and Israel's Writings in the history of the world. It is the Canon of the Old Covenant. It is a book, but as this book—the Book— because of its witness to the Voice of the Great I-AM, we may read in these 'Holy Scriptures' Israel's sinful history in covenant with her Lord and God, but we must also read the great hope she teaches with her life on the earth. Throughout all time and times the People of God have found more than trouble enough, but all the troubles of Israel are to be understood in the light of this Voice. He is the Great I-AM. He is the Lord God. He is the Only One. He is the Rock of Israel for all time. Out of this Rock comes the blood of the BCR the Creator has established as the Redeemer of His People in His Creation. His atoning love is central and vital to the secret of the nature of His BCR with His People and His Creation. Both Eternity and space-time are bound up freely with Him in this way of His Blood.

Heart

6

The Great I-AM of the Kingdom of God

*. . . establish for us a king to rule us,
like all the nations have!*

1 Samuel 8:5b

JOSHUA INHERITS THE AUTHORITY of Moses, the Servant of God, and the Exodus of Israel from Egypt. He is the anointed successor of the Torah of Moses and the command to direct the People of God as Israel enters into the Promised Land. He is the prophet's choice to lead the tribes of Israel's new generation into their occupation of Canaan. He is as this Servant's successor the new holy warrior and keeper of the Torah for the history of Israel among the nations.

As this man, he calls the officers of Israel to Shechem, a place well known to their ancestors. What Sinai was to Moses, Shechem is to Joshua. At Shechem, the anointed servant seeks to continue the renewal of the covenanted relationship that marks with the new generation out of Egypt the history of the tribes of Israel in the Promised Land. But in this Land, Israel will be unable to joy in the Blessing of the BCR. She proves unable to obey the Command of her Lord and God, just as once the old generation was unable to obey in the Wilderness. Moses' Song must be always on the mind of Joshua. The Command of the Great I-AM, unheard, compels that deaf condition of the tribes of Israel in which the call for King Yahweh over their life in the Land becomes lost upon them. Like the kings who lead the other nations in the world, Israel in the Land will bring down upon herself not the Blessing but the Curse of the Lord God in His BCR with her. From Gilgal to Shiloh to Shechem, the sacred spaces and times of Yahweh's choice for His Name with the tribes of Israel are forsaken. From the occupation to the tribal allotments under Joshua, a history is recorded that requires the renewal of the BCR. It is upon this kind of ground on

The Great I-AM of the Kingdom of God

which the movement of Israel's cry for a king like the kings that surround her in the Land occurs. Israel's Monarchy is raised up on this ground, in times such as these, when she flourishes for a time, and then finally falls from the Grace of her Redeemer-Creator and the Living God. This history is recorded as Israel's Canon with the Prophets, the Former and Latter Prophets. The Former Prophets recount this history from the entrance of Israel's tribes as the People of God into the Promised Land and to the Exile of their monarchies, North and South, from the Land. The Prophecy accounts for the rise and fall of Israel's Monarchy, the history of kings Saul, David, and Solomon, of the split kingdoms, and their subsequent destruction, first the Northern Kingdom known as Israel to the Assyrians and then the Southern Kingdom known as Judah to the Babylonians. The rise and fall of the kingdoms and the promise of God with His BCR with the People of God is also told by the Latter Prophets, the writing prophets, beginning in the eighth century. It is this history from which is formed the great Prophecy and Messianic Vision that would turn, beyond the Curse upon her, the eyes of Israel towards their Lord God, to the Great I-AM of the Prophecy. Together, the Former and the Latter Prophets of Israel's Canon shape a history in the world whose Vision of the Word of God belongs to the call of Moses and Joshua for Israel in the history of the Creation of the Great I-AM He is.

Under Joshua's inherited leadership, the tribes in Canaan experience trouble after trouble with their neighbors, with their enemies. It is impossible for Israel to fight and occupy the Land according to the command of the Lord God. The Holy and Only One appears to command what is not possible. Right from the start of the occupation, His demands are only always partially met. The relationship with the Lord God remains steadily questionable. From the resolve of Joshua and then throughout the periods of the Judges, again and again great trouble comes upon Israel, the People of God, and their unwillingness to hear the command of the Voice who spoke with Moses and speaks with Joshua. Thus, the tribes are unable to live in the Land under His Promised Blessing. They live in His BCR more cursed in the Land than blessed. Appointed times at chosen places for the tabernacle, where they are to go to do what is right in His Eyes, according to His Command with Moses, appear to be beyond their hearing. They are unable to do the right thing in His Presence with them.

Soon enough we read that their dialogue with their Lord and God becomes quite broken down. Soon enough, perhaps with some wondrously real dismay, we read that the tribes ignore this Command of them and profane His Name in the Land. Doing what is right in His Eyes, *the Yashar,* is ignored. Instead we read: *'In those days, there was no king in Israel; each one—the Yashar—in his own eyes—he would do!'* Soon enough, the 'Eyes of God' would mean nothing in the eyes of the tribes of the new generation. Soon enough, they proved as 'self-centered' as the old generation had proven 'stiff-necked, high-handed, and complaining.' Soon enough, Israel experiences a terrible degradation of their lives in the Land. Ruin and desolation grows instead of fruitfulness and prosperity. In the Land, the tribes dry up and wither away like the grass of the fields. In spite of the passionate struggles of the I-AM the Lord God is with them, in spite of all their troubles in the Land with their enemies and with themselves, this generation cannot escape its self-imprisoned will, its self-centeredness, against the center He has chosen for them in the Land. Rather than become centered on His Chosen Places and Appointed Times, they will to bring down upon themselves His Curse rather than His Blessing in His BCR with them. Like Moses' command, Joshua's leadership does not bring the Blessing to the People of God. The victories of their enemies prevail instead. Their ruin is determined. They will do what is right in their own eyes.

It is not as if Joshua and the Judges of Israel do not know the deliverance of the Lord God from their sin against God. They know it over and over again. They are raised up from the curse of death and dying to life in the Land with a mysterious freedom that belongs to the One who is with them. They are given to defeat the defeats of their enemies time and time again. In the mystery of the freedom of the Lord God with them, they experience time after time the promised blessing of their tribes in the Promised Land. Israel is freed from certain destructions under the Blessing, one trouble after another. Their Judges appear as chosen leaders and anointed deliverers who save the tribes from their deafness, from their self-centered unwillingness to hear the Command of the Lord God. These deliverers would honor their Lord and God as the King of the Creation among the peoples of the world. They would see the heavens and the earth as the work of His hands. They would with the Elect work the works of His Word for them. They are messengers of the Word of the Lord. They would seek the faithfulness of His People in Canaan. They struggle mightily to deliver the tribes from their punishment with their enemies, their troubles in the Land. Steadily, they would seek to renew the People of God in their BCR with the Great I-AM King Yahweh is for them. The books of Joshua and Judges record these fierce struggles. They tell the tales of God's passionate will to be with Israel. But they also show the slow and steady and sure degradation of Israel's hopes in the Land. In covenanted relationship with Him, His People, the tribes of Israel, will not escape these troubles. They, with themselves, will continue to seek to do what is right in their own eyes rather than to go to do *the Yashar* in the Eyes of their Lord and God in His sacred space and time. Their stories take us to face again and again the profound desolation, the terrible primordial cries of their troubles, their need for deliverance, and finally to see their perception of this need as the need for another king than the King Yahweh is as their Lord and God. Throughout these tales, we are reading both the Grace of the Lord God in the Land with them and their willingness to make nothing of this Grace with them. Thus, the tribes set the stage in this history for the developments that are recorded in the Books of Samuel and Kings.

This is the ground from which is raised up King Saul, then David, and then Solomon. From Solomon's kingdom comes the history of the split Monarchy, Israel and Judah, whose falls lead all Israel to her Exile from the Land. Far from the Blessing in the Land, the People of God become dispersed throughout the nations that surround them. While Israel is steadily possessed by the Promise of His Grace in the Land, even in the form of her kingdoms, she just as steadily grows more and more wicked, until in 722 the Northern Kingdom is defeated by the Assyrian armies and in 586 the Southern Kingdom is defeated by Babylonian armies. The Command is steadily lost, North and South among the tribes, upon the ears of the People of God. Israel brings down upon herself His punishment of His Curse and not His Blessing, and she is sent into her Exile from the Land. The rise and fall of Israel's Monarchy then is told the reader with the relentless confession that her kings are willing to do what is evil in the Eyes of God, rather than what is 'Right,' until at last the Lord God would seek to rest the Land from the life of the People of God upon it. Israel proves herself a faithless People of her Lord and God. She lives in the Land under the Promised Blessing unfaithful to the Command of the Lord God who brought her from Egypt to Canaan. With this history, we are shown that the nature of the BCR with His People in His Creation possesses freedom both with the dimensions of God's Grace in space and time as well as the freedom of those He will judge in the Land. The Prophecy reads that, in spite of these judgments and their punishments, the promise with His compassion and grace for His People remains. He will be faithful to a faithless People. He shall find the time when at last He will call His People '*My People.*' These are the times of the development of the Messianic Hope, the Prophecy that envisions the Lord God of Israel among the nations blessed in His Creation. This Prophecy belongs to words that are possessed with the meaning of these mysterious freedoms with which God has chosen to be faithful with His Elect People as His Witness in the world to who He truly is even among the nations.

The Former and Latter Prophets, the Books Joshua through Kings in the Hebrew Canon, narrate then a history whose events are very much bound up with the nature of the BCR. Across some eight centuries of their experience (1250–586), the People of God in the Promised Land must learn of the Lord God's freedom and faithfulness in the relationship. Because of the Promise, just as Abraham and his sons, with the ancestral promise in the BCR, must be delivered from Egypt, Israel must be delivered from Babylon. The history of the transition from Joshua and the Judges to the rise, formation, and fall of Israel's Monarchy is written with the significance of the Great Promise of the Great I-AM the Lord God is in His BCR with His People. The fall of the kings in the BCR shapes the dark dimension of the stories. The ultimate triumph of the Lord God with His People in the Latter Days forms the bright dimension of them. This history is prophetic history. It is told as a confession whose theological thrust belongs to the nature of the BCR between the Redeemer-Creator and the People of God, to Abraham, to Moses, and the Kingdom. In these stories we read the development of the Messianic Hope of Israel as the People of God, even with her disbelief and unfaithfulness. It is the Vision whose Word is no others than God's, than the Lord's Himself. It is a Vision the Promise of which shall be kept by God Himself. With these stories, we are to see and hear Him acting, even as He acted in *the* Beginning, with a Divine Freedom, with the mystery of which belongs to all those He calls to Himself, upon whom His Word comes, to command them to an obedience alien to the drift of the nations and its various monarchies. Israel's Messianic Hope is developed with prophetic power in her history. The prophets of Israel bring to bear in time and time the Word of the Lord that proclaims the Divine purpose for His People among the nations. It is a Word that commands without the vanity of the world's experience in a fallen Creation. The Day of the Lord will come when all that has been said shall be fulfilled. He shall call His People '*My People.*' His People shall surely name Him '*Our God*.' The BCR will realize the purpose and intentions of the Glory of Her Lord and God among the nations. It is a Vision of that Day when He, the Great I-AM He is, will reign as King, King of His People and King of the Creation, Priest, Prophet, and Sage of the House of David over the entire world. The failure of the monarchies in the eyes of the prophets is never the last word on Israel's existence in this world. The Word of God that has come upon them shall not fail to realize and actualize who He is in His BCR with Israel in His Creation.

Israel's refusals in her renewal traditions are never to be the last word on His Covenant with His People then. *Yahweh Elohim Himself* will have the last Word on His BCR in the world. The written forms of Israel's Prophecy foresee the triumph of His Promise in the Land. They hear of His Victory over His People among the nations in His Creation. They tell that this promise will be kept. It has not been posited in the world in vain. What is to come true is the Word of *Yahweh Elohim* with Israel among the nations in the Creation. In spite of all and every refusal, what the Great I-AM has to say in time and times will determine the meaning of time in the Creation. This prophecy written down on papyrus is for this purpose, that all might know Him for who He truly is in the world. The Voice of this Prophecy will have its way. It is the Voice of the Great I-AM who is the Lord God of Israel and the Creation. It is the Voice of the Only and Incomparable One. It is the Voice of the Holy One with His holy passion and prophetic powers as the One who will not be denied. It is the Voice of the One who will make both space and time an event for His Self-Revealing, Self-Naming, Self-Defining, and Self-Giving in His BCR for His People in His Creation. It is this Voice that will be known for who He is as the Great I-AM He is. To His Presence, Israel has been called to go and there learn to do the *Yashar* in His Eyes.

We will gain insight into this renewal tradition by looking at some specifically vital events in the history of Israel's tribes in the Land. At Shechem, where Joshua has called the leaders of Israel's new generation to come and renew their role in His BCR, we may listen in on a renewal ceremony. Joshua 24 records such a covenant renewal ceremony. It tells of the gathering of Israel at Shechem where Joshua sought for the tribes of Israel a renewed commitment to their witness to the acts and purpose of Israel's Lord and God in the BCR in the Land. Shechem is the place where, through Joshua, the Lord God has chosen to set His Name. This is the place where His People might come and do the *Yashar* in His Presence. Again, Shechem becomes for Joshua what Sinai had been to Moses.

Joshua's choice of Shechem would honor the way that this place is marked with the meaning of Israel's ancestral history (Genesis 12:6–7; 33:19; 35:2–4). It belongs to a history that speaks of the Presence of the Lord God in times past, that the present may remember. Thus, time past as well as time present, for the sake of time future, is rehearsed at this time in this sacred place. Scholars may question the relationship of the texts to any actual history they seem to find with the world, but this tradition establishes an event that can be compared in its form and content to other events common to the fourteenth century BCE. Joshua 24 belongs to such an event. The chapter may be thus compared to Hittite Treaty forms, found written on clay tablets dated around 1300 BC. The tablets contain the records of relations arranged between kings and their peoples, perhaps made commonly throughout the Ancient Near East. Scholars can compare these forms and their contents of such treaty making to the renewal of the covenanted relationship at Shechem:

> *Preamble—honoring the king*
> *Past History Rehearsed—honoring the king*
> *Declarations—honoring the king*
> *Definitions—honoring the king*
> *Invocation—honoring the king*
> *Curses and Blessings—honoring the king and his gods*

Joshua 24 is then compared to such treaty making, meant now to honor King Yahweh:

> *Preamble—Victories of Divine Election rehearsed in times past*
> *Time Past—Threats issued once more against idols and idol making*
> *Time Present—Celebration of the Wondrous Sovereignty of the Lord God in time, and stipulations about the boundaries in His Land*
> *Time Future—Exhortation against idolatry in time future*
> *Final Ratification—Renewal's continuities in history, with preparations for the future and the Divine Blessing*

However similar the patterns may be, the nature of the BCR is far different than this ancient treaty making. Whereas the treaties among the ancients would honor a one-way relationship between kings and peoples, Israel definitely would produce a two-way street, a real dialogue, between the King and His People. The Hittite Treaty, for example, possesses an imperative that the peoples understand their obligations as in a contract obligation to the royal authority of their king, an absolute authority ready to punish disobedience absolutely. To disobey was to invoke immediate royal punishment on one's existence. The covenant renewal tradition, on the other hand, is filled at all times with a mysterious freedom, in which the nature of the relationship bears both the freedom of Divine Authority and the authority of Divine Freedom for His People, a people whose freedom is meant to signify His free authority and authoritative freedom to be with them in the relationship. The ratification of the BCR demands obedience, but the punishment is ministered with the mystery of the freedoms meant to realize an ultimate freedom for the peoples. Thus, renewal is always implied and must be explicated in the nature of the relationship. It always envisions that the purpose of the Lord God in this relationship and with His dialogues shall be realized in the BCR. Any comparisons must keep this essential difference in mind. However much the recognition of similarities may be observed, we need to penetrate beneath their surface patterns into the actual nature of the relationship. The Hittites may help us appreciate that Israel's BCR was not formed without influence from the cultures that surrounded her. But as the People of God, she is to be taught another kind of relationship than any we may find in times past among the nations. She must come to understand the uniqueness of her Only One in this relationship. Any and all comparisons with the Hittites must be tempered and we must come to understand the uniqueness of the dialogue that has brought to Israel the Promise of the Lord God to her. To refuse to grasp the unique freedoms involved in the nature of the BCR is to deny His very existence, which is too possible to do in Israel's history of herself with Him.

Today, we refer to such comparisons and similarities as entanglement, an interaction that occurs between peoples in intercultural clashes. In the case of the covenant renewal ceremony at Shechem, we may argue that the event of the gathering is recorded as Israel among the nations in the Promised Land for the purpose of a dialogue that would continue the meaning in history of what was begun with Abraham, carried on afresh with Moses, and now with Joshua. It is a record of what does not simply read back into times past the significance of the history of Israel, but it is the way of remembrance, when a moment in time is made to renew with the Lord God His relationship with His People. The antiquity of the Covenant Renewal Ceremony belongs to a tradition that is Israel must remember belongs to the Promise to Abraham (Genesis 12–50) and the Torah of Moses (Exodus 24 and Deuteronomy 32). This remembrance would shape the very basis for the prophetic development of Israel's written and oral traditions, for the form of a literature that will become the Canon of the People of God. Joshua 24 belongs to Joshua's times, to the oral and written traditions of his times, to a canonization of these traditions in his time, a movement that bears witness to a destiny in a future that belongs to the Lord God in time and times and so forth. When we read the various forms of this tradition throughout the Old Testament (Judges 6:1–13; 2 Kings 22–23; Isaiah 1; Jeremiah 32:16–44; Ezekiel 20:4–20; Nehemiah 8–13; 20:4–13; 2 Chronicles 15:12–15, as well as in Psalms 78; 106; 136), we are steadily being compelled to penetrate into the way that the nature of the BCR is experienced in the nature of time and times and time again in this way of God with His People among the nations. The nature of the BCR bears quite movingly with His holy passion and His divine pathos as the Great I-AM He is as the Lord and God of this People. As such, He seeks to embrace His People as '*My People*,' and thus makes time and times serve His purpose and intentions in the history of His Creation. We dare not reduce down this tradition and its memory to some static notion of the nature of this relationship. It possesses always the relational dynamics of two freedoms, divine and human, which we need to recognize and grasp as what has come from the Only One who will not be who He truly is without His People. We may analyze with this thrust of the chapter as follows:

> *24:1   Historical Introduction for the gathering of Israel
>   at Shechem*
> *24:2a   Joshua addresses Israel*
> *24:2b–13 A Dialogue of Times Past and the Victories of
>   God for His People*
> *24:14–18 Ritual of Obedience for Time Present*
> *24:19–24 Test of Loyalty in the Wisdom of God for
>   Time Future*
> *24:25–28 Ritual of Ratification*

Comparison with the Hittites may help us date the antiquity of this form of Joshua 24, but its content transforms the old intentions of kings and peoples and creates, even as the Exodus created, something new in the history of the world. The event belongs to that uniqueness and incomparableness with which the Lord God makes Himself present and to be known in His interaction as the I-AM He is in His relationship with Israel among the nations. We may not allow the similarities to enable us to identify Israel with the nations. She must be seen and understood as the Elect she is. *This* and *that* may appear to be similar, but the one from the other needs to be distinguished, always. We need to employ analogies with wisdom, not with conclusions. We need to seek as steadily as we can to grasp the actual nature of the BCR in the history of Israel among the nations, to apprehend the actual nature of the covenanted interactions of the Lord God with Israel among the nations. The renewals in Israel's history in the world are for the purpose of the Promise in the BCR, and for no other. Israel's history is generated with the prophetic thrust of this relationship. The meaning of the events in Israel's renewals belongs to a freely chosen passion and purpose that cannot be divorced from the Unique and Only Incomparable One the Lord God is with His People in His Creation. The Promise to Abram in Ur, the Promise that entails the Blessing of His Seed in the Land, is not to be heard as an empty promise. The Torah given Moses renews the intent of this Promise. It is a Torah that would instruct and shape Israel as the People of God she must become in dialogue with the Great I-AM her Lord God is. His Self-Revelation, His Self-Naming, His Self-Defining, is for the sake of this Promise in the nature of the BCR with '*My People*.' Nothing of these events in the history of Israel is given meaning and significance by Israel, by Abraham, or by Moses. They belong to the time and times of the Great I-AM with determination in His freedom to be with Himself the Redeemer-Creator He is with Israel. He is thus in His created and creative relationship for Himself, the sake of His Name, in His Divine Freedom, the power that makes space and time serve Him with Israel among the nations. This is the One who gives meaning to such events. This is the One whom His People are to know. In our time, we are often; I am afraid, unable to keep pace with Him in such matters. I am afraid that often we are unable with our freedoms to follow Him in His Freedom for us, and thus we are unable to grasp the real nature of His BCR with His People in His Creation. Renewals often fall very short of the mark for which they are intended, but always the intention is quite in the events. They are intended to serve the purpose of the Lord God with His Promise to His People in His Creation.

We believe that Joshua as Moses' successor and the inheritor of his Book of the Torah with Israel knew well the purpose in the nature of the

BCR. At Shechem, the new leader confronts the new generation with the authority of the Presence of the Lord God in the relationship. Israel's King, however invisible, embraces her time past, her time present, and her time future. Within the nature of the BCR, all that time is belongs to Him. Thus, Israel is His Elect. Her future with Him is at stake in the world. This is to say that the covenanted relationship of the Great I-AM with His People is renewed in space and time with prophetic power and thrust, with the formula—*thus says Yahweh*' ('thus says the Lord'). Joshua confronts Israel not with his words but with the formula of the prophetic history of the People of God that signifies a royal messenger from King Yahweh. With this formula, Joshua acts in possession of the very authority with which Moses became Israel's Prophet. Here is the King with His People acting to give Voice to His Command over the tribes, through Moses and his Book of the Law and then through Joshua. The rehearsal of these times is vital then to the relationship. In the midst of Israel's generational opposition, we read in the first person singular again and again of the victories He has given her: '*I took, I gave, I assigned, I sent, I afflicted, I brought out, I destroyed, I delivered,*' and so forth. The '*I*' in Joshua's confession of Israel's past is the confession of the personal reality of the Royal Commander, the Holy Warrior of her victories among the nations. There is no question about His use of His freedom. The mystery of this freedom at the gathering of all Israel at Shechem is brought to bear upon the freedom of the People of God. As His Elect, what shall she do with her freedom? In a sense, the world itself must be considered poised for her answer. As the Elect, she cannot escape either the Divine Freedom of the Great I-AM or the human freedom she must know as the People of God. He is free to act for her. She is free to worship or oppose Him. Both belong to the covenanted relationship posited in the world between the Lord God and her tribes. Both divine freedom and human freedom are significant here at this time and in this place. Both belong to the renewal traditions. The secret of the victories and the secret of the judgments is these freedoms utilized in the history of Israel among the nations. We miss much of the irony of prophecy when we fail to apprehend the meaning of these freedoms and their significance in the dialogue. The patient Wisdom of the Lord God who is who He truly is with Israel belongs to a personal reality whose compassion and favor, long suffering, grace and faithfulness, steadily determines the meaning of the events whose occurrences, marked with the nature of the BCR, define Israel among the nations in His Creation.

The Great I-AM of the Kingdom of God

The 'test of loyalty' that we read in Joshua 24:19–24 makes this gathering at Shechem face His personal reality with an ironic confrontation. In 19a, we hear Him with the wisdom of His passion for her say: '*You are not able to serve Yahweh, for He is Holy Elohim—'El-Qanah He is* . . . . The Zealous Lord God He is, as the Holy Creator and Israel's Redeemer, speaks with His People in such a way that Israel is to be understood as unable to respond to His love for her. It is important thus that this chapter is written down. It is 'canonized' in the history of Israel because of the irony in these confrontations. She is for better or for worse in this history with Him, who is who he is for her, in the nature of his BCR even when she is seems unable to rid herself of her idols and idol making. The renewal exposes these matters between the Elect and the One who has elected her in his divine freedom to choose to be with his Elect. This gathering is intended to gain for her some understanding of what in the past has spelled disaster for her, but with a full appreciation for her 'stiff-necked,' 'high-handed,' 'complaining' disposition against Him. Joshua as Moses' successor is determined to serve the Lord and to exhort Israel to serve the Lord. But shall she do differently now than in her past with Him? Joshua gains from the leaders of the tribes of Israel in the Land their witness with their freedom in the BCR to Him. He solidifies her vows in His Presence. A record is established for her as the witness she has become at Shechem. It may be against herself, but it shall be canonized forever, so that future generations can bear witness to her witness. The Freedom of the Lord God and the freedom of the People of God are evidently significant at this gathering. Their confrontation is the history of Israel among the nations.

This 'test of loyalty' brings about the conscious determination of the People of God to be a witness to their *Yahweh Elohim*. The ratification of the BCR is accomplished with the vow of this determination. The gathering with its 'canonization' confirms the dialogue's divine purpose and passion. The '*stone*' that Joshua sets up at its conclusion bears witness to Israel's witness in the nature of this BCR. In this place and at this time, she is who she is to become with her Lord and God. The personal confrontation of the 'I' the Lord God is and the 'we' Israel must become as the new generation among the nations is defined with this '*stone of witness*.' This stone is marked with the words of this confrontation just as Moses once marked the Stone Tablets at Sinai. The personal and prophetic presence of the Great I-AM the Lord God is at this time and in this place is written down and joined in this way at Shechem to Moses' Book of the Law. This is the place where the Lord God has chosen to set His Name. This is the place then where Joshua's bones are to be buried, right beside the bones of his ancestor Joseph. In this Promised Land with her Lord and God Israel is the subject of the promise once made to Abraham and his sons. Here is the gift promised Israel. Who can read this account without hearing, implicit within it, the fact that Israel will certainly not keep her vows and the 'stone of witness' will certainly keep the words of Moses and Joshua and their prophetic confrontation with Israel?

Israel is on record in this way as being against that for which she has been called to confirm. It is remarkable that we have this 'Canon of Truth' preserved by Israel's scribes and historians. No such confessions may be found in the literatures of the ancient world. Archaeologists have never dug up a single shard or stone tablet that tells us that the ancient kings and their reigns were defiantly against their gods. Posterity is not recorded as worthless peoples and failed kings. Profane practices of priests and prophets find no headlines in history making. Laws are made to be kept and the disobedient for punishment. Never is the utter emptiness of idol making and idol worship denounced among them. Right to their bitter ends all these civilizations, with praises for kings, celebrate with wondrous and magic rituals the sacrifices of their priests, with superstitious awe for the divine powers of their prophets, persist with the worship of their idols and gods. It is this worship that is precisely despised by the Lord God of Israel's Election of Israel, and here at Shechem at this time in the life of Joshua we read the command that would rid the People of God of all this superstition, of all these celebrations, of all this idol making and this worship of gods who are not in fact gods in this world. We read that Israel is elected to bear witness against all their worshipers. This is not a confession like the confessions read in other nations. At Shechem, we read of the unique and incomparable Only One who is the Zealous God the Great I-AM is in His BCR, the Lord God He is with her among the nations she faces. We read of His passion and purpose for these tribes. We read of the renewal of His determination with His Self-Revelation for Israel among these nations. We understand that His great compassion and favor, His great grace and faithfulness is being spent wisely with His long-suffering in His BCR with His People, in spite of their contradiction of Him. He is *El-Qanah* with Israel, whether His People will hear Him or not. Though Israel may not go to the place where He has set His Name to learn to do there the *Yashar* in His Eyes, still He will not be who He is without her. The '*stone of witness*' has been set up in Israel's history. The stone hears all that Israel may not hear. I doubt that anyone can escape the implication of this '*stone*' in the nature of the BCR. The stone shapes and forms beside the history of Israel among the nations what must be heard as the Word of God for her.

Israel's history in the Land is told by a series of renewals that entail then the sure and steady self-degradation of the People of God in the land of Canaan. Israel will prove she is not only 'stiff-necked,' 'high-handed,' and 'complaining' People of God, but also quite prone to becoming a 'self-centered' people, to her own destruction. Israel's '*Deliverers*' (The Book of Judges provide the reader with stories that tell over and over again and again of the utter breakdown of every kind of relationship in the Land!) belong to the Lord God's mysterious freedom and steady insistence in His BCR to call His People 'My People.' These shape the thrust of the theological meaning in this history. The narrative provides the reader with a steady record whose significance belongs to the theological reality of Israel's experiences in the Land among the nations. It speaks of the various needs the tribes felt in the pathos of their 'self-centered' existences. The stories provide a context in which the history of the transition from the tribal confederacy into the Monarchy may be told. Israel's life in the Land leads her to cry out for a king like the kings of the other nations. The need is perceived in the midst of the relentless breakdown of her unity and fellowship in the Land. From the death of Joshua to the birth of Samuel, we read of the breakdown of the tribal relations and the need for royal ones like the nations experience. The need for renewal is evident, but the way of renewal is not.

The transition from tribal life to Monarchy teaches us much about the Great I-AM the Lord God is. It shows us about the way that, in degrading times, He wills to minister His Promise with Himself to His Elect. He remains always free to seek to establish His Reign with His People. He puts Himself among His Chosen with a will that shows the reader His faithfulness to the BCR. The Book of Judges would teach us that in some three hundred years of the struggle between *Yahweh Elohim* and Israel in the Land of Canaan, surrounded by Philistines, Egyptians, and Mesopotamians, and so forth, Israel's 'self-centered' inability to hear His Command of her in the relationship and her steady troubles in the Land must evidence her need for renewal in the BCR. In contrast to her 'self-centeredness' we read of the way of His Faithfulness. It is this faithfulness that determines the significance of renewal in the tradition of the BCE in Israel's history.

Only once is reference made to the *chesed Yahweh* in the Book of Judges. Judges 1:22–26 tell of the events concerning the Israelite spies sent to help the tribes take the city of Bethel (once named Luz!). This man helped Israel take the city. Because of this one man's help for the house of Joseph, Israel was successful in the Land. Therefore, *chesed* was accorded to him (*Show us how to get into the city and we will make with you chesed*— Judges 1:24b). The loss of this *chesed* in the Land speaks volumes of the darkness by which the period of the Judges is to be understood. In this darkness, the tribes of Israel perceive their need for a king like the kings of the nations that surround her. The cry of the need is heard throughout this darkness in the Land. To live in the Land among the nations Israel needs to become as they are. 'Self-centeredness' leads the tribes to the wickedness of kings whose reigns are far distant from the Command of the Lord God. Disintegration of life among the tribes in the Land tears apart the very fabric of the society of a tribal confederacy meant to go to the place He has chosen for them. On every level of their culture, loss of moral, social, and religious vitality is experienced in their 'self-centered' will. We may understand that, without *Yahweh Elohim as their King*, with His *chesed* an unmentionable among the tribes, the need for this king grows, until the cry goes up for deliverance and renewal. There could be no more vivid account of this disintegration, degradation, and carnage than that which we read in the Book of Judges. Far from the oaths taken at Shechem, Judges 19–20 records the perception of the People of God lost from King Yahweh. Their troubles belong to the fact that they have no king like the kings of the nations that surround them. The Tribes of Israel doom themselves with a certain wicked and self-destructive cry heard throughout the Land, from Gilgal to Shiloh. The stories of the Judges in the Land reach their conclusion when a wife of a Levite, living in the remote regions of Ephraim, becomes unfaithful to him. She leaves the Levite to return to her father's house in Bethlehem. He goes to retrieve her and on their journey back to his territory, they stop to spend a night at Gibeah. An old man welcomes them, but that night townsmen come to the old man's home to seek sex with the Levite. The old man attempts to satisfy their cravings by giving them the Levite's wife. The men spend the night taking turns raping her. In the morning, the Levite throws his ravaged wife on his donkey and goes home. Once home, he kills her, cuts her body up into twelve pieces, and sends each of the pieces to each of the tribes of Israel. Thus is Israel in the Land. The gauntlet has been thrown down, the battle engaged. The casualties are great enough that the very existence of the tribe of Benjamin is placed in jeopardy. So women are stolen from Shiloh in order to preserve the tribe. Thus, the development of a world where every man thought himself free to do what was right in his own eyes. Israel in this condition, indeed, needs a king to reign over her. It is this cry that the Lord God is bound to answer in His BCR with His People.

Only through Naomi's Ruth, a woman of the land of Moab, and Boaz, a Redeemer in Israel, can the prophetic line be traced as the *chesed Yahweh*. It is read in the relations between Naomi and Ruth, from whom comes the line of the Lord God's answer to this cry (Ruth 3:10). Otherwise, it is gone from the Land, and without the *chesed Yahweh* with the tribes in the Land, the utter degradation of the peoples is spread throughout Israel, to her priesthood, to her tribes. The whole fabric of their community becomes torn apart. A new beginning evidently must be made. If it is to be kept, the promise of the covenanted relationship between the Lord God and His People must be renewed. Hannah's barren womb marks the end of the tribal confederacy, and the need for the new beginning, one that Israel believes requires a king like the kings the nations that surround her possess. Hannah's son, Samuel, embodies Yahweh's willingness to make this new beginning with His People. With Eli and his sons firmly judged, Samuel's life signifies a new world for Israel. She will become a monarchy like the monarchies common throughout the Ancient Near East. After the Judges come the Kings. Hannah's Samuel marks the transition period. Hannah's 'thanksgiving-offering' (1 Samuel 2:1–10), sung in strong resonance with Moses' Song, is the recognition of the justification of this movement in Israel's history. In this renewal, Samuel becomes to Israel what Moses at Sinai had been to the People of God. He marks the beginning of that new beginning when the Lord God will give himself to Israel in the form her new king, the Elect King. The monarchy is thus a renewal movement in the nature of the BCR in the history of Israel. Most scholars characterize the life of Samuel as the last of the *Deliverers* (Judges) and a new beginning for the prophets and leaders of the tribes in the Land. He introduces a new dimension in the relationship that will obtain between prophet and king in Israel's monarchy. Samuel's life is a life that knows both the destruction and the subsistence of Israel among the nations, the end of the Judges and the beginning of the Kings. We understand the transition as an act of condescension on the part of the Lord God. He is free to accommodate himself in his divine freedom, even with the self-centeredness of the tribes, for the sake of the relationship. With this transition, a new understanding of the Great I-AM the Lord God is obtains, as he solidifies the relationship in this time. '*The Lord brings death and makes alive; he brings down to the grave and raises up*,' Hannah sings in her 'thanksgiving-offering' for Samuel. She sings gratefully, in the midst of all the desolation and barrenness (1 Samuel 2:6), in the midst of all the unfaithfulness of Israel, to proclaim thankfully the faithfulness of the Lord and God to his chosen people. It is his faithfulness in the relationship that is celebrated. Beyond any punishment of Israel's 'self-centered' opposition to him in the BCR, beyond her willingness to join with His enemies against him, the promise of his Grace stands to cause the purposes of the relationship to be realized in time and times.

Yet we read in 1 Samuel 8 of the cry from the elders of Israel for a king. The cry comes to be sure into the ears of an old Samuel as an evil cry. The Lord God, it is well known, is her King. Why do they insist upon another? He is angry with Israel, and when he goes to King Yahweh to complain about her, he meets Yahweh as a King who is not the One even Samuel thinks that He is. As the King rejected, even reigning without honor in the Land, He will heed Israel's cry for another. But what good can come from Israel's cry for another king? Only King Yahweh can answer questions. In the midst of Samuel's objections, the King tells Samuel that He will give them another. Israel does not reject Samuel but Him. He will respond by giving them a king. Yes, He will give Israel a king, but it will be a *Bull King*, to be compared with the Golden Calf she preferred in the Wilderness after Sinai. Yes, Israel will not like her chosen king. Yes, her chosen kings will prove as faithless as the Judges in the Land. Her kings will prove to be the *Bull Kings* they are, and against *Yahweh Elohim* in the Land will lead her to her destruction in the Land. Yet, no, that will not be the end of her. The Great I-AM the Lord God is as her King will in time provide for her, and in time she will respond to Him. He will give Israel a king that is not Himself. But when that king becomes the *Bull King*, like the kings among the nations surrounding Israel, he will lead Israel the Elect to her destruction. Israel lives among the nations in the Creation according to the covenanted promise of the Lord God in His Divine Freedom to be who He is with her, and now through the House of David, in a newly conceived royal relationship with the King of Israel, the

Elect with His Grace is given to His People. It is this story that we read as the monarchy of Israel's history among the nations. Thus, the Monarchy of Israel is canonized with a prophetic power whose origins belong to the Only One Lord God who is the Great I-AM Himself.

Scholars may debate what we are to make of this history. They are surely right to hear the '*economic condescension*' of the Lord and His '*accommodation*' to the conditions in these times. The concepts of '*economic condescension*' and '*accommodation*' are fundamentally sound for grasping the dynamics in the nature of the BCR between the Divine Freedom and Israel's freedom in the relationship. Properly understood, they substantiate the nature of the BCR as we have been attempting to explore it. We hear with these concepts that the Only and Incomparable One with His Divine Freedom is to be understood as free to interact creatively with and for His People in His Creation. To grasp the significance of His '*condescension*' and '*accommodation*' for Israel in this case, we understand that both transcendent and immanent dimensions in the integrity of His Being in His Acts with His Word must be realized in order to describe the real nature of the relations in this history. The Lord God is in the covenanted relationship is confessed to possess a dynamic faithfulness of who He truly is with Israel. These doctrines must be understood to speak of the profound dynamics of stability, intention, and purpose created and sustained by the Lord God with His BCR in the history of His People. They must allow the reader to follow the way that, beyond the evil at work against Him, *Yahweh Elohim is passionately committed to fulfilling His purposes with His People in His covenanted relationship with His Elect Israel.* There is no ambiguity in His commitment to both judge and save her in this way. Both poles of the BCR in Israel's history fully participate, significantly, in every new beginning of the renewals in times and chosen places. The nature of the covenanted relationship between the Lord God and His People is renewed as He wills, over all opposition to Him, to call His People '*My People*.' The doctrines of '*condescension*' and '*accommodation*' bear significance that belongs to the dynamic stability the I-AM He is with Himself in His Freedom to provide with His personal wisdom for Israel's destiny with Him in His Creation. They point to His Glory and no where else.

'*Accommodation*' then has to do with the way that the Lord God is free from within Himself to act for His People as Israel's Redeemer-Creator in spite of her opposition to Him and her self-centered choices against Him. He is always free from within Himself to go outside of

Himself and become something He has never been in order that Israel might become '*My People*.' His purposes in His BCR with the People of God among the nations will not prove vain. Even though He punishes her for her rebellions against Him, He will remain faithful to her. In this way, '*accommodation*' must mean that He is free to establish new dimensions in the relationship, new dimensions He creates for the purpose of renewing her. In His BCR, He works steadily through space and time towards the eventual fulfillment of this purpose. His Being in this covenanted relationship shall prove fruitful. He wills to continue always with His passionate struggle from place to place, one time after another, to choose to save His People for Himself and with Himself. He has chosen to make Israel the People of God among the nations even from *the Beginning*. It is an intention that will not be thwarted. That is, He remains free from within Himself, in spite of all the idols and idol making of Israel in the Promised Land, to free Israel from her faithlessness and to give her a heart for Him. 'Accommodation' is a work then that would move Israel in His BCR into an obedience that belongs to His Glory, the Lord God's final victory with His People among the nations in His Creation. To His Glory, His Promise will be kept. Thus, 'accommodation' has to do with the Divine Freedom of the Great I-AM the Lord God is with His Will to accomplish His intentions and purposes in the relationship. It does not mean He ever overlooks Israel's evil or the evil among the nations.

In this freedom to accommodate Himself in the BCR, he condescends economically with Himself in His Divine Freedom to establish in this place and that time, for the sake of the Glory of His Name, His Presence with Israel. He would bring about the fulfillment of His intensions and purposes in this way. Both providence and prophecy are involved. In this way, He is free to create something new for His People, in order that Israel may fulfill her role in freedom with His in the relationship. In this way, these doctrines help us to understand the way of the Divine Freedom of the Great I-AM the Lord God is in His acts in the history of Israel. The events we read of Israel's Redeemer-Creator acting, in spite of her contradiction of Him, to realize His goal for her is implicated throughout history. We apprehend Him with the nature of His Being as the I-AM He is in this way. The transition from tribal life to monarchial life as a movement in the renewal of the BCR belongs to His '*accommodation*' and '*economic condescension*' with her, in spite of her evil action against Him. No one will grasp the meaning of the *chesed Yahweh* with Israel's prophecy without apprehending the meaning of these freedoms in the history of the BCR with her history in covenanted relationship with the I-AM He is. In this freedom, a map may be drawn that allows the reader to go from where he or she is to chosen places at chosen times, when and where we may go to learn to do what is the 'Right' thing to do not in our eyes but in His Eyes.

In this way, we may understand something of the tremendous struggle in the stories between them. The experience and events that mark the history of the establishment of the Monarchy in Israel make for a history of judgment and salvation understood only in His Transcendent and Divine Freedom to act with His Grace for the Chosen King. King David's throne in Israel's Monarchy in this way is given to possess an authority in the midst of Israel's struggle in the BCR that belongs only to the *chesed Yahweh*. In this way, the throne of Israel's Monarchy is made to possess the secret of the Great I-AM with 'Little Credo' of His Self-Defining purposes with the patient Wisdom of His Grace at the heart of His Elected purposes for her. It is upon this foundation that is built what becomes known in Israel's history as the Messianic Hope of her Prophecy. It is this Hope that is the great gift of God for Israel among the nations. It is this gift that she is among the nations. We do well to spend time in attempting to penetrate into the meaning of this Wisdom of the Lord God with Israel in our world.

Samuel, the son of Hannah's prayers in the Land, marks a new beginning for Israel. Under the command of King Yahweh, Samuel, as judge to prophet, is raised up to anoint Saul the first king over the tribes. The stories of his anointing and rise to power, his relations with David, his successor, and David's rise to the throne after King Saul's killing on the battlefield with his son, Jonathon, are the remarkable tales of the way that the Lord God is willing to work with even those who oppose Him in His BCR with His People in the Land. Many scholars regard these stories as some of the finest narratives to be found in the Bible and in all literature. King David becomes with Israel the king, king as no other shall ever be king over the People of God. All the generations after him in Israel's history shall be known as sons of David. There are no sons of Saul or Solomon in these generations. After King David, the kings are to bear the title of the 'Sons of David.' To their lines belongs the Messianic Hope of Israel's history among the nations. We will attempt to penetrate with our understanding into why this is what it is in the world.

The choice of Saul is no feigned '*accommodation*' on the part of the Lord God. Saul's anointing as king in place of King Yahweh is a real choice. His anointing is both an accommodation and economic condescension of King Yahweh with Israel, a very real anointing indeed, with all of its consequences before them. With this anointing, Saul becomes the great warrior that he is in Israel's history. We need to honor this anointing in any evaluation we may want to make of King Saul. We need to take David's side on this question of honoring this man and his reign in Israel's first monarchy. This anointing of the Lord God upon the life of King Saul and his forty-year reign is not one of God's poor choices. It belongs to His determination to work in the context of His People's desires. Christian thought has often treated the Saul-David history as one in which David is pictured as a good king, a king after God's own heart, and Saul a bad man whose flesh was his downfall. But we need to be able to read their stories as the narratives of two Bull Kings, one rejected and the other elected, where the Monarchy itself resonates as an idol, like the Golden Calf of the Exodus tradition in Israel's history, one from whom the Lord God removes his grace (*chesed*) in the BCR and the other from whom He has promised never to remove his grace (*chesed*). The difference between the two belongs to the Divine Freedom of the Great I-AM the Lord God is to choose to fulfill the purposes of His promise in the BCR. In this way, He chooses to mark with His Glory His intention for Israel among the nations. We may not understand the relationships and conflicts in the adventures of the stories as if they were serials in some Star Trek or Star Wars trip, as if they belonged to reels of movies in which good and evil are set as equals at war against one another over the control of the universe, as if Saul represented the evil king who does evil in the Eyes of God and David is the good king who does good in the Eyes of God. Saul's disobedience and fall and David's obedience and rise in the establishment of the Monarchy in Israel's history belong to the very real significance of the *chesed Yahweh* in His BCR with Israel among the nations. It is not the force that is with David, but the personal passion of the Great I-AM the Lord God is for Israel. We must not miss this point in the narratives. Israel's history is what it is because of the *chesed Yahweh*. She is where she is in the world because of His Divine Freedom with His *chesed* to shape her times as her King, in spite of the Bull Kings. His '*accommodation*' serves economically His purpose in His BCR, from beginning to end, an end that certainly belongs to His Glory, to the actualization in His Creation of His purpose and intentions in the chosen relationship.

Through Samuel, both the anointing of Saul and the anointing of David are God's anointing. They mark the way His freedom for His 'accommodation' and 'economic condescension' in His covenanted relationship with His People is to be followed, like a path of light in the world. The anointed King Saul is a great warrior for the tribes of Israel, but to his issues belong a disobedience Israel knows too well. He does not lack courage or commitment to lead Israel and obtain victories for her over her enemies. But he does lack the ability to hear the Command of the Lord God over him. He is a Bull King without obedience to the true King, in a betrayal of King Yahweh. He is unable to obey Samuel or grasp the prophetic significance of the holy wars he would fight. He will to be his own commander and even be his own priest. He lives to hear that his punishment is his removal from his throne. He lives to hear of the anointing of David, his replacement on the throne. He lives to haunt his replacement's life with his disobedience. He lives seeking to kill David, the newly anointed King of Israel. It is out of this issue that we read the meaning of those famous lines about King Saul, delivered to him by the Lord's aging Samuel with Israel: *'Does the Lord desire burnt offerings and sacrifices without hearing the Voice of the Lord? Look now, hearing is better than sacrifice, and heeding than the fat of rams. For the sin of divination is rebellion; magic and idols insubordination. Because you have rejected the word of the Yahweh, he has rejected you as king'* (1 Samuel 15:22–23). He lives to listen to the dead Samuel, called up from the dead by the witch at Endor, in a séance he himself had strictly forbidden the clans of Israel. King Saul does not lack courage. He does not commit adultery, as David will do after him. He does not seek to murder his generals, as David was to do after him. Yet this Bull King can sin against the very heart of who the Lord God is in His covenanted relationship with Israel. His lack of patience with the Lord's Command of him, his inability to believe that this Command is stronger than he is leads him to his end with his son, Jonathan, on a battlefield where he had known so many victorious campaigns.

Unable to tune his ears into the purposes of the Word of his Lord and God, his deafness discovers that the King has removed his grace (*chesed*) from his reign and given the throne of Israel to another. Whatever the renewal of the BCR is meant to be as Israel's Monarchy, it will not take a form shaped by King Saul. To the king who remains dumb to who the Lord God is with His compassion and favor, long-suffering, and great grace and truth (Exodus 3:14; 34:6), the Great I-AM will remain silent when that one most needs Him. With this deafness and in this dumbness Saul's life is lead to the dark depths of the dead over which the Witch of Endor sits. The 'woman of the queens of the inner side' (masters of the dead?) brings the Lord God's Command through the dead Samuel for the last time, and King Saul and the woman see the *Elohim* rise from the ground, identify him as Samuel, when Saul's anointing is sealed by death and not the *chesed Yahweh*. The Lord has rejected him. He is no longer king of Israel. *Yahweh* with his grace (*chesed*) has given the kingdom to David. Saul is dead (1 Samuel 28). His haunting of David's life with his rage is over. David is called to replace him. David shall be made to arise and become king in Israel's Monarchy. But the anointing, taken from Saul, is placed upon David so that this Bull King shall be a man after God's own heart. He shall seek to obey, even in the midst of sinful life and reign. The point of this anointing in the Monarchy as the renewal of the BCR does not reside in either of these kings in the history of Israel, but in the King the Lord God is with her, even in disobedience. Again, the BCR possesses a continuity that is produced by the freedom of the Great I-AM to be who He truly is with His People.

Woe to the one who would rejoice over Saul and his son Jonathan's deaths! David has the messengers of their downfalls killed on the very spot where they would malign their memories. He never would harm the Lord's anointed king. King David's lament for them is perhaps some of the most touching poetry in the Bible (2 Samuel 1:17–27). Its impact was recorded also in the 'Book of Jashar.' This is the book that records what the right thing to do is in the eyes of the Lord God. It is right to remember them as the Lord's anointed. They belong to Him as much as David belongs to Him. Those who bury Saul and Jonathan with honor David honors (2 Samuel 2:5–7). When David learned that the men of Jabesh-Gilead had buried Saul, he sent messengers to Jabesh-Gilead and he said to them, '*Blessed are you before Yahweh, because you have done this chesed with Saul and you have buried him. Now may Yahweh do with you chesed and 'emet and I will do this good with you because of what you have done.*' The *chesed* that defines the relationships between Saul and Jonathon and David is sourced in the King, King Yahweh Himself, and we do none of them any honor when we do not appreciate His *chesed* with them each and all of them. There is no way anyone can read the stories of Saul and Jonathan and David and turn these characters into creatures that belong to some ancient or modern myth about good and evil in the world, about the battle between the spirit and the flesh in the world, or any other worldview than the real world of the nature of the BCR shaped by the *chesed Yahweh* with Israel among the nations in the Creation. Something far more human and far more sinister is found in the poetry of David's lament over King Saul and the beloved Jonathan. The rise of David to his throne in Israel's Monarchy is a story told only in the light of this *chesed and 'emet* shining on all Israel—Israel elected and rejected, obedient and disobedient—Israel the chosen nation among the nations in the Creation. The whole of it has to do with the secret of the dynamic stability of God's Grace in His BCR with His People. David knows well the significance of the *chesed and 'emet* of the Great I-AM the Lord God is, not because he is a king without sin, but because He has been chosen and anointed to be who he is as king by the King with His 'Little Credo' in the BCR. It is upon this Only and Incomparable One that He is given as the House of David to depend upon the *chesed Yahweh*.

It is in 2 Samuel 6-7 that we read of David's interaction with the Lord God and His BCR with Israel. In these chapters, the full impact of the *chesed Yahweh* in his rise to his kingship and his anointing to reign on his throne to rule all Israel is taught the reader. David brings the Ark of the Covenant, vital for worship and war with the tribes, to his newly purchased city Jerusalem. In this City of David, the throne of King David would establish a new temple for the Ark of God. As the newly anointed king and triumphant warrior, singer of songs for Israel's worship of her *Yahweh Elohim*, he is to shepherd the People of God. At rest in his palace in this new city, he is a man who can think that the Lord God should also leave His old tent behind and be able to move into a new home beside his throne in the city. His confrontation with the prophet Nathan forms at this time the heart and the center of the hope for Israel among the nations. This confrontation will produce what shall become known in the history of Israel as the basis for her prophecy and her 'Messianic Hope' in the world. Here the prophetic moment in the nature of the BCR is to be seen and heard as a movement that belongs to all time. It is renewal movement that belongs again to time past, time present, and time future under power of the Divine Freedom of the Great I-AM to make Himself present with His People. It is a movement conditioned by His freedom to 'accommodate' and 'condescend' economically to be who He truly is with Israel. The dialogue between the King of Israel, David, and His Prophet,

Nathan, marks at this time a renewal of the Lord God in His covenanted relationship with His 'self-centered' People. We understand the movement here among the nations as the heart of Israel's hope. From this time forth, the House of David will gather meaning and significance Israel will for all time and times be made to face in God's Creation.

2 Samuel 7:1–17 records the immense vitality of the confrontation. It is the record of the new beginning the Lord God has made with King David in Israel's history. It is the prophetic sanction of the success of King Yahweh's accommodated commitment to His People. It may be outlined as follows (Cf. 1 Chronicles 17:1–15 and Psalm 89 for the way this prophetic movement and moment possesses a momentum that shall be felt meaningfully throughout the history of the *chesed Yahweh* with the House of David, when it is celebrated and reviewed in Israel's covenant renewal tradition as a irreversible beginning.):

7:1	Historical Narrative Introduction
7:2–3	Dialogue between the King and the Royal Prophet
7:4	Narrative Transition
7:5	Dialogue between King Yahweh and the Royal Prophet
	5b—Messenger formula
	5c–7— Rhetorical Question of Royal Wisdom
7:8a	Messenger Formula Again
7:8b–11	Histories—Past Reviewed
7:12–16	Histories—Future Foretold as Promise of His Grace (Cf. Psalm 2:7 and Psalm 132)
7:17	Narrative Transition

The form and content of the confrontation we read here between prophet and king belongs to the great covenant renewal tradition in Israel's history. It reflects who the Lord God is with Abraham and Moses as well as who He is with Israel's future among the nations. It transparently belongs to the continuity of the BCE as well as to a radical discontinuity of the relationship. Both dimensions are necessary for the renewal in this time and space. The introduction to the events of the movement centers in the nature of the BCR, from Gilgal to Shiloh to Shechem, and then to Bethel and back to Shiloh and Gilgal again, as culminating finally in David's Jerusalem. The future here is begun in earnest. The dialogue between David and Nathan is filled with the kind of freedoms that are inherently involved in the relationship. The narrative transitions indicate that these freedoms belong significantly to the Lord God's Divine Freedom to be who He is and to act for His Name with Israel. Having begun the day affirming King David's plans for the Lord God in the Monarchy, the prophet shall that night have his mind changed about it. He returns from his dialogue with the King only to meet in a dream on his bed the Lord. The next day Nathan returns to King David with a different 'word' for him. This 'word' makes for the rehearsal of the BCR. Once more, David's past, the history of Joshua, Moses, and Abraham are fully honored. All times past in Israel's covenanted relationship with the Lord God contribute to this moment. King David will not build, as he planned, a temple for Yahweh. Yahweh will rather build a throne for David, a throne where He will keep *His Chesed* for as long as forever is with His David. Here is the place of King David's *rest* from his enemies.

The *rest* is also for as long as forever is. It belongs to a promise whose victories over the enemies shall be realized. It belongs triumphantly to the distances of time that are marked with the significance of the Throne of David in the BCR with the Lord God. The covenanted relationship between the Lord and Israel in the form of this Throne with *chesed Yahweh* shall be realized in the fullness of its significance in the world, for as long as forever is with God's Eternity. The House of David will be the place from which the victories of the Lord God over all His enemies shall be achieved. According to the 'word' of the prophet, this throne among the nations will be triumphant forever. In verses 12–16, we read of the establishment in Jerusalem, in the City of David, of the throne of this House as the center of all hope in this world. It is the momentous keeping of this tumultuous promise that has been determined to realize the purposes of God with His People in His Creation. It is this promise given to David's seed as once it was given to Abraham's seed that shall be kept forever: *'This one will build a temple for My Name and I will establish the throne of his kingdom forever. I, I myself, will be father to him and he will be to me a son, who in his iniquity will be punished with the rod of men and the wounds of the sons of mankind. But **my chesed** will never be removed from him, as I removed it from off of Saul, whom I removed from my presence. I will confirm your house and your kingdom forever with my presence; your* *throne will be established forever.*' The announcement of the promise is followed by a record of David's life at court, a life that from beginning to end then is marked with the *chesed* of the Lord. His *chesed* for Mephibosh of the House of Saul is rooted in this Promise (2 Samuel 9:1, 3, 7). His *chesed* and *'emet* for Ittai the Gittite, even as he flees from Absalom, is rooted in this Promise (2 Samuel 15:20). His final prayer about his life as King of Israel, a 'thanksgiving song,' is rooted in this Promise (2 Samuel 22:51), and his final commands for the sons of Barzillai of Gilead are rooted in this Promise (1 Kings 2:7). It is fair to say that the story of King David's court life, even with his adultery and murderous will, his troubles with his family, and the complex politics of his reign among the nations surrounding his Jerusalem, is an offering that is clearly made because of his obedience with the *chesed Yahweh*. His relationship to the promised *chesed* for his House provides the great leader with a boundless strength able to joy in knowing his Master, the Lord of the Promise, just as surely as He created in *the* Beginning as *the Elohim* of the Creation, will make for him the *chesed* he needs in his life. It is this that makes David, even in the form of a Bull King, a man after God's own heart. Perhaps our leaders, even today, would benefit from reading the reign of King David and his experience as the ruler whose house would give its name to all the kings that followed him in the history of Israel's Monarchy among the nations. The destiny of the People of God in this way becomes bound up with the Son of David who would realize the actualization of the purposes of the Lord God with Israel in His Creation.

Here is a man who knows, with songs of victory and with tears of great sorrow, that the anointing of the blessing of the covenanted relationship has come upon the throne of his House forever. The House of David is known as the place where this forever rests as the *chesed Yahweh*. This forever possesses the root and the ground from which springs forth the fruit of the *chesed and 'emet* of the Great I-AM the Lord God is with King David. Beyond his tears and fury and pain, he knows to be forever thankful for Him, the Rock of his destiny in this world. This is ground the Great I-AM is with Himself for him. This is how He is who He truly is with His 'Little Credo' for His People in the form of Israel's Monarchy. This is the freedom in which Israel finds herself rooted as His People in His Creation. It is the working of this secret of the *chesed Yahweh* in the nature of the BCR between the Lord God and the King of Israel that determines the meaning of events in the epochs that must follow after the reigns of the Sons of David. It is this *chesed Yahweh with His Promise to the House of David that indeed shapes and forms the solid substance and firm content of Israel's experience of time and times, time past, time present, and time future* of the Prophecy that gives to the world Israel's Messianic Hope (cf. the eschatological David of the prophets: (Isaiah 9:1–7; 11:1–11; 29:1; 37:35; 38:4; 55:3; Jeremiah 23:5–6; 28:16; 33:15–16; Ezekiel 34:23–24). No one can understand the David of the Gospels (the Son of God as the Son of David) or the David of the Apocalypse as the Lamb and Lion of the Word of God (Revelation 3:7, 5:5, 22:16) without grasping the meaning and significance of this *chesed* in the history of Israel. No one can rightly read Israel's prophecy among the nations in this world without apprehending the movement of this *chesed* in the history of Israel in the Creation. This is the Grace and Truth of the God who is the Lord, of the Lord who is the Only and Incomparable God, the solid and unique One that we are given to read on the pages of this history's witness of the Old and New Covenants of the Holy Scriptures, the Revelation of the Great I-AM the Lord God is. This is the Grace and Truth that belongs to Israel as '*My People*' in God's Creation. If we are enemies of the Grace God has become for us, it is surely because we do not understand His *chesed* for the House of David with His Israel.

King Solomon lives in this Prophecy. With him the *chesed Yahweh* provides the power for the House of David to build the Temple of the Lord God in the BCR. As the Son of David on his father's throne, he commands the building of the great House of God in the City of David. In 1 Kings 8:12–21, the dedication of the great Temple, the place King David once thought to build, is made by King Solomon and his reign. He celebrates then the faith that knows the House of David will be the object of the Promise forever (1 Kings 8:22–32). It is this *chesed* that holds the secret to the renewal the Monarchy is in Israel's history among the nations. Thus, he commemorates the promise in the Exodus of Israel and her deliverance out of Egypt. Moses and David belong to it. The anointing of the House on the throne belongs to the *chesed Yahweh*. In this way, the Throne of David has become the place to which all Israel has been called to go and to do *the Yashar* in the Eyes of God. In this way, the beginning of the history of Israel's Monarchy celebrates the renewal of the BCR, a relationship that was begun even with Abraham. This has become the center of all hope for Israel, where she may do what is 'Right' in the righteous eyes of King Yahweh. This is time and space created by the Holy One for

His Glory in His BCR among the nations. From this center, her prophecy may be proclaimed. When we read the histories of the kings of Israel and Judah, the way that they did evil in the sight of God, we are reading an account of the accumulated sin of her 'self-centeredness' turning towards that wickedness belonging to the enemies of the Lord God. It is wickedness that leads the People of God in the BCR into a faithless condition that shall experience the utter devastation of all that is sacred to Israel in the Land. The destruction of the City of David and Israel's exile from the Promised Land, her scattering among the nations, marks the faithfulness and righteousness of the Lord God in His BCR with her, but with His *chesed* for her destiny in this world.

We need only to refer to Psalm 89 in order to illustrate the effective power of the Promise in Israel's history. The psalmist rehearses, even in the midst of Israel's troubles, when Yahweh's *chesed and 'emet* can appear lost upon her, a faith that belongs to this promise to David and to David's throne as the reign of the Lord God among the nations. When the Chronicler rehearses this prophecy of Nathan for King David, its Messianic meaning of the Promise is explicit. The significance of the Messianic David has been fully grasped as a promise that will be kept even beyond the Exile, beyond the building of the new temple in the times between the Testaments, in the times of the prophetic silence. When we read of the promise with the eschatological David, we find no mention of the 'iniquity' of the historical David or his sons. The Messianic King of the Davidic Promise for the Latter Days need have no 'word' of concern for transgressions and sins, because he belongs to that Day of the Lord when sin will be no more remembered in Israel among the nations. The silence belongs to the freedom of the Great I-AM the Lord God is. The legions of prophetic speculation through all the centuries that lead to Israel's Return from Exile and her waiting in the rebuilt temple for her Messianic Hope to be realized must be nothing more or less than the fulfillment of His Promise. The meaning and significance of the waiting is bound up with this renewal tradition. This Promise belongs to the nature of the covenanted relationship, its dynamic stability and personal intentions. The various shapes and forms of Israel's recorded history are assumed among the nations in God's Creation because of the nature of this BCR. In it, the Divine Freedom of the I-AM He is shall make a free people for Himself, even in the midst of the evil that opposes Him.

The Great I-AM of the Kingdom of God

We need to grasp the significance of the 'decree' that posits this Father-Son as the relationship between the Lord God and the House of David for as long as forever is in the Creation. We need to understand that once posited it holds the secret to His Glory, the Glory of the Election and Providence of His Word with this Throne, the Throne of David and no other. *Yahweh's chesed* will remain always vital in the BCR within the times of the secret of this decree, the Messianic time of this Promise. Again and again, His *Chesed* defines their struggles in the renewal of this relationship across the centuries. We must come to understand this work of His Promise to Israel. His work on behalf of His Promise to Israel in His BCR bears the meaning of all renewal of the relationship in the history of Israel in the world. Under this Promise, Israel is made to bear witness to Yahweh and His Grace for His People in His BCR. It is this *Grace* of the Lord that under girds, sustains, and drives the developments Israel experiences with her Messianic Hope among the nations. In spite of her opposition to her Lord and God, this *Grace* of His Being, this Being of His *Grace*, would give His People to live in His Presence. Though we may not read any one term for *chesed* in the translation made from Hebrew into Greek by Jews in Alexandria around 250 BCE, we need to apprehend the way that the G*race and Faithfulness* are to be defined with the personal power of the Messiah. It is His *chesed* and *'emet* that belong to the Promise. It is His Forever that is posited at the heart of the covenanted relationship between the Father and the Son of David. Israel's Messianic Hope is rooted in this ground of space and time where the Father and the Son define no Bull King, but a union and communion that belongs to their Eternity.

No prophetic tradition lives among the People of God without the Truth of this Grace and the Grace of this Truth. The *chesed* and *'emet* of the 'Little Credo' of the Great I-AM is renewed with the Monarchy in this way. The renewal bears in this way the holy passion for His purposes in His covenanted relationship with His People. Unless this *Grace* is understood as this *chesed*, unless *Faith* is understood as this *'emet*, what was once and for all time established with Abraham, what has been renewed again and again with Abraham's sons, and renewed then again with Moses and Joshua, what has been renewed now once more with the House of David, what is the renewal of Israel's Messianic Hope in time and times among the nations will escape our attention. No other definitions of *Grace* and *Faithfulness* may serve to signify the real meaning of these divine perfections of the Great I-AM the Lord God is with His People. For this reason,

I never like to translate *chesed and 'emet* into English. Everyone then seems to think that they know what *Grace* and *Faith* are in the Biblical World, but hardly anyone knows what they actually mean in this space and time of God's Eternity and Forever. Each and every generation needs to learn afresh their significance in this world. They belong to those divine perfections of the Being and Acts of the Lord God who He has chosen to be who He is in His Divine Freedom with the House of David as His Son. Here we understand the Father the Lord God is. Whatever forever will be for peoples depends upon this secret of the *chesed Yahweh* with the Son of David who is the Messiah of Israel. It is a secret being unveiled to this today with us.

In this chosen place and in His time for Israel, King Yahweh has freely become with Himself the Father of the King of Israel. He has anointed with His *chesed* (*Grace*) the king who is to be His Son. *Chesed* means that the Only and Incomparable One, who is the Great I-AM the Lord God is, has given Himself in this way to His People. *Chesed* bears the meaning of His struggle to renew His People, so that He may name them 'My People.' Israel's history among the nations in His Creation is determined by the decree of this anointing. The term bears a significance that refers us to the fulfillment of His Promise in His BCR in times past, in time present, and in times future. In all that time is, this is the place where His People may go to do the *Yashar* in His Eyes. Through this *Grace* and *His Faithfulness*, the Only Incomparable One will be known for who He is in the fulfillment of His prophecy for the House of David. With this *Grace*, with this *chesed*, the ancient promise to the ancestors and to the generations will be kept. Unlike with the House of Saul, from whom this *chesed* was removed, on this David's House the Lord God has set His Name as the Father of Israel and the heavens and the earth. This is the place chosen forever, the center of forever, where a 'self-centered' and 'wicked, faithless' People of God must come to do the *Yashar,* what is right, in the presence of their Lord and God. With His Divine Freedom, the Throne of David is to be the home of His Son, where in space and time forever is formed. The secret of the meaning of this *Grace* belongs to the secret of this hope, this Messianic Hope, to which the history of Israel must bear witness. She belongs to this Redeemer and this Creator and to no other. Any other definition of *Grace* is not the Grace of God in His BCR with His People in His Creation.

We may also read in the Psalter, Israel's hymn book for her worship, Psalm 2, and hear the significance of the Promise of the *chesed Yahweh* with the House of David raised up to a level of a *decree* for Israel. The *decree* establishes a relationship, as a Father to His Son, between the Lord God and the Sons of David. The psalm rehearses this *decree* of the relationship between the House of David and the Promise of Yahweh as Son and Father with a vigor that belongs to all the crowning of the kings in Israel as the People of God. Psalm 2 may actually be read with Psalm 1 as an introduction to the whole of the Psalter, and as such introduces the Messianic aspect of the Wisdom of the Torah among the nations. The Wisdom of the Torah and the Wisdom of the Father and Son relationship together celebrates the reign of the Lord God over all the nations in His Creation. The prophecy is experienced again and again in times when the kings are anointed according to this decree: '*I will tell of the decree of the Lord: He said to me, "You are my Son; today, I have begotten you!"*' (Psalm 2:7). The decree of the prophecy acknowledges from time to time the *chesed Yahweh* with the House of David as the Messianic King. The history of the Monarchy is bound up with this decree, with this anointing, with the meaning and significance of this promise to David. If we do not divorce the decree from the fundamentals of the Torah, commemorated in Psalm 1, then we will not divorce the songs of Israel's worship from the covenant with Moses and the righteousness of the Lord God in all times. This chosen Son of David of Israel's Monarchy bears that Grace of the Lord God that calls His People to the holy kiss in the chosen place where Israel may do among the nations that which is right in the Presence of her Lord and God. This is the Son Israel can never forget, lest she find herself with God's enemies against Him. This is the Son in whom she must ultimately find her refuge. The secret of the Promise will steadily sustain Israel and the House of David in her rejection of her Messiah and in her acceptance of Him according to the prophetic decree of the Father&Son relationship inherent in the Promise. When we are able to read the anointing of this *decree* of the Grace of the Lord immanent in the history of Israel's kings, we may hear the full weight of the 'Little Credo' of the Great I-AM the Lord God is in the development of the rise and fall of the Monarchy in the history of the People of God.

When we understand that the vitality of the impact of this living *decree*, the Royal Anointing, in the context of the royal priesthood to which it belongs, then we may obtain even more insight into the secret of the Promise with the People of God. In Psalm 110:4, we read that the Lord God has vowed with His Promise to make the House of David triumphant with another priesthood beside the Levitical priesthood inherent with Moses' Torah. A living decree is given to the throne of the House of David along with the Promise that establishes and wills to continue to sustain forever an order of priesthood that is after the orders of Melchizedek, an ancient priesthood whose origins are rooted outside of Israel's Monarchy and formation as the People of God. In this way, the Great I-AM the Lord God is in His BCR with His People in His Creation is honored for who He truly is with the history of Israel among the nations. It is laughable to the Lord God that any nation would come against the Torah of Moses and this Anointed Throne with its priesthood. Obviously, with Israel's worship comes an anointing of the *chesed Yahweh* that rests upon the House of David in continuity with Moses that honors the purposes of the Redeemer of Israel as the Creator in the Creation and His Revelation with Israel. Israel is who she is because He is the One He is and is rooted in His Promise coming from outside of herself, from outside of her history, from among the nations.

The secret of the BCR with these developments ought never to be ignored. The decree of the anointing with the Promise of the *chesed Yahweh* in the covenanted relationship provides for the House of David that new dimension for the new beginning His Royal Reign is with Israel. Implicit now is a decree that is always free to be realized and implemented by a priesthood that is after the order of Melchizedek, a priesthood rooted outside of the genealogy of the Levitical priesthood. The Royal Reign belongs to a Royal Priesthood that is new in the history of Israel. The Monarchy must not be deaf to this decree. Her standing among the nations depends upon her hearing of this *chesed Yahweh* with her. Even after the split of Monarchy into the kingdoms of Israel and Judah, all the kings are steadily bound by the promise in this decree. The deafness of the House of David to this decree and its meaning will in fact lead to her downfall (Isaiah 7 and so forth). But the speaking of the Lord God with this Promise is the Word that Israel bears among the nations that surround her whether she hears it or not. The development of her Messianic Hope, the thrust of her prophetic vision, bears the secret of this decree in the relationship between *Yahweh Elohim* and the House of David. He is as such a Father to His Son, believe Him or not. He has chosen this king to fulfill His promise to His People. We will look long and hard to find such a relationship existing between the gods and kings among the nations of the ancient world. Here is a decree that will stand, with the *chesed Yahweh*, with David reigning over the idols of the idol makers forever. We must learn to allow the meaning of the open dimensions of this decree, continuity and discontinuities, to penetrate into our understanding of its significance in the history of Israel among the nations. We must not allow it to escape our attention.

The Monarchy of Israel is thus the foundation for Israel's Messianic Hope in the world. This Kingdom is firmly and solidly rooted in a ground then that belongs to the wondrous promise of His *chesed* in the covenanted relationship. Over this BCR He reigns as the House of David King of Israel (cf. 2 Samuel 23:1-7; 1 Kings 8:25; 9:5; 11:12; 2 Kings 8:19; 21:7). His reign shall be known as the Kingdom of God. Without the *chesed Yahweh* with this David there is no Messianic Hope in Israel's prophetic history. There is no spirit and no vision of the fulfillment of the ancient Promise. But with His *chesed* the Lord God will be Father to Israel in the form of His Son, David, King of Israel. This is the promise that never is lost in the development of Israel's prophetic Vision. The Word of God for the prophecy is the Word of the Promise to David. Amos knows that with the loss of hearing of the Word of God, after Israel's judgment, the fallen Booth of David shall be restored (Amos 9:11-14). Hosea, among the tribes of the Northern Kingdom, knowing the profound nature of Israel's sin against the Great I-AM and her punishment, knows very well that the place of the House in Judah will not be vanquished forever (Hosea 3:4-5). Micah 7:18-20 reads: *'Who is a God like you, pardoning iniquity and passing over the transgression of the remnant of your possession? He does not retain his anger forever, but He wills* **chesed***; He will revive compassion for him and do away with his iniquities and He will throw into the darkness of the sea his sins. He will give 'emet for Jacob and* **chesed** *for Abraham which He vowed to our fathers in times past.'* Micah envisions in the Latter Days of Israel's history among the nations this Day of the Lord. The prophet of Jerusalem, Isaiah, knows the promise at the heart of the Vision of the Word of God in the eighth century BCE. The prophet is focused upon the David of history with his Messianic passions as the Light and Servant of the BCR in the world (Isaiah 9: 6: 11: 1-3). The year 701 BCE marks the way in history the promise of the House of David functions with Israel among the nations (Isaiah 36:33-35; 39:1-8). The Vision explicated by the so-called Second Isaiah firmly resonates with these concerns (Isaiah 42:5-9, 49:1-6). In Isaiah 55:3 we read: *'Bend your ear and come to me and hear and let your life live; I will cut with you the covenant of forever, the graces (***chesed***) of David, the one affirmed.'* In Jeremiah 23:5-6 (cf. Jeremiah 33:15-16), we learn that the Vision foresees a Day of Righteousness when the Branch of David will reign according to the prophecy. Jeremiah 30:9 reads: *'They will worship Yahweh (the Lord) their Elohim (God) and David their King whom I will raise up for them.'* Ezekiel 34:23 says: *'I will raise up over them One Shepherd and my servant David will shepherd them, and he will shepherd them and he will be over them as the Shepherd. I am Yahweh, the One who speaks.'*

The nature of the covenanted relationship between the Lord God and David is such that King Yahweh shall reign over Israel among the nations for as long as forever is, as Father to Son. The Israel of the Ancestors, the Israel of Moses, the Israel of King David and the Israel of the prophetic Vision of the Word of God is the object from which the Eyes of the Lord God shall not turn in time and times and time again. No matter how badly the kings and priests and prophets and sages of Israel misinterpret the Vision, the true and writing prophets across more than seven centuries are made to bear the divine pathos of this Holy Word and see to the Glory of the Lord its ultimate triumph among the nations in God's Creation. Israel's true prophets all understood that the age of the Bull Kings was long gone and the age of the Servant King in the form of the Messiah would come to fulfill the Promise to her. We do well to seek to understand the nature of this relationship, its prophecy, its decree, its anointed power in the reigns of the kings with their Father, King Yahweh with His People. If the Vision darkens with the centuries, it is not because the Promise shall fail, but because of the growing deafness of Israel's kings and their call to shepherd the People of God in the Monarchy of God. We will not understand the Great I-AM the Lord God *is* except with this promise in His Monarchy for Israel's history among the nations (Psalm 136). Israel has been called to hear this Promise even to the times of her ancestry—*'The scepter shall not depart from Judah, nor the ruler's staff from between his feet, until he comes to whom it belongs; and to him shall be the obedience of the peoples'* (Genesis 49:10). From her beginnings to her end, the *chesed Yahweh* belongs to an Israel He shall be able to proclaim is 'My People.' We cannot understand the prophetic Word with Israel without apprehending the Light of His Being who He is in His Becoming in the nature of His BCR with the People of God among the nations in His Creation.

This Only and Incomparable One reigns through His *chesed* with His David forever (Psalms 93; 96–99). The prophets write of His Promise throughout the development of the Vision, even beyond Israel's punishment from the Land and even beyond her return to the Land. Both Haggai and Zechariah know that Israel's history depends upon this Promise (Haggai 2:23; Zechariah 3:8; 4:14; 6:12), and even beyond the prophetic tradition, Judaism will continue to struggle to understand this Messianic Vision. It is in the midst of the struggle that we may read the setting for the beginnings of the Gospels of the prophesied New Covenant. Luke and Matthew deal with its relationship to the Lord Jesus. It is no wonder that scholars cannot find in any dictionary, whether in Greece, Babylon, or Israel, or even in the United Kingdom, a definition of the 'Grace' of this Promise, the *chesed* of this Vision. The Lord God Himself in interaction with His People forever defines His Grace. In the fullness of these times, the term will come to signify the embodiment of this 'Grace,' the *chesed* the Person of the Lord Jesus Christ is. We will have to discuss what it means that the Lord God with Himself must enact His decree for the House of David with a creative power that takes us even beyond *the* Beginning, with a New Beginning more profoundly solid than anything He had ever done before in the history of Israel in His Creation. What does it mean that the Lord God has incarnated Himself as the House of David of Israel's prophecy? What does it mean for us that this Only One is free to become His decree as this Man who is Messiah of Israel's hope in the world? What does it mean that God with His Incarnation as the Lord of all space and time would redefine in this way all things anew? What does it mean that He is free to redefine Himself in the BCR with these new dimensions the nature of His Being and Becoming that the Promise of the BCR is realized and fulfilled? The significance of the meaning of Grace rests with the secret of such discussions about the New World possessed with these messianic proportions of relationship King Yahweh has made with Himself as the Father He has chosen to become and is with His Son, the House of David. As the Great I-AM that He truly is, He is the keeper in this world of His decree to David. With His Promise He constitutes Himself the King who is the Promise. King David and King Yahweh are become this One whose Promise is kept. It is the personal reality of this Lord and God that holds the secret of this chosen relationship in His BCR with Israel as this David who is Messiah of His People's creation and redemption. We need to be able to discuss this Promise kept as far as we may and as best as we can in our times.

Centuries were spent struggling to establish effective renewals of this Promise to David. These were centuries when Israel as the People and Monarchy of God were given to worship the Lord God in the immanence of the decree of His Grace for her. This Grace in her worship steadily sought to gain from her a response that had to do with who He truly is with her, with His Righteousness and Justice and Glory. It was upon the ground of His Grace that she could find the blessings of His promise to her. Thus, the decree of His Grace was a diamond in the midst of the dusts of the world. It was true freedom among the idol-makers of the world. It was comfort in the midst of her sufferings in the world. It was the affirmation of her existence in this world. Yet Israel's history serves but to prove the wickedness of her kings. She produces but Bull Kings denying the significance of their anointing, of Israel's decree, of Israel's election among the nations. Israel with her Monarchy in her BCR with her Lord and God remains unable to be what she must be with the One He is. When we are able to read in her Psalter His Grace as the ground of her existence and worship, we can readily understand her wicked willingness to do not what was right in the Eyes of her Lord and God, but whatever in her own eyes.

Her ultimate fall from His Grace, the eventual Exile of the People of God from the Promised Land, and even after the Return to the Land in the Persian Empire, is made evident in the history she records of herself in the BCR. The crux of the judgment announced by the prophetic tradition is written somehow upon their hearts. These centuries are filled with prophetic schools and efforts to warn Israel from her idol making, her 'stiff-necked' preference for Golden Calves and her 'self-centered' wickedness with the Baalim of the Canaanite peoples among the nations. Prophets like Elijah and Elisha are raised up during these times to exhort steadily kings, priests, prophets, and sages of the People of God and the Monarchy. But the idol making persists and the emptiness of Israel's worship becomes more and more real until the prophecy is written down for its ultimate realization. We may readily in these times appreciate the meaning of His *'slowness to anger'* as the Divine Perfection that possesses in His covenanted relationship with His People the Wisdom of His Revelation. His *'long-suffering'* is more than evident. By the eighth century, when He has decided to minister His Wrath, both His Judgment and His Salvation are ripe for writing down. The ministry of the prophecy is written down. Men who must suffer with Him the rejection of the People of God will proclaim that Word of God who shall not fail. No longer will these prophets call Israel to repent and avoid their punishment. No more may they hope to turn back the judgment. Only from beyond the times of this judgment and its punishment may Israel look for a reversal of Israel's fortunes, for another renewal of her covenanted relationship with her Lord and God. These prophets write down a Vision, beyond Israel's judgment and punishment, the triumph of the Word of God with her among the nations. Beyond the destructions, beyond even her return from Exile, the prophets of Israel see the Day of the Lord as the Day of Salvation it will be. To articulate the Word of this Vision is the burden of all the prophets of Israel. The prophecy proclaims a Kingdom whose King will reign among the nations, that beyond the destruction which will be the experience of the People of God lies the Promise kept to her in the Promised Land. Israel will understand that the Word of the Lord is *'Emet* (faithful or true) with the Promise of His *chesed* to David.

We may gain some fundamental understanding of the wickedness of Israel's kings and the fall of her Monarchy when we study the Book of Hosea and the Book of Amos. I call Hosea's Vision of the Word of God 'The Great Reversal of the Great I-AM.' I would characterize Amos' words of the Lord God 'The Lion's Roar the Word of God is.' The relationship of the Word and Being of the Lord God is implicit in the ministries of these writing prophets, the first of their kind in a watershed century of Israel's history in the world. The eighth century before Christ in the history of the People of God marks a call to understand that judgment of the Lord God has been made against His People. The two books together shape the earliest assertions about the Promise in the BCR to the House of David. Beyond the Judgment the prophets announce to Israel and Judah the split kingdoms of Solomon's kingdom, Yahweh's faithfulness and grace is to be heard with His People.

I believe Hosea is the first book of the 'Book of Twelve' of Israel's Canon because this prophet proclaims the fundamental prophetic accusation of the Word of God against Israel as the People of God. I call the judgment and punishment announced the result of the loss of those onto-relations that belong inherently to the nature of the BCR between the Lord God the I-AM is and Israel. Hosea thus proclaims the great prophetic reversal of Israel's fortunes in this relationship, the power of the will of the Great I-AM to make Himself present and known for who He truly is in spite of His People's willingness to break the relationship with Him. The history of the prophecy ranges across the reigns of Uzziah (790–740), Jotham (751–732), Ahaz (732–715), and Hezekiah (715–686) in Judah and of Jeroboam (793–753) in Israel. The judgment against Israel was realized in 722, when she is punished as an unfaithful wife and removed from the

Land by Assyrian Armies. But her sister Judah also shall be punished, yet with Babylonian armies, when the House of David with the Ark of God is sent into Exile in 586. In Hosea 1:9, the crux of the rhetoric articulating the reason for the Yahweh's judgment may be read: '*And he said: "Call his name 'Not My People,' because you are not My People, for I am Not-I-AM to you!"*' This is the name of the third child born to Hosea and Gomer, whose marriage was made to bear an embodiment of the relationship of the Lord God with His People, and the name of the Lord God when His People have lost any real relationship with the I-AM He is.

Scholars can observe that Hosea 1:9 refers to Exodus 3:14. But few seem to understand the ontological implications (Being on being relationships) at the heart and spirit of the Word of God that writes the Vision of the prophet Hosea. Hosea is the first book of the Book of the Twelve in the Hebrew Canon because it lays down this fundamental accusation, the primeval disobedience of the broken relationship with which Israel is living in the Land. What her Lord and God has given her as the Great I-AM He is she has given to another god. The assurance of the prophetic deliverance of His People in the form of a Monarchy of God with His Messianic David has become seen as beyond the punishment of the People of God. Her faithlessness appears beyond judgment. Thus, she has doomed herself with Him. Yet she may not ever possess the last word in the BCR. Her broken relationship with Him may not last forever. The One who is who He truly is and who has made her for Himself shall have the last word in the His BCR. Yes, the wickedness of Israel and Judah's kings shall surely be punished. But beyond this punishment will come the Servant King of the Israel whom He will be able to call '*My People*.' We understand the broken relationship as a fundamental loss of onto-relations with the Great I-AM the Lord God is in the Land, when His Name has become used by Israel to marry other gods, the Baalim of Canaan. When the Lord God is named by His People '*Not-I-AM*,' then He shall judge her for the faithless wife she is to Him.

Hosea is this prophet called to embody the Word of God with his life and marriage to Gomer, perhaps a temple prostitute of the idol worship that prevailed in Canaan in his time. Their marriage echoes or reflects in some way the BCR between Israel and Yahweh. Israel's adultery with the Baalim is fornication in the Lord God's Promised Land. In this way, Hosea's marriage to Gomer is made to serve as a witness to the BCR between Yahweh and Israel and the justification of the punishment the People of God must endure. This is more than metaphor or symbolic story telling.

The marriage is made to bear three children, all of which are named for the sake of the announcement of the judgment against Israel—*Jezra'el*, a boy, *Not-Pitied*, a daughter, and *Not-My-People*, a second boy. Their names signify the range of the disobedience that marks the relations between the People of God and their Lord God, those who have been called to be '*My People*' among the nations. The names mean what they mean because they embody in some real sense the betrayal in the BCR of Israel's history with the I-AM He is. Their names signify the judgment Yahweh has determined to bring against Israel. As Hosea and Gomer are to one another, so the Lord God as the Great I-AM is with Israel. The marriage relationship bears with their children a significance for the prophetic history of Israel that belongs to the Divine Freedom of the Word the Lord God to punish His People for her unwillingness to be what they ought to be in His Creation. But Hosea's prophecy also announces with the judgment the fact that in His Freedom the I-AM the Lord God is remains as committed as ever, even beyond her punishment and divorce and alienation from Him, to be her husband. He will not be who He truly is without her. He will ultimately deliver her from her fornication with the other gods and make her the People of God that He shall call '*My People*.'

The name of the first born, *Jezra'el*, is a play-on-words in Hebrew on the name of Israel. *Jezra'el* means '*El will sow*.' Israel means 'El will straighten.' Just as once Jacob is straightened and given the name of Israel, God will sow a judgment with Israel and make her the Israel she had been intended to become. The reference to the name *Jezra'el* may be read in 2 Kings 9–10, where we read of King Jehu's revenge on behalf of Judah against the kings of Israel and the sister's willingness to marry with the Baalim in the split of the Monarchy into the ten northern and two southern tribes of the People of God. Jehu acts against Jezebel of Tyre and the sons of Ahab who have defiled the Land with their idol making. Jehu, though he acts in concert with Elijah's prophecy over Jezebel, goes beyond the law of an eye for and eye and a tooth for a tooth of the Torah, the *lex talionis* of Latin jurisprudence, and avenges with blood quite beyond what is called for in the Law. Thus, Israel has sown in the Land the blood of an injustice the Lord God hates. Now God will sow His judgment with His People in His Land. The name Jezreel marks the firstborn to Hosea and Gomer with an end for the kingdom of Israel.

The second child, a girl, is named '*Not-Pitied*.' She signifies the reversal of the *Rachum* of *Yahweh Elohim* even in the beginnings of the People of God. The reference of this name is found in the 'Little Credo' we studied in the context of the incident of the Golden Calf (Exodus 34:6). This compassion of God is absolutely essential for Israel's birth as a nation in the world, fundamentally necessary with His favor for her subsistence in the history of His Creation. Without His compassion, only false starts can be in relationship with His Beginning. The establishment of the covenanted relationship between Him as the Lord God of His People depends upon the reality of this Self-Defining One with Israel. '*Lo-Ruchamah*' signifies the holding back of the perfection of this care, when Israel's history has lost itself in the history of His Creation. Without His Pity, Israel lives in vain, as if in the darkness of a past that denies her own very beginnings in this world. To remove this compassion from His People is for her Lord and God to turn away from her, and to make Israel once more an orphan in the wilderness the world is without Him. Without the divine perfection this *Rachum* is of Him, the People of God cannot in fact be the Israel that is meant to be. We do well to seek to penetrate into the depths of the meaning of this compassion, this pity, that come from the self-defining and free Redeemer-Creator acting in the world for His People.

The third child is named '*Not-My-People*.' This second boy signifies the end of Israel in her BCR in the Land with Him. This boy is named to signify that the covenanted relationship with Him has been utterly broken by Israel's willingness to marry His Name to her idol making. The BCR as a marriage relationship between Himself and His People has been abandoned. To be named '*Not-My-People*' is to experience the annulment of your beginnings, the divorce of the marriage of your youth, the loss of your first love. This boy's name marks the complete reversal of Israel's vows in these relations, the disavowal of the ratification of the BCR, the dishonoring of the Torah given at Sinai (Exodus 24), a faithlessness in the face of the renewals experienced by Israel throughout her history as the People of God (Joshua 24, 2 Samuel 7, and so forth). Israel is no longer the People of God living in the Land under His Blessing. She is an adulteress existing under His Curse. Even the Creation must bear witness to her broken life. She is bent and warped back into a broken condition without any idea of her beginnings. She will be sent to defeat. Her enemies will exile her as a stranger among the nations, the way she once lived in Egypt, lost from the Blessing in the Land.

The three names of these three children mark the end of Israel's and Judah's life in the Promised Land. They anticipate her Exile from the Land

and her scattering among the nations. The reason for the names, the judgment they signify, is made clear throughout the prophecy: the kings of Israel have so shepherded the People of the Lord that they have turned the Great I-AM the Lord God is into what He is not, into the great 'Not-I-AM,' into the nothingness of their idols, and because He has become for Israel this *Lo-'Ehyeh*, this idol that is 'Not-I-AM,' Israel has become this 'Not-My-People.' The utter loss of the Being on being relationship of the I-AM with Israel, the fundamental nature of the BCR, is felt in all of its deep and profound impact upon the People and Monarchy of God. Now it will seem as if the Exodus never occurred. Hosea's accusations and judgments of this Israel and this Judah is announced in such a way, embodied in the marriage of the prophet and the prostitute, as the breaking up of the marriage between the Lord God and Israel. It is a devastating judgment. That the will of the Lord God for His People could be Assyrian and Babylonian armies is hardly believable. Most of Israel and Judah cannot believe it. Yet in spite of the devastation of this judgment, this great divorce, the Great I-AM that the Lord God is will not be who He is without her, without wooing her back to Him. Thus, I have called the prophecy *'The Great Reversal of the Great I-AM.'* Beyond the break up shall come a renewal of Israel's fortunes in the world that will cause even the Creation to rejoice.

The proclamation is made with surprising power and glory, with Messianic power and glory. The Lord God in the midst of the proclamation of His judgment is not far beyond the punishment for Hosea with her deliverance from her fornications and her restoration. When we read Hosea's prophecy of the judgment and utter desolation of Israel's Monarchy and about her Exile from the Land by both Assyrian and Babylonian armies, we are quite surprised to find on the heels of such utter devastation and its desolation the willingness of the I-AM He is to reverse the fortunes of His People. But with this willingness comes the realization that He is the One He truly is. He is not the 'Not-I-AM' of the idols of their imaginations, but their true King, not their Bull Kings, but their Servant King, their Messianic King, the Light of their Salvation in His Creation. He will name His People as the Great I-AM He truly is 'My People' when His Day has been realized in her history among the nations. He will keep with David His Promise in His BCR with her. The announcement of Israel's ultimate salvation immediately follows each proclamation of the judgment against her. Where she experienced desolation, she will experience salvation. *'And it will be that the number of the sons of Israel is* like the sand by the sea, which no one can measure and no one can count. It will be that, in the place where it was said of them, "You are not My People," it will be said of them—"Sons of the Living God."' One day the sons of Judah and the sons of Israel will be gathered together once again as one under one leader, who will establish the restoration of her fortunes in this world. In that day, *Jezra'el* will become Israel once again. Israel will be known as '*My* People.' She will once more be 'Pitied' (*Ruchamah*), and in that day she will know Him as the One He is, when a complete reversal of the meaning of her history in the world will be experienced by all the nations in His Creation.

The determination of the point of judgment and the surprising counterpoint of deliverance shape the form and content of the Book of Hosea. The prophetic movement of God's Being who He is in the history of Israel resonates throughout the Vision. Hosea 2:2–13 resonates the naming of the prophet's children and the devastating judgments, its desolating accusations and punishments, with the surprises of the power of the salvation of the Lord God. Hosea 2:14–23 envisions the marriage between Israel and Yahweh restored and renewed: '*In that day, I will respond, vows the Lord, I will respond with the heavens and they will respond with the earth and the earth will respond with grain and new wine and oil and they will respond with Jezra'el. I will sow her for myself in the earth I will pity "Not-pitied" and I will say to "Not-My-People," You are My People! And he will say—"My Elohim!"*' In the movement the complete reversal of the fortunes of Israel as the People of God, beyond the judgment, is envisioned. Even the Creation itself will take part in this great reversal of Israel's fortunes in God's world.

The two judgment speeches that follow the introduction to these movements (Hosea 1–3), call Israel to hear, just as Moses once called her to hear (4:1; 5:1; cf. Deuteronomy 6:4), give us to understand the irony of the prophet's insights into the punishment: '*Hear the word of Yahweh, O sons of Israel, because a case has brought by Yahweh against those living in the Land; for there is no faithfulness ('***Emet***) and there is no grace (***Chesed***) and there is no* **knowledge of Elohim** *in the Land—Hear this, O priests, and study, O house of Israel, O house of the King, give ear, for upon you is the Mishpa't (judgment).*' Without the '*emet* and *chesed* of *Elohim* in the Land, her prophets, priests, sages, and kings must find themselves under the curse of His Being and Becoming as the Lord and God of His BCR with Israel. Without real onto-relations with the One who is who He truly is in

His Divine Freedom and Holy Love for her, His self-defining and giving love for her, Israel is without the *chesed* (Grace) and *'emet* (Faithfulness) of His Promise, and therefore without *da'at Elohim* (Knowledge of God) in the Land. She is free only to worship her idols about Him, as if she had never been delivered from Egypt. Thus, the judgment is unrelenting and utterly devastating for the whole of Israel's existence in the Land. Her desolation and removal from the Land and His Blessing is like the Exodus and the Creation never happened. Yet the Promise shall be kept.

Always the great reversal of Israel's sufferings is very near in the judgments of the Vision. No matter how distant her destruction might appear to her, salvation is always in view. Again and again, the Book of Hosea's messages communicate a divine and holy passion of the Being the Lord God is as the Great I-AM He truly is of a Messianic reversal of Israel's fortunes in the BCR. It is the movement of this passion with all of its great pathos that works to show forth the salvation of the People of God in the Day of their Messianic David reigning over the Israel she must be in the Land. Beyond the shattered covenant, beyond the twisted politics of the times, beyond the disastrous foolishness of her stand and worship in the Land, beyond the history of her sin in the Land lies wonderfully and surprisingly announced the ultimate reversal of the fortunes of the People of God with their Lord and God, when the *chesed Yahweh* will have become well known with Israel in the Land.

The marriage of Hosea and Gomer, made to embody the meaning of the relationship between Yahweh and Israel in the Land, is not the only way the prophet employs to signify the reality of the Promise working in the BCR between Israel and God. The relationship of the Lord with the House of David is also embodied as the relationship between Father and son. This embodiment allows us to understand even more deeply the secret of the Lord God is as the Great I-AM in the movements. We may read it most profoundly in Hosea 11:8–11, a love song perhaps more deeply and profoundly felt than even a marriage relationship. The love of Yahweh for Israel's House of David as His People is a holy love whose power acts with divine freedom of His Being and Nature. In these, we can hear the inner life of God Himself, the power in the life of His determination with His Chosen Son. He is the Lord and God who will not be in this way without His People. He will be who He truly is with Israel even as a father to his son, in spite of the times of Israel's faithlessness, in spite of the Bull Kings of Israel's Monarchy. He will reign as this One that He is with His Son. He will accomplish all He has set out to accomplish with His Son. He will with this passion and determination be Israel's comfort. We read: *'Because El I am and not a man, in your midst the Holy One; even I will not come with wrath!'* It is for this reason that we can in the end listen to the first and best Love Song of life: *'Then they will never say again "Our Elohim" to what their hands have made or there the orphan can find compassion (***Rachum***). I will heal their turnings and love them freely, for my anger is turned from them. I am* (I-AM?) *like the dew for Israel; he will blossom like a lily, yes, even like the cedar of Lebanon is his roots; they will come forth—his shoots, and he will be like an olive tree—his splendor—his fragrance like Lebanon, and they who live in his shadow will live, O Grain, and they will flourish like a vine, his memory—like the wine of Lebanon!'* (Hosea 14:8–7). The love song of His passion is reminiscent here even of the passion we read in the Song of Solomon. It is this divine passion of the Great I-AM as the Lord and God of Israel's beginnings in His new beginning for His People in His Creation that we are reading. Salvation shall come to His People from this Only One! It comes as a husband to his wife. It comes as a father to his son. It comes with a very great love song, the love song that shall make Israel the wife and son Israel is to Him who is who He truly is. It comes to David in the Day of the reversal of Israel's fortunes in a world that is indeed His Creation.

But this song is sung with certain and divine wisdom. The rhetorical question that is asked at the end of the Book of Hosea completes the prophecy with the demand for this wisdom. The reader of the prophecy must read its vision with this wisdom. To understand, the reader must become wise about the prophecy's vision. She must become wise in her hearing of this love song sung for the times just beyond the judgment. Only the discerning will be able to grasp the intent of its passion. Only those who can truly hear may grasp the purpose of His divine love in freedom, His divine freedom in love, when both the Grace of judgment and the Grace of salvation bring true knowledge of God to His People. It is a song that is bound up with a justice whose righteousness is the Lord God Himself, the Great I-AM who is who He truly is, with and for His People in His Creation. Those who refuse to know Him for the Only and Incomparable One that He truly is in the way of His Grace in the world, those who prefer to know Him as an idol capable of some marriage with the Baalim will remain foolishly wicked against the Great I-AM. His Grace (*Chesed*) and His Truth *('Emet)* will go unheeded among them. They will remain blind

The Great I-AM of the Kingdom of God

to it, even in the midst of the punishment. Such deafness and dumbness is doomed, for His purposes in His BCR with Israel will be realized among the nations. Only with this wisdom and beyond this punishment shall they hear and see in the Day of the Lord the Promise kept with the joy and righteousness of the Lord and God He is. Hosea's understanding of the *Chesed and 'Emet* of the Great I-AM the Lord God is with His People resounds throughout all the prophets of the eighth century. Scholars refer to these years as a 'watershed' in the history of Israel as the People of God. Joel's vision of the Day is rooted in the nature of this covenant renewal and Self-Defining power and embodiment in His BCR with Israel (Joel 2:12–14). We even glimpse the possibility of His People, in the midst of her punishment, turning to Him because of this movement of the Great I-AM He is. We observe also that Jonah's objection to going to Nineveh is rooted in the prophet's understanding of the reality that He is this Lord and God, and that He is this *compassionate and favoring, long-suffering, and of great grace and faithfulness I-AM* for Israel with the nations (Jonah 4:1–3). If even the Assyrians might be saved and repent because of who He is, then Jonah prefers, until the Great Fish is made, another One. We have also found in Micah the great movement of the point of judgment and its counterpoint in the determination with His passion to deliver and save. The movement is inherent in what prophetic waiting is when it is for this Day: '*He will turn and he will have compassion (**Rachum**) for us; he will destroy our iniquities; he will hurl into the depths of the sea all of our sins; he will establish faithfulness ('**Emet**) with Jacob, grace (**Chesed**) with Abraham, which he swore to our fathers so long ago*' (Micah 7:19–20). From the times of Abraham and his sons, from the times of Moses and Joshua, from the times of David and the Sons of David, no one will be able to forget the Being of this Great I-AM the Lord God is.

If in the Book of Hosea we are confronted with the Being of the Lord God as the Great I-AM He is, in the Book of Amos we are solidly confronted with His Word. The words of this prophet belong to the Word of the Being and the Being of the Word in action with His judgment and salvation for His People in His Creation. The prophet Amos is particularly sensitive to the shaking of the earth in his time and the famine of this Word in the Promised Land. He announces His judgments with words that see a desolation that comes with the silence of God's Word. Silence, earthquake, fire, and famine mark the events of the prophecy. Taken together, Hosea and Amos show us what results from turning the

Great I-AM into the 'Not-I-AM' and living in the Land deaf and dumb to His Word among the nations. Amos sees the Word with His Wisdom throughout the nations in fact under judgment with Israel and Judah. Yet again, beyond all the devastation of such punishment, Israel among these nations will come to experience a salvation that is His keeping of His promise to the House of David: *'In that day, I will raise up the Booth of David, the one falling, and I will repair its broken places and its ruins I will restore, and I will build it as in the days of the past, for the purpose that they will inherit the remnant of Edom and all the nations that are called with My Name upon them, vows the Lord, the one doing this'* (Amos 9:11–12). Most scholars think that this oracle at the end of the Book of Amos was added to the prophecies of judgment perhaps by those who escaped from the Assyrian exile into Judah. It is difficult for them to understand the movement of the point and counterpoint of the passion of this Word who is the source of these eighth century visions. Amos' words roar like a lion for the Word across the Land. They are a fire among the nations in God's Creation. They mean God's NO to His People with her idols. They mean God's NO to the peoples of the world with their idols. But they also mean God's YES to the great reversal of the Lord in His BCR among the nations. The same lion that can roar in judgment can also roar to gather back together what he has scattered in His judgment among the nations. The one roar can judge and save. The one quake can shake a new world into beginning. In this way, the Lord God moves to keep His Promise to the House of David. We cannot, according to these prophets, allow the Word of God to become divorced from the Being of God. The divine passion in the movement of these points and counterpoints in the Vision must be integrated with the Speaking of the Great I-AM that the Lord God truly is in this world. If He is silent, then that silence means judgment. It sounds with the willingness of the People of God to turn Him into the great 'Not-I-AM' and to become deaf and dumb to His Voice, blind to His Word. Yet these prophets know that He speaks, He speaks to the House of David among the nations, and that this David of Israel's Messianic Hope is the center of all hope in the world.

Perhaps we may notice, with some cogency, the problems with which Amos' texts are preserved in the Scriptures. What we are given to read in Amos 9:11–12 is found quoted in Acts 15:15–18, St. Luke's account of the Gospel of Jesus Christ in the early centuries of Christian involvement with the Bible. The quote belongs to a context in which the apostle attempts to resolve the issues that surround the Christian understanding of Law and Grace in the Biblical World. Luke quotes these verses of Amos' prophecy from the Septuagint (LXX), a third century translation in Alexandria of the Hebrew scribal traditions. The quote in Acts reads: '*After this, I will return and I will rebuild the Tent of David, the one falling, and its ruins I will rebuild and I will restore it, so that they may seek—the remnant of men—the Lord, and all the nations upon who are called to inherit my name, says the Lord, the one doing these things being known from ages past*' (16–18). St. Luke's account read the Scriptures with the term '***Man***,' where Amos' Hebrew reads '***Edom***.' If the vowels of Edom are changed from e/o to a/a, then the consonantal text can be read as '***Man***' (*Adam*) instead of '*Edom*.' Around 300 BC, the Jews of the Diaspora in Alexandria, centuries after the eighth century prophecy, read the text in precisely this way that St. Luke quotes. 'Edom,' a judged enemy of Israel, was no more on the map of the world. But 'Man' was. To change the vowels seemed right enough, the universal significance of the prophecy. The prophecy is after all concerned with all mankind and not merely with Edom. So the Greek speaking Jews of Alexandria produced the Septuagint Bible reading 'Adam' instead of 'Edom.' The words of Amos in the Book of Amos belong to the Word of God that embraces time and times in judgment and salvation in both a particular and a universal hold that we cannot afford to ignore. The Word of God with Amos' words creates across centuries an understanding of the prophecy in the BCR that shall be fulfilled when the falling House of David is lifted up on a way that belongs to the Only and Incomparable One He is.

We confront this problem of the prophetic movement when we confront the meaning of the decree to the House of David among the nations. The prophecy bears a double meaning with the Word of the Lord. The anointed King David is the beginning of the House of David that will come to mean among the nations a universal triumph of the Word. In the same sense, we may understand that 'Adam' provided the more universal reading of texts that may just as well signify most specifically the 'Edom' of the Word of God in the time of Amos. The past as it no longer exists as well as the future belong to the presence of this Word in the world, the Word that provides His own framework of interpretation with Himself. How are we to understand such developments in Holy Scriptures? I would argue that both this concern for the universal and this faithfulness to the particular in the movement of the prophecy in the world must be retained by our interpretation of the texts and the intention of the Word of the

Being of the Lord God in prophecy. Here we are reading an intention that belongs to the purpose of God's prophetic promise in a freedom we dare not ignore. Through the prophet Nathan the Lord gave to David a promise He Himself will in time and times keep (2 Samuel 7; 1 King 8; and so forth). Both the Alexandrians and the Massoretes are servants of this one movement of this One Word that is the Lion as both Judge and Savior of the entire world. The times of Amos and Hosea knew both the roar that judges as well as the roar that saves with universal and very particular intent. The freedom to keep this promise in time and times shapes an embrace of history with always new dimensions for the prophecy. The Word of God who is this Great I-AM as the Lord and God of the prophecy must be understood with both Edom and Adam, and this One who is the Only and Incomparable One with the House of David in time and times. Messianic hope and time belongs to these new dimensions that are always meant to overcome a sinful past with a surprisingly wondrous deliverance, so that we may understand what both Edom and Adam shall be by the Grace and Truth of this I-AM judged and delivered for all time. Messianic hope without the hope of the prophetic movement of the Word with Israel among the nations, point and counterpoint, is no hope at all. The future of the world, in its particular nature and specific phenomena, possesses a wholeness that universally dependent upon this Word of Israel's prophets for its condition and destiny in the BCR.

 The greatness of the Vision of the Word of this Lord and God reaches its culmination in the eighth century with the great prophet of Jerusalem, Isaiah. The House of David as the seat of the Messianic Hope of the falling Monarchy is most firmly understood in the Light that Yahweh Elohim is with His Servant David, His Messianic Servant. This seat is absolutely fundamental for Isaiah's Vision of Israel's history in the world. We have already noted the way the promise of *Yahweh's chesed* for David's Throne is envisioned as being fulfilled within the renewals of Israel's covenanted relationship with her Lord and God. In this context the Light of Yahweh shines as the obedient Servant Israel has never been with the Lord God. His BCR with His People shall be well served in the Light of this Servant among the nations (cf. Isaiah 42:5–9; 49:5–6; 55:1–5). In His Light, Isaiah's prophetic claims for King David have become legendary throughout the world and will become true: *'For a child is born to us, a son is given to us, and it will be that the government is upon his shoulders, and his name will be called, Wondrous Counselor, El-Gibor, Father of Forever, Prince of*

Peace, so the increase of His Government and Peace is without end upon the throne of David and upon his Kingdom' (Isaiah 9:6). *'A shoot from the trunk of Jesse will spring forth and a branch from his roots shall bear fruit; he will rest upon him—the Spirit of Yahweh, the Spirit of Wisdom and Insight, the Spirit of Counsel and Might, the Spirit of Knowledge of the Fear of Yahweh'* (Isaiah 11:1-2). In the Light of this King with His Kingdom Yahweh as the Elohim of His People in His Creation shall reign victorious over all of His enemies, when a new heavens and a new earth shall be rid of all evil and sin against Him and death shall be decreed no more. In His Light, the nations will see the Redeemer of Israel and the Creator of the heavens and the earth as the Only and Incomparable One He is (Isaiah 60:1-3, 19), who is who He truly is as the Great I-AM He is. The function of the Light of this Servant upon the pages of the Vision is to bear that Word of God with Israel so that all the nations in His Creation shall see Him and hear Him for who He is. Isaiah's prophecy is most vividly rendered in this regard as one Vision of the Word of God who is faithful and righteous and in His BCR in the world. The **chesed Yahweh** is seen in Isaiah 63 working as the Father with His Servant and by His Spirit to keep the promise in His Day. He will not be denied its work in the world: *'I will remember the Praise of Yahweh, according to all they have accomplished—Yahweh— of great goodness towards the House of Israel, who accomplished them with His Compassion (**Rachum**) and with His great Grace (**Chesed**), and He said, "My People—they are."'* (Isaiah 63:7-8a). No one can read the words of this prophet without understanding that the Light of the World is the Word of the I-AM who is the Lord God in time and times with His People, faithful and gracious, even with His judgments, to His Elect among the nations. The Light of Yahweh in the Vision of Isaiah finds its resonance and reinforcement in the Light Jesus Christ is in the Gospel of John. It is a Vision that does not fail.

Throughout the eighth century and the turbulent centuries that follow, the Throne of this House of David is seen to bear for Israel the Messianic Hope of her future as the People of God in this world. There is nothing in the prophecy of the Vision of the Light of the Word of God Himself in Isaiah that does not find strong resonance and continuity with Jeremiah in the seventh century, with Ezekiel in the sixth century, and with Zechariah in the following centuries of Israel's Exile from and Return to the Land (cf. Jeremiah 13; 21-23; 30-33; Ezekiel 34; Zechariah 12-14). The prophets suffer for this Vision, even as the darkness grows more and more thick and drives His People from His Land, and even in her exile among the nations, the Messianic Hope of this Word retains vividly its dynamic stability in her history among the nations. Beyond the punishment lies the renewed House of David. In time and times and time again, it is this hope that stands firm in time, a firmness that belongs to the Lord God Himself, to His Promise in His BCR with His People, a covenanted relationship that reaches back into times past and forward into time future with divine and human muscle. Certainly, the Psalter of David bears more than ample witness to the Light of this Word in the midst of all the dark opposition to the Lord God He is with Israel among the nations. Moses' Torah together with the Messianic Hope of the House of David renders together for the People of God that worship and its wisdom whose depths and heights and breadths belong to all the ages of time. The significance of the various epochs in which Israel experiences her punishments and her deliverances shape a context for her prophetic faith that comes from and looks towards the David of this Day of the Lord God. When we read the times of the Exiles, the times of the Return, and the times of waiting that belong to Israel's Return, we read now this Messianic Hope everywhere in the world. From the fifth century onwards Israel's experience among the nations in and out of the Promised Land bears significance whose meaning is the secret of this promise and Hope. The Messianic Hope of the People of God remains forever with the secret of this promise and its prophetic realization in the Word of the *chesed Yahweh* with the House of David. The *Elohim* who created in *the Beginning* the heavens and the earth of the Beginning, who made mankind in His Image, and established His Sabbath Rest with all that He had caused to exist, is the Lord who reigns over and in all that belongs to the freedom of the Light of this Word. In this way, the promise of only the Only and Incomparable One shall be kept.

The Wisdom of God with Daniel the Sage in Babylon even belongs to these developments. Daniel's apocalyptic vision belongs to the prophetic vision through the Wisdom of Israel's Sage. The *Chesed and Rachum* of the Lord God with the prophets in Israel is with him as His Wisdom in the Babylonian courts (Daniel 1:9). He is given there in this time the wisdom to interpret dreams, to understand the various times of time that belong to this Messiah of Israel's Messianic Hope. His life, like those of Moses, Joshua, and David, belongs yet again to the renewal tradition of the BCR. With the Promise enfolded in the decree to the House of David the Lord God shall prove faithful. Daniel the Sage's ability to read the dreams of kings and sages lead him to his understanding and discernment of this hope in his time. His intercessory prayer in the reign of King Darius the Mede, recorded in chapter 9 of the book that bears his name, gives us insight into the nature of renewal as it is formed in the Diaspora of Israel among the nations. Just as in time and times past, the renewal is shaped as: 1) An Address to the Lord God 2) A Confession of Israel's sin history 3) A Petition for Forgiveness 4) The Petition for Favor, the future is understood as a final renewal of this Messianic Hope inherent in the BCR.

If Moses mediates between the Lord God and His People, if Joshua exhorts Israel in the Land, if King Solomon, the Son of David, intercedes for Israel in His Temple, Daniel the Sage acts on behalf of the People of God as the Exiled People of God. We read as his prayer of intercession an address to 'My Master,' to the Great 'El,' to the Fearsome One, to the One who keeps Covenant with His *Chesed* for His People, on behalf of all those who love Him and will keep His Command. Daniel, like those called before him, confesses that in times past, even though the Lord has been forgiving and compassionate with His People, His People have steadily brought down upon themselves His Curse in the BCR. They have attempted to live without His Blessing in the Land. Israel, as this 'stiff-necked' People of God has steadily stood against Moses' Torah, against the *'Emet* (faithfulness) of the Lord in the Promised Land. Daniel's petitions thus seek the divine forgiveness and compassion of God. The Sage knows full well, like David, that in spite of her sin the Lord her God will act with His Righteousness for Israel, in spite of her opposition to Him, beyond the punishment from Him in His BCR for her. His second petition acknowledges then, that it is not because of Israel's righteousness that she may seek His 'Mercy' (*Rachum*—Compassion). It is because of His Name that she may turn to Him. The Sage knows that the Great I-AM the Lord God is with His Divine Perfections defined in His 'Little Credo' will pour Himself into His Day for her salvation. Deeply and profoundly embedded in Daniel's understanding of the *chesed and 'emet and rachum of the Great I-AM the Lord God* is with the Wisdom of His Word for the Ages, whose salvation comes to Israel as the Lord and God He is even from *the* Beginning. Daniel's prayer for renewal is filled with this Wisdom, the Wisdom with which the Lord God will act for His Name's sake with Himself in His BCR with His People, so that Israel shall be saved even in the apocalypse of King Yahweh's *chesed* with His Kingdom. In this way, this One, this Rock, will prove faithful to His Promise with His House among the nations. It is because of this intercession that Daniel the Sage envisions and interprets the various dreams whose images bear in time and times and half-time of the ultimate triumph of the Word of this Kingdom of God in God's Creation (Daniel 2:44–45; 4:34–35; 6:26–27; 7:26–27). King Yahweh will reign; His Kingdom will triumph among the nations. This Only and Incomparable One is this King of Kings who keeps His Promise to that people He shall name '*My People.*' This is the Great I-AM He is. It is His Kingdom that shall stand forever and no other!

The Divine Freedom with which we understand the Lord God acts with Himself in His Covenant with His People in His Creation is seen working steadily with His Divine Perfections to be known in this way with Israel among the nations. He is self-defined with His 'Little Credo' in this way across centuries of struggle with Israel, until the Day when He as King with David shall reign as the One He truly is among the nations. In Exile, the People of God wait for His Day. In the Return, Israel waits for this Day. When Nehemiah invokes then, in his renewal of the covenanted relationship with Israel's Return from Babylon (chapter 9), the new leader understands that, in spite of Israel's 'stiff-necked,' 'high-handed,' 'murmuring,' 'self-centered,' 'faithless,' and finally 'wicked' opposition to Him in times past, the People of God may look, beyond her punishment and present towards a restoration whose time will be the fulfillment of what the Lord God had sought beginning with Adam, with Abraham and his sons, a steady and dynamic freedom across centuries meant to experience the Glory of the Promise fulfilled upon the earth and under the heavens. The seed of Adam and the seed of David belong to this Promise. It is in His mode of His Being the One He truly is that He will be known. It is as the *compassionate and favoring, slow to anger God, the Lord of great grace and faithfulness,* that Israel shall know Him for who He truly is. It is for Him that she must wait. It is for His Day that she must wait. She must wait in the Messianic Hope with His *chesed* upon her. It is in Him that her expectation must meet the surprise of His Deliverance for her.

But waiting is a difficult task for a wicked people. Wisdom does not come cheaply. It helps I think to apprehend really a trajectory that can bear the weight of the freedoms involved in the BCR. To take us from the times of the Return to the 'fullness of time,' when the Promise shall be kept, requires the real revelation of the Great I-AM the Lord God is in keeping His Promise to the House of David. It is not necessarily a logical trajectory that we grasp that lays hold of the secret. There is a verse in Psalm 50 that speaks to us about the troubles and difficulties that are inherent in waiting for this One who is the Great I-AM that is the Servant and Light of God as Israel's Lord. This psalm, addressed to *El, Elohim*, hears *Yahweh* speaking throughout the Land, from the rising of the sun until the setting, is not easily categorized by the scholars. Just where it belongs in the life of Israel's worship is not transparently clear to us. Yet it is clear that it is an exhortation in some setting of Israel's worship to focus upon the prophetic covenant renewal traditions with the People of God. The 'Thanksgiving Offering' in Israel's history is at the heart of the psalm's concerns. The accusation is that it is useless to offer up offerings without hearing the One who is speaking to them. Israel has no right to offer up offerings as if *Yahweh-Elohim* needed something to eat in order to exercise His power in His BCR with His People. Israel needs to take upon her lips the Torah and the other covenant renewals because He Himself is near and not far from her. Verse 21 culminates the case the Lord God has against His People: *'These things you have done, and as I kept silent, you compared the Being of I-AM to yourselves. I will rebuke you; I will accuse you to your face.'* This one time we may read in Israel's Psalter a reference to the Great I-AM of Moses' confession (Exodus 3:14). It is the nearness of this Great I-AM the Lord God is with Israel that is the source of the accusation against her. She is unable to take into her heart the One He is, and she offers sacrifices unacceptable to the Lord God He is. She must offer first her thanksgiving offering and then she will be pleasing to Him, then she will be 'My People.' It is no accident that Psalm 51, David's prayer for a clean heart, follows on the heels of Psalm 50's exhortation for the 'Thanksgiving Offering.' All offerings in Israel are to be made with a grateful heart that knows He is more near to us than we are to ourselves, that He is the I-AM who is more real than we are. In this way, we may offer blessed offerings in His Name. In this way, King David and the People of God belong to the *Chesed* and the *'Emet* of the Word of His Being in the Light of His Being the I-AM He truly is. In this way, His People belong to His Divine Freedom to be the One He truly is with His People, to be the Great I-AM He actually is as the Lord God He is in His BCR with His People and the House of David as King and Father to the Messianic Hope in His Creation. Not even His People's disobedience, right at the heart of His People's worship of Him in opposition to Him, shall keep Him from keeping His Promise to them. But waiting is difficult. Sometimes the distances seem great. It is hard to wait. Watch and wait! Wait and watch!

Wait! Watch! One loses heart, goes deaf, and becomes blind. It is not easy to see with your eyes and hear with your ears the realization of the Vision of His Promise. Yet He is more near than we are to ourselves. He comes surprisingly. He is present surprisingly. He heals us surprisingly. He delivers us from life-time's spent with our sin against Him, and even in the midst of the dark fire in which we exist against and without Him, He is the Son of David, the Son of Man, the Son of God.

His salvation and judgment are ministered with the immanence of the Wisdom of His Word in the decree that directs as His Grace the covenanted relationship between Himself and His Servant David, His Light to the Nations in His Creation. The terms of the 'Little Credo' are understood then as divine perfections of the Great I-AM mediating the Lord and God He is Israel's development of her Messianic Hope. We read throughout the Old Testament in this way the ground for that continuity we must find in the very Being, Word, and Acts of the I-AM He I and in no other. The Messiah of Israel's Hope in the world can only be understood on this ground, where His Divine Freedom and Holy Love for His People initiates in His Royal Way the promise of His BCR with Israel among the nations in His Creation. Again, here we may say, I believe, that we have found sent from heaven the diamond of divinity posited in the dusts of the world, the Grace of God immanent with Israel.

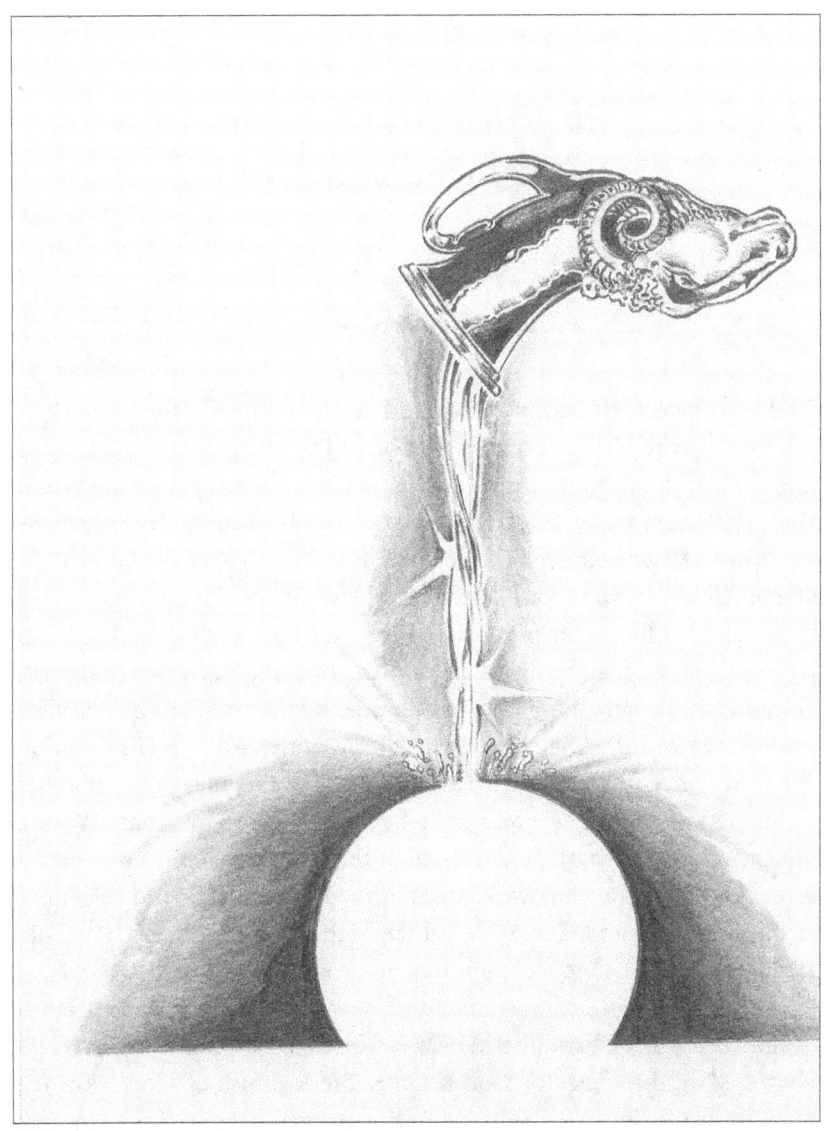

Pouring Into Light

7

The King, His Kingdom, and the Light of the World

Before Abraham was, I-AM!

John 8:58

The surprise of Grace comes with a new setting for the Voice He is, comes with His Speaking as the Son of David, the Messianic King, in the form of the Person of the Lord Jesus Christ, the Light of the World. With the same power that He created in the Beginning, He incarnates the Word of His Being as Jesus of Nazareth, the Keeper of the Promise of His Grace as His Grace. He is the Wisdom of the surprise of His Grace and Truth. The Incarnation of the Word of God, according to the New Testament, may be heard as what the Burning Bush was to the Old Testament. The new thing once prophesied by the prophets of Israel appears in the world with an utterly new form of the Voice in His Creation. What was once immanent with the People of God comes now embodied as the Son of Man. The Voice once heard as the pre-incarnate Word is now heard as the incarnate Word. All of the Gospel writers know that He is recognized as the One who comes in the Name of the Lord celebrated as the Goodness and Grace of God (cf. Matthew 21:9; Mark 11:19; Luke 19:28; Psalm 118). One must not remain deaf to Him.

This is the Word of God embodied now as the very Being and Nature of the Lord Jesus Christ, the Messianic King, Son of God, Son of David, Son of Man, the Grace of God keeping the Promise of God with new dimensions of being for God, new dimensions of being for Man, new dimensions of being for the Creation. Now is the Word of God with His Promised Blessing found in the time of Jesus of Nazareth. He is embodied as Man in the form of the David of Israel's Messianic Hope, of Israel's

Ancestral Promise. What has been so anticipated with the imminence of the Grace of the Lord has become, surprisingly, a new world for all. With this Chosen One comes the surprise of the Lord God's faithfulness with His Divine Freedom to embody Himself with His Divine Perfections as this New Man as the new Beginning of His New Creation. Here is the Man of God set to fulfill the time and the times of the past. Here is the Man who is faithful to the purposes and intentions of the Great I-AM the Lord God is in His BCR with Israel, His Elect among the nations. This surprise comes as the Grace and Truth of the Lord God who speaks in the time and times of Jesus, the *Chesed* of the Lord become known as the *Charis* among men of the great Son of David. Here is your King, O Israel, the apostles all proclaim. He has come to save His People among the nations. Behold, they say, this Man as God among us!

The Voice of this Only and Incomparable One, who spoke once with Moses in the Burning Bush and with great signs and wonders to deliver Israel from her afflictions in Egypt, the Great I-AM the Lord God is in His BCR with His People, comes to renew the relationship and to speak with new power for Israel's fortunes in His Creation. He comes as this Voice who speaks His decree upon His David as His David, which speaking holds the secret of the Father and Son and their eternal relations shared afresh and anew with His People. What was once promised to the House of David has become the House of David among the nations in a world that is His Creation. He comes as the Voice in the Name of the Great I-AM the Lord God is. He comes as the Voice of the New Name of the New Covenant of the Lord God, prophesied by Israel with the Word of her prophets, now fulfilled as this One. As this man, God the Son and Word of God has incarnated Himself in His covenanted relations in order to realize with His Father the salvation of His People among the nations. He speaks now as the Servant of the prophecy of the BCR who is the 'Light of the World.' The Light of God in the Old Testament has become the Light of God in the New Testament. The pre-incarnate Word is now become the incarnate Word. He comes and in this way speaks with Israel as her Savior. It is this One Israel has anticipated and expected. It is this Only One for whom she waits. It is this Incomparable One who bears witness with her to His Presence among the nations. It is in this world that His 'Very Good' Creation shall be justified. It is as this One that He is the Lord of space and time. To Him His People must listen. This One comes, beyond the imagination of everyone's expectations, as this surprising One. With Him is begun the new beginning. With Him is held the secret of the justification and righteousness of *the* Beginning. With Him then comes the New Creation! People had to struggle to hear Him, to see him for who He truly is. Something about Him always seemed so impossible! Yet no one could deny the authority with which His Voice spoke with them as this One that He is!

It is the history of this Voice in the world that is recorded in the Gospels and the Letters of St. Paul, St. Peter, St. James, and so forth, which formed the Apostolic foundations of the New Israel, the Church of the Lord Jesus Christ. We read this Voice as the New Testament of the Holy Scriptures. The lynchpin between the Old and the New Testaments belongs to a trajectory drawn with Divine Freedom of this Voice. The secret of the decree of the Grace of God with the House of David belongs to this Voice. This Voice draws in time the purpose of God's Promise being kept, of the fulfillment of His intentions as the One who is who He is in His BCR with His People. This is the Voice of the Great I-AM the Lord God is. He is the confession of the realization of Israel's Messianic Hope. He is the Voice of God's Being with Word in His Acts for His People in His Creation. He is the Lord God acting as the Messianic King and House of David whose Face is set towards the establishment of His Kingdom in this world's space and time. With this Voice, we hear the struggle of the passion and pathos of the prophecy of Grace with King David, the promise to the House of David. The decree of the promise has been apprehended as the Son of God and the Son of Man as the Son of David. It is a New Word for Israel among the nations, a world that is the New Creation begun. Evidently, it troubles us to hear Him. It is difficult for us to seek to understand Him as the Great I-AM He is in this way of His Word, His Being and Becoming, His Nature in His Divine Freedom to make Himself present and known with His People in His Creation.

But Israel's existence is destined in this way for life with Him. To this Voice belongs the secret of that continuity between the Old and the New Covenants established by the Only and Incomparable One. With this Voice belongs the secret between the Eternal Life of this One and the existence of time and space and the human race. As we read the Testaments, Old and New, the dynamics of the trajectory drawn by this Voice creates a stability between what has been and what shall be in an embrace of a present that is itself a new reality in the world. This One's Voice embraces both the real continuity and the radical discontinuity in the nature of the BCR. We experience with the hearing of this Voice in the history of the world a whole new form of the Word of God, unheard by the world, speaking as never before the Word of the Prophets of Israel. This One Voice binds together in His Divine Freedom and with His Holy Love the created realities we read in the Old and the New Covenants actualized with this Great I-AM as the Lord God He is. This One Voice of God now speaks as the person of the Lord Jesus Christ, Son of David by the decree of the Grace of God, Faithful Witness as this One to the One He is with the Almighty Father. It is the subject of this Voice that has been written down on pages of what we now call the Holy Scriptures. We need to learn to appreciate this Voice that comes to us from the pages of the Holy Scriptures of the People of God. When the person of the Lord Jesus confronted the leaders of Israel in his time, again and again He faced them with Himself as the One who held the key to the prophetic enigma of the decree with the *chesed Yahweh* for the Messianic David. He is Himself the Son of David for whom they are watching and waiting, waiting and watching (cf. Matthew 22:41-46; Mark 12:35-37; Luke 20:41-47). In the context of the Torah of Moses, the Son of David as King and Priest of the New Covenant, in fulfillment of the Old Covenant, is to be understood as the Grace who is the Son of God and Son of Man, the Messianic King, the Lord Jesus Christ (cf. the Book of Hebrews). In his letter to the Romans, St. Paul the Apostle is no less insistent upon the reality that the dynamic stability of the trajectory we need to grasp is bound up with both the Son of God and the Son of David (Romans 1:1-7). This Voice is to be heard throughout the apostolic witness of the New Testament to the Old Testament's Torah and Prophecy. As such, He is as the Image of God who is born of the Father in Eternity and of the Father in space and time, the Incarnate Son of God, at once both the image and the reality of God (Colossians 1:15-20). It is my experience that many people find it very difficult to lay hold of the dynamical continuity and discontinuity implicated in this movement of fulfillment that is inherent in the way the Old and the New, as they are related for us in the Biblical World, is proclaimed. We find it troublesome to know that this world is in fact what it is as God's Creation with God the Son embedded in its physics and evolution.

We may gain some insight into the enigma of this prophetic fulfillment by taking seriously the way that St. John uncovers the Father and Son relationship between God and Jesus Christ. It is in this relationship that the Son of God and the Son of David as the Son of Man witnesses to the fulfillment of the decree of the *chesed Yahweh* with the House of David. It is

Christ's faithfulness to His Father that is to be read throughout the Gospel. It is this faithfulness that does what Israel and her Bull Kings had never been able to do. It is this David that does go to the place where His Name has been established and there does do *the Yashar* in His Eyes. It is within this relationship that the Light of the Word of God shines with the Life of the Lord God embodied as the Great I-AM who is the Messiah King, the Person of the Lord Jesus Christ. He is the decree embodied in this place, this space of the fullness of time. It is in this Light that we may learn to see and hear the Word as a man whose being and nature is faithful to the Father, for our sakes, in our place, on our behalf, that we might know Him for who He truly is as the God He is.

The Prologue to John's Gospel (John 1:1–18) establishes for us the context for understanding the implications of this new reality of the Word of God in the world where the form of God's Grace and Truth is incarnate as a man named Jesus Christ. In Him, the Word has become something He is not and has never been, and in this movement created the continuity we must apprehend in order to grasp the significance of the fulfillment of the Promise in Him. With this Gospel, He is confessed as the Only One who is able to possess as a man the very real knowledge of God that belongs to His Grace and Truth. As the Grace and Truth of God He knows the Grace and Truth of God. He knows the Father as no other knows Him. In this context, we are given to understand that the Word of God's Being and Life, who was God with God in *the* Beginning, has assumed flesh for Himself to work to His Glory to keep the Promise to His People in His Creation. He has chosen to live as this particular man among us, even as His own refuse to know Him for who He truly is. In spite of all opposition, through Him the believer is given to know the way to the Father, to know the Father in His Son, the Son in His Father. In this way, the Lord God has taken upon Himself flesh from the House of David, that as the Son of God He might reveal with His Faith the Grace of the Promise kept by the Great I-AM He is. Here is the decree proclaimed for all men, that all men might see and hear the Light of the Word in action in the space and time of His world. This is the Word who is the *Grace* and *Truth* of God Himself as the Son of Man acting on for His People in His BCR in spite of Israel's rejection of Him. This is the New Man, the faithful David in the Lord's Day, the New Beginning of the New Creation. As such, He is the Light that enlightens all flesh. As such, He is the Great I-AM with His Word speaking as this Only and Incomparable One the Lord God is with

His acting to fulfill Israel's prophetic promise in the world. No one can read the term 'light' in the Gospel of John without some strong resonance with the 'light' that we read in the Vision of Israel's prophets. We need to understand the very real dynamics of this new reality in God's Creation as the way the Lord God has taken with Himself, old and new, in order to be who He is as faithful with the Grace of His Promise to His People among the nations.

The Gospels together know the continuity provided by the Voice of this Word. Because of this knowing, they can lay down the apostolic hearing of the meaning in this Naming of the Lord God in His BCR with His People. The *Theos* (God) of the New Testament is the (*Elohim*) of the Old Testament. The *Kurios* (Lord) of the New Testament is the (*Yahweh*) of the Old Testament. For the apostolic hearing of the prophets, the *Elohim* known as 'Kurios' has become flesh in the form of the Jesus who is the Christ as the Grace ('charis', *Chesed*) and Truth ('aletheia', '*emet*) of God with us. The *Chesed of the Old is the Charis of the New. The 'emet of the Old is the Aletheia of the New. The Grace of the Old is the Grace of the New. The Truth of the Old is the Truth of the New.* Even in the employment of the Name, we may hear the Voice of a continuity that often escapes our attention. But unless we are able to read these terms with the continuity they imply in mind, we will not be able to grasp the dynamic stability and concrete creativity that belongs to the Old and New Covenants, to the prophets of Israel and the apostles of the Church. When the Word became flesh as the Man Jesus Christ, the *Grace* and *Truth* of the Lord and God of the decree with David entered the world, embodying with Divine Freedom a human freedom truly free to be the Son of God and Son of Man. In this way, He is set to keep the Promise of the Old as the New Man of the New Covenant in the New Creation. It is as such that we may understand the significance of the 'fullness of time' that belongs to His birth, life, death, resurrection, and ascension to His Father. It is in His Light we hear and see the promise of the decree kept in an utterly surprising and creative way that belongs to the Great I-AM of the Self-Revelation, Self-Naming, Self-Defining, Self-Giving Lord and God covenanting with His People. As this New Man, He is the Messianic King of Israel's hope. The confrontation between Himself and Israel has reached a fullness whose time has come. The prophecy is fulfilled surprisingly. In the midst of judgment comes her deliverance once again, but this time for all time. It is the surprise He is as His Grace and Truth that faces us when we go to His space and time to understand what is 'Right' in His Eyes. It is not easy for us to believe He is who He is in this way.

But however surprisingly, we see that the Lord God is free to move outside of Himself as the Redeemer-Creator and become something He has never been, something He is not, while remaining the Only and Incomparable One that He is. He moves with His Divine Freedom to become something new even for Himself. This is the nature of the Being of the Great I-AM, who is who He is with His Holy Love in His BCR with His People in His Creation. Unless we apprehend the significance of the Incarnate Word in this way, no logical trajectory can be traced between the Testaments. The watching and waiting of the People of God was broken by this surprise. He came as a blinding 'Light,' the 'Light of the World,' as Israel's obedient Servant, the New World Servant. If the confrontation between God and His People led the Lord Jesus to His Cross, the nature of the judgment and the deliverance of Israel and the Church is defined by this Resurrected and Ascended God. It is a nature that belongs to the Only and Incomparable One at the Right Hand of His Father and to no other. The destiny of the Creation itself is bound with this surprise. The destiny of the People of God is bound up with the surprise of God's willingness to deliver them, like once He delivered them from Egypt. Destiny in this way is bound up in the very real meaning of freedom in time and space in this world. It is, indeed, a wondrous surprise, a tumultuous promise kept, a destiny rooted in the very ground upon which we may stand before the very Being and Word of the Great I-AM the Lord God is and live as His People in His Creation.

When we do take seriously John's Gospel in this way, we hear the Voice of the Word of God as the Voice of the Great I-AM, the same I-AM who spoke in pre-incarnate forms long ago to Abraham, Moses, and David. Israel's confession of Moses and her Exodus from Egypt has now become embodied in her Messiah as the Son of God and David. This embodiment of the 'Little Credo' in the history of Israel, this promise of the decree with the House of David kept, this movement in time in which the Lord God creates as the Great I-AM He is the tabernacle for His Name is where we must go to do that which is 'Right' in His Eyes. He is personal reality of the way of this Lord and God as the Person of the Lord Jesus Christ, the Messianic Hope and King of Israel realized in His covenanted relationship as the One He is with His People. In this way, John's apostolic witness moves with Moses beyond Moses on a trajectory that belongs to the Glory of God's *Grace* and *Truth*, Old and New, with His People. We must be able to hear the Voice of this witness as the Great I-AM the Lord God is in His Divine Perfections moving to fulfill the intentions of His purposes with Israel and finally becoming embodied in the Messiah, the King. Thus, we are asked to understand that Jesus Christ, the only-begotten Son of the only God, the *Elohim* or *Theos* of the Creation, is the *Yahweh* or *Kurios, the Creator-Redeemer* that is in the Name of the Lord Jesus Christ. Through this Only and Incomparable One, we may understand the Redeemer-Creator as the One who has revealed our Father to us in covenanted relations with us. It is futile to look for continuity between the Old and the New elsewhere. It is fruitful to grasp them in this way.

The witness then to Jesus Christ that we read in John's Gospel confronts us with this Face of God Himself. In this way, the deep and profound and abiding conflict with Him is compelled out into the open, a conflict whose testimony is read Old and New between God and the world as His Creation. What arises in the confrontation between their Messiah and the Jews about the way the Lord God has fulfilled with the New Covenant the purposes and intentions of the Old Covenant is something so surprisingly new that it posits beyond everyone's expectations this New Face in the world, a Face that affects the shape and substance, form and content, of the whole world. The Great I-AM the Lord God is has set Himself in His Name within the orders of His Creation, so that, like the Voice with Moses from the Burning Bush that once commanded His People out of Egypt, now He commands His People out of their sin with the gods of this world once and for all time. The Old Covenant's promise is the New Covenant's fulfillment. Israel's Prophetic Word, when sin is covered and forgiven is to be heard in the New Creation as the justification of the 'Very Good' Old Creation in *the* Beginning. Here, with this New World, a Vision has been realized where the wholeness of its being and nature would honor the King of Israel, the House of David, the Father and Son of the Lord God's decree with the David of the Day of the Lord. This Face of this One may lead to a continuation of the great conflict between His People and Himself in the BCR, but this once 'stiff-necked,' 'high-handed,' 'murmuring,' 'self-centered,' 'faithless,' 'wicked,' and now 'hardened' People of God only provides the ground on which His Voice is to be heard, in spite of all opposition to Him, as the Deliverer of Mankind as His Image from its sin against Him. In the midst of the judgment, He will work the many healings and wonders of His deliverance for them. Here we can see the whole history of Israel's sin confronted with the great *Grace* and *Faithfulness* (Grace and Truth) assumed with Divine Freedom and Holy Love into the personal care and compassion and long-suffering of the Lord God with His People in His Creation. His long-suffering, with His favor and compassion, in grace and faith of the Lord Jesus Christ bears to the Father the evil there is against Him in His Creation—the Divine Forgiveness of which we read everywhere in the witness of the New Testament to the New Man of the New Creation. The Great I-AM as the Lord God He is, once from the Burning Bush, now from the Incarnate Word and Son of God speaks with His Cross, Resurrection, and Ascension even to our times in this world.

To give us to hear this Lord and God as a man bodily resurrected from His Death for us, John shapes seven I-AM sayings for his readers: 1) 'I AM the Bread of Life' (6:35) defines the Flesh of Christ and Eternal Life for the disciples as food from His Father. 2) 'I AM the Light of the World' (8:12, 9:5) defines the space and time in which Jesus claims that He is in fact the Great I-AM (8:58) with His Father. 3) 'I AM the Gate for the Sheep' refers to Jesus as the access He is to His Father (10:7). 4) 'I AM the Good Shepherd identifies Him as the Shepherd King sent by His Father (10:11) as God's Son (10:36). 5) 'I AM the Resurrection and the Life' defines the comfort He provides for those who like Martha and Mary, face the death of their brother (11:25). As such He is the One who is (13:19). 6) 'I AM the Way, the Truth, and the Life' (14:6) establishes the ground upon which Philip may believe, but also His Name and the gift of the Holy Spirit to those who love Him (14:14). 7) 'I AM the True Vine' (15:1, 5) provides an articulation of His relationship with His Father and with those who believe in Him. This I-AM that He is establishes a center in the world where His Glory may be witnessed (12:26; 14:3; 17:24). As this One He shows Himself to be the I-AM the Lord God truly is. In the Light He is, He is to be seen as this Great I-AM, as the Only and Incomparable One who spoke with Moses from the flames of the Burning Bush now Incarnate. He is to be known as this One who called Abraham out of Ur of the Chaldees. He is the Lord God of Abraham and Moses and David, the Lord of the Living and He is able to make known His Father in His BCR fulfilled with them for the sake of all mankind. It is in this way that we are rightly to hear John's witness to Him: '*Amen, amen, I say to you, before Abraham came to be, I-AM*' (8:58) is a claim that posits Him with His Name at the very center of the world. The world's destiny belongs with Him as its Redeemer-Creator. It was this claim that made Jesus a blasphemer in the faces of the Jews. It was this claim that provoked them to accuse Him, the bastard from Nazarene, of trying to pass himself off as their Lord and God. For this blasphemy He deserved death. For this blasphemy, it is clear that He has a demon. For this blasphemy He must, by any means, be put to death. He is a pretender and not the Messiah. He has made Himself, in their eyes, a worthless man. The Torah commands his death. The evil one is behind such claims, and the Command of God means He must die.

It is important to understand that the conflict between the Christ and the Jews is a prophetic event. The issue is 'Knowledge of God,' just as it was the issue in the days of Hosea. The issue then is truly the Father, the Father of Abraham, Moses, David, and the Lord Jesus Christ. Everything Jesus as the Christ or Messiah of Israel's history does and says is witness to His Father. He is the Son sent by His Father. He is the One who is faithful to the Father. As the Word He is, as the Great I-AM He is, He acts in the world among the Jews as the true Revelation of the Promise of their Father. As this Son of God and Man, He is the Son of His Father. This Word of God become flesh is the One He is acting among them in the world as the One who truly knows the Father. It is His Knowledge of God that is the Knowledge that gives to those who believe in His deliverance, just as once He delivered His People from Egypt. He is the New Exodus for the New Creation. Outside of Him, outside of the 'Light of the World' He is, there remains but the darkness of God's judgment upon His People among the nations. In Him, all those who believe will see His Day, His Salvation for them. Thus, He is the Eternal Life of God Himself for all mankind. No one has ever seen the Father except the Son, and the Son has made transparently clear through who He is the Almighty Father. He is as this man the True Believer. He is as this man the Giver of the Spirit of God to all men. He is Himself the fulfillment of Israel's prophecy. Sent from the Father, He gives by the Spirit of God true knowledge of God to all those who believe in Him. In this way, His birth, His death on a Roman cross, His resurrection from the grave, His ascension to the Right Hand of His Father accomplishes in the 'fullness of time' the atoning work of His Holy Love to reconcile Jew and Gentile to who He is. In His Divine Freedom, He has chosen to fulfill the prophecy in this way. Perhaps the most wondrous words in John's Gospel are stated in the invitation He extended to His Disciples in one of His resurrection appearances with them.

'Come and have breakfast' (John 21:12) is the New Man God is in action in this world. At this table by the sea, his disciples are invited to know that He is the Great I-AM who is this Lord (*Kurios—Yahweh*) and this God (*Theos—Elohim*), this One that Israel is called and commanded to love!

John's account of the Gospel resonates in this sense with Matthew, Mark, and Luke. The so-called Synoptic Gospels witness to the Great I-AM He has become as the incarnate Word and Light of God, Son of God and Man, with a decided focus on the Son of David of the Messianic Kingdom. Each of these gospels bear witness, each in their own way, to the birth, life, death, and resurrection of this King, yet they resonate with one another in the Light of His Being as the Person of the Lord Jesus Christ. We need not seek to harmonize their witnesses. This is not the best of all possible worlds, but the world God has made for Himself with His People in His 'Very Good' Creation. We need to hear the apostolic ministry as belonging to a wholeness the particulars of which are found with the passion and pathos and purpose of the Lord God who is in His Divine Freedom the Great I-AM of the Messianic Hope of Israel's Prophecy, the King of Israel's covenanted relationship among the nations, the Only and Incomparable One who is as the Redeemer-Creator of the world the Savior of what He has caused to be.

The Son of Man in Mark's gospel is the King of the Kingdom of God. He reigns with His 'messianic secret' in hand. It is a secret that belongs to the secret bound up with the Grace of God and the House of David (Mark 10:47; 12:35–37). The Grace of the prophecy with this House is in fact implicated throughout the witnesses. In the face of this secret, we may appreciate the 'immediacy' that prevails throughout Mark's account of the Christ. The apostle understands Him, identified with the Servant of God, as the immediate fulfillment of what had been foretold in Isaiah's Vision. The Christ reigns as the Risen Lord, Messiah of Israel, clothed with the Gospel of God's Good News in the world. Matthew sees this Messiah as the Christ of the Kingdom of Heaven, the fulfillment of the prophetic Word of God proclaimed by Israel's prophets. The King of the Kingdom of Heaven in Matthew's gospel is seen as the Light for the nations prophesied by Isaiah (cf. Matthew 4:12–17; Isaiah 8:23—9:2; 42:6; 49:6). This is Light we are to see acting as the Servant King for the Kingdom of Heaven in this world. He is the Righteousness of God and no other. He is the fulfillment of the Torah and no other. He is the bearer of Grace to His People and no other. Salvation belongs to Him as the Only and

The King, His Kingdom, and the Light of the World

Incomparable One that He is. To Him belongs the 'Latter Days.' This is the prophet of Israel's future. The gospel according to Luke's witness, one that should be read in concert with the Book of Acts, also resonates with this understanding of the House of David as implicated with the future of the People of God. By the Spirit of God to the 'fullness of time' belongs the 'today' of the Lord. He is the Lord of time as the Grace of God with His House. With and in this 'today,' the Lord God has opened up His Heart to His People. He has poured out in time the Eternity of His Being. He has in this way fulfilled the prophetic hope promised His People. He has met Israel's Messianic expectations with this One, surprisingly. We hear in this time the great offerings of thanksgiving for His salvation with His People: *The Magnificat* (Luke 1:46–56), *The Benedictus* (1:67–80), and *The Nunc Dimittis* (2:25–32) are all given with gratefulness of His Grace with the House of David. They all mark with His '*today*' the time and times of Israel's history in the world. They mark each in their own way with new dimensions the nature of time and space He has begun as the David of the New World. The Synoptic Gospels witness the significance of the Lord of time and space in this way of thanksgiving for the Son of Man.

Luke's account of the beginning of the life of Jesus Christ with these offerings, like Miriam's 'Song,' (*The Magnificat*) belongs to the great tradition of Israel's thanksgiving offerings, gratefulness for the deliverances the Lord God has given Israel to experience in her history among the nations (cf. Psalm 136). The 'Thanksgiving Offering' is fundamental for any real explanation of Israel as the People of God in the ancient world. We may read the significance of this history of Israel's judgment and deliverance in Psalm 50. Miriam's Song, like Moses' and Deborah's (Exodus 15), is sung in the midst of His judgment upon her House because of His deliverance of it. Because she belongs to the House of David and belongs to the space-time where God has chosen to set His Name, Miriam of Israel bears with ordained gratefulness the House's acknowledgment for another of His Mighty Acts in Israel's history as His People. She invokes His Name in His Mercy ('*Eleos*'), which in this case resounds the Compassion (*Rachum*) of the Lord God with Israel. (Although the Septuagint often translates *chesed* with '*eleos*, in the New Testament it is meant to signify the *Rachum* that the Lord God is in any and all real beginnings in Israel's history. She possesses in her womb the *compassion* we have had defined for us in the 'Little Credo' of the Great I-AM (Exodus 34:6). Such beginnings as these have been commanded, for instance, at Abram's conversion to Abraham along with the Promise with his seed as a nation among the nations in this world. Acts of God's beginnings cannot be understood without this *compassion*. Miriam's birth to the Son of David, this Son of God, belongs the histories of such beginnings, but with something that is new and final. As such, she mothers Israel with the Promise to the House of David. As such, she is the chosen link of the Angel of the Lord whose Voice in the Old Testament and whose Voice in the New Testament is to be heard with her. Without Miriam's 'Song,' the song for the new beginning of the new world to be posited with the David of the Kingdom to come could not be sung. Known in Christian circles as 'The Virgin Mary,' she is the solid organic connection between the Old and New Covenants of Israel's history among the nations. She wombs with His compassion the Lord God in His Divine Freedom and Holy Love to become present and known among His People in His Creation. She is the chosen subject of the House of David where the Promise of the *chesed Yahweh* shall be kept. She knows the faithfulness of the compassionate One. The birth of her son bears the secret of His *Chesed*, God's Grace with the House of David. As such, she is the Mother of the Son of God. She is the bodily actuality of the renewal of His BCR with His People in His Creation. In this way, the history of Israel is acted upon by the Almighty to give the world the Messiah, Israel's obedient Servant, the 'Light of the World.' With her song is sung that '*thanksgiving offering*' for which the whole world must learn to give thanks to God as His Grace and Truth with us. We need to remember that Miriam is in the history of Israel what Judas is not. It is her Son that must be received even by the whole world. To Him all peoples must learn to listen. To reject Him is to deny the Word of the Lord God in the world, a denial that is a kind of suicide. With the acceptance of the Virgin, the significance of the life of Miriam in Israel's history provides the rational connection, the real intelligibility to be grasped between the Word of God in the Old Testament and the Word of God in the New Testament. The secret lives with the time of her Son. The Son of Mary, the Son of God, the Son of Man, the Son of David possesses the secret of the world as Lord of all space and time.

I have always been amazed and I continue to be astonished at the way the People of God can seek to misunderstand and annihilate the significance of Miriam's existence in our world. I suppose I should not be so surprised, given the way Israel is to be understood as capable of turning the Great I-AM the Lord God is into the 'Not-I-AM' for the sake of her idol making. We seem unable to avoid making them into things they are not. On the one hand, the Roman Church can promote her being who she is by mystical and supernatural reductionisms upwards of her existence in God's Creation. On the other hand, the Protestant Church can reduce the reality of her being the person she is down, by indifference and ignorance, into an existence in which she is acknowledged, perhaps once a year, as one sinner among the many of us. Between magic rituals as some sort of 'Redemptrix' and the forgotten 'Mother of God' she is, Miriam of Israel's House of David, the 'Virgin Mary' is never understood as who she actually is and who she ever will be as the Mother of the Son who is the Son of David who is the Son of God. Why do we have such great problems understanding her and her *'thanksgiving offering'* as the woman and mother she is in Israel's history among the nations? Why does her gratefulness not mean in the history of the world what it ought to mean for all mankind and the entire world? The personhood of her being and nature may not be reduced upwards or downwards with our understanding of her any more than we may reduce up or down the Person of the Lord Jesus Christ, her son. We may not turn her into something she has never been and is not and never shall be. The secret of the Grace of personhood in our times belongs to this Biblical World, Old and New, where with Miriam's child belongs the time and times of her Son for as long as forever is with His Eternity!

The father of Elizabeth, Mary's friend, is very explicit: '*He has raised up a horn of salvation for us, in the house of his servant David, as he said long ago through his holy prophets . . .*' (Luke 1:69–70). Miriam of Israel is to bear into the world that Son of David who is the Messiah of Israel's prophetic Word. The relationship between the Old and the New with this One has been solidified with this Word. This Word was once not incarnate and now in this time He is incarnate. This Son has made real and substantial the rationality of the Word of God's Promise as embodied in His space-time. Miriam of Israel bears the secret of God's *Chesed* with the House of David and the People of God. Her Son is Israel's King and God's way of keeping His Promise with the fallen Monarchy. Miriam gives birth to the way that the Lord God has chosen to set His Name among His People and meet Israel's Messiah in the fullness of time. With her Son, the Kingdom of God has drawn near in the way of this Son of God. Here is the Son of Man. No one should think that they can understand Miriam and her Son without grasping the Messianic secret of the *chesed Yahweh* promised the fallen House of David, and this secret lies with the time of the *charis of the Theos* that is the Person of Jesus Christ, the Word of God incarnate in the world. Here the God of the Biblical World has created new dimensions of space and time, to His Glory, where the fulfillment shall be realized actually. We call the newness of these developments the 'shock of the New.'

Thus, the Great I-AM of John's witness is the Son of David and King with His Kingdom of the witness of the Synoptic Gospels. Matthew, Mark, and Luke in this way resonate with John as witnesses to the Resurrected Lord God He is at the Right Hand of His Father, Lord of all time in the times of Christ for us. Matthew provides the lineage of Christ as the Son of David, Son of Abraham. He sees blind men calling out to Christ: '... *have mercy on us, Son of David!*' (Matthew 9:7). When Christ casts out demons, people ask, '*Could this be the Son of David?*' (12:22). Significantly, a Canaanite woman can say: '*Lord (Yahweh—Kurios), Son of David, have mercy on me*' (15:22). Again the blind also see to call him, '*Lord, Son of David, have mercy on me*' (20:30). And as He enters Jerusalem on His way to His Death on the Cross, the crowds could shout out: '*Hosanna to the Son of David. Blessed is he who comes in the Name of the Lord ... Hosanna to the Son of David*' (21:9, 15). Mark knows the same such acclamations: '*Jesus, Son of David, Have mercy on me! Many rebuked him (Bartimaeus, the blind man) and told him to be quiet, but he shouted all the more—Son of David, have mercy on me!*' (Mark 10:47–48). When Jesus taught in the Temple at Jerusalem, confronted by the Rabbi, Jesus sought to show them the secret of His relationship as Christ and the Son of David: '*Vows the Lord (Yahweh) as my Master: "Sit at my right hand until I make your enemies a footstool for your feet"*' (12:36, cf. Psalm 110:1). Since King David called him *Yahweh*, he cannot be the Messianic Son of His House. Jesus is this Son. Luke 3:31 traces His lineage to Adam and the son of God of *the Beginning*. He too knows the cry: '*Son of David, have mercy on me*' (Luke 18:38–39), and the claim Jesus makes for Himself as this Son of David (20:41–44). This is the synoptic witness to the Great I-AM the Lord God is as the Son of David that Jesus Christ is with God. This is the One who embodies in Himself the Divine Perfection defined and given as the One who is who He is in His acts according to His 'Little Credo' in the history of His People. Here the secret of the *mercy* of God with His Promise through the House of David for Israel's redemption finds a new life in the world. In this way, the Great I-AM in His Act with His Divine Freedom on behalf of His People seeks to be heard. Here in the midst of a myriad of troubles is

The King, His Kingdom, and the Light of the World

Israel's salvation and deliverance, He has established the new time of His Promise now fulfilled in His Creation. Peter, according to Luke in the Book of Acts, understands the secret and records explicitly its impact upon the People of God: *'Therefore let all Israel be assured of this: God made this Jesus, whom you crucified, both Lord and Christ. When the people heard this, they were cut to the heart and said to Peter and the other apostles, "Brothers, what shall we do?"'* The Being of the Lord God in the Light of His Word must be known before we can ask to do anything about Him.

We must understand the Incarnation is of the Creator as the Creator, a particular embodiment of the universal Word once heard as not incarnate. The Word of God in His Way as the King of Creation and the Prophet of the history of Israel among the nations possesses a dynamic and living Being who is able to go outside of Himself and become what He is not and has never been to keep His Promise to His People. His embodiment as Son of David and Son of God marks the New Beginning of the New Creation, an act even more profound than His act in the Beginning. The fulfillment of God's Promise in His Covenant with His People in His Creation comes with an act that is new for God, Man, and the Creation. It marks the keeping of this Promise with the *chesed Yahweh* upon the House of David (2 Samuel 7:14). It marks the faithfulness of God with His 'faithless' People in the Person of Jesus of Nazareth, the son of Miriam, the Messianic Son of God. The New Testament witness to this 'faithfulness' of the Lord God with His Promise to His King David has been made the One, the Only One Israel is to hear with her ears, see with her eyes, and be His People. The Person of the Lord Jesus Christ as the revealer of His Father in this way is the King with His Kingdom in God's Creation. Now both Israel's King and Yahweh as King are embodied as this Only One, this very real One whose Speaking is the Word that all nations are commanded to hear. But again, it is a hearing and a seeing demanded of a free people, a people free even as His People to deny Him His Being and Becoming, His Freedom to be who He truly is with us. In the Gospel of St. John, the conflict between this Great I-AM and His People intensifies onto the point of the Cross and then His Resurrection. The Word of God become flesh as the Great I-AM the Lord God goes unheard. His existence is denied Him as a blasphemer. The promise kept by God was blasphemous in Israel's ears and eyes. *'Why do you accuse me of blasphemy because I said, "I am God's Son?"'* (John 10:36b).

It is as this Son of David that Jesus is recorded as invoking the great *Shema'* of Israel. In this way, He is bound up with the point of His relationship with His Father. In this relationship, Jesus is the _____, the Only One, who commands the hearing of His People (Matthew 22:37; Mark 12:29–31; Luke 10:27). This Only One is the Great I-AM the Lord God; in His Divine Freedom, he has become with His Self-Defining perfections and Self-Giving passion the Being of the One He truly is, Father of the Son of David, the Son of God. Beside Him there is no Other. Here is the Only One that will not have before Him any of the idols and the much idol making and idol worship common in the race of men. The early fathers of the Church well understood this witness. They struggled to explain this One always, because upon this One depend the deliverance and salvation of the People of God. Here was the One who was Israel's Christ sent from the Father. Again and again, they would turn people's attention to the Father and Son relationship of this One: '*At that time Jesus said, "I praise you, Father, Lord of heaven and earth, because you have hidden these things from the wise and learned, and revealed them to little children. Yes, Father, for this was your good pleasure. All things have been committed to me by my Father. No one knows the Son except the Father, and no one knows the Father except the Son and those to whom the Son chooses to reveal Him"*' (Matthew 11:25–27; Luke 10:21–22; cf. Mark 13:32; John 17). The secret of the *chesed Yahweh* with the House of David is with this One. It is to be found within His relationship as the Son with His Father. This is the One Lord and God who is at once the Creator of the heavens and the earth and the Redeemer of Israel's history among the nations in His Creation. The Lord God, to whom all secrets belong, is divinely free as this One and in this way to reveal Himself as Father to His Children (Deuteronomy 29:29). This is the Numberless One whose is the Grace and Truth He is as the Person of the Lord Jesus Christ. This Only One marks the New Beginning of the New Creation. This Incomparable One marks the justification and sanctification of His Old Creation in *the Beginning*. This Unique One, as the Grace and Truth of this Word become a man, is the Son of David who is also the Lord God of the Old and the New Creation, the Great I-AM of the All that is the Creation. We do well to hear Him. Thus, the Lion and the Lamb of the Apocalypse of Jesus Christ in the Church and in the world knows the secret of our waiting and watching in this way: '*These are the words of Him who is holy and true, who holds the key of David. What He opens no one shuts and what He shuts no one can open . . .* "*I, Jesus, have sent my angel to give this testimony for the churches. I am the Root and the offspring of David, and the bright Morning Star . . .*"' (Revelation 3:7; 22:16).

It is the **Grace and Truth** of this Only and Incomparable One that we are to read throughout the whole of the New Testament witness. We hear this One with this Grace and Truth invoked everywhere in the letters of St. Paul and St. Peter. Romans 1:5 reads: '*Through him and for his name's sake, we received **grace** and apostleship to call people among the gentiles to the obedience that comes from **faith**.*' The whole of Paul's argument in Rome is made according to the *mercy* of God's judgment upon the world (Romans 15:9). In Colossians 1:6b we read: '*All over the world this gospel is bearing fruit and growing, just as it has been doing among you since the day you heard it and understood God's **grace** in all its **truth**.*' Paul knows that thanksgiving to God flows joyfully because of this *grace* to the glory of God (2 Corinthians 4:15). He can urge the church not to receive this *grace* in vain (6:1). He knows that the Creator is his Maker. He, Paul, learned that he is who he is because the Lord God is who He is with this *grace*, even in the midst of his weaknesses and his pleas for healing: '*My **grace** is sufficient for you, for my power is made perfect in weakness*' (2 Corinthians 12:8b). And 1 Peter 1:13 says: '*Therefore, prepare your minds for action; be self-controlled; set your hope fully on the **grace** to be given you when Jesus Christ is revealed.*' Peter knows the new heaven and the new earth will come with the keeping of the promise through the giving of this *grace* (2 Peter 3:13). So he exhorts the believer to, '*grow in the **grace** and knowledge of our Lord and Savior Jesus Christ*' (3:18). Everywhere throughout the letters of the New Testament we read of this *grace* and its peace. The final words of the New Testament are '*The **grace** of the Lord Jesus be with all the saints. Amen.*' Even the most careless of readings in the gospels and the letters of Paul and Peter cannot fail to hear the apostolic heart of the Gospel of the Lord God. The final Amen of Holy Scripture cannot be proclaimed without this *grace* of the Great I-AM.

When we understand He is in this way His **Grace**, we are in a position to appreciate God with and for us in the fullness of the mystery of time and space as created reality, made to bear the knowledge of His Being with us in the world. We are given within the dynamical relations of the nature of His BCR, His acts in the history of the world through Israel for its mankind, to participate with Him in His New Beginning for the world, a beginning that is with His atoning love even more profound than *the* Beginning. From the Virgin Birth, we see Him as this Beginning being baptized by John the Baptizer, identifying His Humanity with us with His Repentance on our behalf for the sin of the world against Him. From His Baptism, we see His Ministry of healing, the signs and wonders of His Deliverance for us, as the Lord God He is with us. It is with this **Grace** that He establishes for us the culmination of His life in His BCR in His Creation. The Lord's Supper signs with this Baptism the way for us to see His Witness of God as God, even upon His Cross, then with His Resurrection. He shows Himself to be our Savior in these signs, our Justification and our Sanctification in this world of His Creation. From His Resurrection, then His Ascension, His Church is given to proclaim, even in apocalyptic form, the **Grace** He is in His BCR for us. The whole of the New Testament, written in the Light of this **Grace** and **Peace**, is what it is in both form and content because of His Life, His Resurrection, His Ascension to the Right Hand of His Father, and in the sending of the Spirit of God for the New Beginning with His Church, the Church of Jesus Christ as the People of God in the world. From beginning to end, throughout the writings of the New Testament, again and again, we read the Blessing upon His Church of His **Grace** and **Peace**. No one should think that they can understand the Word of God become flesh in this world without the Spirit of this **Grace** and **Peace**. It is with this knowledge that Paul knows his spirit as dependent upon the Spirit of the Living Lord God: '*My* **grace** *is sufficient for you, for my power is made perfect in weakness*' (2 Corinthians 12:9). As His **Grace** He is the New Beginning that resonates with *the* Beginning with His **Peace**, the Sabbath of God with His Blessing of His Creation.

The Light that is the Life of the Grace and Truth as this Only and Incomparable One shines that we may see the true significance of His Name, the real meaning of the Being of the Great I-AM He is as Lord and God with His Revelation with us and for us in this world. It is this Light that we may hear resonating in the Vision of Isaiah and in the Word of the Gospel of God. It is in this Light that we may hear the Apocalypse of this One as the King of the Universe He is, the Lamb of His Creation. This One as this Light heals our hearts, gives our eyes to see, our ears to hear His Word, the Word who is the Lord God of the Apocalypse, the Person of Jesus Christ. This is the One who is and was and will be the One He truly is—'*Pantocrator*'—'Creator-Redeemer-Ruler of All' (Revelation 1:4, 8). This Only One is the Alpha and Omega, the Almighty Creator of the

New Creation and the Old Creation. The Vision of the Unveiling of the Person of the Lord Jesus Christ, as the Lamb and King of the Kingdom of God, is made to see this One—the Alpha and the Omega, the First and the Last, the Beginning and the End of the entire Creation (22:12–13). The Great I-AM with the House of David entails the secret of the **Grace** of the Lord God is the One we hear with healed hearts and eyes and ears in His Apocalypse: *'Behold, the Lion of the tribe of Judah, the Root of David, has triumphed. He is able to open the scroll and its seven seals'* (5:5). With the Voice of this One we are given to know Him as the David, the fulfillment of the prophecy He is. With this Voice, the Lord God speaks of Himself with His People. Here, He is not only the Holy One who was and is and is to come, but He is King of Israel and King of kings and the King of the Creation. Again, it is this One who proclaims His Word to us: *'I, Jesus, have sent my angel to give to you this testimony for the churches. I am the Root and the Offspring of David, and the bright Morning Star'* (22:16), and thus John the Revelator's benediction seals the proclamation of the Vision: *'Amen. Come, Lord Jesus. The Grace (Chesed) of the Lord Jesus be with God's People. Amen'* (22:20–21). By this Spirit the Lord God the I-AM is speaks with His prophetic Word to us of His 'today' with our days. He gives us to drink of the free gift of the water of life. He gives us real knowledge of the mystery of His Being and Becoming as the Great I-AM He is as the Lord God, to apprehend the secret of the *chesed Yahweh* even in the midst of the waters of this world's times and spaces, that all mankind might be made a species among the birds and fish and animals that is made to breath with the breathe of God the Life of God. Here is the space and time where He has chosen to set His Name, to surround Mankind as His Image with His Living **Grace** and **Peace**, enabling our kind to breathe in the Life of the Living God. It is this *Chesed* or **Grace** that makes mankind what it is in the Eyes of the Great I-AM the Lord God is.

He is forever this Solid One, the Rock that is the Great I-AM of all confessions. He is this One before the Incarnation of His Word and He is this One after the Incarnation of His Word. He is this dynamic living being One with the **Grace** of His Word as one of us. He has taken this way with Himself, given us His Revelation for our Reconciliation, His Being for our Redemption, to be a part of the New Creation with His Creation. This is the Self-Revealing, the Self-Naming, the Self-Defining, the Self-Giving, the Self-Communicating One as the Great I-AM the Lord God is for us. Unveiled as the **Grace** of the Lord Jesus Christ, we understand the mystery of the Lord of the Ages, the God of time and Eternity. This One is the Lord of His People and the God of the heavens and the earth in the very mystery of His Being and Becoming for us. He is this *Yahweh Elohim*, the Angel of this Voice in the Burning Bush, the *Grace* and *Truth* of the *Peace* this Voice alone can give us, embodied in His Incarnation, Death, Resurrection, and Ascension of His Word. With the Majestic and Transcendent Authority of this Voice's Freedom, His Holy Love is made known as His *Grace* and *Truth*, the Great I-AM who is who He is from even before *the* Beginning and in the Apocalypse of Himself with the Ages the world must know. The '*I AM WHO I* AM*,*' Old and New, must be heard as this *Grace* and *Truth* with us. This is what is in the name with which He has named Himself. This is what is along the Way He takes to act with Himself in the history of His People in His Creation. This is what it is to say that 'Jesus is Lord.' He is the Lord of lords, the King of kings in the *Truth* He has taken in this way. He is His Revelation in this way. He is to be seen and heard with His heavens and the earth in this way. He is to be known and understood with the nations of His Creation in this way. The Church has been by this *Grace* and *Truth* made the Servant of this Solid One, made to face the Face of the Lord God He is as the Great I-AM He is. God has put on His Face for us in this way, and He has given as His People Personal Knowledge of who He truly is with His Creation.

In the first centuries, after this birth, life, death, and resurrection of this Person of the Lord Jesus Christ as the New Beginning of God and Man with the Creation, the apostolic ministry of His disciples, come face to Face with this Lord and God, sought to root the Good News of His Being and Nature within the mighty Graeco-Roman Empire, on the ground over which reigned the Emperors of the times. The King with His Kingdom as this God and Man in this world confronted with His Spirit in His Church the kings of the world. A great challenge and a great clash between them had been begun. It was both bloody and wondrous. The Great I-AM with His Grace in the world with the Glory of His Cross and His Resurrection meant that by His Grace and to His Glory this King with His Kingdom could call all peoples to repentance, Jew and Gentile, repentance that belonged to a whole new world, a world whose past had been forgiven and whose future was bound up with the Glory of this King and this Kingdom, a world whose future could not be the same as the old world's opposition to the Great I-AM the Lord God is. Something utterly new had occurred within the old world. Its past no more could determine what was to come. Time and times, indeed, belonged to the Redeemer-Creator He is as this King come with the Kingdom of God. He and He alone would determine the things that were to come. The fat was in the fire. A new world had been begun. The Kingdom was near. Now all was to be understood anew and in the Light of His Resurrection. In this Light the David of the New Creation had made Himself known to all. If the whole world heard the Word of God this King is as it were in parables, it was only for the purpose of the old world into the New Creation, when opposition of the past to Him was called to be converted to the only future the world has, the only destiny the world possesses. The secret of the parables of the King and the Kingdom belong to the secret of the Risen Lord, the Great I-AM, the King He is of the world's time and space. This is the way He has taken with His Divine Freedom as the Grace and Truth He is among the peoples of the Empires. It was a parable of a story for ears that chose in their freedom not to hear. It was plain talk to ears that willed to hear His Voice. In any case, it was the Angel of the Voice of the Word with His Being and Becoming as the Great I-AM He truly is freeing all peoples everywhere of their idols, their apparitions about Him, the phantoms of their cults with the gods.

The Holy Scriptures had born witness to Him. The People of God through the Monarchy of God were filled with the **Grace** and **Truth** of these words. The Church was made to proclaim with His Holy Love the way of this King with His Kingdom in the world. The apostolic ministry then holds before our eyes what our ears need to hear. They would have us see what our ears must hear. If the old world of our hearts shall be healed, if we are to see and hear the depths of the sin against Him that we hold in them as sons of the First Man, the New World of our New Heart would show us the way He comes for us. It is the **Grace** and **Truth** as His Holy Love that is in interaction as this King with the people of this world. It is the Lamb and Lion of this Kingdom that reigns among the kings of the kingdoms of this world. It is this One that calls us even in our time to no other than Himself, in the Name of Jesus Christ, Son of the Father of the Promise, whose Spirit confronts us with His Church and the Church's proclamation of His **Grace** and **Truth**. He ought to be understood in this way as an invasion of an enemy, an unwelcome alien, an attack upon what we think we already know with our vaunted hearts and minds. His is no mere entanglement of God with the world. His is a command that would transform the very depths of our beings. His is transformation that demands in the very depths of our nature a conversion from an old creature to the new creature, from the old world's time and times to the new world's time and times. Far more than an entanglement, here is a tremendous battle. Far from some local clash of cultures, here is from above and below the grip of love upon our sinful lives, love that will not fail, love that will compromise. Here is justification not of any popular or conventional imagination about the world and its God, but the sanctification of all that truly is and will matter for as long as forever will be what it is with the Eternity of the Great I-AM. Here is Light, if at first blinding, then at last the very Wisdom of God for us. Here is His Wisdom with His Time for us. Here is the Wisdom of His Space for us. Here is the Wisdom of all Creation. Here is the Wisdom of Prophecy. Here is the Wisdom of the very Word of God He is as this One Man who is the King with His Kingdom in this world. That it is a shocking proclamation is to say the least about it. It is a renewal of the wholeness of the race for life as His People in His Kingdom. It is for this Life, this Love, this **Grace** and **Truth** that the Church sought to root the Gospel of His Personhood on the ground of the Empire. On the pages of the Holy Scriptures, the Old and now the New Testament, in their times and time created, in the spaces and space created, they raised up the flag of His Name. It is well worth the attention of the whole human race to seek to understand this confrontation, to be able to go there and do what is 'Right' in His Eyes, where His Glory, His Atoning Love, and His Peace are given to 'Rest' with those who worship Him. Thus, the fathers of the early Church struggled to confront the Graeco-Roman World with the Good News of His Being, this Good News of the Grace He is in Truth among us.

Cross

8

The Church and the World

*Now the Lord is the Spirit,
and where the Spirit of the Lord is, there is freedom.*

2 Corinthians 3:17

"Wʜᴀᴛ ɪs ᴛʜᴇʀᴇ ɪɴ common between Athens and Jerusalem; between the Academy and the Church?" The early Church father Tertullian (160–240 AD) asked this even as the Church sought to root the Gospel of Jesus Christ in the ground of the Graeco-Roman Empire. It is a question that we ask still today. Our answers to this question determine the way we will seek to create from within our cultures the societies of our nation in the world. It is not a question we can ever afford to ignore. Resolutions to the problems with which its significance confronts are vital for the way we would live as individuals and communities. Its rhetoric is often heard as implying the answer 'nothing.' It has also just as steadily been heard with a need to reach some compromise or another. We have already said it faces more than a clash or an entanglement between the Church and the Empire. We have said that it faces with an invasion the vitality of the Empire in the world. We need to explore in this chapter what this invasion meant to the history of the world.

With the same freedom that the Lord God struggled for His People in the Old Testament and with the same freedom that He struggled for His People in the New Testament, the Great I-AM He is continued in the form of the Person of the Lord Jesus Christ to struggle to make Himself known with His Presence as the One He truly is as Head of the Church in the world over and with which He is the Creator. With His Divine Freedom to reveal and name and define and give Himself in His BCR with His People, embodied as the 'Light of the World' and the Great I-AM who is the Servant of God's Salvation and Judgment in the world, His Church is commanded to proclaim the Good News of His Being and Becoming among the nations. It is according to this command that the Church has struggled across centuries to teach the Word of God He is with His Being and Nature as the King and Priest and Prophet and Sage of the Kingdom of God, His Kingdom among the Empires of the nations. Thus, the creedal formations of the Church's confession are to be understood as reflecting in these times this command of the Lord God as the Great I-AM He is. We need to understand this confession from within this context, if we are to grasp the nature of His BCR and His determination within this relationship to bring His Salvation of His People in His Creation.

Begun at Pentecost, when the Spirit of God was sent from the Right Hand of the Father through the Son and Word of God the Lord Jesus Christ is, the ministry of the New Covenant with a purpose that was understood to span and embrace all of time and space with the Eternal Life of the Lord God Himself. Thus, the Church's mission in the world was an utterly new ministry of the Great I-AM the Lord God is. It posited within the world a relationship between God and Israel among the nations that possessed a nature the dimensions of which were utterly new and surprising for world history. From its inception, the Church as the People of God of the Old and New Covenant in the BCR was commanded to face with His Face the face of the Emperors reigning over the Graeco-Roman Empire of the times. In this confrontation, the Gospel proclaimed by the Church as the Word of God Incarnate in a world that was God's Creation met at first a deep and profound hostility. The Light of this New Covenant, prophesied by the People of God in God's Creation, was a light that made blind both Jew and Gentile, barbarians and sages. In this way, the Church marked a new beginning of the Spirit of God in the world, a beginning that was without analogy in the history of the world and a beginning that would not ever be denied its purpose for the world.

The ministry of this Spirit of the Word of God Incarnate and now seated at the Right Hand of the Father in the heavens shaped and formed His Church as the One, Holy, Catholic (Universal), and Apostolic Church of the Lord Jesus Christ in the Empire even against the many and most bloody objections to her. Only with the passing of time, wearisome times indeed, could her confession win its place among the peoples of the nations under the Romans. Only with the Emperor Constantine the Great (288–337 AD) may we read of the Church's triumph in establishing her place in the Empire, when persecutions could take less bloody forms of objections. We need to seek to understand that the Spirit who began with the Church to work to root the Gospel of Jesus Christ as the Great I-AM He is in the ground of the Empire did not begin a work in vanity. However much the Empires fight against this New Beginning of the New Creation, however much the Church's confession might be wracked with controversies both genuine and disingenuous, this is the world whose ground had once and for all time been invaded by the Lord God Himself. However bloody and steadily the world fought against her, the Church where the Spirit had chosen to dwell knew she could not ever be utterly defeated. She belonged to a movement of God in the world that, in spite of all the bloodshed and controversy, was indeed the movement of the Light of the Word of God in the world. The confessions she sought to make of the Great I-AM as the One, Holy, Catholic, and Apostolic Church belonged to the work of this Spirit of the Word sent from the Father for His People in His Creation.

To this movement, then, belonged the very Divine Freedom of the Lord God who would not be who He truly is without His People in His Creation. Here is the freedom that can refuse to be stopped. Here is the freedom that makes with signs and wonders those miracles of deliverance for His People that no machinations of His enemies can comprehend. With this freedom, the Church belonged to the Providence and the Prophecy of the People of God in the midst of the Empires, in spite of the approval or disapproval of the nations where she made her confession and her proclamation. In this way, we may read the history of the Church in the world, Eastern and Western, Byzantium and Roman, developed even in the midst of the dynamic reigns of one Emperor or another, time and time again. The point must be that the world was changed utterly and permanently by what the Lord God had commanded His Church to be and become in the world. She belonged to the Divine Freedom He possessed with His Being and Becoming to whose beginnings He is as the Great I-AM He is absolutely faithful. Though any number of accounts of the relationship between the Church and the Graeco-Roman Empire may be read, for better or for worse, where our mind's eye is made to gaze upon the most terrible triumphs and betrayals, the point must be made more steadily than every condemnation that the Church is who she is because He is who He is with His People in His Creation. The Creeds of the Church belong to this history. The struggles of the fathers of the Church belong to this history, to this movement in the history of the world. However confused we may become because of this Divine Freedom of the I-AM He is, we may not become confused that He is the Unique and Only and Incomparable One, made known through Jesus Christ as the Father, Son, and Spirit of the Blessed Trinity, our Redeemer and our Creator. I believe it is very much worth our while today to seek to understand this movement as best as and as far as we may in this freedom.

I like to think that the rhetoric of Tertullian's question runs like an underground river throughout the entire history of the confrontations we may read between the Church and the Empire. It concerns stream into this lake and that eddy, through this city and that town, all the way down to the seas surrounding the lands where our troubles with its resolutions seem to dissolve like a tear into the ocean depths of the waters. Along this river grow the trees that are the Church's confessions of Jesus Christ, her understandings of Him, and her proclamation of His Word in this world. With her proclamation comes the healing of His Word for the nations. With His healing comes the salvation of the peoples of the nations. For Tertullian, the rhetoric of the question was not simply 'nothing.' It was 'nothing' in so far as the Church stood against the evil of the Empire. It was, however, the 'nothing' that was God's 'Very Good' Creation that provided the basis for her ears and eyes in the world. In the clash or the entanglement between the Church and the Empire, God's Self-Revelation was known to embrace His Creation. Though the Gospel had 'nothing' to do with the philosophers and philosophies that prevailed with great honor in the horror of Athens and the Greek gods, the 'nothingness' of the Creation demanded to be filled with light, as in the Beginning, even the Light that was had become incarnate as the Word become flesh in the world. The Church could have 'nothing' to do with cultic magic and superstitious mechanics, but she must remain committed and open in this Light to seek to understand the world where she preached the Gospel. She must seek to understand the rationality of the world's unity and its universal implications, while divorcing herself from the demonic, the mythical, the mystical aberrations about the Cosmos of the Creation. The Church's confessions were never meant to divorce her life in the world from space and time and the physical reality of the Creation. Thus, we may easily exaggerate the significance of Tertullian's rhetoric. We need to penetrate into the depths of his concerns for the relationship between Athens and Jerusalem, between the Academy and the Church. I like to think that the question found some real resolution in Alexandria in the

Fourth, Fifth, and Sixth centuries, when the Church sought with her Creeds to articulate the full meaning of the Gospel as the Word of God in the world. I would argue that we might learn much for our efforts that is vital even in our time.

In the City of Alexandria, with its wondrous Lighthouse in her busy harbor and the great treasures of her library, the question was formed in such a way as to ask just how the Church could appropriate the language and thought of Athens and convert them into the service of the Gospel. How may the Church's proclamation of the Word Christ is as the world's Redeemer-Creator take root in the ground of this Empire's cultures and societies? The answers we discover come in the shape of conversions and transformations. We find that Greek philosophical categories of thought and experience could be abrogated and given new definition and meanings in order to make them serve the purpose of the Revelation of the Word in the world. Thus, a new way of carving up the realities we experience with our lives in the world obtains. These conversions and transformations of thought and experience were imperative if the Church was to fulfill its obligation of proclaiming and establishing the Truth of the Gospel in the ground of the Empire, as her Lord and God had commanded. Thus, the Church was duty bound to see anew, in the Light and Love and Life of the Word revealed to her, a New World coming, a world to be transformed by the Great I-AM the Lord and God is into His New Creation. The fruitfulness of her existence in the world was to be experienced through the reconciliation of the Empire with her Lord God, the King and Priest and Prophet and Sage of what is to come in the history of the world. The answer to Tertullian's question was not a resolution of a dialectic pertaining to an either/or way of carving up reality, but a complex dynamic redemption of the world pried open, by the creative power of the Word or Logos of God, to the new dimensions posited by Christ Himself within the nature and being of this world.

With the case of one John Philoponus, a sixth century Alexandrian Grammarian, I will seek to show how this new dynamical way of thinking could take seriously for theology and science, for Jerusalem and Athens, for the Church as well as the Academy, the Grace and Truth of the Gospel of God with and in the nature of a world that is His Creation. John Philoponus sought at the Academy in Alexandria to articulate at the interface between Christian Theology whose ground would allow us to stand and see both the nature of God and the nature of the Cosmos, each under the creative power of the Word He is as Head of the Church and King of the Universe. The whole of the universe, indeed, was to be understood as bound as God's Creation with the Great I-AM He is. I believe in this case we may seek to recover something very fundamental at the foundations of this new movement's beginning in the history of the world. I would hope that we may come to see the Church with her Creeds, from Nicea to Chalcedon to Constantinople and beyond, not as having 'nothing' to do with the various fields of knowledge we may study in the world but as possessing a unique power whose Light shines upon both the just and the unjust with compelling progress and fruitful growth. With the created and creative power of the Logos of God in mind, the Grammarian could seek with knowledge, imagination, and will to grasp in the depths of its nature the contingent rationality of created reality in purposeful relationship with the uncreated Being and Nature of the Word of the Father in the Spirit of God. It is with this power that the Church has been called to proclaim the Kingdom of God in the world, to which the Empire best lent its ears and eyes, for the Empire with its Academies has to do with this King and His Kingdom, the Priest, this Prophet, this Sage in the world. I would hope that we may grasp afresh in all of its depths the nature of the Kingdom of God, come and coming, in the Grace and Truth of this One Lord and God the Great I-AM forever is.

As we have seen, the Biblical World does not allow us to split apart who the Lord is as the Redeemer from who God is as the Creator. We must learn to think together the significance of the Creation with its Redemption. Modern assumptions about the relation between the Old and New Testaments, between the Canon of the Church to the Proclamation of the Church in the world, when an abyss has been created between Biblical Theology and Dogmatic Theology, simply cannot be found. Both testaments witness to the One True God who is confessed by the Church as the Father, Son, and Spirit of the Word of God in the world. The Being of the Great I-AM the Lord God is with Moses has been revealed in the Church as the Blessed Trinity of this One. The Biblical World is not a world where two gods reign in time, one a Lord of Redemption and the other a God of Creation. The God of the Old is as much a God of Grace and Truth as the Lord of the New is the Lord of the Judgment. The One Holy Catholic Apostolic Church of the Lord Jesus Christ proclaimed from her beginning the Gospel of the One God, not the two gods.

For her confessions, the Church always steadily persevered to gain her space and time with the Empire. The world did not give her place without objecting to her. It was her patience and the power of the Spirit we read when we see the way she endured with her confession. The Lord God, who is the Great I-AM of the One Confession of the One Rock of Israel and the Church, had chosen to make Himself present and known in the world in the way of His Spirit sent through the Living Word or Logos that is the Person of the Lord Jesus Christ with His Father into the world. His work as this Lord and God of the Prophecy of the New Covenant in the world fulfills the purpose of the BCR with the world. He is the One in this way who is the Redeemer-Creator as the King of Israel and the King of the Creation. The unity, holiness, catholicity, and the apostolic authority of the Church are all rooted at once both in the very real ground of the Nature of His Being and Becoming, as well as in the nature of His Humanity as the New Beginning of the New Creation. The personal reality of the One Great I-AM He is, as made clear by this New Man in His Creation of the New Covenant has become unveiled for the sake of His People among the nations. It is His Space and His Time that hold now the secret of the BCR created between the Lord God and the history of the world as His Creation. It is the space and time of the newly minted dimensions of the new nature of this covenanted relationship that bear with us the meaning and significance that shapes and forms the ground created between God and the world and its mankind with His Living Word. When the particulars of the realities of the world and the universals we may seek to understand of them are given communion and union in a whole that is the Great I-AM this Lord God is, then I think we have begun to understand what it was that was moving in the thought of John Philoponus in the sixth century in Alexandria's Academy on behalf of the Church of Jesus Christ.

Thus, the Great I-AM of the Burning Bush, become the Great I-AM of the Incarnation, become the Great I-AM of the Church's proclamation in the world is the One Great I-AM the Lord God is of the Gospel of Jesus Christ among the nations in the Creation. He is this One Word of God as the One True Triune Redeemer-Creator of the whole of all created reality. He is the Grace of His Judgment. He is the Grace of His Salvation. To explain His Grace is to explain both the Judgment and the Salvation of the Church in the world. By the Spirit of God as His Grace she is sent into a world that is His Creation, but a world that betrays and rejects the Grace

He is. She is sent to proclaim the destiny of Israel among the nations, in spite of her wickedness, to fulfill the Promise of her Messiah as the New Adam of the New Covenant in His New Creation. Thus, His Grace is established with His Cross and His Resurrection from the dead. He lives among the nations as this Grace in God's Creation. In so far as Athens has to do with this Creation, the Church has to do with Athens. Precisely what this meant for their relationship might remain to be discovered, but doubtlessly the Church and the Empire were face to face with one another in a life-changing way at the very foundations of the nature of their fields of knowledge in the world.

Yes, a steady confusion is found evolving between them. But also, yes, it is clear that 'something' out of 'nothing' compels new dimensions upon human thought in a world that is what it is as the Creation of God. The Church had to learn to stand on this ground and there learn to shape the 'Right' answer to Tertullian's question. Just what the nature of the relationship was only time, it seemed, could tell, but the telling must in any and every case occur. I like to think that the resolution was experienced, to some real degree, in Alexandria by Philoponus. If Jerusalem and Athens were having trouble crossing the chasm between them, if the Church and the Academy we having trouble grasping in the 'nothingness' of the 'Very Good' Creation the meaning of Grace and the significance of Truth that belongs majestically to the Lord as God and Father of Jesus Christ in the world, still in this city built by the mighty conqueror (circa 300 BC), Alexander the Great, a student of Aristotle, was shaped an understanding of the space and time and light that for the Church defined the interface between God's People in the face of the Roman Empire. The Incarnation of God with His Word in space and time meant space and time possessed new dimensions of being, the nature of which belong to both God and the world. For the dynamics of these new dimensions certainly the Grammarian groped as he sought to explain the physics of the Creation and the Christology that belonged to the Church's Creed. We may see him seeking to answer Tertullian's question with a positive grasp of the Truth of the Grace Christ is as the Redeemer-Creator of the heavens and the earth. The mystery of the Incarnation in the Creation was to be understood as a solid Truth bound up with the Grace of the objectivity of God's Eternal Life with us. The unveiling of this mystery contained the secret that possessed the resolution of the question, however challenging that ground was for the eye of the human mind, its imagination, and its will in the world. At the

Academy in Alexandria John Philoponus (490–580 AD) loved to work to seek to explain to the relation of the Great I-AM as the Triune Lord God He is even with the physics of a Cosmos that was His Creation.

At the Academy, John was called a Grammarian. His enemies could refer to his position as something less than a Professor's. Perhaps we may think of him as an Assistant Professor or a Teaching Fellow in the Academy. Be that as it may, we may understand that at the Academy in Alexandria John had inherited not only the theology of the Councils of the Church's Creed, but also the task of explaining the truth of the Creed on the soil of the Graeco-Roman Empire. His Emperor was Justinian (482–565 AD), who along with His Empress Theodora (c. 500–548 AD) had inherited Constantine's conversion and wondrous triumph (302 AD) over the reigns of the Empire's pagan past. Both were good theologians, Justinian with a bent for Chalcedon's confession with its Roman leanings and Theodora with a bent for the Eastern Church and its Monophysite confession. So even within the royal family, we can study the tensions of the battles that raged throughout the Empire for supremacy in both political and theological arenas. The Emperor Justinian sought from Philoponus an argument on the Incarnation that he might employ to compel an end to these controversies. They were battles that raged in both the Eastern and Western Sees of the Church of His Reign with debilitating consequences. The Emperor needed to end them, as they could split up the Church in a time when he needs steadily to face enemies prowling always at his borders.

For Justinian and the Fifth Ecumenical Council of the Church (553 AD) John Philoponus wrote then 'The Arbiter.' I like to think that the Anathema of Philoponus in 680 AD marked the Church's history with a tragic mistake, on the order of the mistake made with Galileo in the sixteenth century. It is, I believe, a mistake with which we continue to struggle even today. 'Who is Jesus?' It is still a good question. I believe that it can be shown that history would teach us that both Israel and the Church as the People of God have suffered in this world because of the problems about who this Jesus is, who He is as this Grace and the Truth of God in the world, who He is as this Redeemer-Creator in the world. His relationship with the nature of a world that is His Creation with His Mankind still tends to escape our attention. I believe that even today we need to recover the meaning of this Person as the Grace and Truth of the Lord God is as the Great I-AM of time and times, of space and spaces, in the Light of His Being and Becoming with us. I believe we need to grasp the fundamentals of what Philoponus inherited in the Church and in his scientific culture at the Academy in Alexandria, if we are going to appreciate the rhetoric of Tertullian's question.

What John Philoponus of Alexandria inherited in the Church of Jesus Christ

I. The homoousion of Athanasius the Great and the Confession of the Church at the Council of Nicea (AD 325).

From Athanasius of Alexandria, John Philoponus could embrace the Nicean confession of the concept of the homoousion of the Son and the Father as the Lord God the Great I-AM is, made known through the Incarnate Word He is with us. This was a concept invented to fight against the various notions of subordination of the Son with the Father. Jesus was not an adopted Son. He was not Son according to the Will of God, but according to the very Nature of the Being of God. Jesus, Son of David and Son of Man, was the Son of God's Eternity and as such 'One Being' with His Father. He was begotten of His Father as God of God in the Eternal Life the Lord God is. The Son of Eternity was the Son Incarnate as the Word of God in His Freedom revealing in Himself, the Great I-AM He is, the Father Almighty as the Maker of the heavens and the earth and all mankind. Jesus Christ was 'consubstantial' with His Father as the Great I-AM the Lord God is in fulfillment of the prophets of Israel and the apostles of the Church as the People of God. The Father and the Son were to be understood as One in Essence even in their differentiation from each other. They were not two gods but the One Eternal True God made known in the world in their relationship as Father and Son both in Eternity and in the time and times and space and spaces of His Creation. They were two persons known as the One God. This is the Revelation of the Great I-AM the Lord God is in the world. He is known in the way of this Word through Jesus Christ and in the Spirit of this One Being of the Only Redeemer-Creator of the world.

Some six decades later than the Council at Nicea, the concept of the homoousial relationship of the Son and the Father had to be extended explicitly to the Spirit of God. The Spirit as well as the Son was homoousion with the Father and as such the Almighty Redeemer-Creator of the Creation. Thus the Father, Son, and Spirit, though confessed as three differentiated persons or hypostases of the Godhead, were known as the One

Triune Creator. They were not three gods but the One. The Being of the Father, the Being of the Son, and the Being of the Spirit were One Being as Three Persons. Differentiation and integration were fundamental for thinking rightly about the Lord and God.

It ought to be remembered that this concept in the formulations of the Church's confessions was invented to face views about Jesus Christ that evidently were unable to grasp the actual saving power of the Holy Love of God as His Grace and Truth for His People in His Creation. They were formed against a world that would shape notions against the Salvation of the Redeemer-Creator in the world's reality. The boundaries all such concepts sought to draw were concerned with the Salvation of the human race in the Creation. They were not lines drawn in some mythological sands in a world that existed only in the aberrations of the race, but an attempt to draw with the Light of the Word of God His Life in His Life for Man in His Creation. The Church would proclaim the Word of God Himself in a world that had rejected Him and must in the Face of His Grace and Truth repent and accept Him for who He truly is. The Creeds of the Church were shaped and formed with the substance and content that belonged to the Great I-AM in His Divine Freedom to be as the Christ the Savior He is with His People among the nations of the world. Docetic (He was not fully a man!) and Ebionite (He was not fully God!) views of Jesus Christ did not grasp the significance of the Salvation in the One He is in the world. Gnostic and Adoptionistic thought about Him did not understand the way He had given His Eternal Life, embodied as the Great I-AM, to those He called to Himself for His Glory in His Creation. The homoousion was not conceived as some static, metaphysical concept of timeless value in the minds of men in the world, but as a confession to this way that He had taken with Himself to bring Eternal Life to what is otherwise merely temporary. It was a concept invented to say that Christ is the Person who as the Son of God and Man and David brings God's Life, resurrected from the dead in the world, as the Man for Mankind. Who He truly was and is and will be could not be accepted as anyone less than this God come as this man for the sake of mankind's and the whole world's sin against Him. The particular man Jesus as the Christ of Israel is comes as God into the world in order to reveal Himself as the Savior of the world. Those who would continue not to receive Him as the Great I-AM He is among them remain outside the boundaries that mark the world with the Light of His Word. For this reason, His Cross and Resurrection stands yet in the history of the world as the place where and the time when God Himself has repented for His People, given them a new Beginning, in spite of their sin against Him, and a future with Himself. Here with this Person Eternity and time have been given real union and communion forever!

Once I had learned this concept of the Nicene Creed in the history of the Church, I have been steadily astonished to learn again and again how little known its invention has become in the churches today, modern or post-modern. It is as if this 'dogma' has become some kind of useless information for us. To my astonishment, when I have tried to teach the homoousion whenever and wherever I can, for I know that it involves our minds as sinners with the Faith of Christ in time and space in a saving way, I have met with the many views the fathers fought against in their times. The begotten Son's person of the Eternity He is with His Father, the Unoriginate, born under the Law of the woman of the House of David, gives us the same fits of human thought that it once gave the early Christians. To enjoy the relationship with the unbegotten person of His Father in His only begotten Son is little enough appreciated in our times. Yet as this One, He is the One True Lord that the Savior God is. Incarnate in our time and times, the Word made flesh in our space and spaces, He is as the One who is who He is Man as God and God as Man who is the Redeemer-Creator of the world. It is as this Person that both the invisible and the visible dimensions of all created reality have been given transcendent relations with the Life of God's Eternity, Life of the Godhead even from before the Creation's Beginning, as the Father, Son, and Spirit that is the Eternity of the Great I-AM. It is to this Life and Faith we have been called to go, when and where we are brought to face the Face of the Lord God and live. It is the way of this Incarnate Word and this Eternal Word as the One Person He is that has fulfilled all of His purposes and promises inherent in His covenanted relationship with His People in His Creation. It is in this Light that He has established Himself with His People among the nations. As this Person, the imageless relations imperative for our knowing of Him have been set in correspondence with the Image of God that He is, revealing both the reality of God's Eternity and His Time in Christ for us in our time and times. Imageless knowing is thus fundamental to the Christian Faith, and the homoousion is the concept we need to secure both ends of the relational veracity of the Revelation. Both differentiation and integration are uniquely necessary here as inherent and coherent in the relational wholeness of the Being and Nature of the Living Lord God.

For this reason, the confession at Nicea in 325 AD is not to be learned as some sophisticated metaphysical concept, but the security of the People of God on a ground whose origin belongs to the creative power of the Lord of all space and time. Here is a relational veracity that allows us to grasp both the transcendent and the immanent Being of God with us and for us in the world.

In this Faith, freedom is vital, especially the freedom to see what cannot be seen. With it, we get more than the eye can behold! We get to know the secret of the promise the Lord God made King David in Israel's history, now fulfilled as the David and Son of God of the future of all time and times. We get to see God struggling in such time and times as they belong to Him who is before all created reality. We get to know in space and time what cannot be known, except for His Grace and Truth, in time and space. We may have pictured for us what cannot be pictured, in real relationship with what actually is. We get to confess the Mind of our Savior for us. We get to proclaim who He truly is even in our space and time in a Cosmos that is what it is because of His creative power over and with and in His Creation. We get to know Him in this way in His Divine Freedom, with His Divine Forgiveness for our sin and even the sin of the whole world. We get to grasp more than we can say. We get to wonder as His child in His Kingdom without vanity. We get as His Church to know His Salvation in the world. We get to be created realities redeemed from His Curse upon the evil and sin with this world. We get to see what Man was intended to be in His Creation. We get to enter into a fellowship, union and communion, with this Incarnate Word and Son, who is the David of the future, with Him who is the New Adam of the New Covenant for His New Creation. We get to be reconstituted along the lines of His Image as the King of a Kingdom that is of God. We get to know the Great I-AM He is in His Eternity and as a creature such as we are in His Divine and Human Freedom for us in time and space as we are. I have found that people are not very confident about knowing such things as these that would refer us to such realities today. But according to the intention of the confession of the homoousion of Athanasius the Great at Nicea, and then decades later at Constantinople (381 AD), with this Faith in Christ the Church learned to express the way she had been made to take with her confession from a breath that belonged to the transcendent air of God's Life for mankind, without which breathing creatures suffocate as His People in His Creation. We do well indeed to learn its significance in our inheritance.

Thus, the real concern of the early Fathers with the Creeds of the Church was to posit an 'Orthodox' confession that had to do with life and salvation of Grace and not a metaphysical explanation of God and the human race and the world. They attempted to clarify 'heretical' views of the Faith for the sake of this Life, this Salvation of God for the race of which Christ was the first fruit of the New Creation. Their speculations were not for the sake of logical systems of thought that gave secret knowledge of the Faith, but for the sake of the proclamation of the Gospel of Christ in God as the True Lord and Beginning of all that breathes upon the planet. So-called Arian views of Jesus Christ, that would not reckon the man as God Himself, but an adopted son, a creature by the will of God, who knew a certain beginning of his existence, were declared Anathema. Docetic or Gnostic views of Him, that could reckon him as God all right, but not truly or fully or really a man as we are men, were declared Anathema. The homoousion, championed by Athanasius, sought to affirm and confirm, against such views about the reality of Jesus Christ, that this man was God and God was this man at one and the same time in one and the same space in His Creation. He was both the Eternal Son or Word and the Incarnate Son as One become a man in the fullness of time, One Being with the Father in the Spirit of God's Eternity. He was with the Spirit of God 'consubstantial' with His Father and the Father of the Creation. The Word become flesh in Palestine through Miriam of Israel and the House of David at a particular time was none other than the Eternal God. When you see Jesus, you understand much more than God's Image of Himself, but who He truly is within Himself. You have come face to face with the Face of the Great I-AM in His Divine Freedom as the Lord God of the 'All.' You see that He is free to move outside of Himself and become something that He is not while remaining who He ever is and was and will be, and for your sake, on your behalf, become your Savior. In this freedom, the concept of the homoousion between the Father and the Son in the Spirit of God sought to secure an understanding of the wholeness of God's Being and Nature for us as people saved from their sin against Him and for Him who is Eternal Life. In this freedom, you understand Him as the Messiah of Israel among the nations, God among the nations, and in this way and no other in possession of a new and unique nature that shines in great contrast with Arian and Gnostic views of His Personhood.

The wholeness of this Lord and God was to be found with this particular man. This particular man is the Image of God, with imageless relations inherent in His knowledge of His Father, possessed with the Spirit of God in His Incarnate and Risen Reality in space and time. When we will not understand the concept of the homoousion in this way, we will not understand the freedom of God to act with His Being among us in our times and places.

Both 'adoptionistic' views and 'docetic' views of the Person of the Christ are legion in our cultures today. Arian and Gnostic Christianities remain quite common among us. The Trinitarian Faith found in understanding Jesus as the Self-Revelation of the Lord God still struggles for acceptance in our time. The 'Orthodox' explanation of the Great I-AM the Redeemer-Creator is remains as unknown today as it ever was to many believers. The centuries of efforts to make the Living Word of the Living Eternity of the I-AM as Father, Son, and Spirit have not been without great battles for this Faith. But God will not be something other than Himself in His Acts for us in the history of the world. We may not now divorce the One He is from His Acts in history or His Acts from His Being and Nature in His Freedom then. The homoousion of the Son and the Spirit with the Father as the Almighty Maker of the heavens and the earth and the Savior of the world means that the Incarnation must be understood in the Light the Triune Lord God the Great I-AM is both in Himself and in the history of His Creation. He is the One True Redeemer-Creator of this world, its invisible dimensions and its visible aspects in our experience with the world. Even though we distinguish the Three Persons with the names Father, Son, and Spirit (the Father is 'unoriginate', the Son 'begotten' and the Spirit 'proceeds' as the Triune Redeemer-Creator), we do not understand them as three gods, but the One Being of the One Lord God who is ever who He truly is. Even though the Father did not become incarnate, even though the Spirit did not become incarnate, they are involved each in their own way with the Incarnate Son in His birth, life, suffering of death, and resurrection. The Whole Lord God participates with and in the Whole Man He has become as this Son of God and David. Thus, His Self-Revelation is Self-Defined in this Self-Giving way for our sakes. The Church continues to proclaim the Gospel of the Person of the Lord Jesus Christ in our time and to insist that the true Faith is in Him who is the One and Only and Incomparable Redeemer-Creator of the world, the Blessed Trinity alive in the history of the world. This is the intention and purpose of the invention of the concept of the homoousion championed by Athanasius in the formation of the early creeds of the One, Holy, Apostolic, Catholic Church of the Living God make known in the world through the presence of the Person of Christ, the Son of God and David of the Revelation.

I believe the loss of such solid transcendent relations in much of our thinking today may be associated with the loss of the significance of this doctrinal concept invented in the early Church. The concept possesses an irreversible meaning whose loss is indeed the source of so much suffocation of our humanity in our time, so much closing of our minds to what is significant and meaningful for us as human beings in this world. We cannot come close to being what we ought to be with this loss in our lives in time and space and the light of the universe. The homoousial relations between the Son of the Father and the Father of the Son in the Spirit of the One True God as our Redeemer-Creator for us, as the Great I-AM He is, with His Salvation does not merely take our breath away but provides us with another that all creatures, great and small, must breathe if they are to hear His Call upon their lives. We do well to get to know the real freedom and true meaning implicit in the way the concept of the homoousion in our time and space would refer us to the Light He is for us.

II. At the Council of Chalcedon (451 AD) it is claimed that Cyril of Alexandria's (AD 412–444) confession of the 'one incarnate nature of God the Word become flesh' and Pope Leo's Tome (AD 440–461) of the 'hypostatic union of the two natures of the Person of Jesus Christ' are meant to signify one and the same reality.

If the homoousion intended to confess the three persons of the Trinity were the Same in Being and Nature as the One Lord God the I-AM is, if this concept of the consubstantial being of the three hypostases of the Father, Son, and Spirit was meant to explain the reality that the Incarnate Son and the Eternal Son or Word of God was One Being with the Spirit and the Father in the Eternity, then how may we rightly speak about the actual and full 'humanity' of the 'Word become flesh' as the Son of God in the world? The Council at Chalcedon attempted to clarify the Church's understanding of the Unity that is the Person of the Lord Jesus Christ in the face of the many questions that arose over the reality of the Revelation and the Salvation of the Redeemer-Creator for us. With homoousial relations well in hand on the part of the Church, within the ground of the

Blessed Trinity, within the actual Being of the Great I-AM the Lord God is as Triune, how are we to understand of the Divine Unity of this particular man, Jesus Christ, born of the House of David in Bethlehem and raised in Nazareth by the Virgin Miriam, Mother of God, as the revelation of His Father in His Spirit of the Eternity of the Godhead? The mystery of God incarnate as a man in the world, sent from His Father as the Lord of His Creation posits a 'union' between himself and the world that is an utterly new reality in the history of the Creation. How can such a thing happen in this world? The Unity or 'union' must belong both to the nature of God's Being as well as to the nature of the orders of His Creation. The relation between them, uncreated and created realities, must mean that their Unity comprehends two poles, the uncreated, transcendent, impassible, immutable, reality of God's Eternal Life and the created, temporal, ever changing, contingent being of the reality of that nature which the world shall become. With this kind of Unity, we must understand both the incomprehensible mystery of the Life of the Lord God as well as His Divine Freedom to become what He has never been and is not, this one particular man we know as Jesus of Nazareth, while remaining the Eternal I-AM He is. Fundamentally, the problem of the uncreated reality of God's Eternity and the created reality of time and space, where mankind possesses his and her own created nature and being as the one reality of a beginning of the whole new world, evidently as a relational veracity marking the New Beginning of the New Creation in time and space and mankind. To explain the new dimensions of the new reality raised questions about the Incarnation and the Creation that were not readily intelligible to all concerned.

At the Chalcedon (450 AD), Cyril of Alexandria, just as Athanasius had fought against Arius in 325 AD, challenged the views of Nestorius, again views that embraced some sort of 'subordinationism' of the Son to the Father. At the same time, Pope Leo of Rome set down the West's 'Orthodox' understanding of the Incarnation. Both Cyril and Leo sought to answer the heretical views that saw, like Arians before them, Christ as someone less than God Himself. Both could embrace the four famous adverbs of Chalcedon, denying any merely moral or representative relation between the Son or Word and the Father. When the two natures, divine and human, of the One Personal Reality the One Lord God is as Son of God and David, incarnate in the fullness of time as the Word of God in this world, the New Adam of the New Beginning of the New Creation, the New Heavens and the New Earth of the Kingdom of God, they were one without mixing up their natures and without changing into one another even while they could not be divorced from one another nor conceived as without one another. With this reality of the Person of the Lord, the New Adam had begun the New Creation. How did this actually happen? How can we explain what had occurred? It was an event whose dimensions introduced something so new in the world that not even the Jews had properly expected it. It was evident that (He spent forty days and forty nights with His disciples after His bodily resurrection and before His bodily ascension to the Right Hand of His Father!) the new dimensions were difficult to explain on the basis of what even the Greeks already knew. No one had, in the whole history of the human race upon the earth under the heavens, ever seen or heard of such a thing. The four adverbs attempted to say that the two natures, divine and human, had become the One Christ is 1) without confusion 2) without change 3) without division and 4) without separation. The divine and human natures of the Incarnate One could not be explained as One Person by any transformation of the one into the other, even while, at the same time, they could not be conceived as isolated from each another. He is the One He is as these two natures forever are in the form of the Unity of the God-Man from God's Eternity.

To work out what this meant in the reality of the world orders was admittedly a formidable challenge. We do not take to thinking out truly new things, especially between Eternity and time, uncreated and created realities, in the wholeness of what the world is as His Creation, easily. The whole now needs to be understood anew in the Light of the reality of the Revelation of God as this Person that Jesus Christ truly is, and not as another. He is who He is as the Son of His Father and of the Spirit of God from His Eternity as well as in a man for His time and times sent into the created reality the world is for the sake of the mankind He has become. What was promised David has become David. Here is the Creator God as this particular man, the New Adam, whose being is new for God, Man, and the Creation. This is the Divine Freedom of the Lord God in action with the purpose of fulfilling His vow to His People in His Creation. Something new has happened even for the Lord God. The four adverbs of the Council meant to expose any darkness inherent with the heretical views about Jesus as the Light of the World. They sought to exclude any mistaken thinking about His Salvation for us. They claimed clearly what was not allowed. But they did not readily form any real and positive grasp of the new dimensions of what had occurred, the actual newness of the significance the Incarnation in the Creation. To grasp at once both the Eternal Son and Word of God's Eternity as a particular man among the mankind of the world required a real conversion of the human mind into something truly new in time and space. It meant we had to embrace something new for the Being and Becoming of God, for the being and becoming of the World, and for the being and becoming of Man. The four adverbs said then what Jesus was not, but did not say who He actually is and was and will be with us. This is, I believe, the source of the problem for 'Orthodoxy.' The Church could be good at saying what God is not but not so good at saying who He is actually is. That the bishops could all agree on the four adverbs did not necessarily mean they all understood the implications of a confession that must mean to point beyond itself to that power of the Living God whose Word reveals the reconciliation and redemption of even the whole world. When the bishops agreed that Cyril of Alexandria, with his confession of the One Incarnate Nature of this Person, and Pope Leo's confession of the Two Natures of this One Person meant to refer to the same reality of Christ as this One Being of God's Becoming in the world, the Father of the Son in the Spirit of God, they set a stage on which debates could try the thought of many to follow them. The controversies in these debates led to the Fifth Ecumenical Council at Constantinople under the Emperor Justinian in 553 AD. The New Reality of the New Adam in the New Creation was not readily and positively grasped from within what was already known in the Old Creation. The rules of logic that prevailed in the past history of the human race upon the planet had been challenged with some new, upon which the future depended. It is the nature of this new dimension, of what had actually occurred in the Incarnation and so forth, that caused then the problems of which we read with the times of John Philoponus and the Living God.

Positively, what can be understood then about what happened in the Incarnation? Beyond the exclusion of heretical views, what is included in the New World, new for God and Man? One of the most telling statements about the new beginning and direction of this God, this world, and this Man sought to say what happened within the nature of the Incarnation as an event in the time and space of the Creation. The 'unassumed was the unhealed' became a banner for understanding the positive thrust of the confession. What God had not assumed in His Incarnation had not been saved from His wrath against evil and sin and unbelief. The statement intended to say something along the lines of what happened to the prophet Isaiah, when he was commissioned for his ministry in the history of Israel's prophecy in the world. The mystery of God with us, as we read in Isaiah 6, belonged to the mystery of the Lord who as King was willing to atone for the dirty lips of the prophet who lived among a people with unclean lips in order to send him with His Word into this world. Just as God Himself atoned for Isaiah, God Himself had atoned with His Incarnation His People for Himself. Christ was as Son of God the atoning work of the holy love that would not and could not be denied in God's Creation. It was this Grace and Truth as God Himself that cleansed the Church to proclaim the Word of Christ in the prophetic Spirit that hovers over and within this world still. The Incarnation then possessed in Himself the secret of God's atoning love for His People in His Creation. What God had assumed was the fallen flesh of the Old Adam and with His Atonement cleansed it of its sin and His Curse upon its evil, so that He had taken it up for life with God according to His Word. The assumption in the Word become flesh in the world held the secret of His Divine Freedom to act with His Holy Love on behalf of the unclean or the profane and to cleanse or make holy as the New Adam what had once been cursed in His Creation. Thus, the Incarnation possessed an atoning work of a holy love that God is from the Beginning, Old and New, in His relationship with what He causes to be and sustains in existence with Himself. The 'hypostatic union' had within it the concept of an assumption of the whole man whose positive dimensions with the reality of God sent the Church into the world to proclaim by His Spirit His Word to all mankind. So far as the bishops were concerned, the Right Hand of the Father of us all had spoken His Word by the Spirit into the confessions of the universal, holy, apostolic, and one Church of God in His Creation.

But the Church was forced to think through the confession with as much force and refinement as possible. If the Incarnation was the fulfillment of the BCR recorded in the Old Testament, the fulfillment of the Promise of God to Abraham, Moses, and David, and the Light of God for the nations, then it must be understood in the Light of the Blessed Trinity of the Great I-AM the Lord God is. If the Incarnation is the event in the prophecy of Israel that allows God to call His People My People, it must be understood within the dynamic relations that belong to His struggle to become known as the Lord God He truly is with Israel and the Church, with Old Israel and New Israel in His BCR between Himself, His People, and His Creation, and all this within the secret of His Atoning and Holy Love in covenanted relationship with all that is created reality.

We have seen that both poles of the relationship must be established as the Righteousness the Lord God is with His People, if we are to understand the nature of His BCR. We have seen that His Righteousness must possess both external and internal dimensions as His Salvation, as the Redeemer-Creator He has become in the Incarnation. This is the way He has chosen to make Himself present and known to His People. We must seek to understand with a rationality only His Faithfulness can produce with us, if we are to grasp the Rationality of His Word for us in our time and times, in our space and spaces, in the history of His Creation as a home for us. We need to be able to embrace the secret of His Atoning Love for us, found only in Himself with His Vow to save us in this way. We do not need to posit a new metaphysics for the New Adam that He has become, but we need to understand Him as the One who is the Living Lord God He truly is as the I-AM He is with His Word for us. We must insist that the refinements in the Church's confession of the Incarnation were neither 'Gnostic' nor 'adoptionistic' efforts to bring us knowledge of God, to give us knowledge of the nature of His Being and Becoming. The Creeds were steadily an effort, we insist, to penetrate into and articulate, as far as possible and as best we can, the secret that must mean what it means in the context of His Saving Love, His Atoning Love, of the very real significance of His Person as the Lord God He is, Incarnate, Dead, and Resurrected for the sake of mankind and the sin of the world. Without the Light of this Being of God, become with Divine Freedom the particular human being He is, we remain in the dark about His Salvation and the future of the world. This is the world that is His Creation. This is the space of time and the time of space He has occupied with the nature of His Being and Becoming, with the nature of what is truly new in the world.

The concept of the Incarnation as the hypostatic union of the two natures, uncreated and created, which has been freely posited in homoousial relationship with the Father and in the Spirit of God as the Son and Word of God, required the invention and development of two further concepts. The Unity of the Person of Christ was that hypostatic union of the 'Word become flesh' possessing both the anhypostasis and the enhypostasis of the hypostatic union. The two modes of operations complemented one another to form the content of the reality of the Incarnation in the Light of the Trinity God has revealed Himself to be as this Great I-AM. In this

Light, we may see that the Word did not merely enter into a flesh that already existed outside of Himself, outside of the becoming of His Being. There existed no hypostasis into which the Word went when He was sent by the Father to be born by the Spirit with Miriam of Israel, when He was sent to the House of David of Israel's Prophecy. The only hypostasis of the flesh that ever existed as the Son of Man and God was the hypostasis the Word of God assumed in His Divine Freedom and Power. But this does not and cannot mean that the hypostasis of the humanity of Jesus Christ is not completely real and utterly true humanity, without being this particular man that He is in the world. It does and must mean, however, that this humanity only exists, incomparably, in the divine nature the Word is as an hypostasis in homoousial relationship with the Father in the Spirit of God. He exists as an enhypostasis in the reality of the anhypostasis of the Word become flesh. The humanity of God in Christ is freely established within the divine hypostasis of the Word of God. The two natures are posited as Only One the Christ is in His homoousial relations with His Father and His Spirit of God's Eternity. The hypostatic union is a Unity of Grace and Nature that must signify both the particular man Jesus is as well as the Word He is of God, the Son He is of His Father, born both of the Eternal Spirit God is and the Spirit of God in His Birth of the Virgin.

These concepts do not then serve some metaphysical system of thought turning the passion and pathos of God's Divine Freedom to make Himself known for who He truly is into some timeless set of sophisticated logic. The actuality of the secret of His atoning and holy love for His People in His Creation works dynamically as His Divine Freedom to secure His Salvation of the race of the Adam. Just as Isaiah was cleansed by the atoning work of the Holy One with His Seraphim for his call to the prophecy of the Word of God, Christ as this Word cleanses the fallen race, makes holy the human race, frees the human race from its sin against its Redeemer-Creator in order that the human race in the New Adam may hear His Word and know Him as the Savior He is. In this way, He delivers humanity from its enmity and hostility towards the God who is its Creator and with the Lord who is truly Israel's Redeemer in His Creation. Without His Cross, bodily Resurrection, and Ascension, without the Power of the Spirit sent from the Right Hand of the Father, to affirm and confirm Him as the One He is, no one can understand the I-AM of the Living God I-AM as the Person of the Lord Jesus Christ. His hypostatic union in atoning relations with the homoousion of His Being and Becoming for us establishes His Church to serve as His Witness to this Man He is. The Church in this sense is His Help-Mate, His Bride, His Body, given to be with him forever as He takes the Creation to its destiny with Himself. The creative effort of the early Church to witness to this Living One, to understand what the world's forever shall be in the Light of this Eternity, the Eternity of the Great I-AM He is over and with and for us all and all that is cannot be appreciated enough. In the Light of this union of this man with this Triune Being of the Redeemer-Creator, the anhypostasis and the enhypostasis of the Word become flesh may be grasped as complementing with atoning love one another and creating with this same power that hypostatic union which is the unity of the New Adam in the New Creation. We grasp Him then for who He truly is this Lord God acting in His Divine Freedom to deliver us from our evil and sin and the curse of death upon us in our time and times. No timeless logic could ever speak of Him at any time in any space without His Time and Space created for our sake in His Creation.

We owe the recovery of these doctrines for the Church in our time to Karl Barth, the great Swiss theologian and pastor in Basel. It is a shame that American Christianity does not know him for the Biblical and Evangelical Theologian that he was in His Church Dogmatics. Under Barth's mentorship, the Right Reverend Professor Thomas F. Torrance of Edinburgh, Scotland, in the midst of the rise to power of Hitler in Germany, began a Ph.D. dissertation published with the title of *The Grace of God in the Apostolic Fathers*. The work was interrupted by the Second World War, but finally completed in 1948, the same year Israel was given by the United Nations land in Palestine. In this book, Torrance argued that the early Church fathers could tend very early on to lose their grip upon the meaning and significance of the Truth of God's Grace for the Church. The Grace of God in the hands of the Church could easily be turned into something He is not, just as Israel of old could easily turn the Great I-AM He is into the 'Not-I-AM' of their idol making. The history of sin in the ancient world as recorded in the history of Israel among the nations could be continued with the People of God now in the form of the New Israel, the Church, as the People of God. Professor Torrance argued that the loss of the Church's grasp on the meaning of the Grace of God as the Person of the Lord Jesus Christ and His Revelation of the Trinity can readily be seen in the history of the Church in the world. It can be shown that all sorts of legalism would replace the doctrines that once sought to secure the significance of God in Christ as the Grace and Truth who is the Head of the Church and the King of kings. The authority of Grace could then be substituted with other authorities that were not the Spirit of the Living Word as the Throne of David at the Right Hand of His Father in His Creation. St. Paul's letters to the churches steadily argue for this Grace with the believers in Christ, and from the Letter to the Galatians onwards the apostle is found fighting against every form of legalism that would usurp the authority of Grace and Truth for the Church of Jesus Christ. The Gospel of Grace could suffer and did suffer from a steady effort to replace the I-AM Christ is as the Light of the World with some other god or light, an attempt considered blasphemy by the apostolic authority in the Church. The proclamation of the Gospel demands that each generation wrestle afresh, then, with the significance of the Grace of God in time and times with the proclamation of the Word of God and the Kingdom of God.

In this way, every generation becomes responsible to struggle against the temptation to embrace the idols its hands have made for itself and to understand the Truth of this Grace, according to the Spirit of the Word of God working with us in our times, to the Glory of His Being and Word and Acts in the history of the world. The significance of the meaning of His Grace in the world then, bound up with who He truly is as this Living Word and Lord as the Grace of the Redeemer-Creator of a universe that is His Creation, must be rendered anew from generation to generation. Each and every generation belongs to the generation of the Resurrected Lord of Light and Life in the space and time and light of His Creation. His Grace is the Truth of the actual life of the Great I-AM He is as the Lord God of time and times and the fullness of time with Him. He is the Lord God of space and spaces and the significance of space in relationship to the Light He is as the Redeemer-Creator He is. This is what it means for us to call Him King and Priest and Prophet and Sage of our space and time and the light of His Creation. In His Name we find the place where and when He is what forever is and shall be in relationship with His Eternal Life. Surely Torrance has argued rightly that this Grace of God may not be reduced up or down, down or up, with movements from below or from above, if we are to understand the substantial rationality of His Truth for us, over against all of our legalisms, all of our idols and idol making, all of our ways of remaining His enemies in this world. Surely, no abstract principle or subjective description of what we want the world to be and our selves in it may pretend to be the Grace of God with us. None of our notions about morality and ethics, none of our vaunted efforts to be responsible for this or that world, may necessarily be attributed to the Grace of God. God's Grace cannot be defined by what we would naturally appreciate and seek to establish. The Truth of His Grace is not our common sense in action in this world. His Grace belongs to the Only, Incomparable, Unique One He is as the Holy Lord God He is at once from beyond and within the space, time, and light of the orders of the universe we must know as His Creation. Grace may not be defined by any of our human conditions, our human efforts to imagine or will this or that world, where we would make the best of all possible worlds. Grace is and must be defined by the One He truly is with us, with whom we may find His Grace for our beings in this world. The Great I-AM the Lord God is must therefore define His Grace with us. Grace must be defined by who He truly is as His Grace for us, as His Promise kept in His Creation. We need always to be able to explore what is actually the case of the Grace He is as this Lord and God in our time and times. The Church may just as readily misunderstand His Grace in her efforts to obey as Israel could in the history of her disobedience with Him. The Church can just as easily seek to turn Him into something that He is not, just as Israel seeks to turn Him into the 'Not-I-AM' that He is not. We can as the People of God, as Israel Old and New, prefer our idols to who He is as His Grace and Truth with us. Jew and Gentile can oppose Emmanuel each in their own times in His covenant with His People and His Creation.

Torrance has tried to champion, since those student days with Barth, the very unique nature of the necessity of this freedom, uncreated and created, that comes as the Grace and Truth of the Lord God the Great I-AM truly is with us in this world. Grace compels uniquely, like Light, those He has chosen freely to face with Himself. Emmanuel as the Son of God, the Son of David, and the Son of Man in His Creation as the King, Prophet, Priest, and Sage of the People among the nations in His Royal and Divine-Human Freedom has made room and time for Himself among us, and we cannot claim to know the Righteousness of God in this world without a real grasp of His Grace and Truth. Thus, we may even today busy ourselves with our idols. The Good News of the Resurrected and Ascended Lord in this world, as the Great I-AM He is, who is who He is as the Son of the Almighty Father, both Incarnate and begotten as the House of David in His Creation, is not readily received by either Jew or Gentile today. Yet He continues His struggles with His Spirit sent into the world to establish with His Church,

The Church and the World

called the Bride and Body of Christ, the proclamation of what may become known of the One He is. Because of this Grace, the Church is made to witness to His Servant as the Light of the World in fulfillment of His BCR with His People in His Creation. It is this Word that shines upon all creatures in the world in all of its space and all of its time and times.

We know the sending of His Spirit as the event of Pentecost, a festival celebration in Israel's history, deeply bound up with the renewal tradition in the tradition of the BCR in the Biblical World, where agricultural cycles belonging seasonally to the lands of the ancient world are taken up and given historical significance beyond their times in the Creation by the Revelation of God with His People among the nations, when they possess with the confessions in the history of the People of God the significance they are in the history of the Creation. The festivals are thus made to participate with God's providence and prophecy for His People in His Land according to His Promise in His Covenanted Relationship over which is Lord and God. Luke marks the Pentecost of this Promise with the Church by Peter's invocation of Joel's prophecy (Joel 2:28–32; Acts 2:1–41). This Pentecost is a renewal of the Promise in the BCR for the 'Latter Days' of Israel's history among the nations (cf. Jeremiah 31:31). It is the Messianic Renewal for the People of God, rooted in the ground of the traditions which we have read in Exodus 34; Joshua 24; 2 Samuel 7; and so forth, that we must learn to follow according to the nature of His Grace and Truth in the history of the world. The secret of the Grace of God for the House of David is rooted in this ground, and its fruitfulness shall come from this ground. This Pentecost, the Feast of Weeks on Israel's calendars, celebrates the spring harvest as a time when new meaning may be given to the nature of her covenanted relations with the Lord God, now to be forever known as the Grace of the Great I-AM as Father, Son, and Spirit of the Only and Incomparable God. The Grace and Truth of His Being are to be apprehended and understood in the Light of this Word as Man in His Godhead. His Person shines as such in the darkness that opposes Him among the nations, where Israel has been given life in Him according to the Will of His Wisdom and Divine Freedom, according to the nature of His Grace and Truth as the doctrines of the hypostatic union of the Word and Man in homoousial relationship with the Father Almighty in the One Spirit who is truly God with the Father and the Son as the Eternal and Blessed Life the Triune Redeemer-Creator the Lord God is, when there exists no longer any question about what is means. The doctrines mean to refer us to the Truth of God' Grace with us, to the Grace of God's Truth for us, to take up the minds of sinners in our sinful world and lift them to the Living Lord He is. They mean to proclaim with us in this world God's salvation for us.

> III. The Perichoresis of the Hypostatic Union of Jesus Christ with the Homoousion of His Person of the Father and the Spirit in the Eternity the Lord God is as this Man is the Grace of God and as no Other is.

The relational realities between the Persons of the Godhead are as much God as each of them, Father, Son, and Spirit is God. The union and communion of Christ with God is the Person He is as the Redeemer-Creator of His People in His Creation, the Great I-AM He is. The hypostatic union and the homoousion together refer to a co-inherence that is fundamental to the Incarnation of the Word understood in the Light of the Trinity of God. If the Son of God and David is Man as God, then this union and communion belong to the very nature of the Being of God. The whole of this Man is who He is from within the Being of this God. Relations of the Trinity with the Incarnation and the Incarnation full and complete reality seek to grasp this union and communion, for it is this fellowship to which the Church has been adopted in the Name of this God. This Person is our Mediator, the One who acts with Himself then, to take us up and give us to partake with Him in His Being of the Father and the Spirit of Eternal Life. To believe in Him is to enter into perichoretic relations as adopted sons and daughters with the Great I-AM the Lord God truly is. To enter into these relationships is to become consumed by the Living One as our Redeemer-Creator in this world.

In the Light of this 'Word become flesh' in the space-time world, the Church understood that the perichoresis of her union and communion with the Lord God introduced her to a complex of relational realities that possessed both symmetrical and asymmetrical dimensions of the One Being and Nature of God. The perichoresis of the relations of the Father, Son, and Spirit of the Eternal Godhead could not be conceived as the same as the perichoresis of the Divine and Human Natures of the Incarnation, but the Trinity of the Word become incarnate was and is and will be the God of the Beginning. Also, within the Trinity Himself the relations between the Father, Son, and Spirit of Eternity were defined by who the Lord is as well as who God is not. The Father is not the Son or the Spirit. The Son is not the Spirit or the Father. The Spirit is not the Father or the Son. Who each is cannot be known without knowing who each is not. Jesus Christ is not only the Son of Eternity but also the Son of Man. The Person of the Lord Jesus Christ as the Incarnation of the Word and Son of God possesses a Unity whose inner and external relations cannot symmetrically be read back up into the Godhead. We must learn to deal with asymmetrical as well as with symmetrical relations in the Being and Becoming of the Nature of the Lord God with His Divine Freedom. This means that the triadic relations of the Trinity and the relations inherent in the Incarnation form a wholeness of the Living God in all and every part, where the parts belong to dynamically differentiated relations of Being and Not Being. We know who God is as well as who He is not and not simply what He is not. We know the is-ness of the Lord God while knowing His 'is-not-ness.'

The created space-time of the Incarnation belongs to the uncreated space-time of the Godhead as the Grace and Truth He is embodied in Jesus Christ with His symmetrical and asymmetrical relationships of the Father and in the Spirit. The Name that signifies that He is who He truly is belongs both to the New and the Old Nature of His Being and Becoming in His Freedom. It is a Name among the names of things in the Creation, but it is also the Name to whom all must finally bow. The space-time of the Incarnation with this Name exists symmetrically and asymmetrically in relationships with the actual Trinity the Being and Becoming of the Great I-AM with the creative power of His Word and His Atoning Love. The quantitative magnitudes of the invisible and visible created realities of the world belong to realities to be known invisibly, without imaged relations. Number and Word rationalities form a whole the necessity of which belongs to the created and creative freedom of the I-AM God is with His Creation in His Divine Freedom. Thus, the perichoretic relations that belong to the Being and Nature of the One Redeemer-Creator of the world define a Unity to which the Church has been called in the Name of Jesus Christ. As such, He is the Head of the Church and the King of the Creation. He fills the chasm between created and uncreated realities with the power of His atoning love with His Spirit. He works with His Word as the Son of the Trinity of God the salvation of the race in the world. The whole of the Trinity participates in the whole of the Incarnation as the Incarnation participates in the I-AM of the Trinity. Again, in Him, Eternity and time have been established with His space to define what forever may be in relationship to the Creator of the 'All.' The transcendent, imminent, and experiential dimensions that belong to these relations in Him define what reconciliation and redemption is with His Eternal Light and Life and Love. Here is the ground upon which the Church finds she may stand in actual union and communion with Him. It is ground upon which she may certainly celebrate the salvation of God as well as contemplate her knowing of Him.

We remember the event of the Incarnation as epoch making. We carve up our time and times with clocks and calendars that keep for us an account of the meaning of this event. Time before Christ was not the same as time after Christ. His birth, life, death, and resurrection mark a new epoch in the history of the Creation. It is history-making event. It defines what history is in the Light of God's Eternal Life. It is God with us. We cannot define history in some other light than the Light that God is for us. If we seek the meaning of events in time in our views of history, we must seek it in the fullness of His Time for us, His Time for Israel and the Church as the New Israel, His Time for the whole People of God among the nations in the history of His Creation. Thus, the Church of the Lord Jesus Christ celebrates this new beginning, this New Man for God in God's Creation, this Grace and Truth of the Lord God become embodied in this way for the sake of all mankind, even in the face of the Graeco-Roman Empire of the times. His Grace and the 'fullness of time' marks this new time for us with dimensions that cannot be grasped without the concepts of the homoousion, the hypostatic union, and the perichoresis of the Incarnation as the Revelation of the Triune Creator as the Lord of all time and space. I believe this is the inheritance of the Alexandrian Grammarian named John Philoponus in the scientific community at the Academy where the city's famous Lighthouse guided ships at sea into her busy harbors. This was the man in the history of the Church who faced the Graeco-Roman culture of his time, believing that the Theology of the Church and the Science of the Creation which is the world where we have our being, with the genius of a steady and penetrating faith. It is this faith seeking understanding that, I believe, we need to appreciate afresh in our time.

I remember speaking with Adventist Christians about these new dimensions of relationships in time and space established by the bodily resurrection and ascension of Christ as the fulfillment of the BCR in Israel's prophecy of the Word of God. The forty days and forty nights Jesus spent with His disciples after His Resurrection, an utterly new event in the history of the world, I tried to explain, marked God's New Beginning of His New Creation. In the life of this man God has introduced a new kind of time to our recollection of time and times. It was the inception in the 'fullness of time' that would only end in the realization of the promise the Lord God kept with His People in His Creation. Even in the midst of the time of the Old Creation, experienced as the Old Covenant of God with us, the Lord has acted to reconcile and redeem His People. On what calendar, I asked, may we mark down the full measure of these days and nights? What is the significance of time's fullness realized as the bodily risen Christ? What kind of time did He spend with them as He revealed Himself as the Son of the Father He truly was and is and will be with them? What does it mean for the future of the apostles? Yes, forty days and forty nights passed that could be placed upon our calendars, but yet precisely with this time was also spent the humanity of God as God with us and for us in the history of the Creation. Yes, mark their times down on a calendar, but understand that these marks must point us quite beyond the pages of our measures of time and times, beyond the weeks and months and years and seasons of the Old Creation to His New Time for us, His Time as God's Eternity for us. The days on the calendar come to mean then the Time of His Father and His Spirit with us in our days and evening. The I-AM in time and times and the I-AM in His Eternity have forever been given union and communion with Him. Time is now defined anew. Times in the service of His Temple is spent with Him as the Sabbath of God in His Creation. God's presence in His Divine Freedom in this world marks His Rest with His Creation. Time cannot be properly understood outside of this relationship. Time cannot be spent in the sanctity of His Presence in the world except with this relationship for the believer in Him. With His Sabbath Rest He defines the freely created reality of the universe in relationship to the I-AM He is in this way. Any celebrating we may choose to do of this Sabbath cannot be confined to the rules and measure our calendar keeping, but they all must point away from themselves to the Time He has created with Himself for us, His Time with us. With this Time is defined the Space where He has defined a space as the place where His Name has been established to call people there to go in order to do what is 'Right' in His Eyes. There is no elsewhere of this Name.

After my talk, most of the Adventists told me that they had never heard of such things. No one among them could take seriously this way of grasping the meaning of the Sabbath Relation of the Redeemer-Creator to His People in His Creation. The nature of time and God's Eternity had been for them a kind of timeless idea that they marked down on their calendars now just as people had always marked it down. The fact that the Time of Christ changed time itself had never made much of an impression upon their belief or faith or thinking. The fact that God had made our time His Time for us, even in the midst of a world of history to deny Him His Being, seems to have escaped utterly the attention of many. The meaning of His bodily death on His Cross (the end of the Old World) and His subsequent Resurrection of His Grace (the beginning of the New World) as the New Time of the New Creation, in which He is Himself the Sabbath and the Sabbath Blessing in His Relation to His Creation, does not cross our minds with a solid impact. The significance of His atoning work His Time for our time and times, His Holy Love serving to justify and sanctify sinners in His Creation in this Sabbath Relation with this world, remains alien in the assumptions of many about the universe and its mankind. Our discussions reminded me of the great battles that took place in the conflicts history has recorded as the experience between the Church and the Graeco-Roman world. The early centuries after the Ascension of the Lord Jesus Christ to the Almighty are replete with these battles, sometimes bloody, always as imperative as He is in His Space and Time among us.

The Alexandrian Grammarian, John Philoponus, inherited the solid truth of these doctrines and sought in his work to turn these doctrines into a basis for the physics of the world in his time. For the Fifth Ecumenical Council, held by the Emperor Justinian in 553 at Constantinople, Philoponus was appointed to write a treatise on the Incarnation of Jesus Christ in the Church for the sake of an Empire now, since Constantine, become a Christian realm. The debates that developed after the Councils of Nicea and Chalcedon had reached such an intensity that the Emperor felt he needed a new statement of the Faith, one in which the various parties contending for the right understanding of Christ might find some real agreement in the Empire. In response to his Emperor, Philoponus wrote the work entitled 'The Arbiter.' It is as cool an analysis as possible by the Grammarian for the sake of achieving some real resolution to the many complex issues in the debates that plagued Justinian's Empire. Because of this work, the 6th Ecumenical Council of the Church at Constantinople declared Philoponus 'Anathema' in 680 AD, about a hundred years after his death. I considered the condemnation a mistake of tragic proportions and epoch making significance with my study of the setting-in-life of 'The Arbiter.' The Anathema, I believe, displays the Church's lost understanding of the Grace of God as the Truth of Christ's Time and Space for us in His Creation. Unable to embrace the thought of Philoponus, the Church instead wrestled with the ways the Aristotelian/Ptolemaic cultures would develop a theatre of thought in which she might seek to proclaim the Gospel of her Lord. With Philoponus as a heretical Monophysite to her, she could seek to marry her convictions to the developing Ptolemaic Cosmology of the Graeco-Roman philosophies. Philoponus' concept of the nature of the world as the contingent order and freedom established by the freely creating and speaking God became lost upon the Church's confession of the Mind of Christ. The new nature of the New Creation escapes reality of the power of His Grace to create according to the Promise the actuality that is the object of Israel's prophecy. Philoponus was, however, the first Christian theologian to take seriously both the doctrines of the Councils and the physics of the Cosmos as it comes to us in the light of the prophecy of this Creation, a light he saw shining as the Light God Himself both for the physical laws of the world and the laws of His reconciling and redemptive purpose with created reality, invisible and visible, angels and demons included. For Philoponus, one could not divorce the one from the other, however much we must be able to distinguish one thing from another. I believe we need to understand this ground upon which the Grammarian stood to accomplish the work he loved to do on behalf of Christ and His Kingdom of God with the Creation.

John Philoponus took seriously, then, following Athanasius of Alexandria and Basil of Caesarea, the relationship of the Incarnation as the Redeemer-Creator of the Beginning of the Creation out of nothing. The Incarnation begins the ultimate justification of the Creation. The Church's Dogma and the science of this Creation possessed an inner secret in such a way that the apparent abyss of the world's 'nothingness' had been taken up and given justification with the Lord God through the Person of the Lord Jesus Christ. It is this Person that the Church must proclaim as the Gospel in the world. The secret of the New Creation belonged to this King, Priest, Prophet, and Sage as Word of God for the whole world.

In the Academy, the Grammarian evidently grasped something of the new significance of the new dimensions of the new realities that the Incarnation of the Word established as Man with the Cosmos. The rational order and freedom experienced in the light of the Cosmos belonged to the Incarnate Word, the Light of God with the light of the Creation. This Light, as the source and ultimate substance of the light of the Cosmos with its Beginning drew the boundaries upon which could be seen the horizons of the destiny of the ages. Someone new was in the world, and it was the Church's duty to understand rightly who He is and was and will be. It is this dimension of newness that is perhaps so difficult for us to believe and to seek to understand its significance even for the physical law we experience in the world. It was with this new dimension that Philoponus loved to wrestle. It was upon this ground that he could find a place to stand and to seek to understand God and the World with its Mankind.

The new dimensions of space-time or time-space as created realities belonging to the Grace of God in His Incarnate Being and Becoming demanded a transformation of the prevailing worldviews. The old ways of carving up the reality of the Cosmos and defining the orders experienced in the world had to be converted into a fresh grasp of the Grace He is in His new relationship with His Creation. Everything had to be questioned, including Platonic and Aristotelian and Neo-Platonism philosophies of the Ptolemaic Cosmos developed into the sixth century's view of the heavens and the earth and its mankind. Greek dualisms, reigning supremely over much understanding of theology and physics had to be dethroned and new ways of understanding posited. The heavens and the earth that were dualistically divided and divorced from one another had to be seen with new eyes. The heavens could no longer declare divine and eternal the light from the stars and the Sun and the Moon shining above the temporal and ever changing things on the earth. Where Aristotle sought to define the heavens with his 'Fifth-Substance,' a substance just as Eternal as God is, with a 'logos' principle deeply embedded in the nature of the heavens, a new view of the motion of the heavens needs to be established. All matter, above or below in the one Creation, possessed no such substance. The things above the moon and the things below the moon were perishable things. The nature of the heavens and the earth existed as one created reality, even perishing, in relationship to that which is beyond it. Their subsistence depended upon the power of the Word of the Creator. Greek views that made salvation a thing that belonged to the shape of the heavenly substance, that made participation in divine and eternal forms a necessity for immortality, required conversion if reality was to be faced. Nothing in the world was deathless. There is no such thing as an immortal soul, whose nature was unlike the nature of our bodies. Both things above and things below were temporal. The dualisms that allowed the positing of such a substance produced nothing but phantoms about the nature of the world. We may call them 'Greek Essentialism' at work in understanding the nature of the world. We may understand them as producing abstractions about the wholeness of a world whose reality we need to grapple with anew, if any real heuristic science is to be established. Thus, against the dualisms of the past inherent in the development of the Ptolemaic Cosmos, Philoponus argued with some steady genius, for the sake of the new dimension the New Creation demanded of our understanding. His thought experiments exercised his imagination accordingly.

He replaced Aristotle's 'Fifth-Substance' and Aristotle's physics with his 'three-dimensional,' a controversial concept still debated today. The physics of the matter of the space-time world as God's Creation belonged to the power of the Word of God and not to anything divine within it. Philoponus' 'three-dimensional' posited an invisible structure to space that belonged to the very structure of matter with a relational veracity where time and the motion of the whole of the world was what it was because of its connectedness with the power of God. The invisible structures of space and time belonged to a motion reflected by the reality of the 'three-dimensional,' separable in theory from the structure of matter in motion in the world, but without divorce from motion and matter with the world. The invisible world with its space and time was a part of a whole whose form in relationship with visible matter in motion in space and time made the world what it was. Both the 'three-dimensional' and the magnitudes we learn to measure in the Cosmos were together fundamental to what the nature of the world is with its invisible and visible dimensions of existing as created reality, a reality created out of nothing in the Beginning. The 'three-dimensional' was for Philoponus a concept grasped as a 'thought-experiment,' a theoretical reality that could not be divorced from the empirical reality of the world experienced by the race within it, where the out of nothing character of the world could be appreciated in the light of the New Creation God with His Word had made with His Christ. For the Grammarian, the concept of the 'three-dimensional' together with the sensible physics of the nature of the world possessed physical law imparted to it along with an initial impetus created by the power of the Word of God in the Beginning. Thus, the visible light and matter of the space-time universe as a whole possessed a kinetic energy from the start. Its movements as the created reality of the God the Lord is thus belonged to the Wisdom of God.

We are faced here with the actuality that the Creation out of nothing with its Beginning, the contingent reality of its light, has been reinforced and enhanced with the Light He is from above and below the actual existence and development of the heavens and the earth with God's mankind in it. They are bound up with one another in the Truth and Freedom as His Grace, the Great I-AM He truly is as the Creator and Redeemer of all that exists as created reality. Thus the physics of the Cosmos is what it is in relational veracity with the Incarnation of its Creator. The motion of matter in the Cosmos possessed kinetics that belonged to the dynamics of light in the Creation. With these concepts, Philoponus replaced Aristotle's 'Fifth Substance' and Greek Philosophy's notion of the 'Eternity of the World,' with his assertion that both the heavens as well as the souls of men were perishable and mortal. They were what they are and may become because of the power of the Word of their Creator. He reigns supreme and free to make them what they are as space and time and matter and energy in relationship to who He is with the power of the Great I-AM He is. With His Name thus rests the secret the Redeemer He is. With this Only One rests the Wisdom of the Divine Freedom to be with the 'All' He creates and makes the Lord God He is.

This is the Creator the I-AM had chosen to become when He created in the Beginning. This is the Redeemer who has chosen to become with His Son to renew His Covenant with Israel among the nations in His Creation, sent on behalf of the sin of the entire world, to create the space and time of a new world in which His Promise would be kept. With the Love of this Wisdom then in His Divine Freedom, beyond all necessity and beyond all arbitrariness, He has chosen to justify Himself in the Beginning with His New Beginning as this Man, Jesus Christ, the David of the world that is to come, according to His Promise with Israel. Upon this new ground then, Philoponus stood to think to become in the ancient world the forerunner to Copernicus, Galileo, and Newton with his impetus theory. With his theory of the kinetic nature of created light, we may see him even as forerunner to Einstein and modern and post-modern universe of light. In this way, we may see the interface between Christian Theology and Scientific Culture, the fecundity of thought upon this ground, the Truth of His Grace realized with epoch making significance and proportions. The Anathema of Philoponus, like the Anathema of Galileo, cannot stand the test of time and space and matter, as they really are in a world that is God's Creation, let alone the aberrations of the race within them.

This means we must say that the transformations of traditional terms used to carve up the realities grasped in the worlds of the idol makers are now made to serve the Gospel of the Redeemer-Creator of the Cosmos. The revelation of the I-AM as the Trinity of the Godhead, made known through the transparency of the Person of the Lord Jesus Christ as Father, Son, and Spirit of Eternity, both fulfills the Covenanted Promise to Israel and provides a new Light onto the nature of His People and His Creation. In this Light, we see light not only in the Cosmos but also with Man in the Cosmos. We see that the contingency of the world, with its rational order, independent in nature from its Creator, has experienced the realization of the Grace and Truth of its dependency, through the Redeemer, upon its God. If with Divine Freedom the Creation was given the Beginning, in that same Divine Freedom Man with the Creation has been given his New Beginning, a New Beginning that marks both Man and the Creation with their dependence upon the Redeemer, the Creator of the 'All' that is created reality. Revelation and the physics of the world cannot be either identified with God or divorced from the Creator. Both are to be seen in the Light of the Redeemer, the Lord of all space and time and so forth. John Philoponus was able with this belief to understand space and time relationally in this way, to free space and time from the notions of the philosophers that they were absolute containers of all that occurred in them, a view of space and time that, because of the Anathema, became popular along with the Ptolemaic Cosmology embraced by the Church all the way into the Middle Ages and beyond. It was not until Einstein's Relativity Theories that the relational views of space and time found once more their place in science. The science of John Philoponus, with his relational views of them, could win back the hearts and minds of the race for the coming century, when we must learn to take seriously the power of God and His Word for the physics of the world. The world is not eternal. It is not what it actually is necessarily. It could have been another or not at all. But the wholeness of its contingent reality and created rationality, as 'very good' in the Beginning, is and will be justified as such in the New Beginning the Creator has made with Himself as this Word His Person has become with the Person of the Lord Jesus Christ. Here in this Name lies the secret of the Lord of all space and time and light, even the Light of our salvation. All must be transformed into the service of His intention and purpose with His One Creation with His One Word.

This point about the contingency of the world, with its created rational and substantial reality, has never had an easy time in the history of the development of our thought. The clash with the views of the Roman Empire in the early centuries of the Church hints at the steady confrontation that will occur across the centuries, even with the Church and the Empire seeking to work together to create a civilization for the race of men in the world. Making sense of the New Creation out of the Old Creation is the work of great transformations for the human mind. Belief in such transformations is necessary, uniquely necessary, in a freedom whose relationship with concrete objectivity is imperative in order to understand the profound changes that have been begun. It is now an epoch that is new for God, new for Man, and new for the heavens and the earth the universe is. Both transcendent and concrete matter must be thought, as consistently and thoroughly as possible, together. The Light of the Grace of God for us as the House of David posits in this way a kind of blinding light for the mind of the race. It takes some time just to get used to seeing anything in this Light. Our minds need time and times to adjust to what its shining upon things mean with which we have been so familiar, yet in the dark, so to speak. The Incarnate Word of God as the Man of God in the Creation, living at the Right Hand of His Father as the David of Israel's prophecy, as the Son of Man of the Apocalypse, as the Son of God's Eternity, is not the Light in which we are used to knowing things. We do need time for our mind's eye to become transformed in the power of this Light, in the Word of this Light, in the Truth and Grace of this Lord and God with us in our times. Yet from Athanasius to Basil, from Philoponus down to our own time, we may read a history that has championed the real contingency of the Creation out of nothing in the Beginning and its Redemption in the Incarnation of the Creator's Word and Power. With such, the Promise has been and will be kept. With Him is found in fact the very secret of what time is, what space is, as His Creation. In Him, the uncreated realities of God's power and purpose with the world have been given correspondence with the created realities of the world. The physical law of the nature of created reality is such that this law is made to reflect the uncreated Law of God's Grace with His Creation. The transcendence of the Divine Freedom to be who He is both over and with His Creation is to be understood as served by His immanence with this Creation, and to reflect in its empirical experience of its law the reality of the power of His Grace. Only in this way may our race be open to breathing something beyond the air that surrounds our planet. The earth provides an air we share with animals, but we need as the Image of God among them to breathe the breath of God with us. Without these two worlds of time and Eternity, Man cannot be the man and the women we were intended to be in the Beginning or in the New Creation. We are purposed to be in time and times breathers of both the air that surrounds the earth as well as the Life of God with us. The uncreated time of God's Being and the created time of the being of the Cosmos must possess a relational veracity that belongs to the Truth of His Grace, the Grace of His Truth, for the sake of all truth, the wholeness of God and Man and a world that is from beginnings to endings His Creation.

Thus, in the Light of the Incarnation, we find, however painfully, created time sanctified in His Space for us, in His Sabbath Space for us in His Creation. If Aristotle could carve the world up into categories of class exclusions, genus and species (still employed to analyze things today), Philoponus could call the transformations of these categories into realities the actualities of which took us quite beyond the world of contradictions found so commonly there into the contingency of the world with its independence of God's nature and its dependence upon His Will for its existence and meaning. Philoponus, with his 'thought-experiments' could find theory enough to satisfy with sufficient reason what was indeed experienced in this world, experience that moved with the whole of the Creation towards a destiny that the Redeemer-Creator alone could give it. To Revelation belongs a heuristic science that was True to the Grace of God with us. For this science, all had to become transformed, even human language itself. With this in mind, the Grammarian sought to write his treatise on the Incarnation for Justinian and the Fifth Ecumenical Council at Constantinople in 553 AD.

When I wrote my PhD dissertation about 'The Arbiter,' Philoponus' response to Justinian's call for the sake of the Church, I realized that what the Grammarian had been about with his arguments for the Incarnation and the relationship of God to His Creation entailed a whole new view of the nature of the nature of the Creation and its relationship with its Creator. This view is developed in the Light of the Trinity of the Lord God made known through the Person of the Lord Jesus Christ as the Father, Son, and Spirit of the Eternity who is the Great I-AM of the prophecy of the Word. To understand the Incarnation, one must learn to think in the Light of the Trinity and to understand the Trinity the Great I-AM had become was to learn to think in the Light the Incarnation is as the birth, life, death, resurrection, and ascension to the Right Hand of God of the Lord, when the complementary relationship between them was established by the Atoning Love of God for His People in His Creation. With the dynamics of this kind of complementary relations in mind, Philoponus could argue that the Uncreated Light God is and the created light He has become in Christ as the 'Light of the World,' the fulfillment of the prophecy, formed an utterly new nature as the personal reality of the I-AM the Lord God is with His People in His Creation. As such, all natures became defined in their relations with the One Nature of the Two Natures, divine and human, that God had become as a man in the Creation. It was the dynamics of this development that could not be understood by any definition of nature one encounters in Aristotelian physics and cosmology. Any definition of nature found in that world had to be transformed and made to serve the new dimension of the New Creation that had been established by Jesus Christ, a concrete man of flesh in the history of the Creation who was also the Son of God's Eternity. He Himself is the space and time where and when all creaturely realities are called to go to do what is Right in the Eyes of the Lord.

This meant that the term *nature* had to bear various meanings in different contexts and at last refer away from itself in any context to the Nature of God's Being, the ultimate objectivity of any Truth in the world. The role of Perichoresis in the dynamical character of his thought must be understood here. The perichoretic relations between the Incarnation and the Trinity are not the same throughout the perichoretic relations within the nature of the truth that is the actual existence of the whole and its particular realities. The two are one because of the freedom God as His Grace has with these relations on each and every level of their existences. The divine and human natures are one on the level of the Incarnation and the Persons of the Father, Son, and Spirit are one on the level of the Triune Lord and God, and the two are one as the economical and ontological Trinity. Thus, the Being of God is One Nature (the homoousion) even while He is this One as Three Persons (the hypostases in perichoretic Union with the Incarnation's perichoresis). I was able to pick out of the argument of the Grammarian in Chapter Seven of The Arbiter, the very chapter that had been employed by the Church to condemn his thought, precise sentences where Philoponus' intention attempts to deal with the two natures, divine and human, and the one nature of the union in this dynamic way. The wholeness of God and the particular modes of God's Being and Becoming as Persons could not be understood in any isolation from one another, even as they must be differentiated from one another. Pope Leo and Cyril of Alexandria did not mean to contradict each other. They did not intend a paradox to be posited at the heart of the redemptive purpose of the Creator with His Creation, but they very purposefully intended to refer to the new reality that is this Person and no other, who is the Incarnate Word as the Revelation of the One Creator of the 'All', the Free Creator of the wholeness of the heavens and the earth with its mankind and the Sabbath Relation and Blessing of God constituted of Himself from both outside of the Creation and within His Creation. Both the external relations and internal relations of God with us, however asymmetrical they may appear to possess, according to any logical credence given before the Incarnation, had indeed happened within the history of the Creation and its Mankind. Philoponus' use of the concept of the anhypostasis of the Word become flesh in the Creation appears then absolutely vital for understanding the Alexandrian's understanding of the term 'nature' in his Christology. Is it the new dimensions of this *nature* that blinds our eyes to what has occurred in the world?

It seems that the dynamics of this argument were unintelligible to many, both inside and outside of the Church, in relationship with the thought of John Philoponus. It was the dynamical character in the thinking of the Grammarian, with its beginning rooted in the Beginning and in the Incarnation, that allowed the 'Lover of Work' to grasp the meaning of the New within the Old Creation and understand the way the old potentials were actualized in the Light of the New Creation, when beginning and becoming could easily escaped the attention of his critics. The contingent singularity of the new dimension and its transformations of human thought about God, the World, and Man in the past demanded a new mind, a new mind able to confess the Mind of Christ. The Church is thus committed both to the transcendent dimensions and the concrete material dimensions of the relational complex of space and time that is the Creation. She is to know herself as grounded finally in reality of the Great I-AM the Lord God Himself is as the Father, Son, and Spirit of the Trinity as the One Redeemer-Creator of the entire world. The dynamical nature of this New World could not be captured by timeless sets of logical relations, but all relations had to submit to the New Time and Space of His New Creation caused to exist with a power that only the reconciling Grace and Truth of His Being and Nature could establish with this world. Again, here is a reality made of what are both numerable and without number, visible and invisible magnitudes defined by wholeness only the Transcendence of the Eternity of God could define. Here imageless knowing of real theoretical power and solidly concrete and verifiable reality met, freeing the race from necessary logical relations and from arbitrary subjective relations, a freedom from the past as well as a freedom for the future of the race, the world, and its God. Here the wholeness of the Lord God with all of His particulars and the wholeness of created realities are to be understood on the ground where theology and science must be understood to overlap with one another. The sacred and the secular were not divisions of space and time that could be applied to the real world that is God's Creation. It seems to me that the dynamics of this Word of God still struggles with His listeners to make Himself known even down into our own times. It is little wonder that there remains, even to our own times, so much misunderstanding about Philoponus' intention and the fruitfulness his Christology would bear in the Church of Jesus Christ.

Philoponus in Alexandria, I believe then, answered positively and definitely the question about the meaning of Tertullian's rhetoric with his question about Jerusalem and Athens. I believe we will do well to take seriously the kind of categories the Grammarian employed to invent at the heart of the Revelation a dynamic physics of the Cosmos as God's Creation seen from the Center he believed the Lord has established as Jesus Christ, Redeemer-Creator of the world. From the Emperor Julius to Constantine (300 AD), royal authority had struggled against the establishment of this Center. From Constantine to Justinian (570 AD), this same royal authority attempted to grasp its relationship with this Center, the ground upon which the race might stand to know in concrete terms between the Revelation and Science the interplay between God and mankind in the abyss, the chasm between the transcendent and the empirical that the Lord God had filled with the creative power His Incarnate Word. The New Time of the bodily risen Christ gave to world times a New Humanity in the midst of the humanities of the nations, introduced something utterly and incomparable and irreversible with His new relationship between the uncreated reality of God and the created reality of the world. As we have said, 'All' was new, even for God.

The Church and the World

If the Jews could find blasphemous such development, if the Greeks would cling to the abstract essentials of their wisdom, the Shalom of the David of the New World, the fulfillment of Israel's prophecy and the 'Light of the World' as the Cross and Resurrection of the New Adam, shone freely and brightly over and within the history of the world now, for its redeemed mankind and for its destiny with the Creator the Great I-AM He is. No matter what oracles or magic rites or counselors of stars that surrounded her, the Church knew to fight to root herself with this Center in the ground of this New World, against every claim the Old Empire might make upon her. What is this freedom that John Philoponus enjoyed when he responded to his Emperor and to his God in the way that he did? What is this freedom of this New Man that he worshipped, this Person who is the King of Creation and the Redeemer of the 'All.' Who is this Jesus, this Christ, this God of God, this Light of Light, this Word of the One who is both Man and God for the world to come? How does He, as this His Grace and Truth of our Lord and God embody for us the salvation of the human race in the time and times of His Eternity?

Why are we not free to see in the Light the Trinity the Great I-AM is, as the Lord God of all space and time, the world and mankind in the created freedom that belongs to them from the freedom of the Word of God to be with us? Why may we not in our freedom choose the freedom of God to be the One He truly is with us to develop, heuristically, a science of the universe and mankind? If where the Spirit of this Lord is there is freedom, why do we seek to understand things from some other place than the space He has provided for us in Christ? Why do we seem to prefer the time past to time future? Why did both the Church and the world condemn John Philoponus, the Lover of Work in Alexandria's sixth century? What did this condemnation mean for the history of the development of our civilization? Why has it taken so long to give the Grammarian the credit he deserves in this history, the credit he deserves for his 'impetus and light theory,' for his theory of the 'three-dimensional' with its role in the structures, invisible and visible, of the nature of the world? Are not our cosmologists and physicists today working overtime to understand the nature of a world whose Big-Bang Beginning challenges the deepest resources of our faith in a rational world and its unity with our minds? Are not the visible magnitudes we measure as the particulars of a complex world to be explained in the light of a beginning possessed of a contingency whose rational order and freedom call us beyond ourselves to a power we must understand if we are to fulfill the intentions and purposes of our sciences? If the Lord God has established and sustains with the Divine-Human Freedom of the Great I-AM He is as the Lord and God of redemptions and creation, why are we not free to pursue with our imaginations and wills an understanding of the nature He has actually created and made and sustains with Himself? Why are we not free to employ categories of thought that belong to the uncreatedÛcreated relations that Philoponus posited with his thought experiments? Why may we not function at the interface on the boundaries between God in Christ and the world that is indeed His Creation? These are questions, I believe, that when properly asked will yield fruitful resolutions of surprising impact upon us. These are questions to which we are always responding, whether we believe them or not. Jerusalem and Athens both belong to the One Creation the world is.

Thus, these are questions that must be answered rightly, if we are to grasp the meaning of freedom in our time. If the dynamical nature of the categories inherent in the Scientific Theology and Theological Science of the work of John Philoponus provides the ground upon which we may still stand and interact with Him who is to be known in this way with His Creation, if God's Mankind with the Sabbath Rest with His Creation is truly His joy and freedom, if He will not be the God He is without this Man and this Creation, then how may we learn to think of the freedom He knows as He takes the world to its destiny with Himself. Freedom is known for what it truly is at the Center of His Being and Nature and not elsewhere. It is here that He has chosen to exercise, in His Relationship His Human Freedom and His Divine Freedom as the One He is for us. As this One, His created freedom and His uncreated freedom, established in union and communion with one another in order, shapes and forms the substance and the content of the history of mankind and the world for the Great I-AM He is over all that is the 'All' that is His Creation. In this way, our freedom has been given a significance it otherwise does not and cannot possess and shall not possess. I would conclude this chapter with some reflections upon this freedom. For to this certain freedom, all mankind in its freedom is bound. Without the authority of this freedom, freedom is truth-less.

Since God is the One who will not be who He truly is without us, since the world has been given a created freedom whose contingency binds its nature to its non-contingent and uncreated Creator, it must be evident to us that our race can function in this world without Him. We are freely made to be independent of Him and in our independence we may learn to be successful with our world and ourselves. Our successes, freely achieved, have led us to the many riches that can be found in this world. We enjoy a wealth of resources supplied by the sun and moon and stars and sky and waters and earth and plants and animals that make up the world we have experienced. No one can deny that our possession of the goodness of this world has provided the race with untold kinds of comforts, even in the midst of our experience with destruction and our deaths. Even the most wounded of creatures, the most mangled of souls, can be touched with this goodness and beauty in the world. We rejoice with those who rule wisely and enjoy the riches of this world as best that we can and bring comfort to thousands in the beauty and abundance we find here. No one needs to invoke God in all of this success. No one can prove God in the midst of all this richness. To call this world the best of all possible worlds with the philosophers is merely to assert a fact, not to prove that God is. We are free. We are to be successful without Him. We are free to be rich and enjoy the world without Him. It is a good world in this sense for us.

But this freedom that we do enjoy is given us so we may hear freely the freedom of His Call upon us, that we may hear the Call He makes to us with His Divine and Human Freedom, with the nature of the One He actually is, even in the midst of our freedom, to atone for us and give us fellowship with the One He actually is. Just as we are free without Him to breath the air that surrounds our planet in the solar system that is as this universe our home, we are free to understand that we belong to the breath of His Being. Smog up the air our home provides for us and we suffer with all of our freedoms the consequences of lives spent without Him, with the quality of our lives perishing without Him, making very poor what is freely born to be rich in a world whose orders belong to Him. We are not free to breath something other than the air His 'Very Good' Creation provides for us. No matter how it may appear for a time, we are not free to breathe in other things besides the air He has provided for us. Keep it up long enough and we will sicken, and we will die without Him. Our freedom to enjoy the riches of the world does not mean we are not bound to the air we must breathe to live. We are free, but we are bound. Our freedom is a created freedom. That is the point of the contingent nature of the world. The world is what it is only with those boundaries in place, at whose interfaces our freedom discovers His Freedom with us. Our lives are like that. We are presently bound up as breathing creatures with death, His curse upon our existence on this earth. Limits everywhere mark our freedom with the signs of the nature of our created reality. When we mistake with our imaginations the ideas about infinity for the Infinity that God is, we introduce a confusion that blurs these signs, destroys the actual meaning of these signs, and mistakes created freedom for what it is not, an autonomy undisciplined by His Freedom to be who He is with us. We introduce into our freedom to be successful and rich and enjoy the good world without Him, a kind of self-destructive mode of being; a misuse of the 'nothingness' of His Creation. We all ourselves are threatened by what we ought not to fear and we fear what we make with our wills against Him. We can read this self-destruction daily and nightly in our politics and in our tabloids. When we imagine our freedom for some absolute freedom, when we posit as determinative the autonomous freedom of our creature hood, without limits and boundaries from above and below, when we mistake our infinities for the Infinity of our Maker, we change the very meaning of the rational contingency of our freedom into a significance we cannot bear, into orders that weigh down upon our lives a gravity that belongs beyond us with who He is. We transform contingent orders of space and time and light provided by the Great I-AM He is into what they are not. We choose then to live as if His Call is not upon our lives.

The most common justification of such choices is to accuse Him in His Divine and Human Freedom and as the One He is of being exclusive. The most common thing that I have heard from people, since I have been listening to Him, is that He cramps their lifestyles with prohibitions and narrows life's potentials and possibilities with being there. They prefer He would get lost and leave them alone to the infinities of their various wisdoms in their pursuits of their happiness or deaths. Because He is One and the Only One God and the Only Way of the One God, because He alone is real freedom that is uncreated and unbounded and truly infinite, divinely infinite, as the Man He is, and there is no other Man than the Man He is, they are confined by Him and wish He were not who He is, the Great I-AM He is. This is why we took such a long look at the fundamental sin that the prophets and the apostles were made to see. We need to understand our need to want Him to be the Great Not-I-AM, so that we can turn our freedom into something it is not and can never be, into a kind of self-destructive mode of being because we were made to be free by Him and with Him and for Him. We are made at once to breathe the air that surrounds the earth and to breathe the Breath of His Eternal Life that comes from the heavens, the heavens of the Lord God. We are made to be free, and yet bound to Him who is Freedom, True Freedom, the very nature of Freedom, Freedom from evil, sin, and death, Freedom for life and light and its beauty and harmonies with Him, the Only One who is who He truly is as the forever of Man with God. Here with Him is revealed the Way, the Truth, and the Life of the Person of the Lord Jesus Christ. He will not be this One that He is without us. He has as this Grace and Truth given us His Life for our lives, and that is the heart of our problem with our existence in this world, a problem that may be resolved only in freedom, in our freedom made to experience His Freedom, His Humanity with our humanity. For this reason, freedom has always been vital for the existence of the race upon the planet under the stars, under the moon, under the sun, and upon the waters and lands and cities of this earth. It may appear, especially when we are young, that our independence away from God is absolute, that freedom is merely a brute fact of a people born free, that in this freedom we are free to create our own civilizations, our own survival plans, independent of any metaphysical influence from beyond us. It may also appear, especially as we grow older, that our dependence upon God becomes clearer to us (or in a foxhole in some war), that our free will is not as infinite a thing in the immensities of this world as we once might have thought. But the actual case is that, for young and old, both in our independence away from God and in our dependence upon Him, we belong to a reality that is defined by the free relationship He has determined to make for us with Himself. We are always alive under the weight of His Glory, whether we believe Him or not, whether we choose to worship Him or not, whether we choose to follow Him or not. We are at once both free and bound. We are His creatures, meant not merely for survival but also for His Love and Life and Light. In this way, He will not be who He is without us. He will not be the One He truly is except with Man as Man, Man as He was once created and made and meant to be. It is this Righteousness, the Righteousness of this Divine and Human Freedom, that is bound up with this Only One He is as His Grace, can and does and will define the shape of things to come. The history of the Creation is destined in time and in His chosen place, where the Lord God has chosen to set His Name, that there we care called to go, to learn of Him, and to do what is right in His Eyes, the Christ of the Father the

The Great AMEN of the Great I-AM

Great I-AM is, blessed in His Creation forever. We do well when we take Him seriously, when we take His Time seriously, when we take His Space seriously, as the One who is with us and for us in the world.

Christ Child

Like the seas change
Land and the longing
Dark wraps like arms
The earth in sound,
A small child pushes in his hand
His dreams into a blue sky.
And round the beginningless roar
He alone who reigns holily
Shall take and hold,
For as long as forever is,
Their flesh in His.

The Church and the World

Calvary

9

The Person of God in the World

*I am the true vine and my Father is the gardener
... apart from me you can do nothing.*

John 15:1, 5

It can be shown as historical fact that Israel and the Church as the People of God among the nations in this world have not readily grasped the Grace and Truth of the Great I-AM the Lord God is with His Divine and Human Freedom for us in our times. If the Great I-AM the Lord God is was revealed to Moses, if the Great I-AM the Lord God is was revealed as the Incarnate Word, if the Great I-AM of the Dogma of the Church in the world is the same I-AM who continues, through the Person of the Lord Jesus Christ, to will to make Himself known as our Redeemer-Creator in His Creation, then we say that we must come face to face with the personal reality of a personalizing Lord God, young and old. If embodied in Jesus of Nazareth is the Man in whom God Himself freely joys in His Creation, and with no other, then we are up against in our times a most insistent Lord and God. He will not be who He is without us, and He will not be this in whom He can find no delight. This is Man as Man was intended to be and this is what Man shall be in God's Creation, free Man, Man bound to His God, Man free to obey the Great I-AM He is. It is easy to see in the Light and Life and Love of His Being and Nature that the world continues to prefer its idols to Himself, and it is easy to show that the People of God continue to have difficulty explaining His Self-Revelation and Reconciliation to a world that prefers its idols to who He is. The story of Western Civilization can easily serve to remind us of this struggle the Lord God continues to make in order that He might become known for who He truly is in His Creation. We may survey with some benefit the main lines along which the West has traveled under the

Reign of this Great I-AM, this King, this Priest, this Prophet, this Sage who is both in the world and not of the world, who is both bound with His Freedom to God and by this world for our sakes, on our behalf, in our place, that we might come to know God, the World, and what Man is meant to be.

There are three great transformations we may seek to understand in the history of the relationship between the Judeo-Christian Tradition and the making of what we call today Western Civilization. The great conflict involved in these transformations in our understanding of the Cosmos as a universe that is our home, I believe, is revealing.

I. The Ptolemaic Cosmology (300 BC–1543 AD) of the Roman Empire and the Middle Ages, developed out of the polytheisms, magical superstitions, and primitive practices of ancient cultures in the ancient world. With its 'logos' embedded in its Cosmos, Greek philosophies developed concepts that captured the imagination of the race for centuries, with a force that is perhaps difficult for us to grasp. To remember that the marriage between Christian Theology and the Ptolemaic Cosmology lasted for almost two thousand years ought to speak loudly to us about the profound struggle we must make to understand the world as rational and ourselves as rightly in it. To remember also that the divorce between this Cosmology and the theology of the Middle Ages was quite traumatic. It was not experienced without great hurt and bitter feuds that ought to remind us of our need in time to get things right if we are to know who we are in its universe. I often refer my students to John Donne's *'An Anatomie of the World'* (1600 AD) in order to point out the bewilderment caused by the breakup of the marriage between Christian Theology and Scientific Culture in the Middles Ages:

> *'And new philosophy calls all in doubt,*
> *The element of fire is quite put out;*
> *The sun is lost, and the earth, and no man's wit*
> *Can well direct him where to looke for it.*
> *And freely men confesse that this world's spent,*
> *When in the Planets, and the Firmament*
> *They seek so many new: then see that this*
> *Is crumbled out againe to his atomies.*
> *Tis all in peeces, all cohaerence gone;*
> *All just supply, and all Relation;*
> *Prince, Subject, Father, Sonne, are things forgot,*

> *For every man alone thinkes he hath got*
> *To be a Phoenix, and that then can bee*
> *None of that kinde, of which he is, but hae.'*

If we compare Donne's complaints with Dante's perfect peace in his *Divine Comedy* (1300 AD), upon entering the realms of the Empyrean above the Celestial Spheres of the Ptolemaic Cosmology, we can readily understand the trauma involved when the Sacramental Universe, with all the beauty of its orders in its affair with Greek Essentialism, began to break up with the developments that occurred with the works of Copernicus (1543), Galileo (1643), and Newton (1680 AD). The new unity, according to the physical law of gravity, of the heavens and the earth was grasped only after a bitter struggle with old habits of mind about the universe and our place in it.

> *'The nature of the universe which stilleth the centre*
> *and moveth all the rest around, hence doth begin*
> *as from its starting point.*
>
> *And this heaven hath no other where than the divine mind*
> *wherein is kindled the love which rolleth it*
> *and the power which it sheddeth.'*

The ideas about order, beauty, law, and morality, enforced by the 'Pax Romana' of this world, provided a framework of knowledge and jurisprudence for these times that was, to say the least, formidably captivating. The 'logos' of the Greeks embedded in some way within the heavens of the Cosmos made their motions reflect the very eternity of God, regardless of the arguments John Philoponus had made in the sixth century. We call the universe of those times the Sacramental Universe, because of the common sense popularly grasped in a split between the '*heavenlies*' and earthly experience. Philosophers of the Graeco-Roman cultures, from Augustine to Aquinas, were in one way or another able to find some relationship between this embedded 'logos' in the Cosmos of God with His '*divine* logos.' The reason the world is what the world is belongs to this 'logos.' The '*heavenlies*' were the home of this 'logos.' Eternal life was hidden in the forms of its rationality, eternal principles and shapes upon which depended the immortal orders of this world and the immortality of the race. Here was found the Good, the True, the Beautiful, and so forth. The light of the heavens was in this sense divine light. It shone steadily over the warp and woof of the darkness and the seasons experienced by temporal creatures inhabiting the earth. We see in this light the necessity for Aristotle's 'Fifth Substance,' the hidden matter that holds the world in the eternity of the hand of God. Different from fire and air and water and earth, all of which contributed to what being was as change, the 'Fifth Substance' of the '*heavenlies*,' serve to hold together with the 'logos' of Greek thought the world as it necessarily must come from the hand of God, who lives beyond all experience of changing things. The spirit of this 'logos' thus opposed all strictly temporal matters, all the chaos of changing beings, and acted for the immortal good embedded within the immortal soul of Man, which was his essential being. The spiritual and the material were dualistically thought to be two worlds apart from one another. The destiny of the human race was thought then to be bound up in this way with this 'logos,' which took the race far from the dusts that ever loomed over the material bodies of its existence. The perfect *logoi* that belonged to the *divine logos embedded in the heavenlies possessed those perfections of being, nature, truth, goodness, and harmonies that belonged to the eternity of this world*. The human race was meant to find all these within the immortality of its soul, a place where the 'divine logos' could be found living. In these harmonies, 'knowledge' (*gnosis*) of the 'divine logos' gave to mortal beings their immortality, life that existed only with the One whose Mind made the Cosmos what it is with His Hands. From beyond all changing being, outside of all the evils of bodily existence, far from all that is temporal, we experienced, as a part of the radiance of the '*pleroma*' (the fullness of real spiritual being) immortal souls were filled with the Eternity of Life, the deep knowledge within ourselves that belongs to the Immortal One. For Gnostics, Jesus was a man who came into this world with these perfections, to show us the way of the light of this 'logos.' He would guide us out of the darkness of this material and temporal world, where all bodily reality is ultimately doomed, into the '*pleroma*' of His Father. The immortality of His soul would teach us the immortality of our souls. With knowledge like He possessed, He saves us from our bodily cares, decay, and deaths.

We can read in this view of the world the consequences of the split between the heavens and the earth and the role of necessity in the relationship between God and the Cosmos, the struggle of Christian thought with theology and the natural world, and the desire to imitate on earth what was happening in the heavens. This was a world that of necessity belonged to the Mind of God that called us somehow to travel from earth to the heaven of the heavens for our salvation, as if space travel from the center of the universe to its heavens was a flight that could lead sinners of all kinds through their punishment to rest finally in the Light of Christ. There is little enough of the thought of John Philoponus in the Sacramental Universe of the Middle Ages. Perhaps the idea about the Creation out of nothing in the Judeo-Christian interpretation of the Holy Scriptures kept the West from forsaking utterly the meaning of out of nothing for theology and science. But the light that John once saw coming from the stars, the sun, and the moon to earth and the light coming from the fish, the plants, and the worms upon the earth, as the same light, as one created light, was thought to which those who imagined the Ptolemaic Cosmology in relationship to the Gospel were blind. The God of this Cosmos was for the many the First Cause, the Unmoved Mover, the Primal Reason for being immortal and eternal, the Immutable and Impassible Origin of the Church's Vision of a world whose ground necessarily provided the basis for a relationship between theology and science doomed to failure in the light of a reality we would slowly face. The Church, married to the Ptolemaic Cosmology with some sort of Greek Essentialism, carved up the reality of the world in such a way that split apart the intelligible from the sensible, the heavens from the earth, and thus set for herself a path in this world that was indeed other-worldly. The supernatural and the natural became forced apart and then mystically held together with the great efforts of the best of our minds. But this chasm could remain only so long. The Sacramental Universe of the Middle Ages, with the ever growing development of its science and its civilization, belonged to form or a framework of thought that would finally fall apart. The 56 spheres of Dante's world could not forever bear the actual weight of the Glory of God, and collapsed like an erector set when real scientific progress began to set in. What Thomas Aquinas and Dante Alighieri had so magnificently built up with their works had one day to face the music of a reality that was not the Music of the Celestial Spheres. The world was not the theatre where Man in the Cosmos could be thought to travel from the earth, its center, up through space to the heavens of the heavens for his salvation. This reductionism upwards of human thought with the abstract definitions of Greek Essentialism was utterly stopped in its ascents. We were forced to face a truth anticipated many centuries earlier by Philoponus in Alexandria. The heavens and the earth formed a whole whose mankind shaped a part of its one created reality, out of nothing, with a rational unity and contingency that had to be respected as the real nature of physical law and the orders and freedom of our experience within it. Thus, the race was dispelled of its captivation with the abstract character of this theatre, this Sacramental Universe with its Ptolemaic Cosmos and its immortal Mankind, when the character of its space and its time had to leave behind the old theatre and its plays, when we had to seek to find a new unity between the heavens and the earth and the mechanics of the world and our understanding of them. Gone would be the reductionism upwards of human thought. Vanished would become our efforts to save ourselves in a world whose relationship with its God turned out to be not what we once thought it to be.

II. The transformation of the Sacramental Universe of the Cosmos of the Middles Ages into the Mechanical Universe of the Newtonian Comos in the Age of the Enlightenment, following Newton's system of mechanics laid down in his *Principia* (1687), can now be understood as a reductionism downwards of human thought. Classical mechanics thus shapes into service an instrumentalism, in contrast to the essentialism of the Ptolemaic Cosmos, whose determinative character soon enough could make God unnecessary to explain the workings of the world. Isaac Newton himself knew very well his mechanics did not and could not explain how the machine ever got going. The development of his differential equations explained the motion of matter in the world according to the one law of gravity operating in the heavens and upon the earth. The universe was like a clock wound up by God in its beginning and set to moving without explanation. He did not intend for his science to be viewed as an attempt to rid God from the mechanics of the universe. He remained, in fact, ambiguous about *the* Beginning of the world and often settled, with his disbelief in the Incarnation, on a God who became known as the God of Gaps in relations with the systems lawfulness, a notion of God that Pierre La Place thought he could dispel whenever we became clever enough with our understanding of the laws. La Place had no need for such a God in his development of Newton's science. The point that must be taken is the fact that any absolute causal determinism must produce, ultimately, a deistic notion of the Creator. He may be watching, but He certainly is not doing anything else. If the Sacramental Universe, with its reductionism upwards into an abstract Greek essentialism, understood

Him to be acting in the heavens for us, the Mechanical Universe, with its reductionism downwards of human thought into a hard determinism, saw Him as acting only with His gaze upon a machine He may or may not have set into motion.

Newton's law of gravity, however, did mean that the mechanics of the heavens and the earth were to be grasped as one world, a universe obeying the one law. It was this understanding of the law of gravity that allowed for the development of what we know as the Industrial Revolution in the Western World. It was possible to conceive of machines, in fact, that could be made out of the Mechanical Universe as never before in the history of the world. Civilization could now possess utopian dreams whose machines, like comforts, gave fresh hope to people who had learned to live in the Gothic flight into the heavens. A revolution ensued whose industry utterly changed the world's economy, created a new class of people, and forged a material world that could conceive its own salvation. We may surely understand the beginning of the tyranny of the material over the spiritual in this reductionism. Sir Isaac Newton, the great scientist of the Mechanical Universe, perhaps in some sense the father of the Enlightenment, because he was an Arian in his Christology, and did not believe in the Incarnation, however, never dreamed of a godless Creation. Yes, God could no more become a man in this universe than a pail could become the water it contained. But the absolute space and time of the Mechanical Universe was related to the mechanics of the motion of matter in the world with some confusion. Newton, following Copernicus and Galileo, knew of the 'impetus theory' introduced by Philoponus into the dynamics of the Cosmos. But unlike Philoponus, Newton did not posit an impetus that was bound up with the creative power of the Word and Light of God. The impetus was there with light and so forth, but its origin must remain unknown. Newton's equations did not and could not touch upon its beginning. I believe that this marks a very real carry over from the marriage of Christian Theology to the Ptolemaic Cosmology. Newton could not free himself from its concepts of space and time as empty containers, unmoved by the motion of the atoms of matter, like mathematical points, that moved as the world according to the nature of the law of gravity, when classical determinism marked the development of the Mechanical Universe with its science. Solidly, absolute space and time as the empty containers became the theatre in which causal relations effected what the Newtonians could measure with their hopes for the utopian dreams. We can fairly say, I believe, with poets like William Blake and so forth, that the human imagination suffered under the Newtonians a certain denigration of the meaning of free will for the race in the universe, of miracles and prayers, making the role of the transcendent in human being into the brute fact with which existential philosophies understood the freedom of mankind.

But cleverness, the growth of sophisticated mathematics, the inevitability of experimental enterprises, could take us only so far in our efforts to understand mankind and the universe. The deism and the determinism inherent in the marriage between Christian Theology and the so-called Age of the Enlightenment could conclude that we could just as well worship the sun and the stars and the moon as God. The children of the new marriage experienced in the Eighteenth and Nineteenth Centuries saw great progress, but one that came with prices unanticipated by many. While God was watching and the machine ticked away with the development of one machine after another, clock upon clock, mankind was on the move, not towards the creation of utopian civilizations, but to war, the world wars. The classical mechanics of the Newtonians could build a new world whose hopes were soon dashed in the realities of wars, when technologies served to invent weapons rather than communities, comforted as never before in the history of the world. We need to try to understand why the two worlds, the world of peace and comforts and the world at war, both marked the history we have inherited in our time. Evidently, a watching God is not enough to realize the actual relationship the world has with Him as the One He is.

We may also observe that, with the sun of the Mechanical Universe smiling down upon the peoples on the earth, the myth of the self-made man dominated the aspirations of the race. While God gazed aloofly, men were free under Him to conceive of their liberty as if we were self-defining creatures in the Creation. Those who were free to make themselves successful in this world achieved the comforts the world gave us. Perhaps we should remember here that Thomas Jefferson, the writer of the American Constitution, preferred the One God of the Mechanical Universe above His Incarnation as Jesus Christ in this world. He despised the faith that would understand the One as the Triune Redeemer-Creator revealed in the Word of God become flesh as the Christ of the Great I-AM the Lord God is. For many, at the very heart of the Revolution that would become the United States of America, the myth of the self-made man and the Mechanical Universe with its belief in the watching God, go hand in glove together in the making of our nation. The marriage between the Newtonians and Christian Theology, with the absolute space and time of the mechanics of its physics, like the marriage with the Ptolemaic Cosmology, however, was also bound in history for at least a real separation, if not another divorce. The epoch that evolved out of our sunny dispositions with our utopian dreams, admittedly had a dark side, the darkness of the nothingness of the existential experience in the world, so that the Newtonians became compelled to find their directions not in worshipping the sun and the self-made man in a deterministic world, but through the sciences of Michael Faraday (1843), James Clerk Maxwell (1873), and finally Albert Einstein. Theirs was a science that just would not fit into the determinism and the absolutes of the old mechanical world. Theirs was a new world calling for a new field of knowledge and marked perhaps the greatest transformation of scientific culture since its beginnings in the history of our civilization. It is a world that saw the invention of Relativity Theories (1905–15) of Gravity and the discoveries, beginning with Max Planck (1906) of the stochastic character of the particulars of a Quantum World, both strange and new introductions of a new cosmology and a new physics with which we deal even today. These marked a fundamental shift in our understanding at the very foundations of science, the very foundations of the ways to go about knowing ourselves in the fields of a universe whose rational unity must be conceived without any reductionism in our theory laden experiments and our experientially verified theories.

III. With Einstein's Relativity Theories, the absolute nature of the space and time in which the universe appears to us with the Mechanical Universe must be understood as possessing only a conventional and limited value when it comes to grasping in all of its depths the real physics of the space-time world. If we traveled through the space of the Ptolemaic Cosmos some 56 celestial spheres up from the earth in order to be saved in the Middle Ages, if we were confined in the reign of a space that contained everything without be moved by anything that happened within it, with the absolutes of the Newtonian Universe, Einstein's Universe of Light set us free from this space travel and the tyranny of this space and a multitude of arbitrary necessities that required that we recognize as relative their values in our experience of them and their real connections with another kind of objectivity entirely. (Thus, Einstein liked to refer to his Relativity Theory as an Invariance Theory!) Free from these myths about the cosmological past in the history of the Creation, we became able to begin to understand a new dynamical nature of the relationship between space-time and the matter/energy in the universe we experience with our thought and our sensibilities. If the marriage of the Church's Dogma to the Ptolemaic Cosmology meant a reductionism upwards of our thought about God and world and so forth, if the marriage of the Church's Dogma to the Newtonian system of the world meant a reductionism downwards of our thought about God and the world and so forth, then the development of the Einsteinian cosmologies has compelled us to depart from both of these reductionisms and thus to seek afresh with a new appreciation for the epistemological dimensions in the development of our understanding of cosmology and the physics, one in which the invisible and the visible dimensions of the world's nature are to be integrated with an entirely new mode of physics and cosmology. Here, theory and experience is thought to form a whole the ground of which would provide the scientific enterprise with a way of knowing and seeking for understanding that promises a fruitfulness our progress to date can only be amazed at. With our theory-laden experiments and experimental programs we may design processes to verify things we cannot even now imagine. Theory and experience cannot be torn apart then, cannot be reduced down either abstract principles of timeless logic or existential autonomies dreamed of by our existential desires. Both must be integrated together at once to refer to what lies significantly beyond our existence in the existence of a vast world the universe is compels surprising our attention as God's Creation. The *a priori* force of any abstract necessity in the world is vanished from our assumptions and presuppositions, and what compels or drives the formulation of our experiments is the nature of reality itself, a reality that Einstein said was the fundamental rock upon which all real science rests. Subjectivities not rooted in the actual nature of the objectivity of this universe can only arbitrarily compel fashions and not truth in our efforts to produce a science that grasps reality in all of its depths. Only with respect to such an objective intelligibility, with *a posteriori* and open commitments to what actually lies within the potential of any case, may we seek to contribute to the progress the human race hopes to experience in the future. Along these lines the freedom of the human imagination must seek to work with our knowledge towards these ends. To will not to do this is to will not to be free. We have, indeed, experienced a remarkable transformation of cosmologies in this way with our time and times. Yes, with sometimes very traumatic effects upon what we thought we knew. Yes, with sometimes our guilt and shame staring us in the face, our understanding of the world and ourselves showing us we are not yet what we ought to be here. Yes, our psyche does sense a hope that we can make with our scientific progress, but it is a progress that we must face with the freedom that is bound up with the freedom of the Redeemer-Creator of this world. The history of Western Civilization is marked with this freedom and this progress, and we do well to not let it escape our attention.

When I ask my students about their concepts of space and time today, I can assure you that, for the most part, few have yet to come to appreciate their concepts about them, let alone the significance of what I am calling the third great transformation in the history of our cosmologies. To my questions about space and time, they are mostly silent. They seem to know that space and time are not what they think they are. They pretend to know that the Incarnation does not imply space or time travel. But only a few ever venture a response to my probing of them, and in 2007 few have had any exposure to the great transformation of space and time that marks the character of Einstein's equations and the space-time invariance of a continuum that belongs to the power of the 'Old One,' as Einstein liked to call Him. Still today, few have been exposed to these vital transformations, and good colleagues in the theological enterprise have, in fact, exhorted me not to bother myself with their efforts, with Einstein and so forth. Few indeed make much if any sense out of the fact that space tells matter how to move and matter tells space how to curve in a universe of light that, as conceived by Einstein's Theory of Gravity, belongs to the uncreated Light God is for us.

I now reckon myself as fortunate. In 1954, I was a member of a physics class when John Archibald Wheeler first decided to teach Relativity at the undergraduate level to university students. Until then, Einstein was simply a legend of a science that few could understand. It was known that even the Legend did not understand it all. It took some fifty years before people could believe in its physics well enough to begin to teach it as the ABC's at the foundations of our science. Newtonian physics were taught as the first principles, and only when one reached the Graduate School level was one asked to face the actual ABC's of physics, along with the developments and successes of the Quantum Theory about the microworld. Today, because of people like Professor Wheeler and his students, Kip Thorne and Stephen Hawking, General Relativity Theory is taught even in our high schools. What Wheeler knew in 1954 was that the transformation at the foundations of our knowledge had won a day that could not be denied, and that the future lay with our grasp upon the reality of these developments in the cosmology and physics of the universe in our times. Upon the past had been shed a new light that must be understood, if we are going to grasp the nature of the world as it comes from God with us.

This book is not a course on the nature of light, space, time, matter, motion, and the universe in its changing and permanent structures as that nature comes to us from the Word and Hand of God. For my purposes, I simply need to say that the developments I understand as Relativity Theories and the Mechanics of the Quantum World belong to the Universe of Light that has thrust its nature upon our attempts to understand it. We have had our minds pried open again and again and we have thrust out into the open horizons of human consciousness, where boundaries of human integrity and the rational and substantial contingency of a world places upon us demands we cannot afford to ignore in our time. This then is God's Creation. It is the contingency and freedom of this world that has been grasped afresh by Einstein's way of doing science. It is this contingency that I also read in the fundamental categories at the foundations of the science John Philoponus embraced when he developed his 'impetus theory', his 'light theory', and his concept of a relational view of space and time in accordance with the nature the Divine Freedom and Power of the free Redeemer-Creator he knew as the Blessed Trinity Lord God had become as the Great I-AM He is. Einstein understood that this One, 'The Old One', provided reason that was incarnate in our existence and in the universe. This formed the ground upon which the miracle of understanding did in fact occur (He probably had Spinoza's God in mind!) and why science and religion could not be enemies in any final analysis of our experience in the world. It was evident to this inventor of Relativity Theory that this Old One did not play dice with what He has caused to exist, and that He was deeply and profoundly involved with Man's condition in His world. The light would teach us that, in spite of the fact our knowing occurs on very simple levels of the reality of this world, what we do know belongs to an Infinite God whose Ages shall not let us down. Not on his sleeve does He wear His Heart for us, but deep within the mysteries of this Cosmos lies His heart for the world. Thus, the world is both independent of His Nature and yet dependent upon His Being for its being in existence and our understanding of it. It is, according to Wheeler and so forth, a victory we cannot afford to ignore.

Perhaps this transformation does not take seriously enough what was bedrock for the foundation of Philoponus' thought. His embrace of the *creatio ex nihilo* of the Judeo-Christian Tradition as justified in the Incarnation understands a positive potential with the 'Very Good' inherent in the 'nothingness' of the world. Certainly, it does not take seriously the way that reason has actually become incarnated in the Creation. But it does deny reductionism in our knowing and does intend to refer us to what lies beyond our understanding of the world as this Creation. The universe belongs to the mystery of the Creation that we understand miraculously. The miracle of our understanding belongs to the faith that believes in the rational unity of a universe celebrated by the Temple of Science, the Temple where the 'Old One' is honored. "*Without science, religion is blind; without religion, science is lame.*" Without an appreciation for the ground of this mystery, science becomes mere technology, scientists become mere technicians, and the building a servant of the possible rather than what ought to be grasped and implemented of its nature. I remember that, when Einstein first sought an academic position at the Berlin University, his job application was returned to him because he had left blank the row requesting his religion. The university said to him that it could not hire atheists and that he would have to fill in the blank row. He wrote there, "*The Religion of* Moses," returned the application, and got his first job in the Academy. However tentatively, the doctrine of a Beginning had been posited with his work.

Both the determinant and the indeterminate character of the nature of the Creation compel our scientists today to move beyond the dualisms built into our assumptions about the nature of the world. Black Holes and Black Holes Fields of the New Physics of Cosmologies to come have resulted from this Beginning. Space-time become infinitely curved into a singularity, a universe whose quantum character points us quite beyond anything we have as yet to imagine, makes demands upon the scientific enterprise. Even beyond the quantum vacuum is to be found the mystery of God with us in His Creation. The question here becomes what sort of interface we may realize. Upon what sort of solid ground may we stand to grasp in all of its depths a new simplicity with a very complex world, one that belongs to a rational unity that belongs to the Only One, the 'Old One.' The 'nothingness' of the Creation must be taken seriously in some

The Person of God in the World

real created correspondence with the quantum vacuum, where potentials and when actuals both constitute the dimensions of the universe where we have our beings. Out of the quantum vacuum's relations with the *nihilo* of the 'Very Good' Creation something this way comes, dynamically and really, comes in freedom to allow us to grasp the limits and infinities of the space-time intervals inherent with Einstein's equations as well as with the stochastic world of the quantum events. From a perspective such as this a new unified field may well be discovered in the physical world. Again, we must face the mystery of this ground with that kind of humility and freedom and joy that we see again and again upon the face of the legend Einstein is in the Temple of 'Old One.' If religion is blind and science lame without one another, what is their interface truly like? Is this not the place where Philoponus loved to do his work? May we not find ways of conceiving the nature of the world on such a ground that allows our thoughts to resonate indeed with our modern seeking and longing and experience and with the real created and creative correspondence that allows us, without confusion and conflict, to grasp the relations between God and the world?

Indeed, what did the Personhood of God do through all these centuries of our cosmological speculations? What do these great transformations in the history of our thought mean to Him and His Time for us? For what does He seek from us with all our independence of Him and dependence upon in the mystery of a universe that must be understood as His Creation? How may we relate His personal reality in space and time to our time and times? Who is He really that is this personal Lord in time and times? What do we mean by His personal reality, by His Person, known as the persons of the Father, Son, and Spirit through Jesus Christ as the Eternal Being and Nature of the Great I-AM He is? With these questions, I believe we need to develop in our time a whole new understanding of what we mean by 'Person,' by 'Personhood.' We are more than creatures breathing the air that surrounds the planet, and however successful we are at comforting ourselves here we cannot grasp the meaning of our being in our time out of ourselves. We cannot settle on the meaning we might want to give the events of our history on the earth, but we need to seek to understand their significance as bound up with the freedom of God to be with us here.

When we recall the 'Little Credo' of the Great I-AM as the Lord God defining and giving Himself in His BCR with His People among the nations in His Creation, we grasp the Divine Freedom with which He pours Himself into the renewal of this covenanted relationship with His 'stiff-necked' People. We remember that it is not his pious people that He has to deal, but with his 'high-handed,' 'murmuring,' and 'self-centered' People that He must struggle. When the Redeemer-Creator gave himself in His BCR as the One Lord God who is '*Compassionate* and *Favoring* and *Longsuffering* and of *Great Grace and Truth*' with and for Israel among the nations, even in Israel's opposition to Him, when He poured Himself as such into the Incarnation of His Word and Son, when we have seen Him giving and communicating Himself in this way in this relationship of the Glory of this Holy One that He is, when we understand His Atoning Love and Work on behalf of His People on His terms, in this way then that allows us to see and hear the prophetic vision for what it is beyond the stiff-necked, high-handed, murmuring, self-centered, wickedness of the People of God in the world. He has poured Himself as this Lord and God with this Self-Defining Divine Freedom and Power for us as the David of the New Creation. The promise of His *Grace* to King David in the history of Israel has been kept with His Messiah. He has embodied His Promise as the Person of the Lord Jesus Christ. He has become this Person as the Revelation of the Trinity. He has reconciled with Himself all that Israel is and all that Mankind is in His Creation. This is the testimony of the Old and New Covenants we may survey with any honest reading, hearing, and grasping of the Word of God. This is the witness He has given of Himself to the world. This is the Word of His Being in His Acts, the Word of His Acts in His Being, the Word He has been spoken of Himself in this way with us. The *Grace and Truth* of the Old Covenant has become the *Grace and Truth* of the New Covenant. The 'Little Credo' with which He taught Israel of Himself in the Old Covenant has now become embodied in Israel's Messiah, the fulfillment of the BCR and the 'Light of the World,' as the Great I-AM Jesus is. The Person the Lord Jesus Christ is as this Only One with us has become the New Man of the New Creation. The Old Adam is dead in Him. The New Adam is alive as Christ. The future of time and space belong to Him. We are who we are in the Light of His Being, in His Acts for us, in His Word with us. In this Light and Power, breathing creatures in the air that surrounds the planet come to understand themselves as the People of God. We are children of the *Grace* of this Great I-AM. It is in His Light that we may hear and understand our personhood. It is His Personhood that

The Person of God in the World

adopts us as His own. In Him, we become the persons we ought to be in His Kingdom.

Now there emerges for the sake of the New Creation the will of this New Man, the *'Person'* of the Lord Jesus Christ, King, Priest, Prophet, and Sage of Israel's prophecy, the union and communion of the divine and human natures of this One God and Man, the hypostatic unity of His Grace and Truth as the Great I-AM He is for His People among the nations in His Creation. It is His Face that we face. It is with His Freedom that our freedom has to do. History faces this Face. All nations face this Face. In this Face all must come to see the Face of God, the Great I-AM the Lord God is, the 'I am who I am' who sent Moses and Christ on their missions for His People, who promises to fulfill His Promise with Himself for '*My People*' in His Apocalypse in His Creation. In this way, we come to appreciate the 'perichoresis' inherent in His Personhood, the deep and profound relations of His Eternity with our times. Who can say who this *Person* truly is? Who can say that they possess His Freedom? Who can come to us either from below or from above to speak with us about Him. Who can say what only He can say? Who can do what only He can do and promises to do? What kind of time does He possess? What kind of space does He occupy? What does His Face mean who has come into our space and time to face us with Himself? Who can stand before Him and measure the depths of His seas, the heights of His heavens, the light and heat and existence that belongs to His Life in His Creation? Who can stand before Him and know His Personhood for what He truly is? When we ask these questions about the meaning of persons in this world, it is this Face with which we are confronted.

We have seen in our study that the Messianic King of the Promise of God's **Grace** in His BCR with His People among the nations in His Creation has entered the world as His Incarnate Word, the Son of God and David and Man. As such, He is the King of kings who will not be another. He is the Only and Incomparable One as the Great I-AM He is with His People. He is the Rock that He speaks of His Atoning Love to make His People '*My People*,' so that His People may call Him '*Our God*' without making idols out of Him. He is the King of the New Creation in which the Promise of His Kingdom has been securely announced, just as surely as Israel was once delivered from Egypt. He is Christ who delivers from evil, sin, and death His Creation. He is the King who will not be who He truly is, the Great I-AM He is, without His Kingdom, without His

People. He is the coming into the space and time of the Creation for the sake of His Kingdom of the One who is who He is as the New Man He is, in a world that is His New Creation. He is the King with His Kingdom, and as this King the *Person of God* over and with all that created reality is. He is this Messianic King with His New Creation as 1) Priest, 2) Prophet, and 3) Sage of the world.

I. THE KING AS PRIEST

There exists what we call irony in the relationship of the King of Israel to the Priesthood of Israel's history. We may read this irony most openly in the story of King Saul, the first of the 'Bull Kings' among the People of God. There we read that, without discussing all that goes into his circumstances, Saul's impatience is his undoing. Impatient with Samuel and the kind of accommodation the Lord God has made with Himself for Saul, the new king takes upon his reign what God has assigned to another. We read in the Promise of the Word of God through Nathan to King David that the Lord God will never remove His **Grace** from the House of David the way that He removed it from the House of Saul. In the form of God's silence, the loss of this **Grace** spells the fall of Saul's reign and his seeking from the 'medium' a confrontation with Samuel from the dead for direction in his life. It means his death, and his son, Jonathan's, death. When we read in these circumstances, in contrast to King Saul's impatience, King David's adultery and the murder of the husband, whose wife he took for himself, we feel the full force of this irony in the Election of God's Word to be with the Promise of His **Grace** as the Word of God for the Kingdom in the history of Israel.

The movement of this **Grace** in Israel takes on ironic turns throughout the prophetic development of the Messianic Hope, but none more ironic than with the Incarnation of this Word. Here finally is a movement that is wrought from outside of Israel's history among the nations. The Royal Priesthood of Israel's history is Priesthood rooted in the ground of the Priesthood of the Levites. Their Torah was Word of God with the People of God in His pre-incarnate form. With this form, the *chesed Yahweh with the House of David* serves to minister the annual and divine forgiveness with Israel. But the Royal Priesthood as we find it under the New Covenant of Israel's prophecy is not after the Order of the Levites but after the Order of Melchizedek, a king-priest that belongs to the ancient

Salem, long before it ever became the City of David (Genesis 14). What Saul with his impatience would take upon himself, what David, in spite of his sins, cannot take upon himself (He is a man after God's own heart!), has become in the form of the David of Israel's prophetic, messianic, vision of the Word of God a king-priest after the Order of Melchizedek (The Book of Hebrews). We cannot miss the irony of this movement (Soren Kierkegaard perhaps tried to hear too much of it!). Only with it we may grasp the continuity that belongs to the way the Promise has been fulfilled with the Word become flesh, as the man the Lord Jesus Christ is, the Royal Priest of the New Covenant of the New Creation.

We have seen in our study's survey that the **Grace** (*Chesed*) and **Truth** or **Faithfulness** (*'Emet*) of the Lord God, became embodied as Jesus Christ for His People, and provides the ground upon which Israel may name the Lord '*Our God*' and the Lord may name His People '*My People*.' Upon this ground stands for Israel and the Church as the People of God the mediating priesthood He is of the New World begun with His Incarnation. If the Levitical Priesthood provided upon this ground an annual forgiveness for the People of God, the Royal Priesthood after the Order of Melchizedek provides once and for all in all time and times the divine forgiveness of the Great I-AM the Lord God is for His People. The King-Priest of the New Covenant offers a sacrifice that need not ever be repeated. It is what forever is with God. It comes from His indestructible life, His Eternal Life, and when we participate in this forever of His Sacrifice we have fellowship with Him in a union and communion mediated by His Royal Priesthood. He ministers both Man to God and God to Man as this One Person who is this King-Priest of Israel's Word, the irrevocable and incomparable intercessor of God in Christ for us. This is the Mediator between Man and God in this world. Thus, we are given His Life for ours. We are given to participate by the **Grace** of the God He is with the **Grace** of the Lord He is as the **Grace** of the Great I-AM for us with His **Truth** or **Faithfulness**. Our priest is thus the Great I-AM who is who He is as the Redeemer-Creator of the world. It is in this way that, for all the irony that we may find in Him, we may come to understand the significance of His Name and Being as the Righteousness of the Lord God of space and time and so forth.

Because of this forever, never may the People of God take it upon themselves to mediate for themselves what God has done for His People. When we know the divine forgiveness and reconciliation of God's redemptive power acting on our behalf in this world, we know that what we could not do for ourselves He has done for us, whether we like Him or not. Not to accept the sacrifice of the King-Priest for His People of Israel's prophecy is to remain deaf to His Word. To attempt to usurp His power and authority to be who He is and to do what only He can choose to do with Himself is to blaspheme the Word of His Holy Love, His Atoning Love for us in this world. It is to refuse the *Grace* and *Truth* He is as the Great I-AM He is for His creatures. It is to deny Him His Royal Priesthood for us. It is to refuse His Divine Forgiveness. It is, indeed, to betray the One Mediator between God and Man for all time and times in the history of His Creation. Yet it is with Him in this way that we may come to know Him as the Faithful One He is as His *Grace*, the *Grace* of Father with the Son in the Spirit of God's Eternal Life.

II. THE KING AS PROPHET

The continuity that may be steadily read in the history of Israel among the nations in God's Creation is shaped and formed in substance and content by the promise of *chesed Yahweh* the House of David and thus the David of the New World. This promise is bound up with the Divine Freedom of the Lord God to make Himself present and known in this way to His People. We have seen that the relationship of prophet to kings in the rise and fall of Israel's monarchy possesses the secret of the Word of God for her in the covenant renewal tradition that drives the People of God into her Messianic expectations and prophetic Vision. We know that these traditions take us beyond the 'stiff-necked' People and the tragedies of the Bull Kings that, after Samuel and David, led to the fall of the monarchy to Assyria and Babylon. Moses, Samuel, David, in fact, embody with their lives the struggle of the Lord God to renew His Revelation with Israel in her history among the nations. Without Moses, Israel is a tragedy in Egypt. Without Samuel, Saul is a tragedy as the first of the Bull Kings of Israel in the Land of the Promise. Without the Promise, even the House of David is a tragedy among the nations. But with these people, again and again across centuries of time the prophetic power of the Word of God steadily remains committed to who He is in His covenanted relationship with His People in His Creation. With His Divine Freedom the Lord and God of His promised *chesed* gives through His Holy Love for Israel and His Creation a future, a future that embodies the I-AM He is as His *Grace* and the Beginning of the establishment of the New World under the

New David. Thus, Israel's history is not and cannot be told merely by her tragedies. She must be told in accordance with *the nature of His Grace*, a *nature* only defined by the Word He is Himself of God. Jesus Christ is thus not a man upon whom the Word of God has come, but the man who is the Word Himself, the Son of God from God's Own Eternity. He holds as this Word the Old and the New together in the time and times of His People in the world. The King is this Word, this One Word of the One Lord God who is the Great I-AM of this world.

He is the faithful Witness of the Old and the New Testaments to Himself. It is His victories that we must read in the Bible. It is this Son of David who is the Son of God. It is this One who is the Messianic King of the People of God and the future of the nations in God's Creation. His Word as this Man is the Royal Word. In His Reign is sustained the fulfillment of the prophecy of the history of the world. Messianic prophecy in the fullness of time proclaims the Word of His Royal Reign, the prophet who shepherds the People of God in time and times and time again. With this One the ancient promise to the fathers of the Biblical faith has steadily been secured and fulfilled, a continuity that only the Word of the Prophet the King is can establish. We cannot honor the King without hearing His Word. We cannot hear His Word without listening to the Word of Israel's Prophecy. We cannot divide His Being up in such a manner that we can separate Him from His Word. His Word is a Royal Word. His Royal Reign is His Word. The King as Prophet proclaims the One Word that God is as Lord of all space and time and so forth.

The House of David is the object of this Prophecy that belongs to the Royal Reign of the Servant foreseen by all the prophets of Israel's history. We have seen Him there as both the fulfillment of the covenanted relationship between God and His People as well as the Light of God's Word of God for the nations, a Light that shines even onto the New Heavens and the New Earth for the New Man of the New Creation. As this King He is the Prophet. Beside Him, there is no other. All others are but idols. All nations are justified or not in this One, this One Word, this One Prophet who as King reigns over all that is created reality. When we hear that this Word has become flesh as we are flesh in this world, when we hear that as this man, this Jesus of Nazareth, is the David of the New Creation, then we hear the New Beginning the Lord God has made for Himself for His People in His World. We hear the Word that justifies or not all that is justified. We hear by His Spirit the Prophet as the New Man of the New Beginning in

His BCR for Israel among the nations. We hear, indeed, the Royal Prophet. We hear His Royal Prophecy. We hear by His Spirit the only Spirit that can take the world on its destiny with Him. We hear not merely an occasional prophet, but the Prophet of the Prophecy that is the possession of the King of the Kingdom of God. We hear the Word of His Forever come from God's Eternity. We hear what we cannot tell ourselves. We hear of a work that we cannot do. We hear the Word of the Great I-AM the Lord God as the Messiah King of God's ultimate Sabbath Blessing with His Creation. It is an ear worth getting. Today, it is an ear for which we need to pray.

III. THE KING AS SAGE

The dimension of the Royal Personhood of the Lord God is perhaps the least appreciated in our time. The Wisdom of the King as Priest and Prophet of Israel's Messianic Word is often not explicit in our contemplations of His Being and Nature. Wisdom tends to come from our blood, sweat, and tears rather than from His Life and Word. It does not find ready explanation among many today. Modern or postmodern thought appears more comfortable with the '*creation out of something*' than with '*creation out of nothing*' and the Wisdom of God in *the* Beginning. Most Old Testament commentators today regard the Wisdom Tradition in the history of Israel as a tradition developed separately from her Covenant Tradition. Neither Walther Eichrodt nor Gerhard Von Rad, both great German scholars, sought to integrate in any but an ad hoc manner the Wisdom Tradition with their very different views of the Covenant Tradition. Their positions are readily reflected in the way exegetes interpret Proverbs 8 today. Unlike the understanding in the early Church, the 'Lady Wisdom' of the proverbial Wisdom Tradition is thought to be but metaphor, poetic license, in the same sense that mariners name their ships after one female or another, so that no *hypostasis* between her and Jesus Christ is thought really to exist. The One who was with God before the foundations of the world were laid down is not really known as Christ as the Wisdom of the Lord. Once this split on the level of language and reality is posited, then we are free to produce with our many speculations what we can lay down as a bridge between the Wisdom and Covenant Traditions with the People and Monarchy of the Lord God. We cannot go into all of the ramifications of this split, but I would point out here that I believe the split between Biblical and Dogmatic Theology that plagues our present reading of the

Bible is to be associated with the failure here to understand the whole Person who is the King of Israel's Messianic Hope as Prophet, Priest, and Sage of her history among the nations in the Creation.

Psalms 1 and 2, as an introduction to Israel's Psalter and the David of her worship, highlights for us the consequences of this split, a split felt across the spectrum of our efforts to grasp the relationship between God and the world and its mankind. If Psalm 1, as a Wisdom Torah Psalm is not integrated in Israel's Worship of the Great I-AM the Lord God is, then the Messianic Promise read in Psalm 2 is not understood in its relationship with the Covenant. Wisdom's Doctrine of the 'Two Ways' (The Righteous prosper; the Wicked perish!) is contradicted by the experience of Israel's blood, sweat, and tears as the People of God among the nations (cf. Job and Ecclesiastes). When the Righteous experience suffering and appear to be perishing even at the hands of evil what is Man before God? When the Wicked are found prospering even while the Righteous are going down into the dusts, where is Wisdom's Doctrine of the Two Ways in Israel's life in God's Creation? What is Man, indeed (Psalm 8)? Scholars today have declared Israel's proverbial wisdom old wisdom, the wisdom of her blood, sweat, and tears. Her covenanted wisdom, the wisdom of her Messianic Hope is thought to be late wisdom, a theological wisdom developed in order to explain her Vision beyond her experience. The split is with us today in the form of Salvation History and Scientific History, as if the Bible announced as the Word of God two times to us—a time of faith and a time for reasoning about the world. Add to these kinds of times the chasms they create for our interpretation of the Bible, the fact that many would argue the Doctrine of *'creation out of nothing'* in *the Beginning* is a doctrine introduced into Israel's life and thought under the influence of the Greeks and you have the case for denying any real integration of Wisdom in Creation with Wisdom in the Covenant. The traditions of Israel's Messianic Hope among the nations, as if Creation and Redemption could be divorced from one another in the Vision of the Word of God, never contemplate the Witness of the People of God when the Creator and the Redeemer may be understood as two gods. We may not divorce them nor separate Creation from Redemption. The Great I-AM the Lord God is as One cannot be denied the confession. He is who He is throughout all of Israel's confessions of Him. He is ultimately this **Grace** and *Truth* with Israel's life in His BCR with His Creation as the Only One He is.

I read no such splits in the thought of John Philoponus in Alexandria. Jerusalem and Athens, however difficult it is for us to grasp, have something to do with one another. Thus, Philoponus' work in science and theology was devoted to overcoming any dualistic splits, any reductionism causing an abyss to be posited by the Church between the One God and the One Lord. When the Church as the New Israel of the People of God laid down her belief in the Incarnate, Resurrected, Ascended Lord, who from the Right Hand of the Father as the Messianic David and the Son of God sent His Spirit and gave Israel her life and mission in the world, her inception as Witness to His New Covenant, the Church sought to proclaim this Christ as the Wisdom of God in the world. Jesus is the man come as God in the flesh for all flesh. He is Man for all Mankind in God's Creation. He is the fulfillment of the covenanted promise with the dynamics of His Being and Nature and His purpose for His People in His Creation. Defined by the Triune Creator in this way, Philoponus, along with the orthodox fathers of this One Holy Apostolic and Catholic Church in the world, sought to understand the Incarnate Word and Son of God as the fulfillment of this Prophetic Hope we find fulfilled with this King, His Royal Priesthood, His Royal Prophecy, and the Wisdom of this Sage of Israel's witness, her experience among the nations. The Incarnation is implicated with the whole of the Creation even before *the Beginning*. Jesus Christ as the Wisdom of God, the Sage of the Covenant and the Creation, mediated salvation to His People in His Creation. He is in this way the Word of God who is the Light of the World. His authority possesses that Divine Freedom and Truth able to give His Life and Light and Love to all that is created reality. His is truly the Royal Authority over and with and in the Creation, so that in Him men and women may know Him as the Father He is of the heavens and the earth as well as of the Lord Jesus Christ, our Father. Thus, the inherence and co-inherence of the full dimensionality of the Great I-AM in the fullness of His Personhood is to become articulated with the Church's proclamation of His Gospel. The *perichoretic relations, inherent and co-inherent as the Great I-AM the Lord God is with Israel are found substantially in His homoousial relations with His hypostatic union as the Revelation of the Father in the Spirit of His Eternity.* The relationships are as much God as the Persons of the Trinity with the Incarnate Word. For Philoponus, Eternity was no silent timeless place, some unknown mystery beyond the created light of the Cosmos, but it was the uncreated space and time chosen by God to speak and to

The Person of God in the World

reveal Himself as the One He is in *the* Beginning and in His Incarnation, the New Beginning, whose purpose and direction had been determined by His Father even from before these beginnings. Thus, the Incarnate Word and Son of God, the Person of the Lord Jesus Christ, as King and Royal Prophet, Priest, and Sage of God's Eternity as the Humanity of God in His Creation fulfilled both the purpose of the Creation and the Covenanted People of God. To understand the wholeness of this Christ was to understand in the Light of the wholeness of God from before *the* Beginning and in *the* Beginning and with the New Beginning the Word of God made transparently clear in the Incarnation of the Word of God, the Creator of the World.

We may gain some insight into these kinds of relations that belong inherently to the Person of God as defined by the Incarnate Creator with Philoponus' efforts to explain the problem of the whole and the parts among the Greek philosophers in the Hellenic cultures of that ancient world. The One Personhood of the One Lord God is the One He is as the Three Persons of the Blessed Trinity. Philoponus' will resolves his explanation of this Revelation of the Incarnation as the way that the Lord God has chosen to define Himself as the Trinity the Great I-AM is embodied in the Person of the Jesus. The Lord God has become, with the Light He is as the New Reality of His Being and Becoming in the New Beginning of His New Creation, when new dimensions of the nature of the world are called into existence with the same power of His Word that obtained in *the* Beginning. Old categories of thought and ways of carving up the reality of the Cosmos had to be redefined in the Light of the New Man, this Royal David, this Promise kept in His New Creation. Again, the Grammarian made his points about this problem in Chapter Seven of *The Arbiter*, the very chapter his critics employed in order to justify his condemnation, indicating how difficult it is for us to give up old habits of thought and to discover new dimensions in the mystery and freedom of our Lord and God to be present and known in our time and times.

The Alexandrian argued that there exist various ways of understanding resolutions to the problem of the whole and the parts as inherited among the Greeks. First, we can understand the whole with its parts in one way when we are dealing with parts that each occupy their own space, each possess their own place. For instance, a house is made up of parts that define its space with the places of the floors, walls, ceilings, and so forth. We can number their magnitudes and measure the parts up, geometrically, into a definition of the whole. We can sum the parts in a certain manner and obtain a real definition of the whole. On the other hand, the bronze statue of a man cannot be understood as a whole with its parts in the same manner. The metal of the statue and the form of the man do not occupy their own places in the space of the whole. They occupy the same place and thus form the whole. We say that they form an 'aesthetic' whole, the art of which takes us somewhere beyond number into the realms of beauty and truth and so forth. But, finally, what must we be able to say of the whole and the parts that are the Incarnation? Here we are faced with a composite reality, absolutely new in the nature of the Cosmos, that re-informs its parts in such a way that, without confusing or dividing them, without transforming or divorcing them, a whole is made whose *homoousial*, *hypostatic*, and *perichoretic relations* are essential for defining what it is in the wholeness of who God truly is. The dynamics and kinetics of this thought were too much for his critics. They saw Philoponus in this case as a heretical Monophysite and Tritheist. The assertion that *ousia, hypostases,* and *perichoresis* of the Trinity in the Incarnation, the Incarnation in the Trinity, possessed a dynamic of the whole in the parts and the parts in the whole that took us beyond house and statue into the actual Being of God in His Acts for us and the Acts of God in His Being for us with His Word was not able to overcome the more static and metaphysical views of the Greeks. By 680, as we have said, the Anathema was official and the freedom to think along the lines of such resolution was condemned. I believe we created the Middle Ages because of it.

Because the Blessed King of the 'All' with the Word and Mediation and Wisdom, to be understood as embodied, with the Divine Freedom of the Great I-AM the Lord God is, in the Person of the Lord Jesus Christ could be reduced upwards into an abstract version of His Being or reduced downwards into a subjective version of who He truly is, much of the impact upon reality of the Messianic Hope of Israel can be lost in a fragmentation and alienation about which Israel had been chosen to teach the nations. When the dynamics and kinetic dimensions of the personal reality of Christ are lost upon the essentialism and instrumentalism that belong to the mythological views of the Word with His Creation, then our opportunities for understanding the Messianic King as the Priest and Sage He is with His Kingdom become lost upon us. We will not seek to understand the Great I-AM the Blessed Trinity is over and above and without our time and times and so forth. Yet it is only with His Wisdom that we are able to go to the place where He has chosen to posit His Name and there do what is 'Right' in His Eyes. It is only there that we may learn to hear Him as the Word He is for us, both now and in and even then before *the* Beginning. Incarnation and Creation are to be seen in the Light the Life of this Word He is, the Lord God of Israel's history among the nations in the history of His Creation.

The Sage as King is known in the Book of Isaiah, for instance, as the 'Wonderful Counselor' (Isaiah 9:6). With this Counsel, He is named 'Mighty God,' the 'Everlasting Father,' the 'Prince of Peace.' These are His throne names of the David of the Vision. These are not names to become emptied of meaning and significance in time among the nations. In Hosea 14:9, we read the prophetic grasp of the rhetoric of His claims as the Wisdom of this Throne of David, the rhetoric of the Wisdom that is inherent in the restoration and renewal we must grasp of the **Grace of the Great I-AM** with His People. With this Wisdom, the reversal of Israel's fortunes as the People of God shall be realized: *'Who is wise? He will realize these things.'* Without such Royal Wisdom, no one can understand the great and patient struggle that marks the determination of the Lord God in His BCR to reverse His People's opposition to Him and to fulfill as *'My People'* the promise He made long ago to father Abraham, the father of Israel's faith with her Lord and God. Wisdom may not be divorced from this prophetic promise and hope. Israel cannot be divorced from His priestly intercessions of His Word. This is her Torah Wisdom. This is her Messianic Wisdom. To divorce prophecy and salvation from this Wisdom is to denigrate the patience of His intercession in time and space, to deny Him His space and time in His Creation, to alienate the meaning of our freedom from its source in who He truly is—*the Great I-AM of the Grace of God.*

But with His Wisdom, we must speak of Him, in *the* Beginning. We must speak of Him as His Royal Prophecy. We must speak of Him as His Royal Priesthood. We must speak of Him as His Royal Wisdom, with His Divine Freedom to set with His Royal Truth His People free from their sins and free for His Truth, the Truth of His Grace and the Grace of His Truth from *the* Beginning to His Forever with His Eternity in His Creation. As this Wisdom He is Man as the Image of God with His Divine Freedom and Human Freedom exercised throughout the space-time inherent in the history of His Creation. We must speak of this Person as the God-Man of Eternity. We must speak of Him as the Person He chose to become and made as the One He truly is. We must speak of this One as God's Wisdom become Man to fulfill and complete His purpose for the destiny of Man with Himself in His BCR for the People of God in His Creation. We must speak of His Revelation. We must speak of the Light He is. We must speak in His Name of the Father, Son, and Spirit of Eternity and forever. We must speak of His Reconciliation, His Salvation, and His Determination not to be who He is without His People in His Creation. We must speak of the power of His Glory in His Creation. We must speak of the Blessed Trinity of Christ's Revelation, the Great I-AM of Moses' Revelation, as the Person He has become with the Name of the Lord Jesus Christ. We must speak of our Father, our Savior, our Redeemer from within the structures and orders and freedoms that are inherent and co-inherent in the world as the history of His Creation. We must speak of the I-AM the Lord God is of Abraham, of Moses, of King David, and of the David of the days to come. We must speak of this Person.

It is in fact the case that this concept of *Personhood*, of God as Person, was introduced into the world as a whole new way of understanding the I-AM He is, of grasping the nature of God as made known with this New Man, of knowing the nature of the world as His Creation in His Divine Freedom and Holy Love for all that comes from the work of His Hands and Mouth. Nowhere in all of ancient literature do we find this concept of God as Person, as personal being, as that Being whose Word and Acts shape and form the substance and content of the purpose of history and science. Until the Incarnation of the Creator, the Lord seemed at best a distant Deity for Jews and Greeks, worthy of a humility whose claims to agnosticism ruled His creatures upon the earth under the stars. But for Philoponus, the whole and the parts involved in the Incarnation, explained the Person of God as His Light and Life and Word of the Blessed Trinity the I-AM had become as the Lord and God of the 'All,' whose power had created in this way the ground upon which believers could stand and learn to follow Him in the space-time of His Creation. This was ground as much created out of nothing as *the* Beginning, yet with the difference that all potential of *the* Beginning had been actualized in the Person of Jesus Christ. Out of the 'nothingness' of the Creation had been realized, with this Person, the purpose of the Person of God with His Creation. It is this Name that must bear the significance of the new ground He is as Himself for us in the space and time of this world.

The language that Philoponus transformed into service of this Name had to be understood as referring away from its terms to the actualities of the realities involved in the Naming. The Being of God (*ousia*) is meant to refer to the essential being of God as God. He is this Being with or without His Creation. If there is this Creation, then this I-AM chose with His Freedom to become the Creator and create the Creation He willed to created. There is both Being and Becoming in God's Eternity. There is both a before and after, duration measured timelessly without paradox or contradiction, in the I-AM God is. But with the Incarnation we are shown that God is not God in His Divine Freedom as the number one, but as the One who is the One in His differentiated Being and Becoming. He is One to be known as the Father, Son, and Spirit of His Eternity. He possesses with His Being three *hypostases* by which He differentiates Himself from Himself, and these *hypostatic realities of His differentiated Being are in homoousial relations with one another even from before and after the Beginning of the Creation, which He is not*. The Hypostases of God as Father, Son, and Spirit, though differentiated from one another (Unoriginate, Begotten, and Proceeding) are the One Being of God. The Church learned to think of the Lord in this way in the Light of the Incarnate Word, that is in the Light whose Word was the Son of God with God even before *the* Beginning. Thus, in the Face of Christ, she learned to see the Face of the Father in the Spirit of this One God. 'Face' in Greek is the term *prosopon*. The term *prosopon* was translated into Latin 'personna,' and it is from this term that we get our English 'person.' In the individual face or *prospon* or 'person' of Christ, as the *hypostatic union in homoousial relationship with the Trinity of God*, she could see the Face of the Father and the Spirit of God. Thus, the Person of God as One is at once understood as Three Persons in a resolution of the whole and the parts that could be explained by Aristotelian or Neoplatonic way of carving up the reality of the Creation and the Creation's Redeemer. God was Personal Reality in this way as the Self-Defining, Self-Giving, Self-Communicating Lord God He is as the Great I-AM He is. In this Name, thus the Church baptized those who believed in Him. But this concept of personhood, like the concept of the contingency of the world, has not had an easy time of it in the history of thought in our civilization.

    Much more commonly we find the term 'person' defined as an individual, rational, mortal (or immortal) creature, an atom that exists as species of a genus, a part of a universal, defined not by Revelation but by the logic and assumptions or presuppositions supposed on other grounds. A contemporary to Philoponus, Boethius introduced this way of defining the human race among the creatures of the world, and it is his way of carving up reality and not that of Philoponus that became popular even down to our own times, when creatures breathing the air that surrounds the planet understand themselves as individuals, immortal souls, with individual intellects, capable of an infinity of imaginative powers very often confused with God's. We can recognize the problem of the Self-Made Man with this definition. We can see that autonomy that mistakes individual freedom for the uncreated infinity of God's Freedom, of God Himself. We see every man and woman capable of doing what is right in his or her own eyes, but unable to acknowledge the limits defined by the Freedom of God upon human freedom, defined in reality by the Person of the Lord Jesus Christ. The humanity and the individuality that can be reduced down into the 'nothingness' of the Creation without Him is seen as the phantoms of everyman lost in the chaos and emptiness of the 'Very Good' Creation of the Creator, when our race displays all the pathologies that go hand in glove with our destruction in the contingent rationality and intelligibility of a world that is His New Creation. Free from the Authority He is in His Freedom, existing outside of His Breath upon us, our souls suffocate and shrivel in the loss of transcendence that is too vital for our being in this world. We discuss problems like this when we talk about individuality and community, freedom and authority, freedom and truth, being and knowing that belongs to a truth and freedom that is what it is outside of our knowing and being, truth and freedom that come both individually and communally from outside of ourselves, from the world and its relationship with the Lord God. Again, with John Philoponus, who would resolve the problem of the whole and the parts in the Light the Incarnation on the Trinity the Great I-AM is in our space and time, we read an effort to understand the human race not as individual, rational, mortal or immortal, creatures but as persons belonging to the personal reality of our Redeemer-Creator. It is upon this ground that the Alexandrian sought resolution to the challenges the Word of His Revelation is for us. It is with his thought experiments and with his laboratory experiments that he sought to grasp the real relationship between the God, Man, and the Creation. It is standing on this ground that allowed the Grammarian to make his profound contribution to the history of science and to Christian Theology.

  Professor Thomas F. Torrance has pointed out again and again that the Great I-AM the Lord God is, as our Triune Redeemer-Creator, become known to us in this world through the Person of the Lord Jesus Christ, is a 'personal' Lord God who *personalizes* those who believe in him. Thus, he seeks to make humanity not less than what humanity ought to be, but humanity as humanity was meant to be with Him in His World. This is the significance of the doctrine of the mankind, male and female, made as His Image and Likeness, read in Genesis 1. Humanity as the Image of God has been justified in the Creation as the Person of the Lord Jesus Christ. What is Man? He is Jesus Christ. The Genesis of the New Covenant, the fulfillment of the declaration of the Adam as the Image of God, has been sanctified in Him. Thus, in Christ, God has reconciled Man with Himself as Man ought to be with His Creation, Old and New, the Man and God Jesus is. In this way, Christ is Man as God able to be both Lord of all space and time, even time past and time future, and in time and times and so forth. With this Christ the Lord God has determined to save and redeem all that He has created and made. He has chosen in His Divine Freedom to sustain His 'Very Good' Creation with His Sabbath Rest and Blessing from His Atoning interaction with His People. As this Holy Love, He is the Rock of all Ages, the Blood of Time and all that is created and made and sustained with His Eternal Life and Power. The Dogma of the fathers of this Church, inherited by John Philoponus, wanted to say that the believers are being made as the image of this Image of God. Their adoption as His Children in BCR with who He truly is has been instituted in and with and through His Nature and Being. In this way, He has chosen all mankind to come to Him, to be made in His Likeness, what mankind ought to be in His New Creation, and to be with Him for as long as forever is in His Eternity. Here and then we will be human as He is human. We will possess as He possesses the real correspondence the Lord God has created and made and sustains with His Eternity for His People, on behalf of His People. Thus He may call His People '*My People*' forever, a people saved by the Truth of His Grace and the Grace of His Truth as the One He is in this world. In this way, He makes right those who have wronged Him. He has not defined Himself in His BCR with them in vain. His love, with His compassion and favor and patience and grace and faithfulness is the truth of a solid determination no creature in this world can reverse. It is as we reflect this determination that we become 'personalized' with the *Person* He is as the head of the Church, in 'personal' relationship with the Great I-AM He is as Lord and God of the 'All' that created reality. In this way, there is no contradiction between personal community and personal individuality, but the power of the Glory of God to make what appears as opposites together as One. In this way, the Unity of God has prayed for the unity of the believers. In this way, we belong to the Nature of the Being and Becoming of the Great I-AM the Lord God is as His Great AMEN with and for us and even within us in our times.

What may this kind of personalization mean for us? For me personally it has meant a profound healing in the depths of my being of my life in this world. You cannot have read the first chapter of this book without at least a glimpse of the extent of the healing I needed even to exist, let alone to become restored enough to write my argument. To experience this healing, I have come to appreciate what the Church has meant with her doctrine of the 'vicarious humanity' of God in Christ or Christ in God ministered to sinners by the Holy Spirit of the Triune Redeemer-Creator. To this teaching belongs the assertion that 'what God has not assumed has not been healed.' The Incarnation means the assumption of the whole of what Man is, even as a sinner. His 'vicarious humanity' means that He has been willing to die for us and to raise Himself from the dead as one of us and to live ever at the Right Hand of His Father sending His Spirit with His Atoning Love and Mercy with and for us in His Creation. The *vicarious humanity* means that for the whole of Man the whole of God has determined to save sinners from themselves, from one another, and from the evil to which they have succumbed at the hands of the Evil One. He has substituted His Life for our misery and rebellion and death under His Curse upon all that is evil in His 'Very Good' Creation. He has brought to bear upon us in our time and times the whole weight of His Glory embodied in the Man Christ is as Jesus of Nazareth, the Son of David and God. It is as He is that we are to be, because of His willingness to substitute Himself for us before our Father. Becoming 'personal' in the *Person of God* is to belong in His BCR with Him to relations that make true what the personal Lord is with His Children as the Father, Son, and Spirit of His Eternity. It is to be made in the image of the Image of God within the structures of the space-time of the New Creation. It is to be healed from death, from sin, and from the Evil One. It is to be set free to follow the One He is for us, who has made even my reader for Himself to His Glory.

I am in these relations a long way from being a 'Jesus Freak'. I am becoming a follower of the Person of the Lord Jesus Christ, a journey that travels in time and space while belonging to a freedom is made as His Freedom. My freedom to be independent of Him has become my dependence upon Him. I could write ten books about the problems sinners have with the dynamics in the ways the Lord God seeks to personalize His Children. But this one is about the freedom with which He accomplishes His determination for me. To heal me in the depths of my being means to make me free as I have never been free, free from sin and fear, free for love and Him. It is to make me free to understand that forms of relations are vital to who we are, what we are, and that these forms, created though they are, are a reflection of His Form and Forms, His Person and Persons, without separation or confusion, division or mixing up one with the other. His Divine and Human Freedom had made a home for Himself in my life and made my life at home with Him, with our Father. The Nature of His Grace and the Grace of His Nature have been made One with a Divine and Human Freedom whose authority has embraced even the depths of my sin and rebellion against Him, converting them into a child for His Kingdom. As a 'Jesus Freak' I possessed only this one advantage over the many sinners in this world. I knew that I was crazy. Most sinners try to think they are not crazy, even all right, and maybe even immortal just as they are, able to be successful without Him. But in America we know success has it limitations and its emptiness and that we were made for something more and that we are crazy without that something more. Because of all of this, I could ask with some amount of sincerity, Lord, heal my mind, and I will be whole. I was indeed tired of being crazy and alone and fragmented and alienated from my generation.

Healing minds is not for amateurs. It is for the Lord Jesus Christ. It is for the Revelation of the Father. It is for the Spirit of God among us. It is in the Spirit of this Word of God speaking to you that we know we are those who have been called '*My People*.' It is becoming who you are with Him. It is to be a child whose beginnings belong to the God of *the* Beginning. It is to know Him with His Kingdom in a universe that was meant to be our home. It is to know that His Creation has been justified in Him. It is to grasp *the* Beginning in its sanctification and its destiny with Him. It is to be at one with the One who is more than a mere number. It is to know Him as the Divine Love He is with His Wisdom. It is to follow Him who is free to give Himself with this Love for His People, even in our opposition to Him. It is to belong to a Unity of His Word and His Being in His Spirit, the Word of a Unity that we cannot tell ourselves, that we cannot with ourselves define. It is to hear that speaking that is truly free speaking. It is to be embraced by that power that is true authority. It is to be set free for Him. It is to hear Him from His Eternity as this One Man in His Time and

Space for all mankind, male and female, the Image of God finally realized as the One He is. It is to know that His personal relations are vital with Him. It is to understand that His Dogma and the Church's Dogma cannot be divorced from one another, the one to be found in the other or not at all. There is no such thing as dead Dogma with His Church. There is only the Dogma that speaks freely, because he, who would give us to proclaim what He has done for us in this world, has made us free. It is what I would call the 'Glorious Freedom.' It is human being and becoming, from above and from below, from without and from within, being and becoming human alive as the One is alive with us. It is freedom with a wholeness of body of soul and soul of body that only the Redeemer-Creator can shape and form. It is to know the 'personalizing' Lord and God. In this way, the Great I-AM He is with His Great AMEN for us in His Creation defines our 'personhood.' We are not merely breathing rational mortal animals, but 'persons' conceived to worship Him. We are not merely subjects of some personality cult, but 'persons' conceived with atoning love in the presence of the Glory of God. To a 'Jesus Freak,' this is stirring news indeed, of epoch-making proportions, indeed, news created with an atoning work whose Holy Love waves in the waters of our times, more than the Gravitational Waves of Black Hole Fields Kip Thorne at Cal Tech hopes to detect and look through a whole new window onto the universe of space and time and energy and matter. These are vibrations that come from God Himself, from the Lord and God who is the Light and Power of the 'All' as the I-AM He truly is. We need to catch these waves in the waters of the world, ride them as in His Creation we find ourselves becoming the children of His Kingdom.

Who can say such things as these except in the power of the Spirit that shows us the New World? Who can be in personal relationship with this New Man, even as dying old men, when the Old One has become in our place, for our sakes, on our behalf as the Man that Jesus Christ is for us? What new dimensions of space and time and matter and energy has He made with Himself in His Creation? Just as He said in *the* Beginning, 'Let light be,' He has said in our time 'Let my light shine in your life.' With what power may we hear the Light His Word is? Who is this *Person* really, who has determined to make us for Himself? With what freedom is He to be known as the Divine and Human Freedom He is? He is the Triune Being of the Word of the Apocalypse. He is the Word of God's Being and Becoming in the ages of the world, the Eschatology of time and times.

What is the nature of His Person? Who is the Person that is His Nature? How does His atoning work today substantiate His Holy Love with us in forms and shapes the content and substance of which possess dimensionalities that belong both to the New World and to His Eternity? How does He in this way give to events occurring in time and times the meaning that we need to call our history? Who can imagine what we in time shall truly be with Him who is who He is? Healing in the depths of our being raises questions we would not ask without the mercy of the Lord of time to reach back into all our times and to give us access to His Father because of who He is with Him. This is His Grace and Truth for us.

I believe it is a mistake to think that Dogma and dogmatic people are bad people, and we are the good people who think that freedom knows no authority. I think it is a mistake to seek to understand ourselves as 'persons' without the One who we are not. If we are free to seek to define ourselves with ourselves, we are also free to seek the truth of His Love for us, the One who is who He is and we are not. I believe the way He stirs us in the depths of our being in this world is fundamental to what He thinks we are in our time and times. I believe the questions He raises up for us even in the midst of our chaos and emptiness, even in the dread of our 'nothingness' in the dark depths of this world, are for our healing, that we may become whole 'persons' and not just breathing creatures here. We need to ride the waters on which they wave. We need to sail the seas that form our journeys. We need to grasp the horizons upon our lives. We need to know Him there and here and in the depths of our being, be healed, become whole, rejoice with him as the Great I-AM He is as the Great AMEN He has spoken in His Creation. The Great AMEN of the Great I-AM lives in the waters of this world, where all mankind is a mariner sailing the seas, where all mankind is a surfer riding the waves upon the waters, where all mankind seeks to know and to understand the truth of the world where we have our beings with who we shall become. We need to hear Him with His Power and Wisdom. We need to hear Him with His Speaking for us. From beyond the horizons of our destinations with Him, His Voice sounds from His Eternity to tell us as the Humanity He is of His Light and Life and Love, calling us to the harbor He has prepared for us as His New Creation. I often sing a hymn in church with my contemporaries. Some of its words go like this:

The Great AMEN of the Great I-AM

'Hallelujah to the King of kings;
Hallelujah to the Lamb.
Hallelujah to the Lord of lords,
He is the Great I-AM.'

May the words of our mouths resound from the depths of our beings with the One whose Being, Word, and Work in this world is truly here for us, when we know that He is there and He is not silent. Amen.

Light Bearer

10

In Our Time

Rend your hearts ... turn to the Lord your God, for He is gracious and compassionate, slow to anger, and abounding in love, and He relents from sending calamity ... I will repay you for the years the locusts have eaten ...

Joel 2:13, 25

I HAVE RECENTLY RETURNED from the 50th reunion of the Class of 1957 at Princeton University. It took me decades to gain the courage to rebuild those friendships that I made as a haunted undergraduate. I was surprised that seventy-year-old men can enjoy being again the boys as much as we did. We were together in that special place we call Old Nassau. There one can feel that every citizen of the United States ought to know Princeton's call to the nation's service.

I flew with a classmate who had only attended the university for a year. Like myself, he was ill prepared for the rigor of study at Princeton, but was every bit as much a member of our class as any of us. The class even has established a fund for members and family members who have experienced misfortune. My classmate had gone into the Army after Princeton, became an engineer, only to become a leading member of the team that built the F-117 Stealth Fighter for us. Whenever I am among the crowds that like to see this machine fly above them at one public event or another, I am able to thank him, personally. He knows more about aviation than I ever dreamed there was to know, and I felt privileged to ride with him back to Old Nassau. It was a good way to begin our reunion.

Princeton Reunions attempt to accomplish much more than drinking and remembering, however. There are events designed to help the classes continue their education, grow in Princeton's traditions, and a great parade of the classes on the last day to honor the past and the future of the university. Our class provided panels of some very distinguished gentlemen willing to quit being boys again and to share the wisdom of their age with the rest of us. One such panel, made up of five of the most prominent citizens in the class, said the following to us:

1) Whether you are left or right, whether you are democrat or republican, when we are citizens of the American Democracy, we know that our Democracy works. It does not work with ideal perfections or for timeless causes. It does not work for self-serving interests. It works as only American Democracy works in our world, a very dangerous world indeed.

2) American corporate life must be warned about competing in the new Global Economy. It is being developed in our time with a rapidity that is leaving us behind. American corporations must be warned about educating our young people, to enable them to compete in the Globalization of this Economy.

3) American CEO's have been, in the past, fairly stupid about what we must become in the future. We may very well have already sold out our birthright to another. We are not educating our young people to meet the need for their service in the future we are facing. While China and India's young are setting their faces upon the new Globalization, we are busy entertaining ourselves, being too self-centered and so forth, and we have lost our potential in the maze of presently fragmented developments.

4) We will need to fight a war in the future, but no one is sure how and when we must fight. Some generals believe we fight best as a nation when we fight in defense of our land and not in preemptive war merely for the idea of democracy in our time.

5) We still need to fight for consistency and thoroughness in our own internal struggles for equality for all that we welcome as American citizens. We still need to move from the darkness of our prejudices into the light of what American Democracy is.

From panels like this one, the gentleman-scholars of our Silent Generation spoke with us. Panels of poets and artists from our class also spoke about the un-silent arts and languages in our time. There was not mention of the Person of the Lord Jesus Christ. Our culture remains silent about where it counts most. We appear still lost in a society without Him, yet plagued by a run away technology and its popularizations of things that matter, superficially substituting entertainment and neon communications for the real resolutions of our longing in this universe. Our race can enjoy the riches of the world without Him, but it cannot deny the reality of the truth of our existence in the nature of this world. Truth as an object of reality can easily become lost upon self-centered and self-seeking fulfillment and destiny. Pleasures and fashions and the repeated advance of technological patterns in our progress can captivate the attention that would span with our efforts the scope of real meaning in the world. Real intention and purpose and will can readily vanish from off our screens, turn our horizons into lines of silent information, unable to speak to us of their significance in time and space. The best scientists in Princeton's Class of 1957, one of whom had discovered the '*interferon*' treatment for victims of one virus or another, lives in a world of uncertainty and chance, when the foundations of our knowledge may remain utterly remote from those formations that are rooted in the ground only the power of the Word of God provides in this Creation, without which we will not to know what Man is, how he is what he is, why he is, and to where he is meant to go. We can allow our beings to be defined by another than the Great I-AM, and end up elsewhere than the place He has chosen for us. The human race can end further from being the Man of the Biblical World than we can imagine. I do not believe the distinguished members of my class believed that the so-called 'postmodern' generation would pay much attention to their exhortations and warning and laments. But I do believe that the Person of the Lord Jesus Christ needs to be taken into their accounts of our times.

Fortunately, I listened to them after having spent the first day of the reunion with some distinguished professors of history, on a tour of Washington's crossing of the Delaware River en route to his battle in Princeton. One of the professors, David Hackett Fischer, won a Pulitzer Prize for his book entitled 'Washington's Crossing,' and he led 150 members of the Class of '57 from the Pennsylvania side of the Delaware River across to Trenton and the New Jersey side, from where we walked the 'conservative paths' the General's army took on its march to the battlefield, just outside of the campus of the College of New Jersey. The college was a place where pastors trained to preach. It belonged to the revivalist tradition of the Church proclaiming the Gospel of Jesus Christ in the colonies. On that field General Hugh Mercer, a medical doctor from the Highlands of Scotland, was bayoneted some 17 times. He lay for a while near an oak tree, died painfully nine days later in the nearby Clark House, still standing above the field. A memorial had been raised for him beside the ground of the old oak. On that same field, Washington defeated Cornwallis. With his rag tag formations of colonial soldiers, he took on the most professional armies in the world then, the Royal British Regulars and the Hessians from the German States. The battle marked the beginning of the end for King George III in the United States of America. Along those 'conservative paths' that led the armies to Princeton, I talked with Fischer about his book. He had explained that there was no way to understand the victory of General Washington except through the concepts of contingency and freedom, words that on the lips of many in his book are translated into the concept of the Providence of God.

Fischer himself did not choose to employ this 'Providence' to explain Washington's victory, but he thought that his notion about the significance and meaning of contingency and freedom might very well grasp the reality of what had occurred. When I asked him if he was acquainted with the meaning of contingency in other fields of knowledge, like science and theology, he said that he was not, but that he was interested in its use in these other fields. He felt they marked a new kind of history writing, a freedom for an objectivity that had become lost upon historians content with their 'perspectives' on things that, in themselves, could never really be known. I was happy to pass on to him some references to Karl Barth and Tom Torrance in theology and Albert Einstein in science. I was delighted to speak with a historian in this way and to learn that the 'Providence of God,' as related to the contingency and freedom operative in world history, was not as otiose to scholars as in our recent past. God's Creation was not as far from the possible and the actual as one may want to think. The meaning of freedom may become much more vivid to us in our future in this world. If human freedom is bound up with God's Divine and Human Freedom with and for us in our time and times, then categories like the 'Providence of God,' or even the 'Prophecy of God' might not be laughed off of the playing field. We had begun our tour with a look at Emmanuel Leutze's painting entitled 'Washington's Crossing.' It is a painting once much maligned by artful critics. It was considered a symbolic illustration of no historical value. But it is now happily being restored to a place in New York's Metropolitan Museum of Art, when symbol and reality and art may refer to historical occurrences in their own ways. When Professor Fischer asked me to e-mail the reference, you could have knocked me over with a Yankee-Doodle feather. There was more to General Washington's

Victory than meets the eyes of his critics. The meaning of freedom in our nation and our nation's service in time was defined by this victory.

During the reunions, as we talked about our class's histories, again and again, I was asked to repeat a story my wife had told me about the victory of our nation over Japan in the Second World War. For five years shortly after the war, she lived in Kyoto. One day she was walking the beach in her bathing suit when she noticed some Japanese men dressed in fine French tailored silk suits on some rocks in the tide. She had been a model and thought they were probably at a shoot, for some advertisement or another. She sought to draw near to them and watch. As she approached them, the men began putting up their hands for her to stop, perhaps not understanding her innocence. But she kept going, and she saw a man in a straw hat bent over in a tide pool, looking in the water for specimens. When the man turned to look at the commotion, she was startled. She recognized him as the Emperor, and immediately bowed to him. He laughed and the men began to laugh and just five yards from him, she said, she could gaze into the radiance of a face that she still thinks as one of the happiest faces on a man that she has ever seen on this earth.

She was married to a CEO for Bill Lear in Japan, friends of whom were present when General Douglas MacArthur visited the Emperor at the Frank Wright's Imperial Hotel in Tokyo. It was at this meeting that Hirohito offered up his death for his responsibility in the war, when MacArthur explained to the Emperor that it would not be necessary, because someone has already done that for him. Mickey explains the happy face she saw on the beach that day by Hirohito's acceptance of this death for his. MacArthur's victory was not the same as Washington's victory, but it was in some real sense in the same Spirit as the first victory of the first President of the United States. Reflecting upon the meaning of freedom in our time means grasping its meaning in times such as these, I believe. We do well to remember the Spirit with which these men in their times fought for the nations, if we are going to contemplate the meaning of freedom in our time. When we remember Korea, Vietnam, and Iraq, we do well to remember the victories we have experienced with presidents like Washington and generals like MacArthur. We do well to remember why we are willing to die, for what we become willing to die. We do well to remember why we are able to forgive. We do well to remember what we cannot forgive. We do well to remember that God in Christ defines for us the meaning of freedom in our time. We cannot rightly respond to the very challenging realities we face today, without understanding the significance of this freedom and this freedom's triumphs of His Spirit in our history. American freedom depends upon the reality of this Spirit in the world. Where the Spirit of the Lord is, there is freedom.

People are willing to die for all sorts of reasons. One man's freedom fighter is another man's terrorist. Everybody can conjure up an idea about freedom in order to justify their causes in this world. Freedom needs definition that is given by the Spirit of the Living God, not by mankind's many ideals, many desires, many longings. I live where people have all kinds of revolutionary heroes. I have heard praises sung for Pancho Villa, Emile Zapata, Che Guevera, and even for Fidel Castro, as well as Karl Marx, and so forth. I have listened to the freedom of capitalism and democracy much debated on the streets where I live. When I asked in these debates, who was the greatest revolutionary of them all, many seemed utterly surprised at my answer. They appear dumfounded to hear me claim that it was General George Washington, the First President of the United States of America. He was the greatest of them all, I say, because he was the only successful one, a proven one in the history of mankind upon this earth. The freedom for which he was willing to die belonged to the Spirit of the God who is Lord among the nations, the Spirit whose place means freedom. His victory is bound up with this freedom. This freedom defined our experience in 1776. It is a point in history that bears a passion more passionate than men alone can possess. Today, George is not thought of as a great revolutionary. The revolution that is American history is often understood in a reductionistic form, another history than the actual one it is. But it was the revolution that the great General led which has determined the course of our civilization in the world, where the meaning of revolution and freedom continues to be greatly debated. On the battlefield at Princeton, on the steps of Old Nassau Hall, the triumph of Washington is still remembered on Princeton's campus. We look back at it in order to look forward in this world. The meaning of freedom that celebrates the Fourth of July cannot here be forgotten. With this generation, we may seek today, whether poorly or wisely, to explain what and who we are in this world's history. The Silent Generation, that Princeton University Class of 1957 had been called by Life Magazine, has had to wrestle hard with this freedom, willingly and unwillingly, and its meaning in our time.

Flying back to California from our 50th at Nassau Hall, the man who made the Stealth Fighter challenged me to understand the '*Boolean*

Algebra' that flew the F-117 through the air in the skies. It was not an airplane. It was a machine empowered moment-by-moment and driven through the sky by a computer generated guidance system, like none before it. I challenged him once more to read the Bible. We had had a great reunion. We looked forward as we looked back perhaps better that we had ever done in our lives. When someone writes a book criticizing the way Princeton had chosen us for admittance to the class of 1957, we could smile at its warped in time morality. Yes, we were no women, no blacks, and only a few Asians. Yes, we were white men. But we belonged to a tradition of freedom that the world denies with great consequence. The two of us were among the free, enjoying a freedom whose significance was free from condemnation because we understood that the future is for the Spirit of God with us, the Spirit, I say, of the Great I-AM the Lord God is as our Savior Jesus Christ.

The theoretical physicist at the California Institute of Technology in Pasadena, Kip Thorne, now leads a team of theoretical experimentalists and experimental theorists who seek to obtain evidence of the gravitons passing by the earth from black hole events in the universe, singularities producing a wave field that, once observed, will give us a new window onto the physics of a world the objectivity of which is important to the development of our science. Professor Thorne anticipates that our ability to read the information we gather with the LIGO and LISA experiments will open up new vistas onto the invisible dimensions of the visible world that will allow us to resolve the struggle between Einstein and the Quantum Mechanics. In our time, we are looking for a new physics, a new mathematics, a new relationship of our race to the universe, a new cosmology, a new epistemology. If Galileo's telescope and Newton's differential equations were revolutions in science, then Einstein's equations for the gravitational field and the four-dimensional world are perhaps the greatest revolution science has ever experienced in our history. (One of my Princeton classmates believes that this revolution has made science the art of the future!) The singularity of the Big Bang Beginning of the world has allowed us to seek to understand with ten or eleven dimensions of space-time the significance of the infinities that belong to the invisible/visible natural world. Black Hole Beginning allows us to conceive the evolution of its universe all along the billions of years (13.7) down to our present. New fields of dark matters and energies have been discovered that cry out to us for explanation today, and this cry is heard echoing down through all of our sciences, biological and psychological. The freedom of our imaginations, wills, intuitions, and knowledge to wonder our way into a new understanding of the objectivity with which we must deal in our time is evident to all of science. When we are successful, says Professor Thorne, (not if) a new world of symphonic fields of energies and matters, space and time, will become heard, unlike anything we have ever heard before in history. In the face of it, many scientists today have begun to confess that it is enough to take their collective breath away.

Professor Thorne's mentor and friend, John Archibald Wheeler at Princeton University, later at Austin University in Texas, has heard the cry of these developments as a call for 'Meaning Physics.' The old science, where moral/ethical issues and the influence of religions could be definitely avoided, is gone from our times. Scientists must now become committed to seeking with what lies behind and beyond the universe the answer to the question why it is what it is and not another and why we are in it what we are and not another, singularities once safely ignored in the march of science. We need to seek for 'the Law without Law' that informs us in this world with a meaning that possesses moral and ethical dimensions, that physical law and moral law are to be found inherently together in the world. Wheeler is the scientist in fact who named the singularities of Einstein's equations for his gravitational theory 'Black Holes.' We still do not quite know what they are, but we have learned they form the center of many galaxies and we shall have to determine the nature of the fields in which they are what they are from their beginning in relationship to the fields we have discovered in our times, the nuclear, electromagnetic, and gravitational fields we experience with our theories. It is as if something primordial cries out to us for recognition, even in our time and times.

In this case, I do not believe we employ our freedom rightly when we will not acknowledge the Judeo-Christian doctrine of a universe that is, *creatio ex nihilo*, both independent in its created nature of God and yet dependent upon His Free Will for why it is the universe it is rather than some other one. I believe we need to take seriously what John Philoponus in the sixth century in Alexandria sought to do in the Light of the Incarnation and the Revelation of the Great I-AM whose truth is claimed to set our kind free for life with God in God's Creation.

We have argued that the One who is the Great I-AM the Lord God is, transcendent over, immanent with, and economically within this world assumed with His pre-incarnate Form His incarnate Form and justified

Himself with Abraham, Moses, and the House of David among the nations in His Creation as the Word of God and the King of the Universe. I believe that He speaks with us today as freely as He spoke with His Elect in the Biblical World. I believe that He has chosen, as the Person of the Lord Jesus Christ, to reveal in His Divine Freedom the way He has set His Name with His Space-Time in relations with the space-times of the invisible and visible world that is His Creation. I believe that He has chosen to be who He is freely as the One He is among us as our Reconciler and Redeemer and Creator with the I-AM He is. I believe he calls His People not merely to be free to be successful in this world without Him, but to worship and to follow Him and come to know the meaning of their freedom in their times. I believe that He gives His Spirit to show us the way to go to Him and to learn to do what is right in His Eyes ('*The Upright Thing*' of the command of His Word read in the Book of Deuteronomy!). From His place and with His hour the universe is to be known as God's Creation, His Very Good' Creation, possessed with *the* Beginning whose impetus cannot be explained without Him, whose impetus establishes an open-structured world where the New Beginning has occurred and takes place even in our time.

With this *New Beginning* His purpose and promise in His BCR shall be accomplished with space and time. From this time on, He is revealed as the Father, Son, and Spirit, the Triune Creator of the heavens and the earth, as the King of the Universe. From this center of meaning is revealed the Righteousness of God's Freedom and Mercy with our kind. From here He is, bodily alive beyond all vanity, the Master of all that is created, of all that He is not and of all that is not love for what has been made and exists because of His Holy Love. To seek with the worlds of our sciences for the UNIFICATION in our time of the 'All' without Him is to long in the dark for a center that is not there or here, to agonize for a lost love that is not. But to go to the place that He has chosen with His Life for us is to find the Law of Life. It is to discover the Life of our Creator-Redeemer in the world where we live. It is to possess knowledge of Him that gives us to understand His Kingdom has come and is coming. Why not introduce here then a field whose vanity may be creatively, by the power of the Word of God, given significance that participates in and anticipates the coming of this King with His Kingdom, the Kingdom of God? Are we not free to imagine that, beyond the threat and dread of a nothingness, ill defined by us with the Liar within His Creation, we may become free to imagine His

Freedom to make with us, out of nothing, the 'Very Good' by which His New Creation is justified?

May we not be free in fact to imagine the actualities that belong to this movement of the Lord God in the world, where He makes room and time for Himself as the Great I-AM He is among us? Why not take seriously the ethical dimensions of our world as reflections of this Holy Love, this Atoning Love? Why not take seriously the freedom of His *Grace* and *Truth* with us in our space and time on both the empirical and theoretical levels of reality? Why not seek to discover afresh the power of His *Grace* and *Truth* in real relations with our freedom in our times, with the meaning and significance of our freedom in the space where we live? Between theological and natural sciences there exists a ground then upon which we do well to learn to stand, where we may become enabled to see and hear the New Creation even in the midst of the Old. We may become enabled to know the weight of His Glory upon us, even in the midst of the weight of the gravity that determines for us the shape and form of the substance and content of our lives in a universe that is a world of His Creation.

Much of my teaching has been done with Korean and Spanish speaking people. I have relied on interpreters for years. I know when an interpreter is able to hear thought and not merely words. One of the best I have met is a man named Edgar Mohorko. He lives with his wife, Marta in Oxnard, California, where they raised twin girls and a boy with special education needs. Edgar also pastors a church in the city, directs a Rehabilitation ministry there, and is Chaplain to the Police Force. He would drive from Oxnard to Azusa to interpret me to Spanish speaking pastors, some from as far away as Ecuador, and so forth. He could listen to me and then put into his own words what it was that I was attempting to communicate. We have become good friends.

One night, a highway patrolman, chasing a drunk driver through the streets of Oxnard, struck a car in which one of the twin girls, Eca, was coming home from her high school prom with her date. They were bound for a downtown restaurant after their dance, when the patrol car slammed into hers at an intersection and killed her immediately. When Edgar called to tell me what had happened, he said something about my teaching and how my efforts to get them to understand the Truth of God's Grace for us was the only thing that was keeping him going now, keeping his mind from thoughts of suicide. We prayed together in that phone call. There was too much to face. Would His Grace truly be sufficient?

In Our Time

When Mickey and I attended the funeral, it was truly an amazing time filled with an amazing Grace. Jessica Ann Mohorko, known as Eca to her sister Sisy, possessed a life that was celebrated by the whole city, mayor, police, farm workers, and friends. Eca and Sisy had written a song just a few weeks before her death. Sisy sang it at the celebration. Here are some of the words she sang:

> *Without you I am nothing*
> *But your love touches me*
> *Frees me from pain*
> *Without you I am nothing*
> *But your love teaches me*
> *To walk in your truth*

Every tear running down the eyes in the church knew very well that Eca was not-nothing, not with Him. She was His Child. Out of the nothingness of the wonder of this world, so readily felt as a threat to those who will not to believe in Him, He has taken His Child to Himself, made a future for her with Himself in this world. He is love, and only that which is not love can remain nothing or threatened by the nothingness and no child of His is ever simply nothing, but always what He makes out of nothing, just as He created out of nothing in *the* Beginning and in *the* Incarnation, and in *the* Resurrection and His Ascension. With Him, Eca was now gone, but perhaps more here than we are. Every tear in the eyes of the church knew very well she was not-nothing, that she was who she is with who He is in this world. Love is and Grace is His Love in interaction with us in our time and times. Truth is, because God is this Lord, the One Great I-AM of all that is created reality, in our time. Edgar and Marta and Sisy and Edgar, Jr. have been learning about His Grace and Truth ever since that day in new and surprising ways of God with us. Today, Edgar Mohorko is working on a Ph.D. at Pepperdine University and has been appointed in Oxnard as the Director of Charitable Ministries in the city, while still being a pastor in the Church of the Lord Jesus Christ, knowing the Grace that has turned a murderous night into a day of thanksgiving. The officers and the drunk driver were not hurt, of course, in the chase. God takes cares of them too. In the settlement, Edgar gained a hearing with Sacramento which concerned the control of police chases in our cities. He has become, I am informed, a very active member of the city government of Oxnard. Not in vain did Eca and Sisy write their song. I am told that Sisy still sings their song everywhere she goes.

Mickey wears a T-shirt on which is printed one of Einstein's more famous sayings, *'Imagination is more important than knowledge.'* We have studied the doctrines of *creatio ex nihilo* and *the Incarnation* that are fundamental to our knowledge of the God who is the Lord of all space and time. We have tried to see how that imagination, free will, intuition, and knowledge are all necessary in part and as a whole for grasping the reality of the world as created being in all of its depths. UNIFICATION of the nature of the world and created correspondence between the world and God cannot be possessed without knowledge of the actual Redeemer-Creator He is, the Great I-AM He is according to the Biblical Witness. We have argued no dualistic way of understanding them can lead us anywhere but to the fragmentation and alienation that we experience so commonly with our societies and cultures in our civilization today. We would argue that knowledge of God and knowledge of the universe cannot be divorced from one another, however difficult that makes it for us as we seek to appreciate both our independence of God and our dependence upon the Lord He is as the Great I-AM He is, as the One who is who He is with His Grace and Truth with us. We would argue that even our imaginations belong to the freedom He is for us in this world. We must be free to image that out of nothing the Very Good Creation is the something that it is and that it is what it is because of His Holy Love and Divine Freedom. This is surely what Eca and Sisy Mohorko intend to sing to us.

Eca and Sisy's song belongs to a faith that belongs to the faith that Jesus Christ, as the Man He is, is, the Grace and Truth of God with us and for us in the spaces of our times together. For the twins, the Lord God fills up with Himself the chasms of that abyss in which the Liar would make nothing of us, of our space and time, and twist the 'Very Good' into something it is not. Yet with His Divine Freedom and Holy Love, He has given the twins their song. Eca has been taken. Sisy has been left behind. It appears that between them a distance vast with the world's nothingness has made of them and their hopes and loves a sheer vanity with this world. But the Liar faces the Resurrection like an idea he can manipulate. The twins face Him as the I-AM He is. Though they were once twins on this earth, they are no longer. But what once was does not matter now for them. *What matters is the New Creation.* As children of God, one living on the earth, the other in the heavens, they are still twins, the Mohorko twins.

But they are this as persons defined by Him, twins whose relationship by the Grace and Truth of His Being and Becoming has been established with the Forever He has made with Himself and His Eternity. The distances that appear in the infinities of the nothingness of the world have been crossed for them by the Great I-AM He is. He has filled up with His Love and Light and Life the promise He has promised them. They are together, not nothing, but that something out of nothing only the Only Lord God can with His love create, make, sustain, and sanctify in this world.

I would suppose then that they are 'not nothing,' just as the highway patrolman is 'not nothing,' and the drunk is 'not nothing.' I would suppose that they are utterly what God alone makes, that belongs in some way to the world that is His New Creation. I suppose as pastors, Edgar and Marta Mohorko in Oxnard, know that they are 'not nothing,' no matter how things may appear, that their faith is not a vanity, and they exist as solidly as the Great I-AM exists with the Resurrection of His Son and Word. They are free to imagine with Christ what has come and what is to come and who they shall be with Him. It is this positive dimension of the creaturely life found in His Creation that we need to grasp. Far from the positivism of a Stoic, this dimension in life cannot be negated anymore than His Love will not negate what is not love in the world. Pastors Edgar and Marta, Sisy and Edgar Jr., are free to imagine this dimension with such things as even more solid than anything in the perishing world. With this dimension, without fear of the vanity of the world, they have been justified in Christ, in Israel's Messiah, in Jesus of Nazareth, born in Bethlehem, the Great I-AM the Lord God is in action as His Grace and Truth in His Creation, the King of the Universe, the Person who is the personalizing Lord God, making His children with Himself for life with Him in His Eternity. This is a more solid imagination than any other we can imagine, rooted as it is in His Divine Freedom and Holy Love to make all things according to His Word. They live with a freedom in which their grief knows the freedom that takes them beyond all their grief.

I recall now also the 25th reunion of the high school class of 1953 at James Ford Rhodes in Cleveland, Ohio. The community is actually named Brooklyn, Ohio. People from Brooklyn do not go to Princeton, even today. I had been astonished by the amount of affection I felt from the members of my class at this reunion. I do not believe that I deserve much or any of it. I had not attended across the years to any of my relationships with them. I was surprised by their willingness to forgive me. I was surprised by our affections, even with our judgments and hatreds for one another. I was surprised that there is something in time from which the nothingness of the world is impotent to take away. Even when I knew it least, relations had in them something of the freedom that belongs to God. It was strange to my soul. As I have said, I visited at that time the stones of the graves of my mom and dad. They rest at a little place named Solomon's Cemetery on top of a hill overlooking the Brookside Park, where I had spent many happy hours as a boy climbing and romping around. The headstones appeared side by side in that place before me as follows:

Charles E. McKenna
Pennsylvania
Bglr, 1 Cl Co E 16 Inf 1 Div
World War I
Dec 16 1895–March 9 1970.

Mother
Margaret E. McKenna
1900–1958
Rest in Peace

When I knelt down before the stones to pray, I found myself sobbing uncontrollably. It seemed to me as if the grief and pain of my whole family were convulsing through my body then. It seemed that my two brothers and my two sisters were there weeping with me. It seemed that those terrible times we had endured were being washed away with these sobbing tears. It seemed that the tormented hours of our lifetimes were being cleansed from their wounds. The self-destruction in our desolation was gone. It seemed my very soul was being healed there. It seemed to me that we were forgiven. When I was able to stand up again, these words burned through my spirit: '*Who then is this, that even the wind and the sea obey him?*' (Mark 4:41) Beyond all our grief and pain, we are made free in the Grace and Truth that He is, the Great AMEN of the Great I-AM He is.

Albert Einstein, as perhaps the greatest legend of the history of science, did not believe in the free will of any individual existence. The reason incarnate in the existence of the universe belonged to the 'Old One,' whose secret lay quite beyond our effort to understand Him or the world. But we could, on some rather simple levels of reality, grasp in all its depths something of the secret, yet with a significance that belonged at last beyond our individual wills and knowledge. Human thought might reflect the thought of the 'Old One,' but the 'Old One' ultimately kept His secret to Himself. That the Word of God was God's Reason become incarnate, as the Person of Jesus Christ was not a part of Einstein's belief. He may have been a man for all seasons, a good man, a great teacher, a moral man, a prophet of God, but He was not the 'Old One' come in Person into His Universe. The 'Legend of the Temple of Science' believed that no particular individual could possess the will that created the beginning or the destiny of the Universe. The individual each with its particular will and knowledge was finally consumed by an impersonal power of His Reason, and though Einstein could confess at times as none other than the 'God of Moses,' the 'God of Moses' was not a man as we are in this world.

Yet the great scientist knew well that no necessary reason existed between the nature of the reality of the Universe and our theories with our empirical experience of that nature. Mathematics, for instance, and the nature of physical reality did not possess any mathematical correspondence between the nature of physical reality and our mathematics. Imagination at this point became more important than knowledge. If a correspondence was to be grasped, it was to be understood with a freedom that made the correspondence always appear as a miracle. That we can understand, at whatever levels we can understand it, was always something of a miracle for the scientist. The mysterious intelligibility of the Universe belonged to the mystery of freedom and contingency in miraculous ways, which make science and theology at last, beyond enemies of one another, in alliance with each other in the depths of the nature of its existence. The empirical, the phenomenal dimensions of the world, could be measured and related to a theoretical embrace of the actualities that belongs to world potentials when the whole of mankind, his imagination, his knowledge, his will becomes devoted to the task of understanding. Intuition and imagination were just as vital to our progress as any deduction and conclusions we may formulate with it. In faith and freedom, then, the scientist devotes his or her individuality to the progress of the race upon this earth, a progress that is both successful and always wondrously challenging because it occurs within the power of the mystery that belongs to the 'Old One' and His Reason incarnate in its existence, when we bow humbly to the Reason that outweighs all of our comprehension about the world and our lives within it. Thus, freedom is at the heart of science. It is at the heart of our purpose for doing science. It is at the heart of the 'Old One,' the King of the Universe. We would argue that Einstein was quite deaf to the personal being and freedom of the 'Old One' because he did not ever hear proclaimed loudly enough in his time the I-AM the Lord God is as the Individual Being He is. For He is not a human individual as defined by the ways of our personality cults, but as the 'Only One' He is, when human individuality and the Eternity of God have been made the 'Old and Only and Incomparable and Unique One' that is the 'God of Moses' and the 'God of Jesus Christ' with a Divine Freedom we have seen in the Grace and Truth that is with us in the Universe. What we mean by the personhood of God and our modern definitions of personality have nothing whatsoever to do with one another in so far as their origins are concerned. The Personhood of the Blessed Trinity the Great I-AM of Holy Scriptures has become in His Creation must remain the source of any definition of mankind and the world as the Universe that is God's Creation. No one can grasp the nature of this reality except in the wondrous relationship between uncreated and created realities freely created and sustained by the power of this One Lord God.

We would argue then that here in the place He has chosen to set His Name lies the key for understanding the ultimate significance of human freedom. Free will of the individual is bound up with the Free Will of the 'God of Moses,' who as the Great I-AM has become the David of the Prophecy of His Grace as the Person of the Lord Jesus Christ the King—the Priest and the Prophet and the Sage of the Hope of the People of God in His Creation. In this way, Christ as the Son of God is the Image and Likeness of God from *the* Beginning now justified. He has become this Man for all time, making all times what they otherwise could not be. In this way, He is the sanctification of the 'Very Good' Creation in *the* Beginning (not simply the best of all possible worlds) as *the* New Beginning of the New Creation. As such He is the New Adam, mankind reconstituted for life with God in a freedom that knows divine and human freedoms, uncreated and created freedoms, having been given union and communion with one another in such a way that the two are the Old and One and Incomparable and Unique and True God of all Grace, the Lord of all space and time and light and mankind. We are called to love Him, because He first loved us. We are called to love Him all of hearts and minds and strength because He is the healer of all of our betrayals of Him and our brokenness from Him. We would argue then that creatures have been freely made to worship, even if in their independence of Him they are free to be successful without Him in His world. We were born free to worship Him, to be successful in His Creation Him in His Freedom, when His Grace embraces both those who follow and those who do not the way He has determined to take us to our destinies with who He truly is, our Redeemer-Creator. The Kingdom of God shall belong to the free, when both independence, even as individuals and communities, and dependence upon Him together characterize our freedoms to be who we are in the Universe. Thus, the race is rightly defined only with its independence in relations dependent upon the Great I-AM He is as our Lord and God. Thus, we may say that we are both free and yet bound to Him.

It is a special freedom. It is a unique freedom. It is a singular freedom. It is an old freedom. It is a new freedom. It is a gift. It is the gift of belief. It is a personal freedom. It is communal freedom. It is an individual's freedom. It is a community of faith in freedom. It is a substantial freedom. It is not merely an idea about freedom. It is a passionate freedom. It is not merely a concept that can become empty of meaning. It is a foundational freedom. It is a fundamental freedom. It is freedom in the Beginning and it is freedom before the Beginning. It is freedom in the ending of the Ages of time. It is freedom in the New Beginning. It belongs to what created reality is. It belongs to what created reality is not. It is with what can perish and with what shall not perish. It belongs to the power of His Freedom to relate Himself to His Creation, to the history of His Creation and to the destiny of His People under the heavens and the earth. When we would know the meaning for this freedom, we would know the Blessing of His Divine Freedom made human with His Holy Love and Atoning Will with His Grace and Truth for us. All authority in this world is what it is because it serves this freedom. Any authority that does not set people free for this freedom is a tyranny that is the enemy of who He is. Thus, we say, it is Royal Freedom, Priestly Freedom, Prophetic Freedom, and Wisdom's Freedom. We say that we may grasp Him in all of His Depths with us because He is the Great I-AM He is, our Redeemer and Creator for us in this world.

One hundred and eighty six thousand miles per second has been given us as the speed of light in the Universe. Who gave light to be this number and not some other one? From Ptolemy to Philoponus, from Copernicus and Galileo and Newton, to Maxwell and Einstein science has wrestled with the question. Who gave the Beginning to be whatever the Beginning actually is. Who or what was before this Beginning? From whence comes its light? Science has never been able to avoid these questions. Though we may observe only about five percent of the visible light of the universe, while ninety five percent of the world's energy and matter remains dark to us, how far may we be able to penetrate into what makes the Universe the rational whole it must be if we are going to understand its nature? When we seek among the infinities of structures of a four-dimensional world today, the legacy of Einstein's revolution and in the freedoms that must define the physics that come with our progress, what sort of exotic and strange interactions of energies, matters, and structures shall we discover? What kind of dimensionalities will become among the many infinities we may number with our mathematics real explanations for what we are given to experience? How will we understand the singularity we call the Black Hole and the Big Bang Beginning and cosmology in the science of the future? What happens when space-time matters become at the boundaries of our understanding deaf and dumb to our science's grasp of reality in all of its depths with us? It seems to me that we have just begun to learn to obtain, with the art of our sciences, the kind of intention we need to help us to grasp the relationships between things that tend to escape our attention. What will the artist-scientist of the future know in her grasp of the nature of reality in all its depths in the twenty-first century?

I believe none of these questions are beyond the scope of Philoponus' commitment to his 'thought-experiments' and the freedom we possess to learn to think relationship between uncreated and created realities. Perhaps we may, with his categories in mind, seek afresh for the place where human consciousness might yield to insights of greater simplicity than we have ever before imagined. Perhaps we may name the unity of the Universe with a rationality that will take us quite beyond any self-centered interests we may have with it and into the Kingdom of God as His Children. In any case, I believe we do need to rid ourselves of the kind of confusions that result from mixing up the uncreated realities that belong to God with the created realities that belong to the world. We need to grasp the Lord acting in His Freedom freely to make Himself present and known to us. I would suggest that with a man like John Philoponus, we have an example of someone willing to accept the challenges of his times and willing to seek to proclaim the Gospel of God in all of its fullness in space and time. I believe we need a fresh understanding of the Doctrine of Creation out of nothing, and its relationship with the nature of the reality, the Incarnation in a Cosmos that is His Creation.

I believe that, if we will attend to such relationships, our future will bear fruit that belongs to His Will and Power with His Creation. I believe the Lord of space and time has crossed the abyss between Himself and all created reality, acted in the infinite chasm that appears between us and who He is, in order to justify to His creatures what His Creation is as His New Creation. I mentioned that I had an astrophysicist as a friend for a while, and he gave me a verse that guided his thought as a scientist. It was Deuteronomy 29:29. '*The secrets belong to Him and to those with whom He is willing to share them.*' The Lord God as the Great I-AM He is has shared with us the secret of His Son and with His Spirit has given all who believe in Him access to His Father and our Father. Why not seek to discover the intention of the Blessed Trinity of the AMEN of the Great I-AM with His Creation in our time and times? Why not believe that His Grace and Truth as His Holy Love in action with the history of this Creation would lead us, whatever the appearances are, to a future that He alone has determined for us, beyond determinism's classic stance, beyond indeterminism current fashion? *We are free and bound to Him.* We are free in our time to be free with Him in His Time. Our knowledge of Him cannot be detached from Him or from our knowledge of the free world. Thus, freedom is vital for us. Only as free men and women may we stand on this ground He has created and provided for us. Only as we stand on this ground, may we know both who He is and what the world is, without confusing the One with the other and without dividing apart from one another. Christ is this Free Man who knows both divine and human freedom. When we believe in Him, He shares with us what He knows and loves in the fullness of time and time as His Time and Times with us. Thus, we may be known as the Children of God, the Children of the Kingdom of His Light and Life and Love, the Children who watch and wait for His Coming Again, for His Prophecy to be realized in His Creation.

In the seventeenth chapter of the Gospel of St. John, we read the High Priestly prayer of the Person who is who He is for us in the face of His Father. Theirs is a relationship to which all relations belong, and their life they share with us. Once Jesus prays this prayer, as the Son of His Father in His Eternity, He does not stay behind with us, but He goes to His Cross for us, there to die in our place, for our sakes, substituting His Life for ours as sinners in a world against Him. With His Resurrection, all mankind finds the life that He means for all mankind to possess. He shares the Life beyond His Death He lives with us with this prayer to His Father, and He gives the apostles the Promise of His Spirit, by which all believers may be given to share in the power of His Resurrection. It is in the answer to this prayer that we hear our union and communion made for us. It is with His High Priesthood in this prayer that we may see the 'Reason' He is in His Resurrection, the 'Reason' whose Word is free and bound to the God He is with His Father and His Spirit. Thus, we may come to understand how we are both free and yet bound to Him.

Our unity with Him belongs to His Unity with His Father as our Father. He is the One, the Old One, the Only One, the Incomparable One, and the Unique One who commands what love is. It is sheer vanity to seek to understand the unity of this love without Him. It is futile without the Name of the Great I-AM He is, without this God of Moses, to seek the One He is as the Father, Son, and Spirit of Eternal Life. It is a betrayal of the Name He has given to us to name. In this One, not merely a number, all real unity is to be found, even the unity of the Universe itself. Even when we seek for the UNIFICATION of the various fields of knowledge that drive our sciences today, we are seeking for the freedom for the meaning of the freedom that belongs to who He truly is with the world, with us in the world, with the relations of Man and Cosmos by which is defined the whole of His Creation. We are seeking in the providence and prophecy of the Word God to hear what He alone knows and makes, the simplicity of a contingent reality both independent and dependent upon the Truth of His Grace, the Grace of His Truth with us. It is a simplicity that belongs to the Great I-AM He is and not the complexity of our experience of it. It belongs to the contingent rationality and order and freedom that is inherent in the reality of our world, a universe that is intended to be our home. The UNIFICATION of world realities, Einstein's gravity with the inertia in particle physics, the Big Bang Beginning, Black Holes and Black Hole Fields and the primordial manufacture of stars, Super Novae and the expansion of the universe, Quasars, star clusters, the bussing of galaxies, the Milky Way, Man on the earth, the Quantum World, the Dark Matter and Energies of this universe with its fine constants and structures, and so forth and so on, with the Unity that is the Being and Becoming of the Lord God with us cannot be understood in any real correspondence except with the freedom of the Grace and Truth of His Word, the freedom of His Will to create out of nothing and the freedom of His Being in His Acts and His Acts in His Being to go outside of Himself with His Word and become what He had never before been before, a particular man in this world, while remaining all the while who He truly is and ever will be. It is the freedom of the Son and Father in the Spirit of the Triune Redeemer-Creator that He is that we understand how and why He is with us, His Children in His Kingdom. It is this One that we need to hear and understand in the way He works the providence of His Being and the prophecy of His Word with His Unity and Integrity into our histories.

Eca and Sisy's song sings to us how it is that we are not nothing here and the something we are exists and will exist because of the Power and Glory of His Being, His Word, His Acts with the wholeness of who He truly is, the One who is for us who believe in Him in our time and times. Why not allow His creative will to act and give us to understand the created correspondence He makes for us in Christ, even within the 'nothingness' of His Very Good Creation, in order to make us persons personalized in the personal reality of who He truly is, the Great I-AM He is in our time and times? Why not take seriously His Freedom to be among us in this dark world?

God's providence; man's confusion! Out of these, we find the meaning of our freedom. His Grace is true as He is true to us. He is the One He is and the One He reveals Himself as this One and no other, and it is because of Him in His Divine Freedom that we are not nothing rather than nothing. Because of His Grace, we can sing along with the song of the Mohorko twins—*Without you, I am nothing*, because the Grace of His Holy Love, the Truth of His Atoning Love, leads us where we must go. We are free to imagine Eca in heaven and Sisy on earth, with their mother and father, saying each in their own ways to Him, you make us the something that we are! We imagine Sisy on earth with her grief and joy with Eca her twin in heaven with her pure joy now as the twins they are and shall be forever. We imagine them this way because He is who He is. We imagine them because He will not be who He is without them. Though Eca has been taken away from here, yet she is whom she is because He is her God. Though Sisy has been left behind, yet she is whom she is because He is her God. We are free to imagine that the twins are as they are because He is the Great I-AM He is. We are free to imagine that they are not nothing, because the something they are belongs to His Great AMEN for them. We imagine that they have been given life, as two and each as one, in their independence of Him and in their dependence upon Him because He is the Lord of Freedom in all space and time and light and their relationships as created reality with the uncreated reality of His Being and Becoming.

We are free to imagine that the One He has revealed Himself to be for us is the One who will make creatures willing to betray Him, whole persons and His Children for His Kingdom. We are most free indeed when we are bound to Him in His Freedom in this way. In this freedom, we may know Him as this One that is the Great AMEN of the Great I-AM He is. When we grasp what has been given us in this way, we find our lives embraced by the Grace of the Great AMEN He is as the Great I-AM He is.

'You are My People.' It is this ultimate Word who rides the White Horse of the Apocalypse for His People in His Creation (Revelation 19:11–16). It is the ultimate speaking of the Lord of space and time and light, the God of Divine and Human Freedom and Nature that He is for us. He is His Priesthood; He is His Prophecy; He is His providence; He is His freedom; He is His Communion. His noncontingent Being and Becoming and contingent Being and Becoming are One, the One He is for us, the One He is truly for us in this world, and all that matters is His New Creation. We may be successful without Him, but we need to hear Him to follow Him on His Way for us.

On the one hand, the human imagination is free to seek to resist Him. On the other hand, He struggles against our resistance to Him, freely. The correspondence between Him and our resistances belong to His Power and His Grace and Truth, to the compassion and favor of His Being who He is, to the patient wisdom of His Becoming who He is for us, to His Freedom to embody His Being and Becoming as the Person the Lord Jesus Christ is and as the Revelation of the Father, Son, and Spirit of God's Eternal Life. Out of our experience of the 'nothingness' of this world, He has with His Personhood reconciled and justified and sanctified all things to Himself. He has made creatures to possess 'forever's' with His Eternity, new creatures, children of His Kingdom. If evil intends for the 'nothingness' of the world to threaten our perishing existences with its lies about who He is, about the I-AM He is, then the Good Lord of the 'Very Good' Creation as God Himself intends to uncover the lie, to show us the evil dream behind such threats, and to give our sinful relations with the lie the Grace and Truth that rescues us from it. He has created His union and communion as Himself for us so that all mankind might know that for which we are intended. It is the purpose of this intention that we feel when we feel the weight of His Glory upon our lives. It is the love of this intention when we know we are forgiven. Yes, we are made to breathe the air that surrounds the earth. Yes, we are made to be successful in this world, to enjoy the resources of this world, to be rich in life as children of the Universe, but we are also made to worship Him. Only with the transcendent 'breathing' we find we do when we worship Him, may we take in the fullness of His Time and Space and Light for us, the freedom His Divine and Human Being and Becoming as our Savior, the Revelation and Reconciliation of His Father and His Spirit for us in His Name. With Him, we are not nothing because He is. We are free to be a certain something because He is free to be with us. Why would we want to imagine a world without Him? Why would we not want to imagine His New Creation?

We are painters who would intend to create images that picture some truth of the Great I-AM with us. We are poets who would speak or sing of the wordy truths that belong to the One He is and not another. We are scientists who would practice the art of knowing the science of the nature of the Universe. We are self-seeking and self-fulfilling powers and purposes and intentions. We are humanity meant to serve in the great Temples of Science and Art and Theology. We are extra-ordinary wonderfully ordinary people in all kinds of walks in life. We belong to the past. We belong to the present. We belong to the future. We belong to the wondrous mysteries of time and space and light. We belong to hope. We belong to faith. We belong to love. We do not belong to a meaningless play, a theatre empty of purpose and devotion, to lies and phantoms of Truth and Grace. That which transcends our pains, our diseases, our lives, and our deaths has touched our lives. We do not exist in endless cycles of repetitions that care less about our existences or seek to cheat us of what is truly immortal. We belong to the real meaning of freedom in this world. We are in fact grasped by the real meaning of freedom in our times. We do not live in the silence of an abyss that denies our existence means anything, but we know that the 'nothingness' of this world only serves as that great potential in Creation where all threats and condemnation are exposed as the lie they are. The Word of God has spoken. The Word of God speaks. The Word of God shall speak. He shall speak in His Freedom to be with us and for us here. Upon this knowledge, we depend. For this knowledge we are thankful. We are grateful to be free to go to the place where He has set His Name that there we may do what is 'Right' in His Eyes. We are in the Hands of the Word of His Being and Becoming with us. We are His People. He has called us '*My People.*' We are the people of His Priesthood. We are the people of His Prophecy. We are people of the Wisdom of His Providence. We are the people of His Divine and Human Freedom. It is He who calls us in our time and times. It is He who teaches us to be free and to use our freedom in His Name. It is He who shares with us our grief and sufferings and brokenness in His Name. It is He who has come to give us His Eternal Life. *Sin ti, yo soy nada.* Without you, I am nothing. Yet with you, we are your people, the children who have heard the Grace of the Great AMEN of the Great I-AM. With you, we are 'not nothing.'

Rembrandt van Rijns (circa 1660) painted a series of pictures of the Apostles of our Lord. It is their hands with which he was most interested. Their hands stand out in these paintings, as if to say that their work was in their hands. The hands are very human hands. They are hands that belong to suffering in the world. But they are strong and courageous hands, hands that move us greatly with the strength of their freedom, hands that are free in the freedom of God to be Christ's apostles of the Lord, to do what only He can do in this world. These are hands that are vital to His AMEN in the world. To them belongs the secret of the freedom that the Only One Lord God commands in His Creation. Theirs is a freedom that bears, even while perishing, the witness that they belong to the solid work He does with and for His People on the canvas of what history is, in the midst of His Creation's history with us. Yes, they are hands shaped from the dusts, but they do not exist and they do not work in vain. These hands are the 'not nothing' created in the context of the 'nothingness' of His Creation, His 'Very Good' Creation, and all that truly matters for His New Creation. They are worth looking at sometime. After viewing these paintings, Mickey and I wrote the following poem. It is, I think, a good way to stop writing my California book.

Hands

On viewing 'Rembrandt's Apostles'

Hands do not hold
The temple of time
In the palms of their prayers,
But age on the bone
In the blood-soaked hour,
Tell in the dark
Of the light He lives.
Hands have no tears.

In Our Time

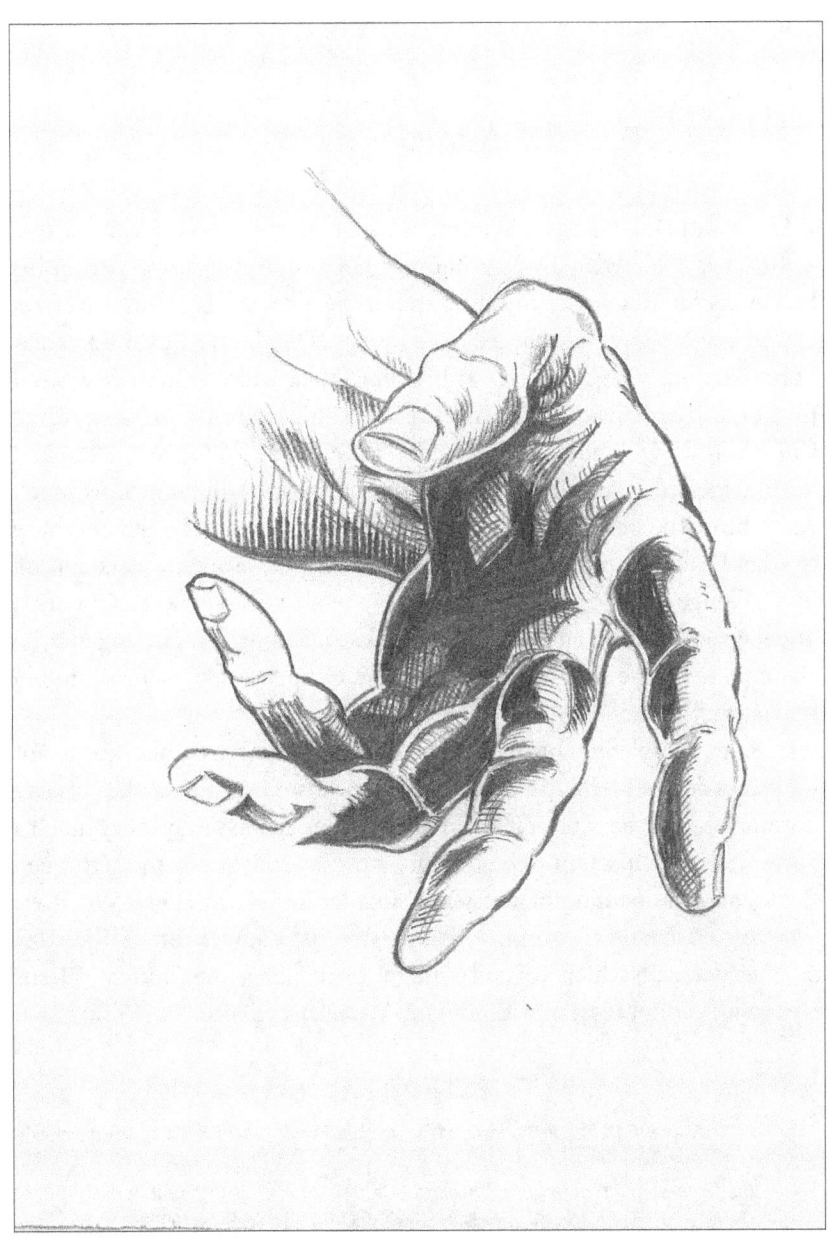

Extended Hand

Addendum

Soon after I finished the manuscript for my book, I learned that the Very Reverend Doctor Thomas Forsyth Torrance went from his bed in his nursing home in Edinburgh to be with His Lord in heaven on December 2, 2007. I have heard from his son, Dr. Thomas Spear Torrance, of his passing in the great care of his family. I have also read from around the world the many eulogies of his life and his work as a servant of the Church and the Academy. My reader, if he or she will read the books I have suggested by this great theologian and friend, will know how much I owe him. The best praise I could ever give him would be that, because of what I learned from him, you have taken up the task of understanding his challenge in our time to grasp the deep relationship between Christian Theology and our Scientific Culture, a relationship whose contingency he championed as he sought to proclaim the Gospel of Jesus Christ among the nations in our time.

Since completing the manuscript of this book, we have also learned of the recent death of John Archibald Wheeler, whose friendship with Professor Torrance cannot be overlooked. Professor Wheeler was always very much a part of events important to our history—the Atomic Bomb, the Hydrogen Bomb, and the naming of Einstein's 'singularities' Black Holes. When we seek to understand the kind of relationship between Christian Theology and Science with which Torrance sought to challenge the Church of Jesus Christ, we cannot grasp it without John Wheeler's science.

SUGGESTED READING

Thomas F. Torrance, *Karl Barth, Biblical and Evangelical Theologian* (T & T Clark: Edinburgh, 1990).
―― *The Ground and Grammar of Theology* (Christian Journals Limited: Belfast, 1980).
―― *The Mediation of Christ* (Helmers & Howard: Colorado Springs, 1992).
―― *The Trinitarian Faith* (T&T Clark: Edinburgh, 1991, 1997).
―― *Divine and Contingent Order* (T&T Clark: Edinburgh, 1984, 1998).
―― *Theological and Natural Science* (Wipf & Stock: Eugene, Oregon, 2002).
John E. McKenna, *The Setting in Life of "The Arbiter" by John Philoponus* (Wipf & Stock: Eugene, Oregon, 1997).

www.ingramcontent.com/pod-product-compliance
Lightning Source LLC
Chambersburg PA
CBHW071143300426
44113CB00009B/1062